CONTRACTS

OBJECTIVE

by

ROBERT D. BRAIN
Clinical Professor of Law
Loyola Law School, Los Angeles

Exam Pro

WEST
ACADEMIC
PUBLISHING

Mat #41352108

Exam Pro Series is a trademark registered in the U.S. Patent and Trademark Office.

© 2014 by LEG, Inc. d/b/a/ West Academic
    444 Cedar Street, Suite 700
    St. Paul, MN 55101
    1-877-888-1330

West, West Academic Publishing, and West Academic are trademarks of West Publishing Corporation, used under license.

Printed in the United States of America

ISBN: 978–0–314–28596–6

I would like to dedicate this Book to Loyola Law School and its students who continue to stimulate me every year.

Preface

To the Student:

This book has two purposes. The first is to give you a number of practice multiple choice questions in contract law. Once your outline is done, the best way to prepare for any exam is to take as many practice exams, and answer as any sample questions, as possible. First year courses tend to be taught by the "case law" method—studying cases, extracting rules, understanding the rationale and policies behind the decision, differentiating holdings from dicta, contrasting the dissent with the majority, etc. However, exams are based on the "problem method"— asking the student to resolve a hypothetical and come up with a solution or answer. It is one thing to know the rules; it is quite another to decide which rules apply to resolve a particular problem. Hence, preparing for exams by answering as many practice questions as possible is important because exams test a different analytical skill set than is used in class discussion. There are over 330 multiple choice questions in this book.

The second reason for the book is to review and teach Contracts principles. As you will discover, the explanatory answers provided in the book are more detailed than would be necessary just to answer the question. Rather, they are designed to explain substantive Contracts doctrine in easy-to-read, basic language. To this end, the questions are arranged in an order so that each question builds on the one before it, and knowledge is reinforced as you proceed through each chapter. Often the explanation of the first few questions in the chapter act as a general review of the subject matter, and provides a step-by-step guide on how to analyze any question in that area, multiple choice or essay.

The book is designed to be both comprehensive and flexible. Hence, it is arranged by subject matter into twenty-three separate chapters. This way you can focus only on the questions that are relevant to those subjects covered in your class and follow whatever path your professor takes on his or her journey through Contract law. It also allows you to skip those subjects that your class may not study, since Contracts classes vary in their coverage. However, there are questions on all the topics that are covered in any Contracts class.

In each "Answer" chapter, there is a discussion and explanation of every answer choice provided in the problem, so not only can you see why the right choice is correct, but also why the others are wrong. There are liberal citations to the Restatement (Second) of Contracts and the UCC in the answer explanations, as well as citations to major cases, which will allow you to review the tested doctrinal point on your own and tie it into your class notes and outlines.

One concern first year students often have is how long should I spend on each of these questions? While most of the questions are ones actually given by a law school professor somewhere, the questions in this book are also designed to mimic the length and difficulty of the Contracts questions on the Multistate Bar Exam, the day long multiple choice test every would be lawyer has to take as part of his or her state's bar exam. On the Multistate Bar Exam, the applicant is given 1 minute 48 seconds per question. Most Contracts professors are a little more generous in their time allocations due to the fact that you are a first year student, and we generally give somewhere between 2 minutes, and 2 minutes 30 seconds, per question. I would suggest that you start by giving yourself a maximum of about 3 minutes a question and then try to improve your speed to conform to the time per question that your professor generally allocates. If you can't answer a question after about 3 minutes, both in your practice sessions and on a graded exam itself, my recommendation is to skip the question and come back later. You don't want to get so bogged down answering one question that it impedes your ability to answer all the questions in the time provided. Hardly anybody gets all the questions correct, so it's OK to miss one every once in a while. There are tear out answer sheets in this book you can use to take the tests, or you can just use scratch paper. The questions and their explanatory answers in each chapter are designed to be taken in the order presented, but they need not be taken all at once. If you only have limited time, it is perfectly fine to do 5 or 10 questions and then come back. Generally it takes about the same time to review an answer as it does to take the question.

A question students don't tend to ask, but should, is how can I maximize the impact of taking practice multiple choice questions as an aid to help me study for my graded exam? Before I give you a recommendation, let me share a story. I was teaching Bar Review classes to recent graduates a few years ago and some students signed up for extra private tutoring. We would give them a multiple choice test consisting of 40 questions and then go over each question and each answer choice with them. Universally at the end of this 3 hour session the students felt they understood the questions, why they got the ones they did right, and why they missed the others. We would then give them the same set of 40 questions 3 weeks later. Those students who did nothing with the questions in the interim (thinking they "had them down" after the review session) invariably got the same score (plus or minus one) as they did the first time around. They got the same ones right that they did the first time and, more significantly, the same ones wrong. So if all you do is take the questions in this book, evaluate your responses, and then go on your way, it is likely you are not maximizing your study opportunities.

What we told the Bar Review students, and what I recommend to you, is to revisit the issues on the questions you missed (and those which you got right as a result of a "guess"). Typically the reason a question is missed is that you didn't know the rule or exception governing that question, or you didn't recognize the rule's proper application to the fact situation given. So what you should do is make flash cards on the questions, or put an asterisk on your outline with regard to the rule, or do something that will make it easy to review the issues involved in the questions you got wrong. <u>Then you should review the cards, or the rules with the asterisks on your outline, every day (or at least every other day)</u>, and especially the night before the exam. The Bar Review students who engaged in that kind of frequent review of their "misses" increased their scores dramatically when we gave them the exam again, and they did much better generally on the Multistate Bar Exam than students who did not heed our advice. Hence reinforcement of the rules and application missed the first go round is very important. If you have already spent the time to take the questions and review your performance, make that time count by forcing yourself to review the reasons you erred.

I would love to hear from you if you have comments about the book or any of its questions. Good or bad. The easiest way to get hold of me is to use my Loyola Law School, Los Angeles e-mail address: <u>bob.brain@lls.edu</u>. If you would put "Exam Pro MC" on the subject line, it will help me—and our school's e-mail filter—identify the legitimacy of the inquiry.

Best of luck as you navigate your way through the quintessential law school class: Contracts.

> Bob Brain
> Clinical Professor of Law
> Loyola Law School, Los Angeles
> Los Angeles, California

August 2013

Acknowledgments

This Book is the result of much effort—much more than I could have done on my own. I would like to acknowledge and thank Kelly Cochran, Blake Williams and Ashton Riley, all Loyola Law School, Los Angeles Class of 2015 for all their hard work and for doing their best to ensure the Book will be helpful to Contracts students across the country. I would also like to acknowledge Loyola Law School, Los Angeles and its Faculty Research Fellowship Program for supporting the project.

About the Author

Clinical Professor Robert Brain is an Honors Graduate of Stanford University in Biology, has an M.S. in biochemistry from Stanford, and was awarded his law degree from the University of California, Boalt Hall School of Law. He began his legal career in the litigation department of Gibson, Dunn & Crutcher, where he received a pro bono award from the Los Angeles County Bar Association for his work with Public Counsel, and represented the ACLU in a case before the U.S. Supreme Court. He later joined the faculty at Pepperdine University School of Law where he taught Contracts, Torts, Constitutional Law, Sales and Trial Practice. While at Pepperdine, he co-taught a course on the History of the Supreme Court with Chief Justice Rehnquist, tried cases on a volunteer basis for the Los Angeles District Attorney's Office and served as a commercial arbitrator for the American Arbitration Association.

He later taught as a Visiting Professor at McGeorge School of Law before becoming a partner at the litigation firm of Howarth & Smith where he tried fraud, defamation, securities, products liability and assault matters, representing clients like the Republic of the Marshall Islands, Suzuki Motor Corporation and the victims of 9/11. He joined the faculty at Loyola Law School, Los Angeles in 2006 and has taught Contracts, Sales, Ethical Lawyering and Legal Research and Writing at Loyola. He has published three books on Contact Law, and is the co-author of the only casebook on Video Game Law in the United States. He has published articles on commercial law, video game law, and evidence and was a regular columnist for the Los Angeles Daily Journal. He has been elected to the Executive Board of the Teaching Methods Section and the Legal Wiring, Reasoning, and Research Section of the American Association of Law Schools and is a sought after lecturer on subjects as diverse as legal writing, video game law, legal history, and game theory.

Table of Contents

PART 2. ANSWERS

CONTRACTS

OBJECTIVE

PART 1
QUESTIONS

CHAPTER 1
OFFER, ACCEPTANCE, AND MUTUALITY

QUESTIONS

Facts for Question 1

Paula and Dan Draper are a married couple with a new baby named Sarah. Dan hates giving Sarah baths. Just before Sarah's first birthday, Dan says to Paula, "I'll give you $1,500 if you bathe Sarah until she is two years old."

1. Assuming that a reasonable person would think that Dan was serious, is his promise to pay $1,500 enforceable?

    (A) Yes, because Dan is obtaining a legal benefit by the promise, and Paula is suffering a legal detriment from the promise. Thus, there is consideration to support the contract.

    (B) Yes, because a court would enforce Dan's promise on moral consideration grounds.

    (C) No, so long as a court finds that Paula would benefit from bathing Sarah.

    (D) No, unless a court finds the promise overcomes the normal presumption that governs such agreements. H & W

Domiciliary Family members

Facts for Question 2

Sally Seller and her friend Brian Buyer were at lunch one day when Sally told Brian, "I decided last night I am going to sell my motorcycle for $800." Brian, who thought this was a deal he couldn't refuse, responded "I accept, I will buy your motorcycle for $800." Assume $800 was a fair price for the motorcycle.

2. Which of the following assertions is true at the time of Brian's statement?

    (A) Sally and Brian have entered into an enforceable contract and Sally is obligated to sell Brian her motorcycle for $800.

(B) Sally and Brian have not entered into a contract.

(C) Sally is an offeree with the power, but not the right, to enter into a binding contract with Brian to purchase the bike for $800.

(D) Both (B) and (C) are correct.

Facts for Question 3

Homeowner calls up Hardware Store ("Store") on the phone and asks the representative how much Store charges for Acme-brand, two-foot-high vinyl picket fencing. Store's representative said, "$2 per running foot." Homeowner said, "Great. I'll take 200 running feet and will be down this afternoon to pick it up." Assume no further communication or actions by the parties.

3. Which is the most accurate description of the parties' status at this point in time?

(A) Store has made an enforceable offer to Homeowner, but Homeowner has not effectively accepted the offer.

(B) Store and Homeowner are not in a valid contract.

(C) Store and Homeowner are in a valid contract for 200 running feet of the fencing.

(D) Store and Homeowner are in a unilateral option contract where Store is bound to sell 200 running feet of the Acme fencing at $2/running foot, but Homeowner can terminate the contract without consequence and need not pick up the fencing as promised.

Facts for Question 4

Sam Seller tells Barry Buyer that he is considering selling his property. Sam invited Buyer to make an offer. Barry says: "How about $60,000?" to which Sam responds, "No, I wouldn't consider selling it for less than $75,000." Barry then says, "I accept, I'll pay you $75,000 for your property." There was no further communication between the two parties.

4. Is there a contract between Sam and Barry?

(A) Yes, because Buyer validly accepted Seller's enforceable offer to sell the property for $75,000.

(B) Yes, because Seller's failure to respond to Buyer when he said "I accept, I'll pay you $75,000 for your property," constitutes an implied acceptance on Seller's part, since Seller invited Buyer to make an offer on the property in the first place.

(C) No, if the fair market value of the property was really $60,000.

(D) No, because Seller did not make an enforceable offer, so Buyer did not have the power to accept.

Facts for Question 5

Seller put an ad in the paper saying he would sell his land for a minimum of $50,000. Buyer wrote him expressing interest in purchasing the land. Seller e-mailed Buyer telling her she needed to act fast if she was interested, because he had other offers for the property.

The next communication from Buyer to Seller was an e-mail from Buyer stating that she had opened escrow with instructions to the escrow agent to pay Seller $50,000 upon receipt of good title to the property.

Seller wrote back that he had already sold the property to another for $60,000.

5. If Buyer sued Seller for breach of contract, which of the following is true?

(A) Seller should prevail because Seller revoked his offer when he told Buyer she had to act fast.

(B) Seller should prevail because they had not entered into a contract.

(C) Buyer should prevail because Seller breached an enforceable contract to sell the property for $50,000.

(D) Buyer should prevail because she materially relied on Seller's offer when she opened escrow.

Facts for Question 6

Rowdy Records is a music store in Indianapolis, Indiana. Rowdy's took out an advertisement in Monday's edition of the *Indianapolis Star* that read: "Freaky Friday Sale! Ten DVD's for only $1 each to the first customer who walks through our door this Friday!"

6.   Is the ad an enforceable offer?

(A) No, because advertisements are solicitations for offers, not offers themselves.

(B) Yes, under the UCC, but not under common law.

(C) Yes under common law, but not under the UCC.

(D) Yes, because all attributes of an enforceable offer are present.

Facts for Question 7

Sally Seller has an upscale clothing store on Rodeo Drive in Beverly Hills. She puts an advertisement in the *LA Times* that she is selling skinny jeans for $175, a bargain for this particular designer. Betty Buyer, a fashionista on a budget, was ecstatic to hear about the sale and went to the store that very same afternoon, as soon as she got off work. Betty pulled $175 cash from her purse and said, "I'll take the skinny jeans in a size 4, please."

Sally had already sold out of Betty's size. She explained the situation to Betty, who was furious. Betty became even angrier when Sally refused to give Betty a "rain check," allowing Betty to purchase the jeans at the same price when her size came in.

Betty sued Sally for breach of contract.

7.   In the suit against Sally Seller, Betty will likely:

(A) <u>Prevail</u>, because Sally made a viable offer that Betty accepted by showing up at the store, with cash, to purchase the jeans in response to the ad and on the same day the ad ran in the paper.

(B) <u>Prevail</u>, because while Sally was not in breach for running out of Betty's size, she was in breach for failing to give her a "rain check."

(C) <u>Lose</u>, because Sally has not made a valid offer.

(D) <u>Lose</u>, because Betty did not effectively tender performance.

Facts for Question 8

Pam saw an advertisement in the Sunday *Times* stating that Tar–Mart was hiring cashiers, and that all cashiers that are hired would start with, "a base salary of $60,000, with a 5% increase in pay guaranteed every six months the employee remains on the job." Pam applied and was hired for the job.

She started at $60,000, but after eight months on the job, Tar–Mart had failed to give her a raise. Pam complained, and was told, truthfully, that there had been a good number of customer complaints about Pam's performance and therefore she had not performed well enough to merit a pay raise.

8. Can Pam successfully sue Tar–Mart for breach of contract over the failure to increase her salary 5%?

   (A) Yes, because Tar–Mart made an effective offer when it advertised the employment opportunity, and Pam accepted the offer by applying for, and getting, the job.

   (B) Yes, because even though Tar–Mart did not make an offer by means of the advertisement, it set forth the terms of Pam's offer in the ad and is bound by the guarantee of a salary increase every six months so long as Pam is employed.

   (C) No, because advertisements are considered solicitations to make an offer, and not offers themselves.

   (D) No, so long as Tar–Mart was correct and in good faith stating that, under its standards, Pam had not performed well enough to earn the 5% pay raise.

Facts for Question 9

Danny Dude and his friends were having a wine tasting in Danny's wine cellar. Danny was having a good time and had become rather tipsy. He was slurring his words and stumbling a little.

About an hour into the tasting, Danny was furious to find that he couldn't find his most precious bottle, a $2,500 bottle of 2000 Chateau Lafite Rothschild. Danny yells at the assembled crowd, "$250,000 to anyone who can produce a 2000 Chateau Lafite Rothschild."

Everyone laughed at this ridiculous price, but Pearl took Danny seriously. Pearl slipped out of the tasting, immediately went to the nearest wine store, and bought a bottle of 2000 Chateau Lafite Rothschild for $2,500. Pearl brought the bottle back to the event before the wine tasting had finished.

9. Danny's offer of $250,000 for the $2,500 bottle of wine is most likely:

   (A) Not an offer because a reasonable person would not believe Danny intended to offer $250,000 for a $2,500 bottle of wine.

   (B) Not an offer because the subject matter of the offer was missing.

(C) An enforceable offer, but Danny can revoke the offer at any time if he changes his mind.

(D) An enforceable offer, and Danny cannot revoke the offer because Pearl had materially relied on the offer by going to the store and purchasing the wine.

Facts for Question 10

Peter Pixie and Dean Dant were drinking together at Dan's house when Dean tells Peter he is dying to purchase his house. Peter, who was feeling tipsy, scoffed at the idea and said "You couldn't afford it you imbecile." Dean, who was unaware Peter was feeling the booze so much, responded, "Well, sure I could, I'll give you $500,000 for it." Peter shook his head and said, "No, make it $700,000," and Dean replied, "$600,000 and we have a deal." Peter said "Ok, $600,000 it is."

Peter and Dean then wrote up a contract on a napkin that stated that Peter would sell his house to Dean for $600,000, payment was to be made by check on the following Wednesday, and the two even called Dean's wife into the room whereupon Peter, Dean and Dean's wife all signed the napkin contract.

The following Wednesday, Dean went back to Peter with a cashier's check to tender payment. Peter yells, "You fool! I was only joking. I never intended to sell you my property. I was higher than a 747!"

10. Assuming $600,000 was the fair market value for the home, in a suit between Peter and Dean, what is the likely result?

(A) The two were in a contract if a reasonable person in Peter's position would believe they had entered into a contract.

(B) The two were in a contract if Peter subjectively believed they were entering into a contract.

(C) The two were not in a contract if Dean subjectively believed they were not entering into a contract.

(D) The two were not in an enforceable contract because the napkin agreement does not satisfy the Statute of Frauds.

Facts for Question 11

Pam Poodle was opening a dog salon and needed someone to paint the salon. She wrote Bill Brush, a commercial painter, an e-mail stating "I'm opening up a dog salon next week and need someone to paint. If you come by and paint the shop, I'll pay you $2,500. Let me know, or just come by next week and start painting." Pam was out of town buying supplies the next week, but Bill went to the salon and began painting. One week later, Pam saw Bill at the salon and told him she no longer needed him to paint the salon. Pam ordered Bill off her premises and has refused to pay him.

11. Which of the following statements is most correct?

(A) Pam could revoke her offer at any time before the job was completed.

(B) A contract between Pam and Bill was formed when Bill began painting.

(C) Bill could walk away before finishing, but Pam could not terminate him without incurring contractual liability.

(D) Bill is entitled to the fair market value of the painting services he provided before Pam demanded he leave.

Unilateral contract- cannot be Revoked once performance Begins

Facts for Question 12

Paul Pack published an ad in his local newspaper offering "$500 to whoever provides information" that results in the recovery of Alice, his dog. Ann calls Paul on Tuesday and says she saw Alice at City Park near Paul's home. Dana calls Paul on Thursday and tells Paul she saw Alice in the same park. Paul went to City Park and found Alice on Friday afternoon. Paul paid Ann $500, but told Dana that he already had the information about Alice being in City Park before her call, so he did not believe he was obligated to pay her.

Dana sues Paul for breach of contract.

12. In the suit between Dana and Paul, Dana will likely:

(A) <u>Prevail</u>, because Paul did not revoke the reward offer before Dana gave the information.

(B) <u>Prevail</u>, because Dana knew about the reward offer before she provided the information and intended to accept it.

(C) <u>Lose</u>, because Ann had already accepted the reward offer.

(D) <u>Lose</u>, because ads are not offers, but rather solicitations for offers.

Facts for Questions 13 and 14

Camille Rose was an avid record collector. She had an expansive collection of all of the most popular vinyl records, including all but one

David Bowie album. The David Bowie album she did not have was *Space Oddity*. She placed the following ad on Craigslist:

> $100 offered for information on the availability for purchase of a vinyl copy of David Bowie's *Space Oddity* album, in good condition. Contact Camille at (555) 555–5555.

The ad was placed Friday, May 10 and was to run for a week, starting Sunday, May 12.

Therese Tulip was another record collector, and independently knew that Camille was looking for the vinyl. On Sunday morning, she saw the record at a swap meet. Therese called Camille as soon as she left the swap meet and told her where she could find the record. Therese had not seen the Craigslist ad.

Randy Record saw Camille's ad on Monday morning and called her right away to give her a tip on the availability of the record at a local record shop. Randy was the first person to call in response to the ad. Camille thanked Randy, but told him that she had already found the record she needed and did not want a second. Camille also truthfully told Randy that she had already contacted Craigslist at 10:00 a.m. that morning and cancelled the ad for the rest of the week, and therefore felt there was no longer a viable reward offer.

13. A few days after telling Camille about the record, Therese found out about the ad and reward. She demanded payment from Camille who refused. If Therese sued for the reward will she prevail?

   (A) Yes, Camille must pay Therese because she bought the record based on her tip.

   (B) Yes, Camille must pay Therese because her revocation was ineffective against Therese.

   (C) No, Therese cannot collect because she did not know of the offer when she called Camille.

   (D) No, Therese cannot collect because Camille's ad was not an offer.

14. Randy Record also sued Camille for the $500 reward. Will Randy recover?

   (A) Yes, because Camille's attempted revocation was ineffective against Randy.

   (B) Yes, because Randy detrimentally relied on Camille's promise.

    (C) No, because Therese had already called about the record.

    (D) No, because Camille did not buy the vinyl that Randy told her about.

Facts for Questions 15 and 16

Drugs, Inc. began a promotion for Sick–Me–Not, a medicine that is supposed to prevent users from catching any illness. Under the promotion, which was described in an ad that ran for three consecutive weeks on page 30 of *Time* Magazine, Drugs, Inc. told consumers it would refund the purchase price of Sick–Me–Not if purchasers used the medicine correctly for six months and still got sick.

Piper Pepper purchased Sick–Me–Not and used it for six months, but still came down with bronchitis. She did not notify Drugs, Inc. that she was taking the medicine.

Four months after Piper began using Sick–Me–Not, i.e., two months before the expiration of the six month period set forth in the ad, Drugs ran an ad for three consecutive weeks on page 30 in *Time* retracting the offer and saying it would no longer pay for anyone who became ill after using the product during the six month period she was using the product.

Piper thereafter properly filled out the paperwork described in the first series of ads to receive her refund. However, Drugs, Inc. refuses to pay the refund amount.

15. If Piper sues Drugs, Inc. for breach of contract, what is the most likely result?

    (A) Drugs, Inc. must pay Piper, unless Piper saw the ad retracting the offer before she completed performance.

    (B) Drugs, Inc. must pay Piper because she has begun performance and its attempted revocation was not effective against Piper. *(Unilateral Contract)*

    (C) Drugs, Inc. has no duty to pay Piper because Piper had a duty to notify Drugs, Inc. she was participating in the promotion within a reasonable time after she started, and she did not.

    (D) Drugs, Inc. has no duty to pay Piper because it made a general reward offer that was effectively revoked against Piper and any other use of the product who had not submitted the proper paperwork before the revocation ads appeared.

16. Same facts as above except: (1) assume there were no revocation ads, but (2) Alice Anderson used Sick–Me–Not for six months and submitted the proper paperwork before Piper ; and (3) Drugs, Inc. paid Alice's claim, but still refused to pay Piper.

In response to Piper's suit against Drugs, Inc., what is the most likely result?

(A) Piper will lose because she cannot effectively accept Drugs's offer because Alice accepted the general offer first.

(B) Piper will lose because she did not notify Drugs that she was participating in the promotion.

(C) Piper will prevail, but only under a promissory estoppel theory, because she relied on the offer.

(D) Piper can validly accept, despite Alice accepting the offer first.

Facts for Questions 17 and 18

Paula Pound was out to dinner one night when she discovered her good friend, Darla Deed's wallet in the women's restroom. She took the wallet and after dinner started driving the wallet to Darla's home. On the way, Paula took a cell phone call from Adam Ant, who told Paula that Darla had just posted a $200 reward on her blog for the return of the wallet.

Paula brings the wallet to Darla, and demands the $200 reward. Darla, however does not feel she should have to pay a friend who was going to return the wallet anyway, and refuses to give Paula the reward.

17. Does Darla have to pay Paula the reward?

(A) Yes, because Paula learned of the reward before she returned the wallet.

(B) Yes, because Paula materially relied on the promise by driving the wallet to Darla's home.

(C) No, because Paula did not know of the reward until after she began performance.

(D) No, because Paula did not find out about the reward from Darla's blog, she found out about it from Adam.

18. For the purposes of this question only, assume the following: when Adam tells Paula about Darla's reward, Paula responds, "I could never ask her to pay me for returning the wallet. That is what friends are for." Paula then returns the wallet and when Darla tries to pay her, Paula says "Don't worry about it, I won't take your money." Paula leaves without payment. However, on her way home Paula gets in a fender

bender. She now has an unexpected payment to fix her car and could really use the reward money. Paula calls Darla and explains that she needs the reward money but Darla says that it is too late.

If Paula sues Darla for the reward within the statute of limitations, what result?

(A) Darla will lose, because she offered the reward and Darla accepted by returning the wallet.

(B) Darla will lose, because Paula learned of the reward before she returned the wallet.

(C) Darla will prevail, because Paula did not know of the reward at the time she decided to return the wallet.

(D) Darla will prevail, because Paula did not intend to accept the reward offer at the time she returned the wallet.

Facts for Question 19

Merchant Buyer ("Buyer") sends an order to Factory A, owned by Alvin, for 5,000 generic plastic paper clips. The offer could be validly accepted by beginning production of the clips. However, Factory A went out of business before the clips could be manufactured.

As a courtesy to Buyer, Alvin forwarded the order to his friend Byron, the President of Factory B. Without notifying Buyer, Factory B competently fills the order and ships conforming clips to Buyer.

19. Is there a contract between Buyer and Factory B?

(A) No, because Buyer placed the order with Factory A.

(B) No, because the clips were specially manufactured goods.

(C) Yes, because Factory A validly transferred its right to accept when it transferred the order to Factory B.

(D) Yes, because Factory B effectively accepted by sending the clips that Buyer ordered.

Facts for Question 20

In a face-to-face conversation, non-merchant Seller offers to sell his old smart phone for $100 to non-merchant Buyer. Buyer replies: "I'll pay you $75 for it." Seller says: "I cannot reduce the price, but my offer remains open to you until tomorrow." The next day Buyer tells Seller: "OK, I'll pay $100 for the phone."

20. Are Buyer and Seller in an enforceable contract?

(A) Yes, because Seller said the offer remained open.

(B) Yes, because Seller made an irrevocable firm offer when he said the offer remained open.

(C) No, because Buyer made a counteroffer and the power of acceptance was terminated.

(D) No, because in a face-to-face conversation, the power of acceptance terminates when the conversation ends.

Facts for Question 21

Seller offers to sell Buyer her antique record player for $80. Buyer replies, "Wouldn't you consider taking $50?" Seller says no. Buyer then says "OK, I'll take the record player for $80." No further communication existed between the parties.

21. Has Buyer effectively and enforceably accepted Seller's offer?

(A) Yes, because Buyer's response to the $80 offer never terminated his power of acceptance.

(B) Yes, even though the power of acceptance briefly terminated when Buyer offered $50, Buyer then immediately accepted the original offer.

(C) No, because Buyer had only a power, and not a right, to accept.

(D) No, because Buyer made a counteroffer, which terminated the power of acceptance.

Facts for Question 22

On Monday, November 16, Homeowner told Painter she would give him $2,000 to paint the outside of her home by December 5, when she was hosting a party. Painter told Homeowner he would get back to her as soon as he looked up prices for the paint. Later that day, Painter called Homeowner and left a message on her answering machine that said, "This is Painter. I've checked the paint prices and I won't do the job for less than $3,500."

A job Painter planned to work on fell through and Painter now needed the money. So on Friday, November 20. Painter called Homeowner and left another message, "This is Painter, again. Upon further consideration, I accept your offer to paint your house for $2,000. I'll do it this weekend."

Homeowner played the second message just as she was going out of town for a long weekend away, and did not contact Painter. She had made no other arrangements for painting the house. That weekend, Painter went to Homeowner's home and painted the outside, without Homeowner's knowledge. When Homeowner returned from her vacation, Painter gave her a bill for $2,000.

Homeowner refuses to pay the bill and Painter brings suit for breach of contract only.

22. Who will likely prevail in the lawsuit?

    (A) Painter, because he accepted Homeowner's offer before Homeowner materially changed her position in reliance upon the first telephone message.

    (B) Painter, assuming the work he did was actually worth $2,000.

    (C) Painter, because he put Homeowner on notice that he was going to paint the home over the weekend.

    (D) Homeowner, because she did not accept Painter's offer to paint the home for $2,000.

Facts for Question 23

Seller offers to sell Buyer his ticket to a popular music festival for $200. Buyer says to Seller: "I plan to keep your offer under advisement, but while I am thinking about it, would you take $125?" Seller doesn't answer, but Buyer then says, "OK, I'll take it for $200." No further conversation occurred between Buyer and Seller.

23. Is there a contract between Buyer and Seller?

    (A) No, because Buyer made a counteroffer which terminated his power of acceptance.

    (B) No, because the power of acceptance terminated at the end of the $125 conversation.

    (C) No, because Buyer has made an offer to purchase the ticket for $200, which Seller has not yet accepted.

    (D) Yes, because Buyer validly accepted the offer to buy the ticket for $200.

Facts for Question 24

On April 1, Elizabeth offered to sell Thomas the last puppy from the litter her dog had just birthed for $600. Thomas wanted some time to think about it, but Elizabeth knew her neighbor Amanda was dying to buy the puppy, and Elizabeth really needed the money. Because Elizabeth and Thomas had been best friends for a long time, Elizabeth told Thomas she would keep her offer open until April 8, in exchange for $5 from Thomas. Thomas gave Elizabeth the $5 and went home to think about the deal. Thereafter, Amanda gave Elizabeth $600 in cash for the puppy "just in case" Thomas did not want the puppy.

After a long week of indecision about the responsibility of owning a puppy, Thomas woke up on the morning of April 8 and knew he had to have the puppy. He called Elizabeth immediately to tell her his decision, but she had not paid her phone bill and her line was cut off. Instead, Thomas wrote a check to Elizabeth for $600 and put it in a stamped envelope along with a note that he was accepting the offer to purchase the puppy. The envelope was properly stamped and addressed, and Thomas dropped the envelope in the mailbox at 10:00 p.m. on April 8. The note and check were not received by Elizabeth until April 10.

When Elizabeth had not received the letter, or otherwise heard, from Thomas on April 8, she told Elizabeth the puppy was hers on April 9.

24. Who owns the puppy in a jurisdiction that follows the Restatement 2d of Contracts?

    (A) Thomas, because he had a valid option contract with Elizabeth and effectively accepted Elizabeth's offer to sell the puppy for $600 because, under the "mailbox rule," acceptances are effective upon dispatch.

    (B) Amanda, because oral option contracts are unenforceable.

    (C) Amanda, because Elizabeth sold the puppy to Amanda on April 9th before receiving Thomas's check.

    (D) Elizabeth, because the sale of goods priced $500 or more must be in writing or it is void.

Facts for Question 25

Buyer and Seller went out to dinner when Seller said "I will sell you this watch for $50." Buyer never responded and the two went their separate ways after dinner was finished. Three days after their dinner, Buyer called Seller and said: "I accept your offer; I will buy your watch for $50." This was the first communication between the two since the dinner.

25. In a jurisdiction using common law presumptions regarding offer and acceptance rules, Buyer and Seller are:

(A) Not in a contract, because Buyer did not accept at dinner.

(B) Not in a contract, because the terms of the offer were too indefinite.

(C) In a contract, because Buyer accepted Seller's offer to sell the watch for $50.

(D) In a contract, unless Buyer changes his mind in which case he can void the contract since it was oral.

Facts for Question 26

On Wednesday, Seller offers to sell Buyer her dining room table for $70. Buyer says "I don't know, will you give me a few days to think about it?" Seller responds, "Sure, how about until next Tuesday?" A few minutes later, though, Seller says, "I changed my mind, I want to keep the table and I am not going to sell it." Buyer then says, "I'll take it."

26. Is there a contract between Buyer and Seller?

(A) No, because Buyer rejected the offer when he said he was not sure and asked for more time.

(B) No, because the power of acceptance was terminated when Seller said she was not going to sell the table.

(C) Yes, but Buyer can avoid the contract because it was oral.

(D) Yes, because Seller and Buyer entered into an irrevocable option contract when Seller told Buyer he could have until Tuesday, and Buyer validly accepted before Tuesday.

Facts for Question 27 and 28

Buyer and Seller enrolled in their employer's "Get Fit" program, which required all participants to purchase a treadmill to use in their office during lunchtime. Buyer and Seller were on different floors of the employer's office building.

Buyer bought an inexpensive treadmill without any bells and whistles. Seller purchased a $2,000 state of the art treadmill with a television screen and calorie counter. After several months, Buyer was pleased to find that he could not get enough of the treadmill. He used it every chance he got. Seller, on the other hand, lost interest in the treadmill and dropped out of the "Get Fit" program. When Seller heard how much Buyer enjoyed the program, he wrote Buyer an e-mail describing his treadmill and explaining he had lost interest in the fitness program. The e-mail provided, "If you pick up the treadmill at my office during business hours within the next three weeks, I will let you have it for $750."

Buyer got busy at work and was unable to pick up the treadmill. Two weeks after Buyer received the offer, Seller's co-worker was at a meeting with Buyer and accurately told Buyer that Seller had already sold the treadmill to another employee. The co-worker was a good friend of Seller's and a trustworthy individual.

Nevertheless, the next day, Buyer went to Seller's office to pick up the treadmill and presented Seller with a check for $750. Seller refused to sell the machine.

27. The conversation between Buyer and Seller's co-worker (where the co-worker told Buyer that Seller had sold the treadmill to another employee) should be found by the court to be:

(A) An indirect revocation of Seller's offer.

(B) Of no legal effect because Seller's offer was irrevocable.

(C) Of no legal effect because Seller's co-worker is a third party and cannot revoke on behalf of Seller.

(D) A direct revocation of Seller's offer because no contract was formed when Buyer failed to send a letter back accepting the offer.

28. The Restatement (Second) of Contracts rule providing that the death of the offeror terminated the offeree's power of acceptance is:

(A) Consistent with the objective theory of contracts, but inconsistent with the subjective theory.

(B) Consistent with the subjective theory, but inconsistent with the objective theory of contracts.

(C) Consistent with both the objective and subjective theory of contracts.

(D) Inconsistent with both the objective and subjective theory of contracts.

Facts for Question 29

Seller offers to sell Buyer his vintage Corvette for $50,000. Buyer says, "Give me a week to think about it." Seller replies, "Sure, no problem." Buyer dies the next day.

Buyer's son, Buyer Jr., whom Buyer had told about the offer prior to his death, wrote Seller an e-mail the next day, correctly stating, "This is Buyer Jr., Dad died last night, but in his will he left the car to me. I am the administrator of his estate, so on behalf of his estate, I accept. Tell me where to wire the money."

Seller has since decided to keep the car and refuses to sell it to Buyer's estate.

29. If Buyer's estate sues Seller for breach of contract, the estate will:

    (A) <u>Lose</u>, because e-mail is not an effective mode of acceptance given the circumstances.

    (B) <u>Lose</u>, because Buyer Jr. did not have the power of acceptance even if he was the administrator of the estate.

    (C) <u>Prevail</u>, if Buyer Jr. can show that he materially relied on the offer.

    (D) <u>Prevail</u>, because he validly accepted the offer on behalf of the estate.

Facts for Question 30

Buyer ordered a truckload of a particular pesticide from Seller. Before Seller accepted the order, but after Buyer placed the order, the EPA outlawed both the sale and use of that particular pesticide. Seller thereafter accepts the order, believing that because the offer was placed before the EPA's actions, the order could be legally fulfilled.

30. May Seller validly accept Buyer's order?

    (A) Yes, because Buyer placed the order before the EPA outlawed the pesticide.

    (B) Yes, so long as Seller's acceptance was sent within a reasonable time after the offer was placed.

    (C) No, because the time for acceptance has lapsed and the power of acceptance has terminated.

    (D) No, because the pesticide was outlawed before the acceptance was sent.

Facts for Question 31

Sarah Seller offers to sell Brianna Buyer her first year contracts book for $50, on the condition that Sarah's favorite singer, Angela Acapella, win "U.S.A. Icon," a popular singing competition. Brianna accepts. Angela got knocked out of the competition early on. Brianna demands that Sarah still sell her the book, but Sarah refuses.

31. Is Sarah contractually obligated to sell the book?

  (A) Yes, because Sarah made an offer to sell the book and Brianna accepted the offer.

  (B) Yes, because Sarah's condition was not related to the sale of the contracts book.

  (C) No, because Angela did not win "U.S.A. Icon."

  (D) No, because Sarah effectively revoked her offer.

Facts for Question 32

Betty Buyer wishes to enclose her back yard with a fence. She reads reviews online and decides that Sam Carpenter is the best choice to construct the fence. On Monday, she leaves Sam a detailed message that includes the address, the exact type of fence she desires, the time for completing the project, a promise she will pay $600 for the job, and the fact that Sam can either call her back and accept or simply show up and begin work. On Tuesday, without speaking to Betty, Sam shows up at her house and begins to build the fence. When he's more than halfway through, however, Betty runs into her yard and yells "I revoke!" and orders Sam off her property.

32. Betty:

  (A) Has validly revoked her offer because Sam never validly accepted it by completing performance.

  (B) Never made an effective offer.

  (C) Cannot revoke her offer because Sam has begun to perform.

  (D) May validly revoke, and Sam may also discontinue performing without consequence if he wishes to do so.

Facts for Questions 33 and 34

On May 1, Owner orally offered to pay Alex $15,000 if Alex would repair the roof on Owner's beach cottage. Alex requested some time to think it over. Owner told Alex she could have a couple of days to think about it, but that he had to know Alex's decision no later than May 4.

On May 3, Alex sent a properly addressed e-mail to Owner, accepting the offer. She started working on the roof on May 4.

33. If Owner's offer to Alex is considered an offer unambiguously looking for a unilateral contract, which of the following is true?

(A) Alex had to notify Owner of her acceptance before she started repairing the roof, otherwise her acceptance was ineffective.

(B) Alex's dispatch of the e-mail on May 3 was a valid acceptance of Owner's offer.

(C) Alex may cease, without breach, if she has started to perform; but Owner must hold his offer open for a reasonable period of time.

(D) Alex would be in breach if she walked off the job before completion.

34. For the purposes of this question only, assume Alex began performance on May 4, and that Owner knew of this.

If Owner's offer to Alex is considered an ambiguous offer, which of the following is true?

(A) Alex may cease fixing the roof without breach, but Owner must hold his offer open for a reasonable period of time.

(B) Owner can revoke his offer without breach, but Alex may not cease fixing the roof without breach.

(C) Owner would breach the contract if he refused to go forward and revoked the offer, and Alex would breach the contract if she ceased fixing the roof.

(D) They have no enforceable contract.

Facts for Question 35

Buyer is a furniture store and a regular customer of Seller, who deals in vases. Once an order comes in, Seller selects the vases from inventory, tags them as Buyer's vases, packages them, and loads them onto a truck to be shipped to Buyer in trucks owned by Seller.

On May 1, Buyer orders 100 vases with a Purchase Order that states, "Order for 100 green vases, Catalogue No. 223, at price per catalogue. Delivery by 6/1" Seller goes through the usual routine: picking the vases, tagging them and loading them onto the truck.

35. Before the vases leave Seller's garage, which is the most accurate statement?

    (A) Buyer may revoke because Seller has not started to drive them to Buyer's place of business.

    (B) Seller may revoke without legal consequence, but Buyer cannot revoke.

    (C) Seller cannot terminate the deal, and Buyer cannot revoke without legal consequence.

    (D) Buyer may revoke without legal consequence because the goods have not yet arrived at Buyer's store.

Facts for Question 36

On January 4, Buyer, a nationwide electronics store, sent a Purchase Order to Seller, a television manufacturer that read, "Send 1,000 Model X–19 52-inch televisions, with delivery by May 15." Seller did not have enough televisions in stock, and so immediately began to manufacture televisions to fulfill the order.

Seller has no further contact with Buyer until it shipped the televisions on May 8, with delivery guaranteed by May 15.

36. Which of the following is correct?

    (A) Seller has not effectively accepted the order for televisions.

    (B) Buyer may treat the offer has having lapsed before acceptance.

    (C) Buyer would be bound to the contract once he received the televisions.

    (D) Buyer may treat the duties under the contract as discharged.

Facts for Question 37

Retailer sent Manufacturer the following e-mail:

> Please immediately send 500 widgets at the listed price of $5/widget. Widgets are urgently needed due to our big sale next week.
>
> /s/ Retailer

Upon receipt of the e-mail, Manufacturer immediately sent Retailer the following response:

> We are out of stock of widgets. However, as an accommodation, we are sending you 500 of our semi-widgets at the listed price of $4/semi-widget. Most of our retailers have accepted the semi-widgets as a replacement for the widgets and we believe these will satisfy your customers.
>
> /s/ Manufacturer

Manufacturer sent the semi-widgets the next day. Retailer never responded to the Manufacturer's e-mail, and the semi-widgets arrived in time for the sale. Retailer returned the semi-widgets rather than put them on sale.

37. What is the best description of Retailer's rights arising out of this transaction?

    (A) By failing to respond to Manufacturer's e-mail, Retailer is obligated to accept the semi-widgets and must pay Manufacturer $4 for each one.

    (B) Retailer was not obligated to accept the semi-widgets; however, because it chose not to accept the semi-widgets, it has no right to sue Manufacturer for breach of contract.

    (C) Retailer is not obligated to accept the semi-widgets, and it is entitled to sue Manufacturer for breach of contract because Manufacturer sent non-conforming goods.

    (D) Retailer is not obligated to accept the semi-widgets; however, if it chooses not to accept them, it must allow Manufacturer a chance to cure by timely sending conforming widgets before Retailer is entitled to sue Manufacturer for breach of contract.

Facts for Question 38

Owner, a resident of San Francisco, has a vacation home in Palm Springs that he only visits from November–March. Owner makes an offer in June to Painter to repaint the vacation home for $6,000, by September 1. In the offer, Owner let Painter know that Owner would not be at the vacation home until November.

38. How can Painter accept?

    (A) Painter can accept by promise or performance, but if Painter accepts by performance, she must notify Owner or the payment duty of Owner is discharged.

    (B) Painter can accept by promise or performance, but does not need to notify Owner if she accepts by performance.

(C) Painter must accept by promise.

(D) Painter must accept by performance.

Facts for Question 39

Barry, a broke but aspiring chef heard that Francis French–Fry, a famous chef, was giving a free demonstration at a local cooking school. Barry went to the demonstration and was impressed with Francis's culinary skills. After the demonstration, Francis and his assistants went through the crowd to answer questions and let audience members know that Francis was giving cooking classes every Sunday morning for the next fourteen weeks for $550. For the next fourteen Sunday mornings, however, Barry showed up at the cooking school and participated in the baking lessons. Due to some administrative mix-up, Barry was not initially charged, but Francis is now seeking payment.

39. What, if anything, will Barry be required to pay for the lessons?

  (A) Whatever is determined to be the reasonable value of the cooking lessons.

  (B) The full $550, under an implied-in-fact contract theory.

  (C) Nothing, because of the mix-up, it was reasonable for Barry to infer a gratuitous intent.

  (D) Nothing, because the price of the lessons was over $500 and there was no signed writing memorializing the contract.

Facts for Question 40

Musician signed up for a monthly streaming music service like Spotify called Musicstream. Under their agreement, Musicstream automatically charged Musician's credit card $9.95 on the first of each month for that month's services. The agreement could be cancelled by Musician for any reason, but he had to give thirty days' notice to do so. Musician had checked out Spotify, which had a promotion going which allowed immediate cancellation with no extra payment, but Musician liked Musicstream's music library better, and signed up with that company.

Musician was fired from his latest gig and so wanted to trim expenses. He e-mailed Musicstream on February 2 to cancel his account and to promise truthfully that he would no longer listen to any music from the service. Musicstream responded by telling him in a return e-mail that he would be charged for February, but that he would be charged for only one day in March. Musician wanted the charges stopped as of February 1.

40. If Musician sued Musicstream in small claims court for a refund of the last $9.95 charge on his credit card for the period between February 2 and March 1, Musician should:

    (A) <u>Prevail</u>, because the terms of the Musicstream agreement are unconscionable.

    (B) <u>Prevail</u>, because charging of the credit card is an unenforceable acceptance by silence or inaction by Musician of Musicstream's offer for services for thirty days.

    (C) <u>Lose</u>, because Musician had given Musicstream reason to understand that assent for thirty days' worth of service may be manifested by silence or inaction.

    (D) <u>Lose</u>, because there is no consideration to support Musicstream's promise since Musician never listened to any music on the service during that last thirty day period.

Facts for Question 41

Owner owns a plot of undeveloped land in the state of Washegon. Owner went on an extended trip to Europe for several months. While Owner was gone, Contractor, who was having a slow month in terms of business, decided to build a home for Owner on the plot without talking to Owner. Contractor worked day and night for the several months Owner was gone and built a beautiful home. When Owner returned, Contractor told him, "If you use this house, you owe me $500,000 under contract law." Owner used the house, but was furious and refused to pay.

Contractor sues Owner for breach of contract.

41. Contractor will:

    (A) <u>Prevail</u>, because in using the home when Contractor told him that if he did so, he would owe her $500,000, Owner is deemed to have accepted by silence.

    (B) <u>Prevail</u>, but will only recover the reasonable value of the home under quasi-contract principles.

    (C) <u>Lose</u>, if $500,000 is an unreasonable price for the home.

    (D) <u>Lose</u>, because Owner did not have reasonable opportunity to reject the services.

Facts for Questions 42–44

Sam was a landscaper. Both Ashley and Betty owned homes and explained to Sam that they needed their front yards completely landscaped.

On June 15, Sam mailed Ashley and Betty offers to landscape their yards. Sam offered to landscape Ashley's for $1,000, and offered to do Betty's yard for $1,500. Both offers stated that Sam's offer would be open until June 30.

On the morning of June 20, Ashley mailed Sam a properly stamped and addressed letter stating, "I accept your offer." That afternoon, Ashley spoke with Zack, who said he'd do the job for $700. Ashley immediately mailed a letter to Sam by express mail that read, "Please disregard my other letter. I found someone else to landscape my lawn."

On June 21, Sam received the letter Ashley sent by express mail. The next day, on June 22, Sam received Ashley's first letter. Sam demanded that Ashley permit her to do the work for $1,000, but Ashley refused.

On June 24, Betty mailed a letter to Sam stating, "$1,500 is too much, I would agree to pay you $1,000 if you will agree to do the job." On June 25, Betty spoke to a few other landscapers, who said they would not do the job for less than $2,000. Realizing she could not get a better price, that afternoon Betty sent a letter by express mail to Sam stating, "Disregard my letter of 6/24. I accept your offer." Sam received both of Betty's letters on June 26.

On June 27, Betty spoke to Thomas, another landscaper. Thomas said he could to the job for $1,000. Betty immediately called Sam and said (before Sam could say anything), "This is Betty, and the deal is off." Sam then demanded that Betty permit him to do the work for $1,500. Betty refused.

42. If Sam sues Ashley for breach of contract, Sam will:

(A) <u>Lose</u>, because Sam received the letter Ashley sent by express mail before he received Ashley's first letter.

(B) <u>Lose</u>, because the acceptance in Ashley's first letter could be revoked up until the time Sam received it.

    (C) <u>Prevail</u>, because the letter Ashley sent by express mail did not have legal effect until Sam received it.

    (D) <u>Prevail</u>, because the offer in Ashley's first letter had legal effect when it was sent, even though Sam did not receive it first.

43. Assume Betty's first letter (the letter not sent by express mail) was received on the morning of June 26, and Betty's letter sent by express mail was received on the afternoon of June 26. If Sam sues Betty for breach of contract Sam will:

    (A) <u>Lose</u>, because Sam received Betty's first letter before Sam received the letter Betty sent by express mail.

    (B) <u>Lose</u>, because Betty's first letter had legal effect when it was sent.

    (C) <u>Prevail</u>, because Betty's first letter did not have legal effect until Sam received it.

    (D) <u>Prevail</u>, because the letter Betty sent by express mail had legal effect when it was sent, even though it was not received first.

44. For the purposes of this question only, assume that the letter Betty sent by express mail was received on the morning of June 26, and Betty's first letter (the letter not sent by express mail) was received on the afternoon of June 26. If Sam sues Betty for breach of contract Sam will:

    (A) <u>Lose</u>, because the letter Betty sent by express mail did not have legal effect when it was sent.

    (B) <u>Lose</u>, because Betty's first letter had legal effect when it was sent, even though it was not received first.

    (C) <u>Prevail</u>, because Sam received the letter Betty sent by express mail before Sam received Betty's first letter.

    (D) <u>Prevail</u>, because the letter Betty sent by express mail had legal effect when it was sent.

Facts for Questions 45 and 46

Owner calls professional plumber to his home and describes the work he wants done. Plumber says, "I estimate the work will take four hours and I charge $60/ hour. So my estimate is $240." Owner says, "That sounds reasonable. Go ahead."

45. Assuming no further communications between the parties, which is the most accurate statement?

(A) The parties are in an enforceable bilateral contract for the plumbing work to be done for $240.

(B) The parties are in an enforceable bilateral contract, but the price charged by the plumber could be more or less than $240, depending on how long the job actually takes, assuming she was acting in good faith both in making the estimate and in doing the work.

(C) The parties are not in an enforceable contract.

(D) The parties are in an enforceable unilateral option contract whereby the plumber is bound, but Owner may revoke any time before Plumber actually starts work.

46. Assume for this problem only that Plumber does the work described by Owner, but it reasonably and in good faith takes her 4 ½ hours to complete. She submits a bill to Owner of $270, constituting 4 ½ hours at $60/hour.

It turns out Plumber is expensive for the area. Most plumbers would only charge $50/hour, although it would take them 4 ½ hours to do the work as well. As such, their bills to Owner would be $225, constituting 4 ½ hours at $50/hour. However, assume they, too, would have estimated that the job would only take four hours, meaning their estimate would have been 4 hours at $50/hour, or $200.

How much does Owner owe Plumber?

(A) $270 (4 ½ hours x $60).

(B) $240 (4 hours x $60).

(C) $225 (4 ½ hours x $50).

(D) $200 (4 hours x $50).

Facts for Question 47

Dr. Brown, the Head of Trauma Care at prestigious University Hospital, comes across an unconscious car accident victim in the road on her way home. She applies her considerable skill and stabilizes the severely injured man. However, the injuries were too severe, and the man dies in the hospital.

As one of the foremost trauma care specialists in the world, Dr. Brown routinely charges $2,000 per visit when she sees patients in her office. A normal trauma doctor in the area where she practices charges $400 per visit.

47. If Dr. Brown sought payment from the injured victim's estate, which is the most accurate statement:

(A) She would be entitled to $2,000.

(B) She would be entitled to $400.

(C) She would have been entitled to $2,000 had the victim lived, but is due nothing from his estate.

(D) She would be entitled to nothing because she never entered into a contract with the victim.

CHAPTER 2
UCC § 2–207

QUESTIONS

Facts for Question 1

On October 1, Doggy Daycare ("Daycare") sends its own "Purchase Order" form to a dog food supply company ("Company"). The Purchase Order has blanks for type of food, quantity, price and delivery date, all of which Daycare fills in. Pre-printed Clause 15 in the Purchase Order requires Company to use the United States Postal Service for delivering the dog food.

Company receives the Purchase Order, and fills in the blanks in its own "Acceptance of Purchase Order" form. Company fills in the same information regarding type of food, quantity, price, and delivery date as were in the Purchase Order and sends the Acceptance form back to Daycare. However, pre-printed Clause 25 in the Acceptance form states that delivery will be done by U.P.S.

Daycare received the Acceptance form and checked to ensure that the type of food, quantity, price, and delivery date was correct and placed the form in its files.

The stated delivery date comes and goes, however, and Company never delivers the dog food. There is no communication between Company and Daycare other than set forth above.

1. Is Company liable to Daycare for breach of contract?

   (A) No, because of the discrepancy in the shipping terms between the Purchase Order form and Acceptance form, the two parties never had a contract.

   (B) No, because Daycare never assented to the different term.

   (C) Yes, but only if Daycare had materially relied on Company sending the dog food.

   (D) Yes, even though there was a discrepancy in the shipping terms between the Purchase Order form and the Acceptance form.

31

Facts for Question 2

Contractor orders windowpanes from Supplier. Two clauses of Contractor's Purchase Order provide:

All windowpanes supplied under this resulting contract shall be of stainable quality.

Acceptance of this Purchase Order is limited to terms of the Purchase Order. ("Limitation Clause")

Supplier immediately sends Contractor an Acceptance of Purchase Order form that is identical to the Purchase Order form, with the exception of: (1) there is no Limitation Clause; and (2) there is a clause which provides:

Supplier warrants that its products are only of paintable, not stainable quality.

The windowpanes are timely shipped and are accepted by Contractor. However, a few weeks later, when Contractor installed the windows and began staining them, he discovered they were not of stainable quality, but of a lesser, paintable quality only.

Contractor sues Supplier for breach of contract, claiming the contract was for stainable quality windowpanes, not the paintable quality windowpanes Supplier sent.

2. In his suit for breach of contract, Contractor will likely:

(A) Prevail, because Supplier breached the contract when it sent windowpanes that were not of stainable quality.

(B) Lose, because Supplier sent its form second.

(C) Lose, because the contract was for paintable quality windowpanes.

(D) Lose, because Contractor accepted the windowpanes.

Facts for Question 3

Buyer submits a Purchase Order for 500 pounds of grapes at a price of $3 per pound. Seller then sends a "confirmation" acknowledging Buyer's order for "500 pounds of bananas" at a price of $18 a pound. No further communication is exchanged between the parties.

3. Are Buyer and Seller in an enforceable contract?

(A) Yes, the two have a contract for 500 pounds of grapes at $3 a pound.

(B) Yes, the two have a contract for 500 pounds of bananas at $18 a pound.

(C) No, the two do not have a contract because their forms were too different.

(D) No, the two do not have a contract until and unless Seller ships the 500 pounds of bananas, regardless whether Buyer accepts them.

Facts for Questions 4 and 5

Buyer sent Seller a Purchase Order for 1,500 laptops at a price of $400 per laptop, and the Purchase Order had a clause stating that Buyer would have one year to make any breach of warranty claim. Seller sent Buyer an Acknowledgment confirming it would send 1,500 laptops at $400 per laptop. The Acknowledgment was identical to the purchase order, with these exceptions:

1. Any warranty claim for a laptop supplied under this contract must be asserted within ninety days.

2. Seller's acceptance is hereby expressly made conditional on Buyer's assent to the additional and different terms of this Acknowledgment.

The Purchase Order and Acceptance were the only communications regarding the contract exchanged between the parties. (Assume there are no unconscionability issues).

4. The laptops have not yet been sent. Which is the most accurate statement?

(A) The two are in a valid contract and there is a one year warranty claims period.

(B) The two are in a valid contract and there is a ninety day warranty claims period.

(C) The two are in a valid contract with the warranty claims period determined by what the law would provide if the parties had not included the one year or ninety day period in their forms.

(D) The two are not in an enforceable contract.

5. Assume the laptops were sent and Buyer accepted and paid for them. Which is the most accurate statement?

    (A) The two are in a valid contract and there is a one year warranty claims period.

    (B) The two are in a valid contract and there is a ninety day warranty claims period.

    (C) The two are in a valid contract with the warranty claims period determined by what the law would provide if the parties had not included the one year or ninety day period in their forms.

    (D) The two are not in an enforceable contract.

Facts for Question 6

Buyer sent Seller a Purchase Order for 1,000 apples at a price of $1/apple. Buyer's Purchase Order expressly limits its acceptance to the terms of the offer.

Seller responded with an Acknowledgement form and the form is identical to Buyer's Purchase Order, except for the following two clauses:

    1. Any dispute under the resulting contract shall be settled by arbitration by the American Arbitration Association under then-pending Commercial Arbitration Rules.

    2. Seller's acceptance is subject to all the terms and conditions in this document, including arbitration.

Seller delivered apples and Buyer accepted. However, several months later Buyer and Seller had a dispute. Buyer sued in district court and Seller moved to dismiss the suit, claiming the dispute had to be arbitrated. Both Buyer and Seller are merchants.

6. Should the court rule that the dispute must be arbitrated?

    (A) Yes, because Seller made its acceptance subject to the arbitration clause and Buyer paid for apples under the contract.

    (B) Yes, if Buyer read the arbitration clause and did not object.

    (C) No, because the "subject to all the terms" clause was insufficient to turn the acceptance into a counteroffer.

    (D) No, because the arbitration clause proposed by Seller is inoperative due to the "knock out" rule.

Facts for Question 7

Buyer sends Seller a Purchase Order for 1,000 t-shirts at $5 per t-shirt. There is no clause limiting the acceptance of the Purchase Order to its terms.

Seller timely sends an "Acceptance of Purchase Order" that has the same terms as the Purchase Order except the following, which was prominently and conspicuously displayed: "Under this contract there is no implied warranty of merchantability." This clause is known as a "warranty disclaimer."

Both Buyer and Seller are merchants, and assume that Seller's Acceptance of Purchase Order is an effective acceptance.

7. Is the warranty disclaimer part of the contract?

   (A) Yes, unless Buyer objects to it.

   (B) Yes, because both Buyer and Seller are merchants and the warranty disclaimer does not materially alter the contract.

   (C) Yes, because Buyer did not expressly limit acceptance to the terms of the offer.

   (D) No, because both Buyer and Seller are merchants and the warranty disclaimer materially alters the contract

Facts for Question 8

Buyer, a department store chain, sends Seller a Purchase Order for 1,000 t-shirts at $5 per t-shirt every month for the next ten months. Payment is due thirty days after receipt of the shirts. There is no clause limiting the acceptance of the Purchase Order to its terms.

Seller timely sends an "Acceptance of Purchase Order" that has the same terms as the Purchase Order except the following: "Seller has the option to cancel this contract and refuse to send any additional shirts under it upon Buyer's failure to meet [pay] any one invoice when due." This clause is known as the "one invoice default clause."

Both Buyer and Seller are merchants, and assume that Seller's Acceptance of Purchase Order is an effective acceptance.

8. Is the one invoice default clause part of the contract?

   (A) Yes, unless Buyer objects to it.

   (B) Yes, because both Buyer and Seller are merchants and the one invoice default clause does not materially alter the contract.

(C) Yes, because Buyer did not expressly limit acceptance to the terms of the offer.

(D) No, because both Buyer and Seller are merchants and the one invoice default clause materially alters the contract.

Facts for Question 9

Buyer, a department store chain, sends Seller a Purchase Order for 1000 t-shirts at $5 per t-shirt every month for the next ten months. Payment is due thirty days after receipt of the shirts. There is no clause limiting the acceptance of the Purchase Order to its terms.

Seller timely sends an "Acceptance of Purchase Order" that has the same terms as the Purchase Order except the following: "Seller will charge interest at 6% per year on overdue invoices." This clause is known as the "overdue interest clause."

Both Buyer and Seller are merchants, and assume that Seller's Acceptance of Purchase Order is an effective acceptance.

9. Is the overdue interest clause part of the contract?

(A) Yes, unless Buyer objects to it.

(B) Yes, because both Buyer and Seller are merchants and the overdue interest clause does not materially alter the contract.

(C) Yes, because Buyer did not expressly limit acceptance to the terms of the offer.

(D) No, because both Buyer and Seller are merchants and the overdue interest clause materially alters the contract.

Facts for Question 10

Buyer sends Seller a Purchase Order for 500 laptops at $600 per laptop. Seller sends Buyer an Acknowledgment that is the same as Buyer's Purchase Order with the exception of a clause that states that all disputes arising under the contract must be resolved in arbitration, rather than litigation ("arbitration clause"). Buyer receives the forms and immediately reads the arbitration clause. He immediately calls Seller and tells her that he objects to the arbitration provision. Both Buyer and Seller are merchants.

10. Is the arbitration clause part of the contract?

(A) No, because Buyer gave Seller notification of objection within a reasonable time after Buyer received notice of the additional term.

(B) Yes, unless Buyer expressly limited acceptance to the terms of the offer in its Purchase Order.

(C) Yes, unless Seller agrees to remove the clause.

(D) Yes, unless the court finds that the arbitration clause materially alters the contract.

Facts for Question 11

Rip–Off, a retailer, advertised vintage Ed Hardy t-shirts for $200 on Amazon.com. Buyer, an individual, e-mailed an offer to purchase one of the shirts, giving his credit card. Rip–Off e-mailed back an "Acceptance of Offer," which had identical terms to the offer except that it included a clause requiring that any dispute under the agreement had to be decided by arbitration and not litigation ("arbitration clause").

Assume that Rip–Off's Acceptance of Offer is an effective acceptance.

11. Is the arbitration clause part of the contract?

(A) Yes, unless Buyer objects to the arbitration clause.

(B) Yes, unless a court finds the arbitration clause materially alters the contract.

(C) No, because arbitration clauses do not materially alter contracts.

(D) No, unless Buyer specifically agrees to the arbitration clause.

Question 12

12. Which of the following statements is (are) FALSE:

I. If there is a contract made by telephone, and Seller thereafter sends a "Confirmation of Order" to Buyer, the situation is not governed by UCC § 2–207 since there is only one form exchanged between the parties.

II. If an offeror provides in its offer that it refuses to engage in arbitration of disputes under the resulting contract, absent a change of heart by the offeror, there can never be an effective arbitration provision in the parties' final contract (so long as the agreement is formed by an exchange of forms), even if the court determines that an arbitration clause does not materially alter the deal.

III.   A clause limiting the time under which the seller must act on complaints made by the buyer will always materially alter the deal.

(A) I only.

(B) II and III only.

(C) I and III only.

(D) All the statements are false.

Question 13

Author's Note:

The remaining questions in this chapter deal with an issue many first year contracts professors skip, believing that it will be covered in upper division Commercial Law or Sales courses. I would recommend you look at Question 13, which introduces the issue, and if you discover that this is not an issue your professor covers, you should probably skip the remaining questions in this chapter. After all, UCC § 2–207 analysis is hard enough without going around looking for issues.

13. If an expression of acceptance states "different" terms from those found in the offer, which approach has been, or which approaches have been, used by courts to determine if the different terms become a part of the contract?

(A) The "different" terms will judged under the same standards as if they were "additional" terms, which finds support in UCC § 2–207, Cmt. 3.

(B) The "different" terms will never become a part of the contract without the offeror separately and specifically agreeing to them under what is called "the literalist" approach.

(C) The "different" terms in both the offer and acceptance will be "knocked out," and either there will be no term on the issue (and the law that normally applies in the absence of a term will become operative), or a gap filler is used to provide the term under what is known as the "Cmt. 6" approach.

(D) All of the above have been used by courts.

Facts for Questions 14–16

Buyer sends Seller a Purchase Order for 1,000 notebooks at $3 per notebook. The Purchase Order specifies that the notebooks will be delivered to Buyer's store by October 1. There is no limitation of acceptance to the terms of the offer clause in the Purchase Order nor is there a clause by which the Buyer states that no other delivery date will be acceptable.

Upon receipt of the Purchase Order, Seller sends Buyer an Acknowledgment form confirming the purchase of 1,000 notebooks at $3 each. However, Seller's form states that the notebooks will be delivered to Buyer's store by October 5.

The exchange of the forms is the only relevant communication between the parties.

14. Under the approach to "different" terms that finds support in UCC § 2–207, Cmt. 3, what will the delivery date be?

    (A) October 1, unless the delivery date materially alters the offer.

    (B) October 5, unless the delivery date materially alters the offer.

    (C) October 1, unless Buyer specifically and separately agrees to an October 5 delivery date.

    (D) There is no delivery term and a gap filler will have to be used to establish this term.

15. Under the "literalist" approach, what will the delivery date be?

    (A) October 1, unless the delivery date materially alters the offer.

    (B) October 5, unless the delivery date materially alters the offer.

    (C) October 1, unless Buyer specifically and separately agrees to an October 5 delivery date.

    (D) There is no delivery term and a gap filler will have to be used to establish this term.

16. Under the "Cmt. 6" theory, what will the delivery date be?

   (A) October 1, unless the delivery date materially alters the offer.

   (B) October 5, unless the delivery date materially alters the offer.

   (C) October 1, unless Buyer specifically and separately agrees to an October 5 delivery date.

   (D) There is no delivery term and a gap filler will have to be used to establish this term.

CHAPTER 3
INDEFINITENESS AN
FILLERS

QUESTIONS

Facts for Question 1

Priscilla and Sarah enter into an agreement by which Priscilla would build a custom patio cover for Sarah's new home. They agreed as to the price ($1,200) and the design, but they did not agree on a start or completion date, but rather they agreed to figure it out at a later date.

Six months after they made the agreement, Priscilla had not started construction on the patio cover and there was no other communication between them. Sarah has now sued Priscilla for breach of contract.

1.   In a jurisdiction that follows common law rules, Sarah will likely:

   (A) <u>Prevail</u>, because six months is not a reasonable time to wait before beginning construction.

   (B) <u>Prevail</u>, if the contract was put in writing.

   (C) <u>Lose</u>, because the terms of the contract were too indefinite.

   (D) <u>Lose</u>, if the contract was not put in writing.

Facts for Question 2

Landlord leased a commercial space to Tenant who wanted to use the space as a restaurant. The lease was for ten years and contained an "option to purchase" clause, allowing Tenant to purchase the property at the end of the lease term. The lease provided that the Tenant had to give notice of its intention to exercise the option six months before the lease ended, but contained no language about the purchase price or language indicating the parties agreed to agree on the price later.

Tenant gave timely notice of its intention to exercise the option to purchase the building nine and a half years into the lease, but Landlord refused to sell, arguing there was no enforceable agreement as to the sale of the building because no price was set and no mechanism for determining the price was mentioned in the lease.

In an action by Tenant against Landlord for breach of contract in a jurisdiction that follows the Restatement 2d, what is the likely result?

(A) Judgment for Tenant, and the sale must take place at a reasonable price.

(B) Judgment for Tenant, and the sale must take place at a price set by Tenant as winner of the action.

(C) Judgment for Tenant, but Tenant can only seek monetary damages as the terms are too indefinite to order specific performance.

(D) Judgment for Landlord, because there was no enforceable agreement as to the option due to indefiniteness.

Facts for Question 3

Mr. and Mrs. Smith contract with Paul's landscaping service to "landscape our home in Orange County," twice a month for $150. Unknown to Paul, Mr. and Mrs. Smith have three homes in Orange County: one in Huntington Beach; one in Newport Beach, and one in Irvine.

Paul shows up at the Huntington Beach home on a Saturday when the Smiths are there and they let Paul in the gate to perform the landscaping services. The grounds of the Huntington Beach home were the smallest of the Smiths' three homes, and the fair market value of his services at the Huntington Beach home was only $100.

Now, Mr. and Mrs. Smith refuse to pay anything, claiming the contract was for the Irvine house. Their argument is the contract was unenforceable based on indefiniteness as to which residence was intended.

3. In an action by Paul for payment, what result?

(A) The contract is unenforceable because of the indefiniteness as to which residence was intended, but Paul can recover for the $100 fair market value of his services for the Huntington beach home on a *quantum meruit* basis.

(B) The contract is unenforceable because it was not in writing, but Paul can recover for the $100 fair market value of his services for the Huntington Beach home on a *quantum meruit* basis.

(C) The contract is enforceable because the contract is sufficiently definite regardless of the Smiths' conduct.

(D) The contract is enforceable because Paul was allowed to landscape the Huntington Beach home by the Smiths, and Paul is entitled to $150.

Facts for Questions 4–6

Buyer and Seller entered an agreement by which Buyer was to purchase 200 widgets at $1 per widget. This is the first transaction between the parties and there is no applicable usage of trade. The parties agree that Seller is to deliver the goods to Buyer, but the parties do not determine the exact date of delivery.

4. Under the UCC, when would the Seller be required to deliver the widgets?

(A) Never, because the parties have not formed an enforceable contract.

(B) Within a week of the agreement, if that date is set by Seller.

(C) Within a week of the agreement, if that date is set by Buyer.

(D) Within two weeks of the agreement, if the court determines that is a reasonable time.

5. For this question only, assume that delivery was set for January 1, but the parties did not agree where delivery of the widgets was to take place or when payment for the widgets was due. Under the UCC, where would delivery take place and when would payment be due?

(A) Delivery and payment would not be required because the parties do not have an enforceable contract.

(B) Delivery is to occur at Seller's place of business, with payment due when Buyer receives the goods.

(C) Delivery is to occur at Seller's place of business, with payment due within a reasonable time of receiving the goods.

(D) Delivery is to occur at Buyer's place of business, with payment due within a reasonable time of receiving the goods.

6. For this question only, assume that delivery was set for January 1, Seller was to deliver them to Buyer's place of business with payment on delivery, but the parties did not stipulate if the widgets were to be delivered in one single lot or in multiple installments. Under the UCC, how would Seller be required to deliver the widgets?

    (A) Seller is always required to deliver the widgets in a single lot unless otherwise specified in the agreement.

    (B) Seller is always required to deliver the widgets in multiple lots unless otherwise specified in the agreement.

    (C) Buyer can demand delivery in multiple lots if he does not have the storage space for a single delivery and it would not be an inconvenience to Seller.

    (D) Buyer has the unfettered discretion to demand delivery in a single lot or multiple lots because delivery is set to take place at his place of business.

Facts for Question 7

Contractor reaches an agreement with Supplier under which Supplier will provide a "truck-load" of lumber for a single-family home that Contractor is building. The parties agreed that the "truck-load" would cost $2000 and delivery was to take place at the jobsite on June 1. The lumber is to be Coastal Pine of excellent quality. Supplier believes that a "truck-load" is 1,000 pounds of lumber.

7. Which of the following is an accurate statement?

    (A) The contract would be enforceable for 1,000 pounds of lumber if contractors in the business of building single-family homes understand a "truck-load" to be 1,000 pounds.

    (B) The contract would be enforceable for 1,000 pounds of lumber if Contractor has ordered seven "truck-loads" of lumber for past jobs from Supplier and each time Supplier delivered 1,000 pounds of lumber without objection from Contractor and were accepted by it.

    (C) The contract would be enforceable for 1,000 pounds of lumber if this were the third such "truck load" order for this specific job site under the current agreement between Contractor and Supplier and Supplier has delivered 1000 pounds of lumber in response to each of these orders without objection from Contractor and were accepted by it.

    (D) All of the above are accurate.

Facts for Question 8

Dealership and Manufacturer reach an agreement on July 1 under which Manufacturer is to deliver to Dealership a shipment of new cars for Dealership's summer sale, but the parties do not agree on the date for delivery. The cars are to be delivered in one lot, which is the first and only order and delivery under this agreement.

It is customary in the car business that delivery is to take place two weeks after agreement. However, Dealership and Manufacturer, in all of their past dealings, which included multiple shipments of cars for special sales, have set delivery for one month after agreement.

On July 10, Manufacturer receives an order from another car dealership, and begins work on that order which delays delivery of Buyer's order until July 30.

8. Under the UCC, has Seller breached the contract for failing to deliver the cars on time?

  (A) Yes, because the usage of trade would require delivery by July 15.

  (B) No, because delivery by August 1 would be operative due to course of performance.

  (C) No, because delivery by August 1 would be operative due to course of dealing.

  (D) No, because the contract was too indefinite to be enforced.

CHAPTER 4
CONSIDERATION AND PROMISSORY ESTOPPEL

QUESTIONS

Facts for Question 1

Uncle David, a successful businessman, made a promise to his 14-year-old nephew Paul in front of the 100 people present at David's 50th birthday party. Uncle David promised that if Paul refrained from playing football in high school and college, when Paul turned 21, David would give him $25,000. David was very fearful that Paul would suffer a concussion playing football and hoped that, with football out of the way, there would be nothing to stand in Paul's way to a successful business career and taking over David's company later in life. Paul refrained from playing the sport. Upon turning 21, he demanded the $25,000 promised, but David refused to pay.

1. In an action to enforce the promise, who will prevail? (For purposes of this question, ignore any issues regarding the capacity of a teenager to contract and assume that Paul could enter into a contract in the relevant jurisdiction, and otherwise assume Restatement 2d of Contracts rules apply).

  (A) David, because David received no legal benefit from Paul's not playing football.

  (B) David, because the promise was oral.

  (C) Paul, because Paul's refraining from playing football was adequate consideration to enforce the promised payment.

  (D) David, because the promise is between people who are related.

Facts for Question 2

Aunt Mary was a rich widow who loved her adult nephew Bill. However, Bill had come across tough times and had become addicted to cocaine. In order to help him put his life together, she invited him to her home and sat down with him in front of friends, family, clergy, and the local newspaper and told him, "Bill, if you forego cocaine for 5 years, I will give you $100,000 to build a new life." Assume the jurisdiction follows the Restatement 2d.

2. If Bill later seeks to enforce the promise after foregoing cocaine, will he prevail?

  (A) No, because the promise was not supported by consideration.

  (B) No, because it was oral.

  (C) Yes, because Bill's actions constitute a forbearance which is adequate consideration.

  (D) No, because the promise is between people who are related.

Facts for Question 3

Patty, a young college graduate, had saved up $5,000 while working on the weekends during her college years. She needed a car to go out for interviews to obtain a professional job and knew her uncle Donald had a car he was not using. She explained her situation to Donald who offered to sell it to her for the $5,000 she had saved to help her out with her job hunt, even though both Patty and Donald knew that similar cars were selling for no less than $8,000 on Autotrader.com and other car selling sites. She accepted on the spot and wrote him a check there and then, which Donald put in his wallet. However, the next day, when she went to pick up the keys and arrange for title to be transferred, Donald said he could no longer give her the car for that price and gave her back her check.

3. In an action for breach of contract, who will prevail?

  (A) Donald, because the promise to sell was not supported by adequate consideration.

  (B) Donald, because until Patty picked up the keys and had the title transferred, the deal was not final and so he had the right to change his mind.

  (C) Patty, because there was a bargained-for exchange.

  (D) Patty, because of the moral obligation theory of consideration.

Facts for Questions 4–6

All of the following took place in a jurisdiction that follows the Restatement 2d.

Professor Smith looked out his front window one day when he heard some screeching tires. He immediately turned and saw his neighbor Peter hit by a car driven by Daniel.

Dr. Jones, who was driving by, stopped and treated Peter and took him to the hospital. Despite Dr. Jones's rapid response and competent, expert treatment, Peter died from his wounds at the hospital a few days later.

Professor Smith felt horrible about the whole situation because he had called Peter and asked him to come over because Professor Smith had some homemade cookies he wanted to give Peter.

In order to cheer up Professor Smith, three of his students washed and groomed his prized poodle. The following day, to show his thanks, Smith promised the students he would pay them each $20. (The reasonable value of the wash and grooming was $150).

Although Professor Smith was not legally responsible for Peter's accident, he felt responsible because Peter was coming to see him and because of that, he promised Peter's widow $10,000 a week after the crash.

4. Who, if anyone, is obligated to pay Dr. Jones for the treatment of Peter?

(A) Professor Smith.

(B) Peter's Estate.

(C) Both Peter's Estate and Professor Smith.

(D) Neither Smith nor Peter's Estate is obligated to pay Dr. Jones.

5. What are Professor Smith's obligations regarding the students?

(A) He is legally obligated to pay the students $20 each as promised.

(B) He is legally obligated to pay the students $150, which they must equitably split among them.

(C) He is legally obligated to pay the students under the moral theory of consideration.

(D) He is not legally obligated to pay the students anything.

6. What are Professor Smith's obligations regarding Peter's widow?

   (A) He is not obligated to pay the widow anything.

   (B) He is obligated to pay $10,000, assuming her financial loss due to the death of her husband is at least equal to the $10,000 Smith promised to pay her.

   (C) He is obligated to pay $10,000 under the doctrine of promissory estoppel.

   (D) He is obligated to pay $10,000 because the promise was supported by consideration.

Facts for Question 7

While negligently driving his father's uninsured car, Aaron crashed into a car driven by Brittany. Both Aaron and Brittany were injured. Aaron's father Carlos, reasonably but incorrectly believing that he would be liable as owner of the vehicle in the jurisdiction, told Brittany that he would "see that she was reimbursed for any losses" she incurred as a result of the accident. At all times relevant, assume Brittany had no thought of suing Carlos.

7. In an action by Brittany against Carlos for lost wages while she recuperated from the accident, which of the following would be Carlos's best defense?

   (A) Lack of consideration.

   (B) Mistake of fact as to a basic assumption.

   (C) Statute of frauds.

   (D) Indefiniteness of Carlos's promise.

Facts for Question 8

While on a cruise, Alex, Brett's adult son, fell ill for several weeks. Another passenger on the ship, Cornelius, took care of Alex in his ill state. Alex did not have any additional money to pay Cornelius for his care, but Brett wrote to Cornelius expressing his thanks and promised to reimburse Cornelius for any expenses incurred in caring for Alex. Alex and Cornelius returned to their respective homes after the cruise, and Cornelius sent Brett a list of expenses from Alex's care. Brett refused to pay the expenses.

8.   In a suit by Cornelius to enforce Brett's promise, Cornelius will:

(A) <u>Prevail</u>, because the promise was supported by bargained-for consideration.

(B) <u>Prevail</u>, under a moral obligation theory of recovery.

(C) <u>Prevail</u>, because the treatment of Alex is sufficient past consideration.

(D) <u>Lose</u>, because the promise was not supported by adequate consideration.

Facts for Question 9

Borrower owes $10,000 to Lender, but fails to pay it back. The debt consists of a loan with a $7,500 principal, and $2,500 interest on the principal. The statute of limitations has expired and thereafter Borrower tells Lender that he is sorry and promises, "I will pay you back $7,500 by January 31 of the following year" ("January 31 Promise"). Borrower fails to pay the agreed amount by January 31.

9.   In a jurisdiction that follows the Restatement 2d of Contracts, which of the following most accurately states Borrower's obligation to Lender?

(A) Borrower enforceably owes Lender $7,500.

(B) Borrower enforceably owes Lender $10,000 as the January 31 Promise effectively revived the debt.

(C) Borrower owes Lender nothing because the January 31 Promise lacked consideration.

(D) Borrower owes Lender nothing because the statute of limitations on the original debt expired.

Facts for Question 10

Dell Computers entered into an exclusive dealing agreement with Best Buy whereby Best Buy was granted the exclusive right to sell its computers nationwide in return for 60% of the sales price of any Dell computers sold, if any. The parties agreed to an initial shipment of 10,000 computers, with more computers to be shipped later, upon mutual agreement, once the initial shipment was sold.

10. Which of the following best describes Best Buy's obligations to Dell Computers under the agreement?

(A) Best Buy is not obligated to do anything to try to sell any Dell computers because Best Buy's obligation was illusory and not supported by consideration.

(B) Best Buy is required to use "best efforts" in trying to sell Dell computers, but is not obligated to sell any computers.

(C) Best Buy is required to sell 10,000 Dell computers, but is not obligated to order any additional computers.

(D) Best Buy is required to sell all of the Dell computers delivered in the initial shipment, and is obligated to continue to receive shipments to sell in the future once those are sold.

Facts for Questions 11 and 12

Sammy's Scrap Heap entered into a written contract with Carl's Car Parts under which Sammy's would supply, and Carl's would buy, all of the excess scrap metal that Carl's required from Sammy's. Sammy's obtained its supply of scrap from old cars that were donated or that it bought from the city impound. Carl's ordinarily needed 200 pounds of scrap every month, and that quantity was put in the contract as a good faith monthly estimate that Sammy's would be required to furnish.

For six months, orders by Carl's varied between 175–225 pounds. However, one month Carl's received an extremely large order of car parts and ordered 1,000 pounds from Sammy's, which Carl's actually and in good faith needed, but Sammy's refused to supply that much.

11. If Carl's sues Sammy's for failing to deliver the 1,000 pounds, Carl's will most likely:

(A) Lose, because the contract lacked consideration.

(B) Lose, because the offer to sell can be revoked at any time.

(C) Prevail, as long as Sammy's is acting in good faith.

(D) Lose, because of the stated estimate and previous purchases made by Carl's.

12. Assume that Carl's in good faith ordered the stated estimate of 200 pounds instead of the 1,000 in the pertinent month. Sammy's states that it is no longer going to deliver any scrap under the contract because, while it was making a few cents a pound when the contract started, it is now losing a few cents per pound under the deal because of increased energy costs.

If Carl's sues Sammy's for failing to deliver, Carl's should:

(A) Prevail, because 200 pounds is reasonable in light of course of dealing under the contract.

(B) Prevail, because Sammy's is acting in bad faith by basing its decision on losing money.

(C) Lose, because Sammy's has a valid commercial impracticability defense.

(D) Lose, because the contract is unenforceable because it is illusory.

Facts for Question 13

Tony's Trucking agreed to transport lumber from Larry's forest property in Oregon to Larry's lumber yard in Northern California. The price was fixed at $1,000 per truckload and the contract was for a four year term. Three years into the agreement, the price of gasoline unexpectedly and suddenly rose from $3.10 per gallon (the gas price at the start of the contract) to $4.50 per gallon. As a result of the increase, Tony is now losing money on each delivery.

Tony asks Larry if he would be willing to raise the price from $1,000 to $1,250 per truckload for the remaining year of the contract which would allow Tony to stop losing money and break even. Larry agrees to this.

13. In a jurisdiction which follows the Restatement 2d of Contracts, is Larry's promise to pay $1,250 per delivery enforceable?

(A) No, because Tony is under a preexisting duty to deliver the lumber.

(B) Yes, because the modification is fair and equitable in light of circumstances not anticipated when the contract was entered into.

(C) No, because there was no consideration for the promise to modify their agreement.

(D) Yes, because modifications never need consideration to be enforceable under the Restatement 2d of Contracts.

Facts for Question 14

Uncle told Nephew that he would give Nephew a valuable gold watch (worth $12,000) if Nephew would drive 400 miles to Uncle's house to pick it up. Uncle didn't like Nephew all that much, but Nephew was his only living relative and Uncle felt that his valuable watch should stay within the family. Nephew took two days off from work and drove the 400 miles to Uncle's house. When he got there, Uncle told Nephew that he had changed his mind and did not wish to part with the watch at this time.

14. Does Nephew have a viable claim under any theory against Uncle?

   (A) No, because Uncle's promise lacked consideration.

   (B) Yes, if a court finds that justice requires enforcement.

   (C) Yes, because there was a bargained-for exchange.

   (D) No, because the promise was made to a family member.

Facts for Question 15

At a family reunion, Pauline sat next to her grandmother Daniella. She told her that she was hoping to go to Paris the following summer after graduation. That spring, she received a card from her grandmother wishing her safe travels with a note stating: "Because of your trip, I will transfer $2,000 into your savings account when you return." Relying on the card and note, Pauline went to Paris and spent $1,000 of her savings on the trip. However, when she returned, Daniella refused to transfer the $2,000.

15. To what extent, if any, can Pauline enforce her grandmother's promise to pay her, in a jurisdiction governed by the Restatement 2d?

   (A) The promise is unenforceable because past consideration is insufficient to make a promise enforceable.

   (B) The promise is unenforceable because it was a gift promise.

   (C) The promise is enforceable, entitling Pauline to $2,000.

   (D) The promise is enforceable, but only for $1,000.

Facts for Questions 16

Donee calls a St. Jude's telethon to contribute to the charity and pledges $500. However, when the charity later calls Donee back to inquire when to expect its payment, Donee tells them that she has changed her mind and that she will no longer be donating.

16. In a jurisdiction controlled by the Restatement 2d of Contracts, in an action by St. Jude's seeking the pledge, who will prevail?

    (A) Donee, because the promise was a gift and not supported by consideration.

    (B) St. Jude's, because it is a charitable organization, even if St. Jude's did not rely on the pledge.

    (C) St. Jude's, but only if it can prove it relied on the pledge.

    (D) St. Jude's, but only if Donee is acting in bad faith.

CHAPTER 5
STATUTE OF FRAUDS

QUESTIONS

Facts for Question 1

Contractor is a successful businessman known for being very expensive, taking longer than expected on jobs, but doing the best quality work. He is awarded an oral contract for $3 billion to build an office tower in Los Angeles twice the size of the Empire State Building in New York. No completion date for the project is specified.

1. Is the contract within the Statute of Frauds?

   (A) Yes, if a court finds it is "factually unlikely" that the contract will be performed within a year.

   (B) Yes, because it is impossible that the contract will be "fully performed" within a year.

   (C) No, because it is not impossible for the contract to be performed within a year.

   (D) No, because construction contracts are not subject to the Statute of Frauds.

Facts for Question 2

Seller and Buyer enter into an oral agreement for the purchase of an easement across Seller's property. Seller tendered the correct title, but Buyer refused to complete the transaction. Seller sues Buyer.

2. Which of the following is a correct statement?

   (A) Seller will prevail because an agreement for the purchase of an easement is not within the Statute of Frauds.

   (B) Seller will lose if Buyer asserts the Statute of Frauds as a defense.

(C) Seller will prevail because a party to be charged can waive the Statute of Frauds since a contract within the Statute of Frauds which is not satisfied is only voidable, not void.

(D) Neither (A), (B), nor (C) is correct.

Facts for Questions 3 and 4

On April 1, Seller orally agreed to sell his land, Blackacre, to Buyer for $45,000 to be paid April 30. Buyer orally agreed to pay $24,000 of the purchase price to Lender in satisfaction of a debt which Seller said he had promised to pay Lender.

On April 10, Buyer dictated the agreement to his secretary but omitted all reference to the payment to Lender. Neither Buyer nor Seller carefully read the writing before signing it April 15. Neither noticed the absence of the payment to Lender nor objected to its absence.

Consider the following statements:

  I.   Buyer could successfully raise the Statute of Frauds as a defense because the Buyer–Seller agreement was a suretyship agreement whereby one party agrees to answer for the debt of another.

  II. Buyer could successfully raise the Statute of Frauds as a defense because the Buyer–Seller agreement was for the sale of an interest in land.

3. In an action by Lender against Buyer for $24,000, which of the following is (are) correct, if any?

(A) I only.

(B) II only.

(C) Both I and II.

(D) Neither I nor II.

Fact Variation for Question 4

For the purposes of this question, assume that when Buyer's secretary typed up the agreement, she mistakenly listed the purchase price as $44,000, instead of the "correct" figure of $45,000. Neither Buyer nor Seller carefully read the writing before signing on April 15. Neither noticed the incorrect price nor objected to it. Buyer tenders $44,000 and refuses to pay more.

For purposes of this question, ignore any applicability of the parol evidence rule.

4. If Seller sues for the additional $1,000, which of the following is most accurate in describing the effect of the Statute of Frauds in this transaction?

    (A) Seller is estopped to testify to the "correct" terms of the contract.

    (B) Seller alone may testify as to the "correct" terms of the contract as the party contesting the inaccuracy in the price.

    (C) Buyer alone may testify as to the "correct" terms of the contract as the party to be charged.

    (D) Either Seller or Buyer may freely testify as to the "correct" terms of the contract.

Facts for Question 5

Grandfather had a thirty-acre parcel lying fallow. On their wedding day, Grandfather orally promised Granddaughter and her groom, Beau, that they could have title to the land on their fifteen-year anniversary if they moved onto the property and worked the land, and paid him 10% of any revenues derived from the property during the interim.

Granddaughter and Beau gave up their legal jobs and moved onto the property right after the wedding. Over the next fifteen years they always sent Grandfather 10% of the revenues and had established a working ranch with a barn and a house, and corrals for fifty horses. Grandfather was aware of their efforts and both allowed and encouraged the work. However, after their fifteen-year anniversary, Grandfather said he now wanted the land back, and refused to convey title.

5. Which is the most accurate statement?

    (A) Granddaughter and Beau cannot enforce Grandfather's promise because it was an oral agreement to transfer an interest in real property.

    (B) Granddaughter and Beau cannot enforce Grandfather's promise because it was too indefinite.

(C) Granddaughter and Beau can enforce Grandfather's promise due to reliance.

(D) Granddaughter and Beau can enforce Grandfather's promise only if they can establish that Grandfather never intended to give them the land when he made the promise at the wedding.

Facts for Question 6

Seller authorized Agent <u>in writing</u> to sign a contract for the sale and purchase of land for him. Buyer <u>orally</u> authorized Broker to sign the contract for him.

Agent and Broker signed a written contract for the sale of the land: "Seller by Agent" and "Buyer by Broker." Buyer refuses to complete the purchase and Seller sues Buyer who pleads the Statute of Frauds.

6. In a suit by Seller in a jurisdiction that recognized the equal dignities rule, Seller will:

(A) <u>Prevail</u>, because the sales contract was in writing.

(B) <u>Prevail</u>, because his agency contract was in writing.

(C) <u>Lose</u>, because he did not sign the contract personally.

(D) <u>Lose</u>, because Buyer's agency contract was not in writing.

Facts for Questions 7 and 8

Donna operates a retail television store. Phil operates a wholesale distribution business which specializes in televisions, such as the Samsung Model X. Donna telephoned Phil May 1 and said, "I need a Samsung Model X television, can you get me one?" Phil replied "Yes, but it will take a month . . ." At that point Donna interrupted Phil to say "I have to go, an important customer just walked in. You will deliver the T.V. in a month for sure?" Phil responded "Yes," and Donna ended the call by saying, "I'll be waiting for it. Good-bye."

The next day Phil sent Donna a brief note (with Phil's initials at the bottom) that said, "Per agreement with Donna: one Samsung Model X television to be delivered on June 1." Donna received Phil's note on May 4. Donna later sent Phil a letter that stated, "I never agreed to buy a television from you. We didn't even agree on a price."

Phil sued Donna; in Phil's complaint all of the foregoing facts were alleged.

Consider the following facts:

I.   Donna sent her letter to Phil on May 16.

II. The price for the Model X was $2000 and Donna's letter was sent on May 5.

III. The price for the Model X was $400.

7. Which of the above facts would be helpful to Phil in countering Donna's Statute of Frauds defense argument?

(A) I only.

(B) II only.

(C) I and III only.

(D) III only.

Fact Variation for Question 8

Assume the following for this question only: a contract was formed, Donna did not send any letter to Phil, Phil failed to deliver the television, the reasonable value of the television was $6000, and Donna has sued Phil in an action in which <u>Phil</u> has asserted the Statute of Frauds defense.

Consider the following statements.

I.   Donna is the "party to be charged" for purposes of the Statute of Frauds.

II. The contract is enforceable because there is an adequate memorandum signed by the "party to be charged."

III. The contract is unenforceable because Phil's letter fails to satisfy the requirements of a confirmatory memorandum.

8. Which of the above statements is (are) correct?

(A) I only.

(B) I and III.

(C) II only.

(D) III only.

Facts for Questions 9 and 10

Manufacturer designs and builds industrial pressing machines for commercial dry cleaners.

On March 1, Buyer telephoned Manufacturer and ordered two of their Model A pressing machines at $10,000 each. Both parties agreed that delivery of the first was to be April 15, and the second on May 30. Payment was to be no later than thirty days after delivery. On April 15, Manufacturer delivered the first machine, which Buyer accepted. On May 25, Manufacturer completed the second machine, but had not yet tendered it to Buyer, i.e., had not yet notified Buyer it was ready for delivery. The next day, Buyer's President, with Buyer having made no payments yet, called Manufacturer and said she hoped Manufacturer was not planning to deliver any additional machines as Buyer would not pay for it.

Model A pressing machines are standard models and could be used by any professional dry cleaning establishment without alteration. Assume the parties are in a jurisdiction that does not recognize the estoppel exception to the Statute of Frauds.

9. In a breach of contract action brought by Manufacturer, in which Buyer, not admitting that any contract was made, raises the defense of the Statute of Frauds, Manufacturer will recover:

(A) Nothing.

(B) $10,000 only, the price of the one machine that had been accepted.

(C) $20,000, constituting the price for both pressing machines, because Buyer accepted by part performance under the contract.

(D) $20,000, constituting the price for both pressing machines, plus whatever consequential and incidental damages that can be proven by Manufacturer, because the goods were specially made for Buyer.

10. For this question only, assume that the machines that Buyer ordered from Manufacturer were to be made according to Buyer's own unusual specifications. The first was delivered and accepted April 15. Buyer then canceled the agreement on May 26 and Manufacturer immediately tendered it to Buyer. Manufacturer's cost to make the machines was $7,000, meaning that it made a $3,000 profit on each machine.

There is no market for the second machine and the scrap value is nominal. In a contract action by Manufacturer, in which Buyer, not admitting that a contract was made, raises the defense of the Statute of Frauds, Manufacturer will recover:

(A) Nothing.

(B) $13,000 only.

(C) $17,000 only.

(D) $20,000.

Facts for Question 11

April was a slow month for Ace Novelties. So, on its own and without ever talking to Harvard, it manufactured 1000 key chains with a clip on the end which said, "Congratulations Harvard Law School Graduate as you 'Drive Into Your Next Legal Life,'" and sent them to Harvard along with an invoice for $2,500.

11. What is the most accurate statement?

(A) Harvard will be liable to Ace for $2,500 unless it objects to the invoice within ten days after receiving it.

(B) Harvard will lose its Statute of Frauds defense in any litigation brought by Ace unless it objects to the invoice within ten days after receiving it.

(C) Both (A) and (B) are correct.

(D) Harvard has no Statute of Frauds defense in any litigation by Ace regardless whether it objects to the invoice or not.

Facts for Question 12

Buyer and Seller orally contracted whereby Seller promised to deliver a single load of firewood to Buyer for the winter season in December. In return, Buyer promised to make fourteen monthly payments of $25 to Seller. In December, Seller delivers the wood but Buyer refuses to pay.

12. In a contract action by Seller, who will prevail?

(A) Seller, because an installment contract is outside the Statute of Frauds.

(B) Buyer, because there was no writing evidencing the formation of a contract.

(C) Buyer, because Buyer cannot perform her obligations within a year.

(D) Seller, because the Statute of Frauds has been satisfied.

Facts for Question 13

Advertiser had the following conversation with Owner, the owner of a vintage Ferrari with the license "DEPP'S," on September 1:

A: You are positive this was Johnny Depp's car?

O: Yes, I bought it at auction last month, and have a letter from the auction house authenticating the car. I wouldn't ask $200,000 for it otherwise.

A: Great, that is important to me because I have an advertising campaign that revolves around re-living the elegant lifestyle of Johnny Depp. We plan to feature the car as authentic in our ads and to send the car around the country to shopping malls to increase the volume of our department store sales. However, the campaign will only go forward if we are able to secure the authentic car.

O: I understand. However, I would not have bought it from the auction house if I wasn't sure it was the right car.

A: Well, okay, I'll take it. I would like delivery October 1.

O: That will be fine.

The next day, Owner telephoned Advertiser and they had the following conversation:

O: When we spoke yesterday, we neglected to set any payment terms. Is it acceptable if we agree that you will pay $20,000 down by September 15, and the remaining balance on delivery?

A: That will be no problem at all.

On September 15, Owner received a check from Advertiser's agency for $20,000, which had the following phrase typed on the check's "Memo" line: "Dn. Pymt. For DEPP'S Ferrari." Owner immediately deposited the check in her account.

On October 1, Advertiser came to Owner's house with a cashier's check in the amount of $180,000. However, Owner appeared at the door and said she had changed her mind and no longer wished to sell the car. Owner offered Advertiser a refund of $20,000 in cash and said: "We never really had a deal anyway. Our agreement was never put in writing."

Consider the following statements concerning the Statute of Frauds defense:

I. The defense should <u>succeed</u> because of the "part performance" exception to the Statute of Frauds.

II. The defense should <u>fail</u> because of the "part performance" exception to the Statute of Frauds.

III. The defense should fail because the notation on the "Memo" line of the $20,000 check is sufficient to satisfy the UCC's Statute of Frauds, assuming the check was signed by Advertiser.

13. In a suit by Advertiser against Owner for breach, which of the above Statements accurately describes how the court should rule on Owner's Statute of Frauds defense?

(A) I only.

(B) II only.

(C) III only.

(D) II and III only.

Facts for Question 14

Wilma and Fred fell in love and after three years, Fred proposed. Wilma comes from a very wealthy bedrock mining family. A few weeks after the proposal, Fred and Wilma began discussions and eventually agreed on a pre-nuptial agreement which spells out how much Fred would get upon a divorce from Wilma.

14. Is the pre-nuptial agreement within the Statute of Frauds?

(A) Yes, pre-nuptial agreements are always within the Statute of Frauds.

(B) Yes, if Wilma can show that Fred is only marrying her in contemplation of getting a divorce settlement.

(C) Yes, because contracts made in consideration of marriage are within the Statute of Frauds.

(D) No, because Wilma's payment obligations under the pre-nuptial agreement were not bargained for in return for a promise to marry.

Facts for Question 15

Upon graduation from high school, Niece couldn't decide whether to go to college or start working for a living. Grandfather told Niece that if she would go to college, he would pay Niece's tuition and expenses for her first year, and that he would pay a $1,000 bonus for each "A" she earned. Niece told Grandfather that she would attend college.

The next day Uncle called Niece and told her that he had learned of Grandfather's offer and told her that if Grandfather failed to pay as promised, he (Uncle) would do so. He said he knew that Niece was torn about college or work and he wanted Niece to know that college would not cost her a dime and might earn her a bonus if she studied hard.

Niece went to college because of the promises of Grandfather and Uncle, and earned four A's in her first year. Both Grandfather and Uncle refused to pay Niece the $4,000 bonus for her four A's.

15. In a suit against Uncle to enforce Uncle's promise, Niece will lose because:

(A) The contract was illusory.

(B) The contract was oral.

(C) There was no consideration flowing to Uncle.

(D) Contracts among family members are unenforceable.

Facts for Questions 16

Deacon owes Priscilla $2,000. To collect, Priscilla is about to levy an attachment on Deacon's house. Deacon's other creditor, Saul, is afraid that if Priscilla levies on Deacon's home, Deacon will declare bankruptcy and the chance of Saul getting paid will be greatly reduced.

In order to ensure that does not happen, Saul orally promises Priscilla that if Priscilla will wait to levy on any attachment for two months, Saul will play Priscilla the $2,000 if Deacon fails to pay it during the two-month period.

16. If Deacon fails to pay and Saul refuses to make good on his promise, will Priscilla be able to enforce the oral promise from Saul?

    (A) No, because the promise does not satisfy the Statute of Frauds.

    (B) No, because only Deacon is ultimately liable for the debt.

    (C) Yes, because the main purpose of Saul's promise was to benefit himself.

    (D) Yes, but only on a promissory estoppel basis if Priscilla can show justifiable and actual reliance.

CHAPTER 6
CAPACITY

QUESTIONS

Facts for Questions 1 and 2

Teresa just turned seventeen and is looking for a new car. She buys a brand new Volkswagen on credit from Seller. Six months later, she got accepted to a college that banned cars on campus, and on the same day was negligent and ran the car into a tree, denting the bumper. She immediately sought to disaffirm the contract against Seller.

Consider the following statements:

    I.   Teresa can disaffirm the contract.

    II.   Teresa must pay a reasonable value for use of the car during the six month period she had it.

    III.   Teresa must pay to repair the bumper.

    IV.   Teresa must wait to disaffirm the contract until she is eighteen.

    V.   Teresa would not be required to pay for the use of the car during the six month period she had it, or for the damage to the bumper.

1. Which of the above statements is (are) most accurate in a jurisdiction that follows the Restatement 2d?

(A) I and V only.

(B) I, II, and III only.

(C) I and III only.

(D) IV only.

2. For purposes of this question only, assume that Teresa went to college that allowed cars on campus, turned eighteen, and continued to use and make payments on the car for another year. Halfway through the year, the dealership contacted her regarding the remaining years of payment due on the car and she told the dealership "Of course I will continue to make payments on for the car. I really like it." She did, in fact, continue to make the payments for the rest of the year.

However, during her sophomore year, she moved into an apartment where parking would be too expensive to keep the car.

She now wants to disaffirm the contract. Which of the following would be reasons she could <u>not</u> disaffirm the contract?

(A) She has expressly ratified the contract when she said, "I will continue to pay for the car."

(B) She has impliedly ratified the contract by continuing to use the car for a year after turning eighteen and making the payments.

(C) She has impliedly ratified the contract by not disaffirming the contract within a reasonable time after turning eighteen.

(D) All of the above would be reasons not to disaffirm the contract.

Facts for Question 3

Sally Student, who just turned seventeen, wants to buy a new Mac laptop to use when she goes off to college. She goes to the Apple store and picks out a new computer that she likes for $900. She puts $300 down that she had saved up from babysitting, and will pay the remaining balance at $100 per month with no interest. Two months go by in which Sally has made two monthly payments when she realizes that she will not be able to make the remaining payments and wants to void the contract.

3.   Assuming she can disaffirm the contract, in a jurisdiction that follows the Restatement 2d, what will be her recovery? (For purposes of this question, assume a judge would conclude that a computer is not a "necessity").

(A) $300, the value of her down payment only.

(B) $500, the amount of money she has paid thus far, not subject to any offset due to depreciation in value of the computer.

(C) $500, subject to any offset due to depreciation in value of the computer

(D) $900, the total value of the contract.

Facts for Question 4

Ben is an adult male that was diagnosed with a mental illness. His mother has been appointed as his guardian by the court. Ben recently entered into a contract to purchase a new television set with a retail store. He said nothing to the sales representative that would indicate any mental illness and the representative otherwise had no knowledge of Ben's illness.

Ben's mother found out about the sale and wishes to avoid the contract as a guardian on Ben's behalf.

4. In a jurisdiction that follows the Restatement 2d, can Ben's mother, in her role as guardian, disaffirm the contract?

    (A) Yes, because Ben does not have the capacity to contract, and Ben will owe nothing to the store for use of the television.

    (B) Yes, but Ben's estate will have to pay restitution if the salesperson did not have any reason to know of Ben's mental defect.

    (C) No, if the store can prove Ben was sufficiently aware of the nature and consequence of the agreement.

    (D) No, because the sales representative neither knew, nor had any reason to know, of Ben's mental illness.

Facts for Questions 5 and 6

Terry was a public school teacher who participated in the school's retirement system for twenty years prior to her going on medical leave for mental illness. No guardian was appointed for Terry, but the school district was aware of the reasons why she went on leave.

After going on leave, Terry was required to make a decision regarding her retirement benefits. One option provided a greater payment per month, but payments would continue under this choice only as long as she lived; while a second option called for a smaller monthly payment, but allowed the payments to continue to her husband if she died first.

Prior to her mental illness, Terry showed great affection for her husband throughout their marriage and often spoke about her desire to protect her husband financially during her retirement. However, during the period in which she was affected by her mental illness, she chose the first option described above. Terry died two months after making the change and her husband sues to void her decision due to mental incapacity.

5. In a jurisdiction which adopts the "cognition" test for mental illness, would he be able to do so?

 (A) Yes, because Terry had a mental illness, so the contract is voidable.

 (B) Yes, if Terry did not understand in a reasonable manner the nature and legal consequences of her decision and the transaction.

 (C) No, because the school district was aware of Terry's mental illness.

 (D) No, even if Terry did not understand the legal consequences of her decision.

6. Under the "volition" or "acts" test, would he be able to do so?

 (A) Yes, because Terry had a mental illness, so the contract is voidable.

 (B) Yes, because Terry did not understand the legal consequences of her decision.

 (C) Yes, because Terry was unable to control her actions and the school district knew of her mental illness.

 (D) No, because Terry acted willfully in choosing the first option.

Facts for Questions 7 and 8

B.B. owns a Gibson guitar coveted by Lucille. Lucille has often offered to purchase the guitar in the past, but B.B. continually refuses. One night at B.B.'s blues club, Lucille gets B.B. very drunk, and while intoxicated, B.B. agrees to finally sell the guitar to Lucille for a fair price. The next morning, after B.B. had sobered up, Lucille came by the club with the money and demanded the guitar. B.B. shouted "No way! I was drunk, I'll never sell the guitar!"

7. In an action by Lucille for breach of contract, who will prevail?

 (A) B.B., if he was unable to act reasonably in making the deal.

 (B) Lucille, because B.B. voluntarily got drunk.

 (C) B.B., if he was unable to understand the nature and consequences of the deal.

 (D) Both A and C.

8. Assume for purposes of this question only that the next morning, when Lucille comes by the club, B.B. says "well, I know I was drunk, but I'll stick by my word and sell you the guitar." Does he have the power to do so?

    (A) No, the contract was void because Lucille was aware that B.B. was drunk at the time the contract was made.

    (B) No, the contract was void regardless of whether Lucille was aware that B.B. was drunk at the time the contract was made.

    (C) Yes, because B.B. has ratified the contract now that he is no longer intoxicated.

    (D) Yes, because the contract was enforceable from the time of its making.

Facts for Question 9

Mike is a diabetic who takes prescription medication for his condition. Recently his doctor changed his medication and gave Mike an experimental drug that had some incapacitating side effects that Mike was not aware of. While under the influence of the medication, Mike's neighbor Isa came by Mike's house in order to try and buy Mike's old lawnmower. Isa offered a fair price for the lawnmower and Mike, in a dazed state, said "sounds like a good deal, let's do it." Isa did not know that Mike was a diabetic and thought that Mike was being a great neighbor in selling the lawnmower.

Isa takes the lawnmower home, but a couple of days later, Mike went to mow his lawn and couldn't find the lawnmower. He asked Isa if he had seen anyone take it and Isa explained their transaction. Mike immediately claimed that he would not have sold it but for the influence of the medication and wants to disaffirm the contract.

9. Mike thinks the contract is void while Isa thinks it is valid. In a jurisdiction that follows the majority common law rule as to this issue, who is correct?

    (A) Mike, if he was unable to understand the nature and consequences of the transaction when he told Isa he would sell the lawnmower.

    (B) Mike, regardless of whether he understood the nature and consequences of the transaction.

    (C) Isa, because he was unaware of Mike's diabetic condition.

    (D) Isa, because incapacity due to drug use is no excuse.

CHAPTER 7
MISTAKE AND
MISUNDERSTANDING

QUESTIONS

Facts for Questions 1 and 2

Two experienced cattlemen sign a contract to buy and sell a young bull that is only two months old for $2,000, with payment to be made 11 months after its making. If the bull turned out to be fertile, it is worth over $5,000, but if it turns out to be sterile, it is only worth $250. It is common knowledge in the cattle industry that one cannot tell if a bull is fertile until it is six months old. Buyer takes the bull back to his farm pursuant to the contract. Several months later he finds out that the bull is sterile and refuses to pay the full price.

1. In an action by seller against buyer, who will prevail?

    (A) Buyer, because the price for the bull is disproportionate to its value.

    (B) Buyer, because he did not know at the time of sale that the bull would be sterile.

    (C) Seller, because buyer knew there was a possibility the bull would be sterile.

    (D) Seller, because the contract was enforceable when the buyer took delivery of the bull.

2. Assume for purposes of this question only that the buyer was not an experienced cattle rancher. Instead, he was a teacher looking to break into a new business. He did not know much about the cattle trade, but figured that it couldn't be that hard and purchased the bull for the same terms outlined in Question 1. As before, the teacher later discovers the bull is sterile and refuses to pay the full price. In an action by the seller against the teacher, who will prevail?

    (A) Seller, despite the teacher being unaware there was a possibility the bull could be sterile.

(B) Seller, because the contract was enforceable when teacher took delivery of the bull.

(C) Teacher, because he was unaware of the possibility the bull could be sterile.

(D) Teacher, because the price for the bull is disproportionate to its value.

Facts for Question 3

A Chipotle franchisee opens up a restaurant and leases the restaurant space for ten years at $600 per month. There is a mix up the first month of the lease, and so the franchisee asks his accountant to send a check for $1,200 the second month. Incorrectly believing the rent was always $1,200, the accountant continued to send checks for that amount for the entire first year of the lease. When the franchisee realizes the mistake, he demands credit for the excess payments from the landlord, who refuses.

3.   In an action by the franchisee to recover the excess payments made, will he prevail?

(A) No, if a court determines the accountant was negligent in making the payments.

(B) No, because the franchisee assumed the risk in letting his accountant handle the rent payments.

(C) Yes, because the franchisee did not know of the mistaken payments.

(D) Yes, if a court determined that it would be unconscionable for the landlord to keep the excess payments.

Facts for Question 4

General, a general contractor, sought bids for electrical work from three different subcontractors. Sub 1 bid $35,000. Sub 2 bid $32,500. Sub 3 bid $16,000.

When General was awarded the job by Developer, it accepted Sub 3's bid. Upon reviewing its records, Sub 3 realized that it had made a clerical error and mistakenly failed to add in the electrical costs for one of the two buildings that constituted the development. It refused to go forward.

Assume that the court finds that requiring Sub 3 to go forward would not be "unconscionable."

4.   Is Sub 3 entitled to avoid the contract on mistake grounds?

(A) Yes, if a court finds that General had reason to know of Sub 3's error.

(B) Yes, regardless whether the court finds that General had reason to know of Sub 3's error.

(C) No, unless a court finds that Sub 3 was not negligent.

(D) No, because enforcing the agreement would not be unconscionable.

Facts for Questions 5 and 6

Buyer was a home builder in Houston, Texas. Seller owned a forest near Portland, Oregon. They agreed upon the sale of timber from Seller's forest, with delivery to be made in Houston at Seller's expense in October via "The Dreamliner." There is both a plane and a ship known as the Dreamliner.

At the time of making the contract, Seller believed it had agreed to send the lumber by the ship Dreamliner, whereas the Buyer thought it had bargained for delivery via the aircraft Dreamliner.

The aircraft Dreamliner landed in Houston as scheduled on October 10, and had no wood on it. The ship the Dreamliner docked in Houston on October 30 and had all the lumber ordered by Buyer.

Assume the correct Dreamliner was a material fact for both parties.

5.   In an action by Seller to enforce the contract, can the Buyer validly assert a defense of mistake?

(A) Yes, because the elements of mutual mistake are met on these facts.

(B) Yes, because neither party will be deemed to have assumed the risk of the mistake.

(C) No, because Seller delivered the wood in Houston by October 31.

(D) No, because this is not an appropriate situation for the doctrine of mutual mistake.

6. In an action by Seller to enforce the contract, if Buyer were to raise the defense of misunderstanding, Buyer should:

(A) <u>Prevail</u>, if neither party had reason to know of the other's meaning attached to "Dreamliner."

(B) <u>Prevail</u>, even if Buyer knew that Seller mistakenly believed delivery would be by the aircraft Dreamliner while Buyer believed delivery would be by the ship Dreamliner.

(C) <u>Lose</u>, because the lumber was timely delivered, regardless whether either party had reason to know of the other's meaning of the term "Dreamliner."

(D) <u>Lose</u>, and Seller will be entitled to recover damages for Buyer's breach so long as neither party had reason to know of the other's meaning attached to "Dreamliner."

CHAPTER 8
DURESS

QUESTIONS

Facts for Question 1

Dawn is dying to purchase Portia's season tickets to her favorite basketball team, the Pouncing Poodles. Portia has no desire to sell the tickets and has repeatedly turned down Dawn's many offers. Dawn realizes that Portia will never take money for the tickets, so instead threatens to poison Portia's husband, Albert, if Portia does not sell the tickets to Dawn. Portia finally agrees to sell the tickets for face value to Dawn in order to save Albert's life. Assume that face value is the price the tickets are selling for on the open market.

1. The contract between Portia and Dawn is:

   (A) Void.

   (B) Voidable.

   (C) Enforceable.

   (D) Unconscionable.

Facts for Question 2

Damon, a bank manager, believes Penelope, a teller, has embezzled $15,000. Damon threatens to turn Penelope over to the police unless she signs an agreement to "repay" the $15,000. Penelope signs the agreement because she is frightened of having to undergo a police investigation.

2. The agreement between Penelope and Damon is:

   (A) Void.

   (B) Voidable, but only if Penelope did not embezzle money.

   (C) Voidable, whether or not Penelope embezzled money.

   (D) Enforceable, so long as Damon was reasonable in believing Penelope embezzled money.

Facts for Question 3

Dane hired Parker to repaint only the outside of his home. When Parker is finished Dane is very pleased with the paint job. However, believing he can bully Parker, Dane threatens to sue Parker for breach of contract and tie him up in court for a long time unless Parker agrees to paint the interior of Dane's home as well.

Parker has other jobs waiting and does not want to paint the interior of Dane's home, even though Dane has said he will pay Parker a reasonable price for the job. Nevertheless, Parker agrees to do the interior painting job in order to avoid the expense and hassle of litigation.

3.   The contract between Parker and Dane is:

(A) Void.

(B) Enforceable, because Dane is paying Parker a reasonable price for the job.

(C) Enforceable, because Parker had the choice of whether or not to take and complete the job to paint the interior.

(D) Voidable.

Facts for Question 4

Doreen is a landscaper. She has a contract to completely redo the landscaping at Peter's home for $5,000. When Doreen is halfway through, she threatens not to finish the job unless Peter also allows her to landscape Peter's vacation home as well. Peter agrees to pay Doreen to landscape his vacation home as well.

4.   The contract between Peter and Doreen is:

(A) Enforceable, so long as Doreen charges a reasonable price for the vacation home job.

(B) Void, but only if the price to landscape the vacation home price was unfair.

(C) Voidable, regardless of whether the price to landscape the vacation home was unfair.

(D) Enforceable, because Doreen is "terminable at will."

Facts for Question 5

David is friends with Phoebe and knows that Phoebe has been having an extra-marital affair for the past several months. David threatens to expose Phoebe's affair unless Phoebe agrees to sell her $3,000 watch to David for $20. Phoebe agrees because she is so terrified that news of her indiscretion will leak to the public.

5.   Is Phoebe enforceably obligated to sell David her watch for $20?

(A) No, only because the price for the watch is so low.

(B) No, because Phoebe can avoid the contract due to duress by improper threat.

(C) Yes, because Phoebe agreed to the contract, knowing of its terms.

(D) Yes, because courts do not inquire into the disparity between the price and value of an item under the "peppercorn" theory of consideration.

Facts for Question 6

For the past five years, Betty's Bakery has delivered 100 cinnamon rolls to Paula's Diner for $90 on the 25th of every month. The cinnamon rolls were made from scratch and had made Paula's famous. Many of Paula's customers came in regularly to order them. On July 26, the local restaurant owner's association was set to meet at Paula's for the first time. At 4:30 p.m. on July 25 Betty calls Paula and tells her she refuses to deliver the cinnamon rolls unless Paula pays $1,000 for the normal 100 cinnamon roll delivery. Paula is out of cinnamon rolls and wants the meeting to go well, so she agrees.

6.   The contract between Betty's and Paula's is:

(A) Void.

(B) Voidable, due to a threat that is a breach of good faith and fair dealing.

(C) Voidable, due to the fact that prior dealing between the parties significantly increases the effectiveness of Betty's threat.

(D) Enforceable, because Paula did not have to purchase the cinnamon rolls for her meeting.

Facts for Question 7

David wants to purchase Phyllis's mountain bicycle. David tells Phyllis: "sign this contract to sell me your bike for $200, or I will stab you with this knife." Phyllis is terrified and signs the contract. Both David and Phyllis are adults.

7. The contract between Phyllis and David for Phyllis's bike is:

    (A) Void.

    (B) Voidable, only if $200 is an unreasonable price for the bike.

    (C) Voidable, whether or not $200 is an unreasonable price for the bike.

    (D) Enforceable if later ratified by Phyllis.

Facts for Question 8

Darren tells Patricia that if she does not sell him her car for $6,000, he will murder her husband, Aaron. Patricia immediately agrees. The two sign a contract and Darren gives Patricia $6,000, and Patricia gives Darren the title and keys to her car. $6,000 is a fair price for the car. About two months later Patricia timely avoids the contract due to duress by improper threat. While in Darren's possession, the car suffered depreciation, reasonable wear and tear and some damage, not exceeding $6,000.

8. At this time:

    (A) Darren must give Patricia back the car; but Patricia does not have to give Darren back the $6,000.

    (B) Darren must give Patricia back the car; Patricia must give Darren back the $6,000.

    (C) Darren must give Patricia back the car; Patricia must give Darren back $6,000, less any reasonable amount for depreciation, wear and tear, and any other damage caused by the use of the car while Darren was in possession of it.

    (D) Darren must give Patricia back the car; Patricia must give Darren back the full $6,000, but she has a valid claim against Daren for the reasonable amount for depreciation, wear and tear, and any other damage caused by the use of the car while Darren was in possession of it.

CHAPTER 9
UNDUE INFLUENCE

QUESTIONS

Facts for Question 1

Paula is a sixteen-year-old girl. Paula had a child out of wedlock and had just given birth to her child alone and in a maternity home, Darla's Home. Immediately after Paula gave birth, and when she was still highly emotional from all that was occurring, Paula's counselor at Darla's stormed Paula's room and encouraged her to give up her baby for adoption. Paula's counselor pressured her for an hour and a half to give the baby up for adoption and said that there was the utmost urgency that she agree to it now, without discussing it with any family or friends, for the benefit of the child. Paula gives in and signs the adoption forms.

1. May Paula avoid this contract?

    (A) Yes, because there is both a "special relationship" and "improper persuasion" in this situation.

    (B) Yes, under a theory of duress.

    (C) No, if the court finds that the counselor was acting in good faith in recommending that a quick adoption was in the best interests of the child.

    (D) No, if a court finds that the counselor is not in a fiduciary relationship.

Facts for Question 2

Pearl, an eighteen-year-old, was working for Doom Construction, Co. at a construction site during her summer vacation. Pearl was not supposed to be working with heavy-duty equipment, but one day they were short-handed at the site and had Pearl use a jackhammer. Pearl was seriously injured while using the jackhammer and was rushed to the hospital.

The adjuster for the company that provided worker's compensation insurance for Doom Construction, Co. followed the ambulance and confronted Pearl in her hospital room. The insurance adjuster badgered her for an hour about signing a release promising immediate payment in return for only one-quarter of the benefits provided for by the insurance policy.

Pearl had no one around to ask for advice, and was unable to leave her hospital room. Eventually, Pearl gave in and signed. Later, Pearl wants to avoid the release.

2.   May Pearl avoid the release?

   (A) No, if a court finds that she understood the terms of the contract.

   (B) No, unless the court finds the insurance adjuster made an "improper threat" that induced Pearl into signing the release.

   (C) Yes, but only if Pearl can prove that the terms were unfair, and the insurance adjuster threatened her.

   (D) Yes, because the insurance adjuster's tactics involved unfair persuasion.

Question 3

3.   Which of the following are factors implicating undue influence?

   (A) Discussion or consummation of the transaction in an unusual place or at an unusual time.

   (B) Absence of third party advisors for the victim.

   (C) Unfair resulting bargain.

   (D) All of the above.

Question 4

4.   If a party to a contract is induced into the contract by means of undue influence from a *third party*, who is not a party to the contract, that contract is:

   (A) Enforceable, so long as the other contracting party has not engaged in unfair persuasion.

   (B) Voidable, unless the other party to the transaction in good faith and without reasons to know of the undue influence gives value to, or materially relies on, the transaction.

   (C) Voidable by the victim, regardless of the circumstances.

   (D) Void.

CHAPTER 10
FRAUD & MISREPRESENTATION

QUESTIONS

Facts for Question 1

Debbie hired a professional surveyor to measure her property prior to sale. The inspector gave Debbie a written report certifying her property at 50.2 acres.

In reliance on the survey Debbie posted the land for sale as 50+ acres. It turns out that the inspector had carelessly measured the property and the property was not fifty acres, but only forty.

Paula contracted to purchase the land for $100,000, a fair price for fifty acres, but 20% too much for a forty acre plot. After the sale, Paula discovered the land was actually only forty acres and has brought suit.

Assume neither Debbie nor Paula is in any way at fault for believing the land was fifty acres.

Consider the following statements.

  I. The contract is voidable by Debbie.

  II. Debbie has innocently misrepresented the property size.

  III. Paula can recover $20,000.

  IV. Debbie has fraudulently misrepresented the property size.

  V. The contract is voidable by Paula.

1. Which of the above statements are correct if Paula sues for breach of contract only?

 (A) II, III and V only are correct.

 (B) II and V only are correct.

(C) I, II, III and V only are correct.

(D) III, IV, and V only are correct.

Facts for Question 2

Dwayne is a famous basketball player who is approached by Paul after a game. Paul hands Dwayne a piece of paper and asks him for his autograph and says, "Don't mind the other writing on the paper; it is irrelevant. This is just the only thing I had with me."

In fact what Dwayne was signing was an agreement to pay Paul 10% of every paycheck he receives from this day forward.

Paul has brought suit to enforce the contract against Dwayne after he refused to make any payments.

2.   Which of the following statements is most accurate?

   (A) The contract is void.

   (B) The contract is voidable by Dwayne.

   (C) The contract is voidable by Paul.

   (D) The contract is enforceable.

Facts for Question 3

Drew negotiated with Patricia for painting services. To help seal the deal he said, "In my opinion we provide the fastest and best quality work." In fact, Drew knew that he could not paint very well or very quickly, and that almost every job he undertook ended up with a customer complaining. Patricia reasonably did not know of Drew's poor reputation and, based on what he said during the negotiations, she contracted with him.

Shortly after contracting with Drew, Patricia went online and found out the truth about Drew's painting skills. She tells Drew she no longer wants his services. Drew says okay, but sues her for breach of contract, seeking the profits he would have made under the contract.

3.   Assuming Patricia was not at fault in failing to discover Drew's reputation before contracting, which of the following statements is most correct if Patricia defends by asserting misrepresentation?

   (A) The contract is void.

   (B) The contract is voidable by Drew.

(C) The contract is voidable by Patricia.

(D) The contract is enforceable because Drew's statements were merely opinions and not statements of fact.

Facts for Question 4

During negotiations, merchant Seller told Buyer, the owner of a grocery store chain, "Our grape jelly is the best on the market." Buyer tasted the jelly, thought it was pretty good, and contracted with Seller to purchase twenty cases.

After signing the contract, Buyer sampled another company's grape jelly, and believed it to be much better than Seller's. Buyer felt that Seller had deceived him and refuses to go forward with the contract to purchase the twenty cases of Seller's jelly, saying the contract is voidable on misrepresentation grounds.

4.   Which of the following statements is correct?

     (A) Buyer is in breach for refusing to purchase the jelly.

     (B) Buyer is not in breach, and may avoid the contract, based on misrepresentation.

     (C) Buyer is in breach because he waived any misrepresentation defense by tasting the jelly.

     (D) Buyer would be able to avoid the contract under the standards for merchant sellers under the UCC.

Facts for Question 5

Seller plans to sell his home but knows that the value would be severely reduced if a buyer knew of the many holes in the walls, which would cost $25,000 to fix correctly. Instead of fixing them correctly, he decided to hide them, by using white paper and glue to cover the holes, and then painting over the paper. The "patching" is very cleverly done and a reasonable person in the position of a buyer would not notice the holes or their being covered.

Buyer viewed the house and reasonably did not notice the patching. Seller was very careful to not say anything one way or the other about the walls. Buyer bought the house for $200,000 cash, which was somewhat of a bargain, since the fair market value according to his appraiser was $210,000.

Buyer discovers the holes shortly after taking title to the home and is furious. He has brought suit to void the contract.

5.   In <u>Buyer v. Seller</u>, Buyer will likely:

    (A) <u>Prevail</u>, and is entitled to $210,000 in damages from Seller.

    (B) <u>Lose</u>, because Seller never made any assertion about the walls.

    (C) <u>Lose</u>, but is entitled to collect $25,000 from Seller to fix the walls.

    (D) <u>Prevail</u>, and is entitled to only $200,000 in damages from Seller.

Facts for Question 6

Seller knows his refrigerator is missing the cooling system that all refrigerators must be equipped with to cool food. Essentially, it is just the body of the refrigerator, but looks like a complete refrigerator from the outside. Seller did not remove the cooling system—when he got it, it was missing the system. Seller sold the refrigerator to Buyer for $500.

Buyer did not ask about the cooling system because he assumed when someone sells a refrigerator it comes with the cooling system. But he did say to Seller, "I don't understand how refrigerators work. I mean, how does a bunch of wires make something cool? But I'm sure glad it does. The guy who invented it should get a Nobel prize or something" Seller said nothing in response. The refrigerator without the cooling system has a fair market value of $50. Buyer would now like to bring suit to void the contract.

Assume Buyer was reasonable in not discovering the missing cooling system.

6.   In <u>Buyer v. Seller</u>, Buyer will likely:

    (A) <u>Prevail</u>, because Buyer has a valid claim for misrepresentation.

    (B) <u>Prevail</u>, because Seller took an affirmative action to conceal a fact.

    (C) <u>Lose</u>, because Buyer did not ask about the cooling system.

    (D) <u>Lose</u>, because Seller never said anything regarding the cooling system.

Facts for Question 7

Debbie is an asset manager for Penny, and has managed Penny's assets for many years. Debbie knows Penny has an unimproved piece of property that Penny is looking to sell in an area where an amusement park plans to build a new Disneyland-type park. The park has been slowly and secretly buying all the other pieces of property in the neighborhood and Debbie learns of the amusement company's plans from another client. Debbie is pretty sure that when the amusement park makes its offer for Penny's property, it will be for a multiple of its current fair market value.

Debbie offers to purchase Penny's property for the fair market value as it exists without the presence of the amusement park. Debbie never mentions the amusement park's plans during her negotiations with Penny. Penny is delighted to get rid of the property and agrees to the sale. A week later Penny learned Debbie was planning to sell the property for four times what she paid Penny for it to the amusement park.

7. Which of the following statements is most accurate as to the Debbie–Penny transaction?

   (A) The contract is void due to misrepresentation.

   (B) The contract is voidable by Penny.

   (C) The contract is not voidable by either party.

   (D) The contract is voidable by Debbie.

Facts for Question 8

Derek applied for life insurance from Pristine Policies ("Pristine"). The application asks whether Derek had ever been diagnosed with cancer. Derek had not been diagnosed with cancer and truthfully answered "no" to the question. The end of the application had a statement that prominently provided, "This is an application only. Insurance policy will not be in force until Pristine accepts the application, which could take three to four weeks."

A few days after submitting the application, and before hearing from Pristine, Derek was diagnosed with cancer as a result of a routine check-up. Derek failed to inform Pristine the subsequent cancer diagnosis and there was no further communication from Pristine other than the approval of Derek's application a few weeks later.

8. Which of the following statements is correct?

   (A) The insurance contract is voidable by Pristine under a misrepresentation theory.

   (B) Derek has not committed an actionable misrepresentation because at the time he answered the application he had never been diagnosed with cancer.

(C) The contract is not voidable because Pristine did not further inquire about, or condition its acceptance on, the absence of any subsequent diagnoses before it issued the policy.

(D) Derek has only committed an actionable misrepresentation if Pristine can show Derek implicitly agreed to inform them of any subsequent diagnosis.

Facts for Question 9

The meeting of City's Road Commission was open to the public, but almost nobody went to the sessions. Rookie Reporter, however, was assigned to the latest meeting of the Commission and learned there that the local interstate was going to be extended into City. Reporter began researching who owned the land around the interstate, believing that the extension of the road would make the land valuable for fast food restaurants, gas stations and the like. Reporter found out that it was owned by Businessman.

Reporter made an offer to purchase the land from Businessman for $40,000. Businessman asked, "Why do you want to buy it? Is that interstate thing actually going to happen?" Reporter answered "Look, do you want to sell it or not." Businessman agreed and a contract was signed. Businessman later found out about the interstate and refused to go through with the deal, claiming the contract was voidable because of misrepresentation.

9. In <u>Businessman v. Reporter</u> to avoid the contract, Businessman will likely:

(A) <u>Prevail</u>, because Reporter misrepresented a material fact by silence.

(B) <u>Lose</u>, because Reporter did not have a duty to disclose facts about the road.

(C) <u>Prevail</u>, because Reporter cannot use information he obtained while working in his job for personal use.

(D) <u>Lose</u>, because Businessman did not inquire about the record of the Road Commission meeting.

Facts for Question 10

Seller offers his home for sale. Buyer is interested in the home and while he walks around the house, he notices some brown spots on the third floor ceiling. He asks Seller about it and Seller replies, "A year ago there were some loose tiles on the roof which caused some water leakage, which are the spots you see, but they're all fixed now."

In fact, there are big holes in the roof, which Seller knows about. The holes would be easy to see if Buyer got to the roof, but there is no easy way to get up there. The holes are not visible from an external inspection in the front or back of the house.

Buyer decided not to go on the roof and bought the home. He sought to avoid the transaction when he discovered the holes.

10. Assume there was no custom of a pre-buyer inspection by a professional home inspector in the pertinent jurisdiction. Which of the following statements is most accurate?

(A) The contract is voidable by either Buyer or Seller.

(B) Buyer will not be able to successfully assert a misrepresentation claim because he did not inspect the roof.

(C) Buyer will be able to raise a misrepresentation claim only if the court determines that the absence of holes in the roof was a material part of the transaction.

(D) Buyer will be able to avoid the contract by virtue of misrepresentation.

CHAPTER 11
UNCONSCIONABILITY

QUESTIONS

Author's Note:

Unconscionability is much more an "essay" issue than a multiple choice one. This is because it is difficult to ask a student to decide, objectively, that a contractual term is substantively "too" unfair, or that the victim has not "enough" meaningful choice in the marketplace. Accordingly, most multiple choice questions in this area ask about the standards and elements to find unconscionability, and the consequences when it is found.

Question 1

1.   If a court determines a contract has an unconscionable provision, it is empowered to:

(A) Refuse to enforce the entire contract.

(B) Enforce the remainder of the contract without the unconscionable clause or clauses.

(C) Modify or limit application of any clause to avoid an unjust result.

(D) All of the above.

Question 2

2.   To find unconscionability, a court must find that a clause, or the entire contract, contains:

(A) Procedural unconscionability <u>and</u> substantive unconscionability.

(B) Procedural unconscionability <u>or</u> substantive unconscionability.

(C) Only procedural unconscionability; substantive unconscionability is not required but supports a finding of unconscionability.

(D) Only substantive unconscionability; procedural unconscionability is not required but supports a finding of unconscionability.

Facts for Question 3

You are the law clerk to a judge. Your judge has made a finding in a case that a variable interest clause in a contract was oppressive and the result of surprise at the time it was made, and thus procedural unconscionability was established. The judge has also found that the interest clause was substantively fair at the time the contract was entered into, but is now grossly unfair in light of the poor economy.

3.   The judge asks you whether she can find the clause unconscionable. Your answer should be:

(A) Yes, so long as the interest term is sufficiently unfair.

(B) Yes under the "sliding scale" test, because procedural unconscionability has been established.

(C) No, because unconscionability is judged at the time of making the contract.

(D) No, unless the agreement is <u>so</u> procedurally unconscionable at the time of its making that a court would forgive the lack of substantive unconscionability.

Question 4

4.   Unconscionability may be found in which of the following types of transactions:

(A) Merchant sellers to consumer buyers only.

(B) Merchant sellers to consumer or merchant buyers only.

(C) Sales of goods transactions only.

(D) Unconscionability can be found in any type of transaction.

CHAPTER 12
"ILLEGALITY" AND CONTRACTS UNENFORCEABLE ON GROUNDS OF PUBLIC POLICY

QUESTIONS

Facts for Questions 1 and 2

Dean's neighbor played music so loudly that Dean couldn't take it any longer. Dean thus contracted with Preston to kill the neighbor for $10,000. Preston demanded $3,000 paid up front, which Dean paid.

Preston went to the neighbor's home and told the neighbor that he, Preston, was going to have to kill the neighbor unless the neighbor moved. The neighbor moved that night, fixing the noise problem.

Dean refused to pay Preston the remaining $7,000 due under their contract.

1. In <u>Preston v. Dean</u>, Preston will:

    (A) <u>Prevail</u>, because he satisfied Dean's primary purpose for entering the contract.

    (B) <u>Prevail</u>, but only if Preston ends up killing the neighbor as the contract specified.

    (C) <u>Lose</u>, because the contract is void.

    (D) <u>Lose</u>, but only if Dean can prove Preston's performance was a material breach.

2. If Dean sues Preston for return of the $3,000, he should:

    (A) <u>Lose</u>, because the law will leave the parties as they found them.

    (B) <u>Lose</u>, because Preston earned the fee under the contract.

    (C) <u>Prevail</u>, under the *in pari delicto* doctrine.

    (D) <u>Prevail</u>, under an unjust enrichment theory.

Facts for Questions 3 and 4

Peter Plumber wants to do the plumbing work on the Big–Time office building, but he knows no one who works for the general contractor which will be awarding the job.

Dan <u>does</u> know the owner of the general contractor and agrees with Peter to recommend Peter for a payment of $10,000. Dan tells Peter while they are negotiating their deal that a portion of the $10,000 payment was going to go for a $4,000 bribe that Dan intended to pay to the owner of the general contractor to secure the job for Peter. Peter said he did not care how the money was spent—he just wanted the work.

Through Dan's efforts, Peter is hired to do the work on Big–Time. Peter found out that Dan simply put in a good word for Peter and had not paid any bribe.

However, a week before the project is to begin, the general contractor fired Peter without cause and hired another plumber. It turns out that the second plumber actually paid a bribe to the general contractor's owner.

3.   Which of the following is correct about the contract between Peter and Dan?

(A) The contract is unenforceable.

(B) The contract is enforceable because Dan never paid the bribe.

(C) The contract is void.

(D) Both (A) and (C) are correct.

4.   For purposes of this question only, assume Dan did pay the $4,000 bribe to the owner of the general contractor, and the reason the contractor went with the second plumber is because the second plumber paid an even bigger bribe to the owner of the general contractor.

If Peter brings suit against the general contractor, Peter will likely:

(A) <u>Prevail</u>, because the general contractor breached by firing him without cause.

(B) <u>Prevail</u>, but will be limited to collecting $4,000.

(C) <u>Lose</u>, unless Peter can show bad faith.

(D) <u>Lose</u>, because Peter's contract with the general contractor is void.

Facts for Question 5

Dave contracts with Paula, who is a carpenter, for Paula to build Dave a custom dining room table. The municipality in which Dave and Paula reside requires that all carpenters obtain a "business license." There is no testing, screening, or qualifications to receive the license, other than a $500 annual fee. As it turns out, Paula had never obtained a business license at the time of contracting. Dave had never investigated whether Paula was licensed or not by the municipality.

5.   Which of the following statements is most correct?

   (A) The contract is illegal and unenforceable.

   (B) The contract is enforceable only because Dave never investigated whether Paula had a license.

   (C) The contract is enforceable.

   (D) The contract is unenforceable unless Dave waives his defense to the contract based on Paula being unlicensed.

Facts for Question 6

Darlene contracts with Patrick, who holds himself out as an attorney, for Patrick to write a will for Darlene. The two freely negotiated agreeable terms, and Patrick does a competent job and creates a legally enforceable will.

The state in which Patrick practices requires all legal professionals to be licensed, which includes having passed the bar examination. Darlene later learns Patrick is not a licensed attorney and refuses to pay Patrick. Patrick has brought suit for breach.

6.   In <u>Patrick v. Darlene</u> for breach of their contract, Patrick will likely:

   (A) <u>Prevail</u>, because the contract is enforceable.

   (B) <u>Prevail</u>, but only because the will was competently drafted.

   (C) <u>Lose</u>, because the contract is unenforceable due to illegality.

   (D) <u>Lose</u>, but he may still recover in restitution for the fair market value of any services rendered by Patrick, otherwise Darlene would be unjustly enriched.

Facts for Question 7

Within the state where Department Store operates, the maximum usury rate is 15%, meaning the maximum interest rate on credit agreements is 15%. Department Store establishes a program whereby, in return for agreeing to a line of credit carrying a 17% interest rate, the customer is given a "Platinum Status Customer" card. As a Platinum Status Customer, customers get special offers and discounts not available to the general public.

Penny lives in the same state, and signs up for the Platinum Status program. The day she gets her card, Penny buys some goods on credit and is charged 17% interest.

7.   Which of the following is accurate?

   (A) Penny may avoid the contract.

   (B) Penny may enforce the contract.

   (C) The contract is unenforceable by either party due to illegality.

   (D) Both (A) and (B) are correct.

CHAPTER 13
PAROL EVIDENCE RULE AND INTERPRETATION

QUESTIONS

Facts for Questions 1 and 2

Buyer and Seller have contracted for the purchase of Seller's home. Their agreement is reduced to writing which states, among other things, that the sale is for "Seller's home located at 100 Maple Drive for the purchase price of $200,000."

After the sale closes, and Buyer moves in, he notices that the above-ground hot tub that Seller had put on display for the open house was no longer there. Buyer files suit, claiming that the hot tub was supposed to be included with the house because Seller orally told him that he would throw it in as part of the deal. There is nothing in the written agreement one way or the other about the hot tub.

1.   In a jurisdiction that follows the rules of the Restatement 2d of Contracts, would Buyer be able to introduce evidence at trial that the hot tub was a part of the agreement?

   (A) No, because the agreement was reduced to writing, the contract is totally integrated as a matter of law.

   (B) No, because Buyer asserts that the parties had agreed to the hot tub term, the written contract is partially integrated as a matter of law.

   (C) Yes, because the very fact that the Buyer asserts the parties had agreed to the hot tub term means the written contract is not integrated at all.

   (D) Maybe, because whether the contract is integrated, and, if so, the extent of the integration, is a question of law for a judge to decide.

2.   For the purposes of this question, assume the writing was the same as in Question 1, but that instead of a missing hot tub, Buyer argues that Seller had, prior to reducing the agreement to writing, orally agreed

to remove a tool shed on the property that interfered with the view from the property. ("Shed Agreement") No mention of the Shed Agreement made it into the written agreement.

In an action by Buyer for breach of contract in which the <u>judge determines the written contract is partially integrated</u>, would Buyer be able to introduce evidence of the Shed Agreement?

(A) Yes, because a party can always introduce parol evidence if an agreement is partially integrated.

(B) No, because a party cannot introduce parol evidence if an agreement is partially integrated.

(C) Yes, if the court determined the Shed Agreement is a term that might naturally be omitted from a land sale contract.

(D) No, if the court determined that the Shed Agreement was a "consistent additional term."

Facts for Questions 3 and 4

Angela was interested in selling some property she owned for $2,500. She was also about to have a new paint job done on her classic Porsche from Matt. Therefore, she approached Matt and asked him if he would be interested in trading her property for the paint job. Matt agreed.

However, to avoid costly tax consequences, the written property conveyance documents listed the purchase price as "$2,500 cash" and said nothing of the bargained-for-exchange. Matt competently painted Angela's car and thereafter Angela transferred the property to Matt. However, she thereafter sued Matt for the $2,500 purchase price based on the written contract, alleging that Matt never paid her the $2,500 cash as set forth in their written agreement.

3.   At trial, would Matt be able to introduce evidence as to the barter agreement, assuming the court finds the agreement partially integrated?

(A) Yes, if a court determined that the barter agreement is the type of term that "might naturally" be omitted from the property conveyance documents.

(B) No, if a court determined that the barter agreement is the type of term that "might naturally" be omitted from the property conveyance documents.

(C) Yes, to avoid Angela's unjust enrichment, regardless of whether a court finds the barter agreement to be a consistent additional term.

(D) No, because it is Matt's duty to ensure all of the terms of the agreement which favored him were reduced to writing.

4. For the purposes of this question only, assume that at the bottom of the written property conveyance documents, the following was included:

The parties to this contract hereby affirm that this writing expresses the final, complete and exclusive statement of the terms of their agreement. There are no inducements to enter this contract other than those appearing in this document, and all prior agreements, written or oral, are discharged and/or merged into this contract.

What is the most likely effect of this language?

(A) It would turn the agreement into a totally integrated one, because such clauses always render an agreement totally integrated.

(B) It would make it more likely that the agreement would be found totally integrated than would be the case without the language.

(C) It would turn the agreement into a partially integrated one, because such clauses always render an agreement partially integrated.

(D) It would allow the admission of a "contradictory additional term."

Facts for Question 5

Gordon Jeffrey executed a written agreement with Fordham Motorsports in which Fordham agreed to build a NASCAR racing car for Gordon according to plans and specifications to be developed by Fordham and incorporated into the written contract. The contract stated that Fordham was to receive $175,000 upon delivery of the completed car, in racing condition, to Gordon.

Prior to signing the contract, Gordon and Fordham orally agreed that the written contract would have no effect until and unless the plans and specifications for the race car were approved by Penske Engineering, a leading engineering company. There was nothing in the written Gordon–Fordham agreement regarding Penske's involvement in the deal.

When Fordham sent the plans and specifications to Penske, Penske determined it would not be of racing quality and would be too slow to be competitive and refused to approve the design.

Gordon then declared the contract unenforceable, but Fordham brought an action for breach against Gordon.

5. At trial, the judge ruled that the Gordon–Fordham contract was totally integrated. Will the evidence of the prior oral agreement regarding Penske's approval be admitted?

  (A) No, because the parol evidence rule precludes admission of any evidence of a prior or contemporaneous oral agreement by the parties to supplement a totally integrated agreement.

  (B) No, because the oral agreement contradicted the terms of the written contract.

  (C) Yes, because Penske was not a party to the contract.

  (D) Yes, because the oral agreement was a condition precedent to the parties' duties under the contract.

Facts for Question 6

Buyer and Seller are parties to a contract calling for delivery of goods on "June 1." This is the sixth contract between Buyer and Seller that dealt with the same subject matter over the years. In each of the six previous contracts, delivery was supposed to be on "the first" of the month under the express terms of the contract, but in each case, Seller made the deliveries on the tenth of the month in question. In all cases, such deliveries were accepted and paid for without complaint by the Seller.

Delivery under the new contract took place on June 10. However, it was rejected for late tender by the Buyer, and Seller brought suit.

Buyer moves for summary judgment stating that the contract clearly shows that delivery was due June 1, and it was admitted that the delivery was not made until June 10. In response to Seller's attempt to show deliveries under previous contracts were made and accepted on the tenth of the month despite the first of the month term ("Previous Evidence"), Buyer invokes the parol evidence rule.

At a hearing, the judge rules that the contract is completely integrated.

6. In a jurisdiction that follows the UCC, which of the following is the most accurate statement?

(A) The Previous Evidence may not be introduced at trial.

(B) The Previous Evidence may only be introduced at trial if the court found it to be a "consistent additional term."

(C) The Previous Evidence may be introduced at trial if the court determines that the parties would not certainly have included a ten-day extension of time for delivery in their written agreement had they, in fact, agreed to such a term.

(D) The Previous Evidence would be admissible if the court determines it is a course of dealing.

Facts for Question 7

Farmer entered into a four-year written requirements contract with Brewer. Under the contract, which was signed by both parties, Farmer was to provide Brewer with all the wheat, barley, and hops it needs for its production over the next four years. Another term provided that "all natural ingredients are to be grown and purchased in accordance with the side oral agreement agreed to by the parties." ("All Natural Ingredient" clause)

The side oral agreement was an agreement by both parties to follow the growing standards for "natural ingredients" under the Federal "Natural Ingredients Act."

In the third year of the contract, Brewer rejected the wheat, barley, and hops tendered by Farmer because he alleged the ingredients were not "natural" as specified in the All Natural Ingredient" clause.

7. In an action by Farmer for breach, can Brewer admit the side oral All Natural Ingredient agreement into evidence to show that its rejection of Farmer's ingredients was proper?

(A) No, because the parol evidence rule will bar its admission.

(B) No, unless the court finds the written contract only partially integrated.

(C) Yes, because the All Natural Ingredient clause in the written agreement is ambiguous on its face and use of the standards of the "Natural Ingredients Act" is a reasonably susceptible interpretation of the agreement under the circumstances.

(D) Yes, because the side oral All Natural Ingredient agreement is not parol evidence.

Question 8

Consider the following situations:

I.   Buyer wants to introduce evidence that his acceptance to a contract for the sale of Seller's home was entered into under duress.

II. Retailer wants to introduce evidence that Manufacturer's "acknowledgement of purchase order" was not in response to an actual purchase order and the parties never contracted.

III. Buyer of a Blu-ray player wants to introduce evidence that the written contract was supposed to include a stereo system that the parties agreed to orally when nothing about the stereo was included in the writing.

IV. Seller wants to introduce evidence that her contract with Buyer which was reduced to writing was modified to adjust the date of performance.

8.   In which of the above situations would the parol evidence not apply to preclude the proffered evidence if the court determines that the relevant contract was completely integrated?

(A) I and II only.

(B) I, II, and IV only.

(C) III and IV only.

(D) I, II, III, and IV.

CHAPTER 14
CONDITIONS AND BREACH

QUESTIONS

Author's Note:

Conditions and breach have similar, but somewhat specialized concepts under the Restatement 2d/common law rules, on the one hand, and under the UCC, on the other. The first twenty-six questions of this Chapter deal with Restatement 2d/common law conditions questions, with the remainder dealing with those issues under the UCC. I would recommend that you do the Restatement questions first, even if your professor focuses on UCC concepts, as many of the UCC principles can best be applied after understanding the common law principles.

Facts for Questions 1 and 2

An insurance contract with Patient provided that Health Insurer would pay for medical treatment, "on the condition that the treating physician provides an affidavit, signed under penalty of perjury, that the treatment was medically necessary." The pertinent state statute requires that any oath under penalty of perjury must be signed, "so help me God."

The religion of Patient's treating physician prohibits signing an oath swearing anything "so help me God." However, Physician provided a letter to the insurer stating that the treatment she recommended for Patient is medically necessary. Health Insurer failed to pay for the treatment, citing the failure of the affidavit.

1. The requirement of the physician's affidavit is best characterized as:

(A) An express condition precedent.

(B) An express condition subsequent.

(C) A promise.

(D) An implied-in-fact condition.

2.   In <u>Patient v. Health Insurer</u> for payment of the medical treatment, which is the most likely result?

    (A) <u>Patient will prevail,</u> if the court finds the letter a "substantial equivalent" to the affidavit.

    (B) <u>Patient will prevail,</u> under the religious waiver exception if a court finds Physician's religious objections to be "credible."

    (C) <u>Health Insurer will prevail,</u> because express conditions are strictly enforced.

    (D) <u>Health Insurer will prevail,</u> but only if the court finds that the requirement of the oath is not unconscionable.

Facts for Questions 3–5

Harvey agrees with Stockbroker that he will purchase 100 shares of Facebook next Tuesday, "unless it rains on Monday." There was some slight precipitation on Monday, and Harvey refuses to purchase the stock on Tuesday as a result. Stockbroker contends the precipitation was not "rain" and brings suit for his lost commission.

3.   The phrase "unless it rains on Monday" is best characterized as:

    (A) An express condition precedent.

    (B) An express condition subsequent.

    (C) An implied-in-fact condition precedent.

    (D) A constructive condition subsequent.

4.   What is the most accurate statement about the burden of proof to establish that it was or was not raining on Monday in the <u>Stockbroker v. Harvey</u> litigation?

    (A) The burden of proof would be on Stockbroker to prove it was not raining because Stockbroker is plaintiff in the suit and a plaintiff has the burden of proof.

    (B) The burden of proof would be on Stockbroker to prove it was not raining on Monday because he is the party seeking to challenge the application of a condition.

    (C) Both (A) and (B) are correct.

    (D) The burden of proof would be on Harvey to establish it was raining because he is the party seeking to take advantage of the condition.

5. If the court found that it was raining on Monday, which of the following statements is the most accurate?

    (A) Harvey would be obligated to pay the commission because parties cannot condition their performance under a contract on events that are beyond their control.

    (B) Harvey would be obligated to pay the commission because whether it rains or not is an aleatory condition.

    (C) Harvey would not be liable because his obligation to buy the stock was discharged by the Monday rain.

    (D) Harvey would not be liable because his obligation to buy the stock was excused by the Monday rain.

Facts for Question 6

In late June, Steve entered into a contract with Al's dealership by which he would purchase a new Audi A7 for $75,000 from the new shipment of similarly equipped A7s recently received by Al. The contract does not specify which A7 would be Steve's since he wanted to check with his wife on the exterior and interior colors. As such, the Steve–Al's Dealership agreement had a clause whereby Steve promised that he would "select which A7 he wished to purchase from the shipment before July 1."

Steve's wife wanted a Mercedes instead, so Steve never went back to Al's dealership. Al sues for breach of contract, and Steve defends claiming that, since he never picked which A7 he wanted by July 1, he was not obligated to pay for any Audi.

6. How will the court likely interpret the clause regarding Steve selecting an A7 by July 1?

    (A) As an express condition that was not met, thus Steve has no duty to purchase a car.

    (B) As an express condition which was excused by Steve's breach of the obligation of good faith and fair dealing, meaning Steve is liable for breach of contract.

    (C) As an express condition that was waived by Steve, thus Steve has no duty to purchase a car.

    (D) As an unconditional duty, meaning Steve is liable for breach of contract.

Facts for Question 7

General Contractor subcontracts with Carpenter for the framing of a home. Under the contract, General promises to pay Carpenter $25,000, "which shall be paid five days after payment to General Contractor by Developer for framing." Carpenter timely completes the framing and did his job well.

Developer has not paid General Contractor for the framing work. As a consequence, General Contractor refuses to pay Carpenter. More than five days have passed since Developer was supposed to have paid General Contractor.

Developer says it will not pay until Developer gets a chance to inspect Carpenter's framing work. There is nothing in any agreement or usage of trade that gives Developer the right to inspect the work, but Developer remains adamant.

7.   Is General Contractor liable to Carpenter for $25,000 under the contract at this point in time?

   (A) No, because payment by Developer to General Contractor was a condition precedent to General Contractor's obligation to pay Carpenter.

   (B) No, unless the fair market value of Carpenter's services was at least $25,000.

   (C) Yes, because Carpenter has done the work and the time for payment has passed.

   (D) No, because Developer has not inspected the Carpenter's work.

Facts for Questions 8 and 9

Jack and Diane entered a written contract on May 15, the essential parts of which provided:

Jack to supply Diane with seventy-five personalized graduation announcements for her daughter Danielle's high school graduation on or before June 15, with a photograph of Danielle in cap and gown to be prominently displayed. Timely delivery guaranteed.

Photograph to be taken by Jack at Diane's house with the picture of Danielle on the announcements to be satisfactory to Diane or Diane shall have no obligation under this agreement.

Diane to pay $200 thirty days after receipt of the announcements.

Jack contemplated taking the picture of Danielle on June 1. However, Diane and Danielle left town for an unexpected family emergency on May 25 and did not call Jack to tell him they were back in town until June 7. Jack took Danielle's picture on June 10. Before taking the picture of Danielle, Jack told Diane that the announcements wouldn't be ready by the 15th given the delay, but that he would do his best. Diane told Jack to go ahead and take the picture.

The announcements were delivered by Jack to Diane on June 17 with Jack working reasonably on them in the interim. Diane refused to accept them.

8.   In an action by Jack against Diane, which of the following would be Diane's best defense?

   (A) The picture of Danielle on the announcement was objectively unsatisfactory, even if Diane liked it well enough.

   (B) The picture of Danielle on the announcement was not satisfactory to Diane, even though everyone else who saw the picture liked it very much.

   (C) The announcements were delivered two days late.

   (D) The contract failed for lack of consideration because the personal satisfaction clause was illusory.

9.   Which of the following statements is most accurate?

   (A) Payment by Diane of the $200 was a condition precedent to Jack's duty of performance.

   (B) Tender of the performances by Jack and Diane were due simultaneously because of the doctrine of concurrent conditions.

   (C) Payment by Diane of the $200 was a condition subsequent to Jack's duty of performance.

   (D) Satisfactory performance by Jack under the contract was a condition precedent to Diane's duty of payment of the $200.

Facts for Question 10–12

Abbott contractually agrees with Costello to purchase Costello's rare Babe Ruth baseball card for $1,000. They agree to exchange the payment for the card that week on Friday at noon at their local Starbucks. Friday comes and Abbott and Costello meet at Starbucks at noon. Abbott shows Costello a cashier's check for $1,000 and says "I'm ready to proceed with the deal," but says that he will not give Costello the money until he can see the card. Costello says he has the card, but refuses to show it to Abbott until Abbott gives him the check. When Abbott does not hand over the check, Costello walks away without ever showing or delivering the card to Abbott.

10. Which of the following statements is most accurate, assuming the exchange to be governed by Restatement/common law principles (even though technically it involves a sale of goods)?

 (A) Both parties' duties under the contract are subject to a concurrent, constructive condition of tender.

 (B) Only Abbott's duty of payment under the contract is subject to a constructive condition of tender.

 (C) Only Costello's duty to deliver the card under the contract is subject to a constructive condition of tender.

 (D) Neither parties' duties under the contract are subject to a constructive condition of tender.

11. In an action by Abbott against Costello for breach of contract, will Abbott prevail?

 (A) No, because Abbott must actually give the check to Costello before a breach action can be successfully maintained.

 (B) No, because Costello had the card with him.

 (C) Yes, because they were parties to an enforceable contract as soon as they agreed to the card-for-cash exchange.

 (D) Yes, because Abbott sufficiently manifested an ability and willingness to pay for the card.

12. For this question only, assume that Costello pulled out the baseball card in response to Abbott's showing of the check, and assume both parties said that they were willing to proceed while looking at the check and card, respectively.

Who, if either, must perform first?

 (A) Abbott, because his performance will take time.

 (B) Costello, because his performance will take time.

(C) Both parties are obligated to perform simultaneously, because performance of both parties can occur simultaneously.

(D) Costello, because Abbott manifested Abbott's willingness to perform first.

Facts for Question 13

Stylist cuts hair in Beverly Hills. Customer makes an appointment and wants "the works," a treatment for which Stylist charges $600. Customer comes in at the appointed time and before beginning Stylist says, "I'm ready to go. Payment up front, please." Customer says, "The works, first; then I'll pay." Neither budges and Customer walks out of the salon without having any work done by Stylist. Stylist did not work on another client during the two-hour period reserved for Customer.

There is no industry custom or other previous relations between the two which would have any applicability to this situation.

13. If Stylist sues Customer for breach of contract, Stylist should:

(A) <u>Prevail</u>, because Stylist tendered performance.

(B) <u>Prevail</u>, because the common law rule requires payment before performance of services to ensure the party providing the service avoids the forfeiture that would result from the customer not paying.

(C) <u>Lose</u>, because the common law rule requires performance of service before payment.

(D) <u>Prevail</u>, because Stylist had booked a two-hour period for Customer and could not fill that slot with other work.

Facts for Questions 14–21

Morris entered into a written contract on February 15 with Linda to build a backyard pool in Linda's new home for $25,000. Under the contract, the pool was to include a working pool light in the deep end, and was to be lined with Acme-brand gunite. A progress payment of $10,000 was due after the hole was dug; $12,000 due once the gunite was poured; with the remaining $3,000 due upon final inspection.

14. For this question, and Questions Fifteen and Sixteen, assume that Morris dug the hole perfectly but Linda did not make the $10,000 progress payment. Morris immediately walked off the job and refused to return until he was paid.

Which of the following is the most accurate statement?

(A) Morris has not committed any type of breach.

(B) Morris has committed an immaterial breach.

(C) Morris has committed a material breach.

(D) Morris is entitled to the $10,000 progress payment, but is required to finish the pool since the amount of the progress payment is less than half of the total cost of the project.

15. Assume for purposes of this question that Linda changed her mind the day after she said she would not make the $10,000 progress payment. On that next day, she apologized to Morris and handed him a cashier's check for $10,000. Morris hadn't gotten any other work during the one day hiatus, was not inconvenienced by the one day delay, and could likely finish the pool on time if he came back to work the next day. However, he says he will not return because he genuinely does not trust Linda to pay him at the end of the job and he does not like customers who "pull these kinds of shenanigans."

Which of the following is the most accurate statement after Linda's late tender of the progress payment?

(A) Linda's breach and Morris's breach are immaterial.

(B) Linda will be deemed not to have breached due to cure, but Morris is still entitled to walk off the job if he genuinely fears that Linda will not pay him.

(C) Linda's breach is immaterial; Morris has committed a material breach.

(D) Linda and Morris have both committed a material breach and neither has any further obligation under the contract.

16. For this question, assume that Linda has refused to make the $10,000 progress payment for over three months. During that time, Morris has not been back to Linda's home and Morris has accepted other work which will keep him busy for the next year. He could not do the newly accepted work and Linda's pool at the same time.

What is the best description of the status of the parties at the end of this three-month period?

(A) Linda is in material breach of the contract, but can cure her breach by tendering the $10,000 progress payment.

(B) The contract has been totally breached and Morris's duties have been discharged.

(C) Linda has immaterially breached the contract, but Morris's obligations have been discharged.

(D) The contract has been totally breached and Linda's duties have been discharged.

17. For this question and for Question Eighteen, assume Morris completes the pool, but forgets to put a bulb in the pool light. This is discovered during the final inspection, before the final $3,000 payment is made.

Which of the following is the most accurate description?

(A) Linda is obligated to pay Morris $3,000.

(B) Linda is obligated to pay Morris $3,000, minus the cost of the light bulb and its installation.

(C) Linda is not obligated to pay Morris anything more until he installs the light bulb.

(D) Morris has materially breached the agreement but can cure the breach by installing the bulb.

18. Linda loves the pool and is in a forgiving mood. Accordingly, upon discovering the missing pool light during the final inspection as called for in the agreement, she says, "Don't worry about it. I suppose I could force you to put it in, but the pool is so great . . . I can get my husband to install the light."

Which is the best description of Linda's statement?

(A) She has made an election under the contract.

(B) She has waived the breach.

(C) She has made an irrevocable decision to treat the breach as immaterial under the divisibility doctrine.

(D) She has made an irrevocable decision to treat the breach as immaterial under the "part performance" doctrine.

19. Because the final inspection took place during the day, no one thought to check for the missing light bulb. In fact, Linda did not discover the missing bulb until five weeks after she had sent the final $3,000 check to Morris. She thought about calling Morris and having him put in the light, but then said to her husband, "Oh, the heck with calling Morris. I don't want to hassle him, we can put in the bulb."

Which is the best description of Linda's decision?

(A) She has made an election.

(B) She has waived the total breach.

(C) She has made an irrevocable decision to treat the breach as immaterial under the divisibility doctrine.

(D) She has made an irrevocable decision to treat the breach as immaterial under the "part performance" doctrine.

20. Assume for this Question that Morris built the pool perfectly and no flaws were found during the final inspection. Linda nevertheless fails to make the final $3,000 payment.

What is the best description of Linda's failure to make the payment?

(A) It is a material breach.

(B) It is an immaterial breach.

(C) It is neither a material, immaterial, nor total breach; it is just a breach.

(D) It is a total breach.

21. During the final inspection, Linda found a bag of gunite in Morris's truck that was labeled "Beta" brand, not Acme brand as required under the contract. Morris truthfully said he was surprised—he ordered Acme-brand from the hardware store and it was delivered altogether in one shipment to the worksite. Morris knew the first few bags were Acme, as he mixed them himself, but thereafter supervised the application and the rest of his crew mixed the gunite, and guessed that some of the Beta-brand got in the mix by mistake. Linda had asked for Acme gunite in the agreement because the company had advertised on TV, but had never heard anything one way or the other about Beta-brand gunite.

Subsequent investigation shows that Acme and Beta brand were virtually equivalent in quality and that to empty the pool, rip out the installed gunite, and reinstall all Acme-brand gunite would cost $20,000.

What is the best description of the situation?

(A) Morris has breached the contract, and Linda is entitled to collect as damages the difference, if any, between a pool with all Acme gunite and one with a mix of Acme and Beta brands.

(B) Morris did not breach the contract under the substantial performance doctrine because the quality of the two brands of gunite was substantially equivalent.

(C) Morris materially breached the contract because the brand of gunite desired by Linda was specifically bargained for and mentioned in the contract.

(D) Morris has breached the contract, and Linda is entitled to collect as damages the cost of replacing the existing gunite with all Acme-brand gunite, but is not entitled to an order of specific performance requiring Morris to replace the gunite.

Facts for Question 22

On June 1 Mary signed a written contract to purchase John's boat for $25,000. The contract had a clause providing, "Mary's payment obligations are contingent on her obtaining a loan from First Bank by June 30 for at least $20,000 of the purchase price, using the boat as collateral." However, there was no provision in the contract requiring Mary to go to First Bank and try to get a loan.

Shortly after signing the contract, Mary had buyer's remorse. So she never applied for a loan. On June 30 she told John she was sorry, but she did not get a loan and thus was not obligated to purchase the boat.

22. In <u>John v. Mary</u> for breach of contract, John should:

(A) <u>Lose</u>, because Mary did not obtain a loan from First Bank as of June 30, and express conditions are strictly enforced.

(B) <u>Lose</u>, because there was no consideration to support Mary's promise, since she had no obligation to obtain the loan under the contract.

(C) <u>Prevail</u>, but only if he can show that Mary would have obtained the loan had she applied for it.

(D) <u>Prevail</u>, because Mary did not apply for the loan.

Facts for Question 23

Debtor took out a loan of $1,200 from Creditor. Under their contract, repayment was to be $100/month on the first of the month, plus interest. Debtor paid for the first six months, but then told Creditor that he was laid off from work, and so would be making no additional loan payments.

23. What is the most accurate statement as of the end of month seven of the agreement?

(A) Creditor is entitled to sue Debtor for the remaining $600 principal, plus interest.

(B) Creditor is entitled to sue for the remaining $600 principal, but must wait until the end of the one-year loan period to sue for the lost interest.

(C) Creditor is entitled to sue Debtor only for $100, plus interest.

(D) Creditor must wait until the end of the one-year loan period to bring suit for any of the missed payments because Debtor could always change his mind and cure the breach.

Facts for Question 24

Maid is to clean Moneybags's mansion every other week for a year starting in January, under a written contract. Under the contract, Maid can only be fired for good cause. Maid does not show up for all of January, so Moneybags hires someone else to clean the mansion for that month. Then, the first week of February, Maid shows up to clean the mansion, and Moneybags, who has heard that Maid does good work, and is very affordable, tells her that it is okay that she did not show up in January, and that he would like Maid to continue cleaning for the remainder of the year pursuant to their contract. Maid agrees and her services in February and March are very good.

24. Moneybags fires her at the end of March. If Maid sues for breach of contract, she should:

(A) Lose, because Maid's absence in January was a material breach.

(B) Lose, because Maid's absence in January transformed her employment into an employment-at-will situation.

(C) Prevail, because Moneybags waived Maid's material breach.

(D) Prevail, because Maid cured her breach by showing up in February.

Facts for Question 25

Mark purchases three rare records from Brian's vintage record shop, each by a different artist, and in different genres: one jazz, one classical, and one rock. Each record cost $100 and the contract called for the records to be delivered the following Tuesday. However, on Tuesday, Brian only delivers one of the records, and refuses to sell the other two.

Consider the following statements:

    I.   Mark is obligated to pay Brian $300.

    II.   Mark can sue Brian for breach of contract for failure to deliver the other two records.

    III.   Mark is obligated to pay Brian $100.

    IV.   Mark need not pay for any records so long as he returns the one that was delivered, and can cancel the contract.

25. Which of the above statements is (are) true?

(A) II only.

(B) I and II only.

(C) IV only.

(D) II and III only.

Question 26

26. Which of the following are examples of valid excuses for the non-occurrence of an express condition precedent?

(A) Buyer is to find a loan prior to purchasing a home but Buyer never applies for a loan.

(B) Nephew is to take care of Uncle for life prior to receiving his inheritance from Uncle, but Uncle, in a rage, forces Nephew to leave the property at gunpoint and orders him never to come back.

(C) A contract calls for Contractor to install Brand A pipe in a home, but he installs Brand B, which is of equivalent quality, and costs the same as Brand A.

(D) All of the above.

Facts for Questions 27–29

Steve Seller contractually agreed to sell Ben Buyer his laptop for $600, with the agreed exchange to take place next Monday at 2:00 p.m. at Room 332 of Law School.

27. Neither Seller, nor Buyer show up at 2 p.m. at Room 332 on the appointed date, and Seller sues Buyer for failure to pay.

In a suit against Buyer, Seller will:

(A) <u>Prevail</u>, because Buyer did not make the payment, but will himself be liable to Buyer for failure to deliver the laptop.

(B) <u>Lose</u>, but only if Buyer provides the payment within a reasonable time.

(C) <u>Lose</u>, because the constructive condition of tender did not occur.

(D) <u>Lose</u>, because Seller did not provide the laptop.

28. For this question only, assume Seller and Buyer show up at the agreed time and place, but Buyer won't show Seller the money until Seller shows the laptop, and Seller won't show Buyer the laptop until Buyer shows the money. Both leave without any further communication.

Has Buyer breached the contract?

(A) No, because the constructive condition of tender did not occur.

(B) No, because Seller did not provide the laptop.

(C) Yes, because Buyer did not provide the payment.

(D) Yes, but it is only an immaterial breach.

29. For this question only, assume both Seller and Buyer show up at the agreed time and place, and Buyer shows Seller the $600 and says "I am willing to proceed," but says he won't give Seller the money until Seller shows him the laptop. Seller says he has the laptop, but refuses to show it or give it to Buyer until Buyer hands over the money. Buyer refuses, and Seller leaves without ever showing or delivering the laptop.

Has Seller breached the contract?

(A) Yes, but only if a court finds that Buyer gave Seller the payment within a reasonable time and Seller did not give Buyer the laptop.

(B) Yes, because Buyer tendered performance and Seller did not.

(C) No, because Buyer had not yet given Seller the payment.

(D) No, because Seller's performance was not yet due.

Facts for Question 30

Buyer and Seller entered into a written contract on November 1 in which Seller agreed to sell her car to Buyer for $10,000. The contract provides that on November 1, Seller was to deliver the title and Buyer was to pay the money. On November 1, Seller fails to deliver or tender title to the car. Buyer immediately sues Seller for breach of contract.

30. Will Buyer prevail?

(A) Yes, but only if Buyer had totally performed her duties under the contract by paying the $10,000 on November 1.

(B) Yes, if Buyer tendered payment on November 1.

(C) Yes, because Seller's tender of the title was a constructive condition precedent to Buyers duty to pay the $10,000.

(D) No, because there was no "time is of the essence" clause in the contract.

Facts for Question 31

Buyer and Farmer are in a contract where Buyer purchases apples from Farmer each month under a valid written contract. Their agreement contains a clause which makes Buyer's obligation to accept and pay for the apples expressly conditioned on their arrival by the first of each month. The parties have operated under the agreement without problem since the first of the year. However, on August 20 Buyer e-mails Farmer and asks for Farmer's agreement to switch delivery for September only to September 15. Farmer responds via e-mail her agreement to the change that same day. There is no further communication or remuneration exchanged between the parties.

31. Is the agreement to deliver the next shipment of apples on September 15 enforceable?

(A) No, because Buyer gave no consideration for the change in delivery date.

(B) No, unless Farmer delivers, and Buyer accepts, the apples on September 15, in which case an implied-in-fact waiver occurs.

    (C) No, unless Farmer can show it materially relied on the August 20 agreement.

    (D) Yes, even though Buyer did not give consideration for the change in delivery date.

Facts for Question 32

In April 2010, Seller entered into a contract to sell three commercial refrigerators to Buyer Restaurant for $12,000. The written agreement requires buyer to make monthly payments of $500 and also states, among other provisions:

> Payments shall be made on or before the first of each month. Time is of the essence. In the event that Buyer shall fail to make any payment when due, Seller may, at its option, repossess and sell the equipment in partial or entire satisfaction of the unpaid balance of the purchase price.

> This agreement contains the entire agreement of the parties, and may not be modified, except by a writing signed by both parties.

Since entering the contract, and for fourteen months, Buyer has made all monthly payments, but usually twenty days late. Seller has accepted each payment without objection, but has grown increasingly annoyed about the pattern of late payments. Buyer made its May 2011 payment on the 20th of the month, and Seller decided to repossess its refrigerator. Buyer has not relied on making the payments late—it is just more convenient for its bookkeeping department to do it this way. Except for the sending of the checks, there has been no communication between Buyer and Seller since the contract was signed. Seller has asked for your advice on the matter. Assume no unconscionability issues and that, to the extent applicable, 30 days' notice is reasonable.

32. What is the best advice?

    (A) Seller should not repossess the refrigerators at this time; rather it should notify Buyer that delivering on the first of the month will be required with respect to payments beginning in July 2011. If Buyer thereafter fails to make the payment by the first of the month, Seller may exercise its right to repossess the equipment.

    (B) Seller may proceed to immediately repossess the equipment as provided by the agreement since the agreement expressly provides that failure to make a payment when it is due entitles Seller to repossess, and that time is of the essence. Express contractual conditions are strictly construed.

(C) Seller should not repossess the refrigerators due to the failure to pay by the 1st ever, because it has waived the condition of prompt payment and established a course of performance allowing payment by the 20th of the month.

(D) Seller should proceed to immediately repossess the equipment as Buyer has provided no consideration for modifying the agreement for payment by the 20th.

Facts for Question 33

Buyer owns a retail store and orders 500 headbands from Seller, a headband manufacturer. The goods were to be delivered in one shipment. The goods arrive on time, but when Buyer counts them she discovers that only 499 were delivered. There is no usage of trade as to headband count and this is the first contract between Buyer and Seller.

33. Which of the following best describes Buyer's rights?

(A) Buyer is legally obligated to accept the entire shipment, because the breach was minor, but is only obligated to pay for 499 headbands.

(B) Buyer is entitled to reject the entire shipment, or accept the entire shipment; but if it accepts, it is only obligated to pay for 499 headbands.

(C) Buyer is entitled to reject the entire shipment but only if the breach substantially impairs the value of the shipment to its store.

(D) Buyer is entitled to accept and pay for only 200 of the headbands and reject the remainder and ship them back to Seller.

Facts for Question 34

Buyer owns a retail store and orders 500 headbands from Seller, a headband manufacturer. The goods were to be delivered in two lots of 250 headbands each. The first shipment was timely delivered, but when Buyer examined the headbands, she discovered one was missing, i.e., only 249 headbands were in the shipment. There is no usage of trade as to headband count and this is the first contract between Buyer and Seller. Assume the missing headband impairs somewhat, but not substantially, the value of the shipment to Buyer.

34. Which of the following best describes Buyer's rights as to the first shipment?

(A) Buyer is entitled to reject the entire shipment.

(B) Buyer must accept the entire shipment.

(C) Buyer is entitled to cancel the contract and stop the second shipment because Seller breached the agreement by sending only 249 headbands in the first shipment.

(D) Buyer may accept 100 headbands, reject the remainder and ship the remainder back to Seller.

Facts for Question 35

On Monday, Buyer and Seller entered into a written contract for the sale of a new motorcycle for $8,000. The agreement provided that the motorcycle was to have a GPS system installed on the handlebars.

Buyer picked up the motorcycle on the designated delivery date, Friday evening at 6:00 p.m. Buyer immediately noticed it did not have a GPS system. The service department was closed for the weekend, but Seller apologized and offered to have a GPS system installed first thing on Monday morning. Seller correctly stated that Seller had ordered a motorcycle with a GPS device installed from the factory and was genuinely surprised to find the motorcycle as delivered was without the device.

Buyer would suffer no real harm or hassle getting the motorcycle on Monday, but was angry at the delay and called the deal off, saying he did not want the motorcycle any longer and would refuse to pay for it. Assume the lack of the GPS substantially impaired the value of the motorcycle to Buyer.

35. Which of the following best describes the rights of the parties?

(A) Buyer was entitled to reject the motorcycle and cancel the contract under the perfect tender rule, and Seller has no recourse to make the contract enforceable thereafter.

(B) Buyer was entitled to reject the motorcycle, but Seller had a right to cure the breach and make the contract enforceable thereafter.

(C) Buyer is entitled to reject the motorcycle and avoid the contract because the lack of a GPS substantially impaired the value of the motorcycle to him.

(D) Buyer was entitled to reject the motorcycle if Seller was a merchant; but was not entitled to reject the motorcycle if Seller was a non-merchant.

Facts for Question 36

A restaurant contracts for delivery of 150 heads of lettuce per month over the next three years from Farmer. In the first shipment, 130 heads of lettuce are spoiled, and Farmer refuses to send replacements.

36. The restaurant:

(A) May reject this shipment and cancel the contract in order to find a more reliable supplier.

(B) May reject this shipment, but may not cancel the contract in order to find a more reliable supplier.

(C) Must accept this shipment, but does not have to pay for the spoiled heads of lettuce.

(D) Must accept this shipment, and may sue for damages based on the value of the spoiled heads of lettuce.

Facts for Question 37

The Academy of Motion Picture Arts and Sciences ("Academy") ordered from Seller fifteen television monitors for use at the Oscar telecast on February 20. The agreement called for all fifteen monitors to be delivered on February 19. Seller shipped the monitors in time to arrive at the Academy on the 19th. However, the shipping company was responsible for a delay and the monitors arrived on February 21. At that point, the Academy legitimately had no use for the monitors.

The Academy refused to accept or pay for the monitors and Seller sued.

37. Which is the most accurate statement in <u>Seller v. Academy</u>?

(A) <u>Seller should prevail</u>, as it was not its fault that the monitors did not arrive on time.

(B) <u>Seller should prevail</u>, so long as there was no "time is of the essence" clause in the Seller–Academy agreement.

(C) <u>Seller should prevail</u>, if it did not know that the Academy was ordering the monitors for use at the Oscar telecast.

(D) <u>Seller should lose</u>, because Seller did not have the right to cure.

Facts for Question 38

On July 15, a retailer of mp3 players discovers that it only has fifty of a certain type of mp3 player left. Because the storeowner does not want to run low on inventory, he orders another 200 of these devices, to be delivered no later than August 1. Late in the day on August 1, Seller delivered the mp3 players, when the storeowner still has thirty mp3 players in stock. On August 2, when storeowner begins to unpack the mp3 players, he discovers that Seller has accidentally sent the wrong brand of mp3 player. Seller's employees made an honest mistake and thought they were actually sending the correct mp3 players.

38. At this point in time:

(A) Seller has an absolute right to cure the imperfect tender.

(B) Seller has the ability to cure the imperfect tender if it would not cause retailer an inconvenience to wait for a promptly sent shipment of the proper brand of mp3 player.

(C) The retailer has an absolute right to reject the mp3 players and cancel the contract, because the time for performance under the contract has expired.

(D) The retailer must accept the shipment if the different brand of mp3 players is of equal value to the mp3 players Seller delivered under the substantial performance rule.

Facts to Question 39

Jackie is about to go on a month long trip to El Salvador. She orders a special mosquito repellant long sleeve shirt that is breezy enough to keep her cool throughout the hot Salvadorian days. Jackie orders the shirt from One Stop Sporting Goods. Because the material is very expensive and unique, One Stop must order the shirt from a reputable manufacturer. Jackie is set to leave for her trip on July 26, and her contract with One Stop provides that the shirt is to be delivered no later than July 25.

The manufacturer delivers the shirt to One Stop near the close of the business day on July 25. Jackie comes in that evening to pick it up and realizes the manufacturer accidentally sent a child-sized shirt that will never fit her. She would have no need for a properly fitting shirt after her trip, and the area in El Salvador she is attending has no mail or delivery service.

The Sporting Goods Store ordered the proper shirt, and any problem was the fault of the manufacturer's order fulfillment department.

39. May One Stop Sporting Goods cure the breach?

(A) No, because Jackie is leaving on her trip tomorrow.

(B) Yes, regardless whether One Stop Sporting Goods knew Jackie needed it for a trip the next day.

(C) Yes, assuming One Stop Sporting Goods thought that the shirt would be acceptable.

(D) Yes, because it was the manufacturer's fault; and not One Stop's.

Facts for Question 40

Smith bought a brand new Chevrolet. While driving the car home from the dealer, the car broke down due to a defective transmission.

Consider the following statements:

I.   The dealer is entitled to cure by repair—by replacing the faulty transmission in Smith's car with an identical transmission taken from another Chevrolet model.

II. The dealer is entitled to cure by discounting the price of the car to take into account the price of a competent transmission repair.

III. The dealer is entitled to cure by providing Smith with a brand new car.

40. Which of the above statements is correct?

(A) I, II, and III.

(B) I and III only.

(C) III only.

(D) II and III only.

Facts for Question 41

David bought an expensive rug from Randy's Rug Mart on Monday. Later that day, David discovers that there was a large snag in the rug, and promptly notified Randy that he was rejecting it. Randy's promised to pick it up from David's home on Thursday. On Wednesday, painters were in David's home and dripped paint on the rug, ruining it. The painters then offer David a check to pay for the rug, which David accepted. The check was made payable to David. Randy's finds out about the check, refuses to pick up the rug, and demands payment. David refuses to pay.

41. In a suit between David and Randy's, Randy's will likely:

  (A) <u>Prevail</u>, because David had already taken the rug home.

  (B) <u>Prevail</u>, because David accepted the check.

  (C) <u>Lose</u>, because the rug was imperfectly tendered.

  (D) <u>Lose</u>, because David notified Randy's that he rejected the rug prior to accepting the check.

Facts for Question 42

Buyer purchases a bookcase from a furniture store. When she brings the bookcase home and puts it together, she realizes that the bottom shelf is missing. She contacts the store, and the representative tells her the store will mail her a bottom shelf. Because the store had agreed to send the bottom shelf, Buyer decides to accept the bookcase and use the unit. However, after three weeks, the furniture store has never mailed the shelf. Buyer now wants to return the bookshelf and get her money back. The missing shelf substantially impairs the value of the bookshelf to Buyer.

Assume that three weeks is more than a reasonable time to effect a cure under the circumstances, and that it is a reasonable time in which to send the bookcase back.

42. Which of the following is the most accurate statement?

  (A) Buyer may reject the bookcase, but may not revoke her acceptance of it.

  (B) Buyer may revoke her acceptance of the bookcase.

  (C) Buyer may neither reject nor revoke her acceptance of the bookcase, but can sue successfully for breach of warranty.

  (D) Buyer may revoke her acceptance of the bookcase, even if she has substantially changed the bookcase by painting it, because the lack of a shelf substantially impaired the value of the unit to her.

Facts for Question 43

Buyer purchases a brand new bicycle from Seller to ride to work. For the first week, the bike works perfectly and Buyer cruises to and from work every day without a problem. At the beginning of the second week, however, one of the "wheel nuts" holding the axle rod in place falls off, causing the wheel to become unstable. Buyer can no longer ride the bike to work as its value is substantially impaired to him, and he wants to return it. Buyer has made no substantial change to the bike.

43. May Buyer revoke his acceptance at this time?

(A) Yes, as all the elements for revocation of acceptance are met.

(B) Yes, but only if Seller "accepts" Buyer's attempted "revocation."

(C) No, once Buyer took the bike home, he accepted the goods.

(D) No, if a court determined that a reasonable person would not find the loose wheel nuts substantially impaired the value of the bicycle.

Facts for Question 44

Buyer is a clothing manufacturer that orders 20,000 "40-lignes" (approximately 1-inch) buttons from Seller in certain colors specified in the contract. Throughout the button industry, it is customary for a supplier to measure buttons by weight, rather than count each individual button. The custom is that 1,000 "40-lignes" buttons weigh ten ounces, and under the terms of the contract all the buttons are delivered in a single shipment.

Seller timely sends Buyer twenty, 10-ounce packages of "40-lignes" buttons in the proper colors. Buyer is obsessive and never wants to be shorthanded, so he counts every single button. He discovers that he was only sent 19,959 buttons. He is furious and calls Seller to demand that seller take back the buttons. Seller refuses.

44. Is Buyer entitled to reject the shipment?

(A) Yes, because the buttons were imperfectly tendered under the perfect tender rule.

(B) Yes, if the shortfall substantially impairs the value of the shipment to this buyer.

(C) No, because this is an immaterial breach and Buyer must accept the goods, but may prorate payment for only the 19,959 buttons received, and not the 20,000 buttons ordered.

(D) No, because the tender of buttons by Seller conformed to the contract and Seller must pay the contract price for 20,000 buttons.

CHAPTER 15
ANTICIPATORY REPUDIATION

QUESTIONS

Facts for Question 1

On June 5 Parker, a homeowner, contracted with Dennis, a landscaper, to do landscaping work around Parker's home beginning June 25. On June 10, Dennis told Parker he wasn't going to show up because he had obtained a more lucrative job across town that would keep him and his crew busy for the next six months.

1. Which of the following statements is most correct?

   (A) Parker may bring suit immediately against Dennis under the doctrine of anticipatory repudiation.

   (B) Parker does not have standing to bring suit against Dennis until June 25, when the contract will have been breached if Dennis fails to perform on that date.

   (C) Parker may bring suit immediately for an injunction prohibiting Dennis from working elsewhere during the contracted for period, but must wait until June 25 to sue for damages.

   (D) Parker will only be able to bring suit once he hires a replacement landscaper because it will not be until then that he will be able to establish damages, if any.

Facts for Question 2

On May 1, Buyer contracts with Seller to purchase Seller's watch for $5,000. Under the agreement, Seller was to give Buyer the watch now, and Buyer was to pay Seller on July 1, when Buyer was to receive a bonus at work. Seller gave Buyer the watch on May 1, but on May 15, Buyer told Seller he would not make the payment when due.

2. Which of the following statements is most correct as of May 16?

(A) Seller may bring suit against Buyer immediately.

(B) Seller may bring suit immediately for return of the watch, but must wait until July 1 to sue for damages.

(C) Seller may not bring suit immediately unless he has made an attempt to find a new buyer.

(D) Seller may not bring suit against Buyer until July 1.

Facts for Question 3

Buyer contracts with Seller to purchase ten tons of steel rebar for use in construction. The price is fixed at $10,000 per ton of rebar with delivery to take place in two months. Just as the delivery date is approaching, Seller contacts Buyer and says, "The price of steel has gone way up. I really don't know if I can go through with our deal for $10,000, I really need $12,000 to eke out any profit on the deal."

3. Which of the following statements are correct immediately after Seller's statement?

(A) Seller has anticipatorily repudiated and Buyer may immediately bring suit.

(B) Seller has neither anticipatorily repudiated or breached, and Buyer currently has no claim against Seller.

(C) Seller has breached, but Buyer must wait until performance is due to bring suit.

(D) If what Seller said is true, Seller's duties under the contract are excused by commercial impracticability.

Facts for Question 4

Paul, a homeowner, contracted with Dave, a painter, to "paint Paul's home" for $5,000. Paul has a very large guest house with lots of trim and complicated surfaces to paint. As Dave was painting part of Paul's house, Dave said, "Man am I glad I don't have to paint that guest house too. That would be a lot of work."

Paul honestly believed that the contract to paint his house included painting the guest house and demanded Dave paint it. Dave honestly believed that the contract only called for him to paint the main house itself, and refused to paint the guest house.

4. Which of the following statements is most correct?

(A) Dave has anticipatorily repudiated.

(B) Dave has anticipatorily repudiated, but only if Paul can establish that painting the guest house was material to him.

(C) Dave has not anticipatorily repudiated his duties under the contract.

(D) Dave did not breach the contract if inclusion of the duty to paint the guest house would produce an unjust result.

Facts for Question 5

Buyer owned a large apple farm. On March 1, Buyer contracted with Seller to purchase a custom apple picking machine for $50,000. It will take four months to construct the machine with delivery and payment due September 1.

On May 1, when Seller was about half way through the manufacture of the machine, Buyer and Seller were talking and Buyer said, "I sure hope we will have the money to pay for that expensive machine come September." The next day Seller read in the *Wall Street Journal* that Buyer's farm was having financial problems and may go bankrupt.

On May 2, Seller wrote to Buyer and asked for assurances that Buyer was willing and able to pay when the machine is delivered in September. Buyer refused to furnish anything to prove his, or the farm's financial stability.

As it turned out, the *Wall Street Journal* article was incorrect and Buyer's initial comment about hoping he had enough money was just a joke as the farm was completely financially stable.

Assume no further communication between the parties other than described above.

5. Which of the following is correct as of June 5?

(A) Buyer has not anticipatorily repudiated the contract because Seller did not have reasonable grounds for insecurity.

(B) Buyer has not anticipatorily repudiated the contract because Buyer never said in definite and unequivocal terms that he would not perform.

(C) Seller can treat Buyer as having anticipatorily repudiated because Buyer failed to provide reasonable assurances, and Seller can stop production of the machine and immediately sue Seller.

(D) Seller can treat Buyer as having anticipatorily repudiated because Buyer failed to provide reasonable assurances, but Seller must finish the machine and try to sell it to another to mitigate damages.

Facts for Question 6

Buyer contracts with Seller for the purchase of 500 televisions for $100,000 with tender to take place in two months. Seller hears from a reliable and knowledgeable source that Buyer is facing financial ruin and has not been paying its bills on time. Seller contacts Buyer and demands to see the latest profit and loss statement ("P/L") for the company. Buyer instead sends a credit report prepared by a reputable company showing Buyer is up to date on all debts, paying on time and is in good financial condition.

6.   Which of the following is correct thirty-one days later, assuming no further communication between the parties?

(A) Buyer has not anticipatorily repudiated because it provided reasonable assurances.

(B) Seller can treat Buyer as having anticipatorily repudiated the agreement by failing to provide the P/L as demanded.

(C) Seller can treat Buyer as having anticipatorily repudiated the agreement only if a court determines the P/L was an "adequate form of assurance."

(D) Buyer has not anticipatorily repudiated because it acted in good faith in sending something in response to Seller's demand, regardless whether a court would later determine the credit report was a reasonable assurance. In such case, Buyer will be required by the court to send something that the court believes would constitute reasonable assurance.

Facts for Question 7

On March 1, Buyer contracted with Seller for Buyer to purchase a custom sign to be installed above Buyer's sandwich shop. It would take almost a month to manufacture and install the sign, so delivery of the installed sign was promised for April 1.

On March 10, Seller was visiting Buyer and noticed a credit statement on the counter indicating Buyer's shop was not doing very well, and was behind on its bills. Seller contacted Buyer and asked for assurances Buyer could pay when the sign was completed. On the day he sent the letter, Seller stopped working on the sign.

Buyer acquired a new credit report as fast as it could, but it took five days to get a new report to Seller. The new report indicated Buyer was in good financial shape and was paying all its bills on time. As it turned out, the first report was based on reporting errors that were being corrected.

Upon receiving the new report, Seller recommenced working on the sign. Due to the delay while waiting for the new report, however, Seller does not install the finished sign until April 6.

7.   Which of the following is correct?

     (A) Seller has breached by finishing the project five days late.

     (B) Seller has breached only if Buyer can show the breach was intentional.

     (C) Buyer breached by failing to provide reasonable assurances in a timely manner.

     (D) Neither party has breached the contract.

Facts for Question 8

On August 1, Seller, a carpenter, contracted with Buyer to make a custom table for her, to be delivered on November 1. On October 1, Buyer definitively and unequivocally repudiates.

Seller contacted Buyer and requested she reconsider, but Buyer did not respond. Seller did not communicate any further with Buyer, and never told her that he was treating the repudiation as final. However, Seller was fortunate to receive new work, and took a job making custom furniture for a chain of restaurants that would require all his time for two years.

On October 25, Buyer contacts Seller to inform him she changed her mind and now wants the table after all. Seller informs Buyer he has taken a new job and will not be able to make her table.

8. Which of the following is correct as of October 26?

    (A) Seller has anticipatorily repudiated after Buyer retracted her repudiation.

    (B) Buyer could not retract her repudiation once Seller took the new job.

    (C) Seller must complete the project or be in breach, but will be given a reasonable time to complete the table before he is in breach.

    (D) Buyer has revoked her repudiation effectively and Seller has not repudiated yet.

CHAPTER 16
IMPOSSIBILITY, COMMERCIAL IMPRACTICABILITY, AND FRUSTRATION OF PURPOSE

QUESTIONS

Facts for Question 1

Dwayne, the owner of a performing arts center in Los Angeles, contracted with Paula, a producer, to rent the building for five nights so Paula could stage a play. In the agreement Dwayne agreed to lease Paula the performing arts center "in good condition."

A few days before the first performance, a lightning bolt struck the performing arts center, which burned to the ground. Paula was unable to hold her play at the center because of the damage.

Paula sues Dwayne for the lost advertising costs and other losses associated with not performing the show. Assume that there was no precaution Dwayne could have taken to prevent the fire from consuming the building.

1.   Which of the following is Dwayne's best defense to the suit?

   (A) Misunderstanding.

   (B) Impossibility.

   (C) Frustration of purpose.

   (D) Commercial impracticability.

Facts for Question 2

Seller is a nuclear fusion company who contracts to supply Buyer with a working nuclear power plant at a fixed price, including supplying the uranium rods that power the reactors. The uranium rods are the most expensive component of the plant. Nuclear power plants take a long time to build, and delivery is promised ten years after the contract was signed.

Historically the price of uranium has remained fairly constant. However, seven years after the contract was signed, but before delivery was due or accomplished, the price of uranium increased twenty-five times the price it was at the beginning of the contract in just one month's time. To supply the uranium rods at the plant now meant that Seller would go from making $3 million on the plant to losing $75 million.

Seller has a source who tells it, accurately, that the price increase was the result of an illegal, world-wide price fixing agreement amongst uranium suppliers. Seller refuses to perform due to the increase in the price of uranium.

2. Which of the following statements is most correct, assuming the illegal price fixing agreement can be established?

(A) Seller will be excused due to impossibility.

(B) Seller will be excused due to commercial impracticability.

(C) Seller will be excused due to frustration of purpose.

(D) Seller will not be excused from its duties based on any of these theories.

Facts for Question 3

Peter owns an apartment with a great view of Central Park. On May 5, there will be a concert in Central Park with a line-up of several famous performers. The concert has been sold out for months. Peter decides to advertise he would rent the apartment on the night of the concert to anyone who wants to view the concert for $5,000.

Denise agreed to rent the apartment for the day of May 5 and agreed to pay $5,000 on the day of the concert. As it turned out, the organizers of the concert failed to get one of the required permits so the concert was cancelled. Denise refused to pay and Peter brings suit for breach and payment of the $5,000.

3. In <u>Peter v. Denise</u> for breach, Peter will:

(A) <u>Lose</u>, because Denise may defend by impossibility.

(B) <u>Lose</u>, because Denise may defend by frustration of purpose.

(C) <u>Prevail</u>, because Denise breached by refusing payment on the date agreed upon.

(D) <u>Prevail</u>, but is only entitled to the fair market value of renting the apartment on a day without a concert.

Facts for Question 4

Derek wanted to open a fireworks store in Celebration County, where, at the time, all fireworks were legal. The fireworks market had been extremely profitable lately, as consumers were buying up as many fireworks as they could in light of recent debate regarding anti-firework laws following an increase in firework related fires.

Derek contracted with Patti to lease a retail space that Patti owned for $1,500 per month. The contract did not specify any particular type of use the retail store must be used for.

Just after the contract was signed, the County passed laws restricting firework sales to only the least dangerous kind, making over 90% of fireworks in Derek's inventory illegal. Derek refused to follow through and lease the retail store. Patti has brought suit for breach of contract.

4. In <u>Patti v. Derek</u>, Patti will likely:

   (A) <u>Prevail</u>, because Derek will still realize some benefits from the agreement.

   (B) <u>Prevail</u>, because Derek had assumed the risk of the laws being passed.

   (C) <u>Lose</u>, because Derek has a viable frustration of purpose defense.

   (D) <u>Prevail</u>, because both (A) and (B) are correct.

Facts for Question 5

The Danbury Hotel is located next door to Pure Fun Water Park ("Pure Fun"). The hotel contracted with Pure Fun whereby the hotel would pay Pure Fun $500/month for the next four years for its hotel guests to have free access to the water park. The Danbury hoped the addition of free access to the park would increase its desirability as a hotel.

Exactly one year into the contract, The Danbury burned down through no fault of its own. As it was no longer taking guests, the hotel refused to continue making the $500/month payments to Pure Fun. Pure Fun brought suit for breach for the remaining payments due under the contract.

5. In <u>Pure Fun v. The Danbury</u>, Pure Fun will likely:

    (A) <u>Lose</u>, because The Danbury has a valid impossibility defense.

    (B) <u>Prevail</u>, because The Danbury has breached by refusing to complete payments under the contract.

    (C) <u>Lose</u>, because The Danbury has a valid frustration of purpose defense.

    (D) <u>Prevail</u>, but only for the fair market value of the admissions used by the average number of The Danbury's guests using the park.

Facts for Question 6

Dwayne is an adventure fishing guide and agreed to take Parker on a trip to fish for blue puffer fish on March 10 for $2,000, with payment due on the date of the trip. It was understood by both parties that Parker only wanted to fish for blue puffer fish, and had no interest in any other fish. At the time of contracting, February 1, it had always been legal to fish for blue puffer fish.

On February 15, a law was passed which made fishing for blue puffer fish illegal in any form due to their declining population. Dwayne informed Parker that he would not be taking him on the trip. Parker made no attempt to contact any other fishing guides to cover. Parker was furious, as he had always wanted to fish for blue puffers, and has sued Dwayne for breach seeking specific performance.

6. In <u>Parker v. Dwayne</u>, Parker will likely:

    (A) <u>Prevail</u>, but Parker must reimburse Dwayne if Dwayne incurs any fine.

    (B) <u>Prevail</u>, because Dwayne is contractually obligated to take Parker blue puffer fishing.

    (C) <u>Lose</u>, because Parker did not attempt to seek any alternative guides to take him to "cover."

    (D) <u>Lose</u>, because subsequent government regulation made performance impossible.

Facts for Question 7

Government put out a Request for Purchase ("RFP") seeking a computer capable of doing a list of tasks specified in the RFP. Start–Up, a new company with three employees, offered to manufacture the computer for $500,000. Start–Up's bid was the low bid by about $80,000, and it was awarded the job.

Making a computer with the required characteristics proved harder than Start–Up anticipated. Eventually it told Government, accurately, that it was impossible for it to make the computer.

Government then went to Apple who had the expertise to build the computer that could do the required tasks. Apple said it could but it would cost $1.3 million to do so.

7. In <u>Government v. Start–Up</u> for breach of contract, Start–Up will likely:

(A) <u>Lose</u>, because it has no valid defense.

(B) <u>Prevail</u>, because it has a valid impossibility defense.

(C) <u>Prevail</u>, because it has a valid commercial impracticability defense.

(D) <u>Prevail</u>, because it has a valid frustration of purpose defense.

Facts for Questions 8 and 9

Seller has 100 lithographs of a beach scene signed by recently deceased Painter, who painted the picture. Under Painter's will, these are the last such lithographs that can be legally made.

Seller has a contract to sell sixty of the lithographs to Gallery #1, and forty to Gallery #2. After these contracts have been signed, but before the lithographs were shipped, an earthquake occurred in Seller's town, destroying half of the lithographs. The lithographs were stored consistent with industry standards and Seller is not at fault for their destruction.

8. Which is the most accurate statement?

    (A) Seller's delivery duties with respect to Gallery #1 and Gallery #2 are completely discharged due to impossibility.

    (B) Seller must offer thirty of the remaining fifty lithographs to Gallery #1 and twenty of the remaining fifty lithographs to Gallery #2.

    (C) Seller can offer thirty of the remaining fifty lithographs to Gallery #1 and twenty of the remaining fifty lithographs to Gallery #2, but is not required to do so.

    (D) Seller's contracts with Gallery #1 and Gallery #2 are discharged due to frustration of purpose.

9. Which is the most accurate statement?

    (A) Gallery #1 must accept and pay for thirty lithographs if they are sent by Seller.

    (B) Gallery #1 must accept and pay for a valid substituted performance if proffered by Seller if a court determines what is offered is a "substantial equivalent" for the destroyed lithographs.

    (C) Gallery #1's duties to accept and pay for any lithographs were discharged by the earthquake.

    (D) Neither (A), (B), nor (C) is an accurate statement.

Question 10

10. Which is the most accurate statement about a "force majure" clause?

    (A) It allows the parties to agree in advance what events will discharge their duties under a contract.

    (B) It primarily protects sellers.

    (C) It often provides discharge of duties for "Acts of God."

    (D) (A), (B), and (C) are all accurate.

CHAPTER 17
THIRD PARTY BENEFICIARY CONTRACTS

QUESTIONS

Facts for Questions 1–3

Jane wanted to help her nephew Bill pay for college, so she sold her diamond necklace to Star for $30,000, and directed Star to pay the money to Bill. Under their agreement, Star was to pay Bill three months after receiving the necklace.

1. Under the Restatement 2d of Contracts, what is the best categorization of Bill?

    (A) A donee-like intended beneficiary.

    (B) A creditor-like intended beneficiary.

    (C) An incidental beneficiary.

    (D) Not a third party beneficiary at all.

2. For purposes of this question only, assume that Jane delivers the necklace to Star who is delighted with it. However, neither Star nor Jane pays Bill. Who may Bill successfully sue for the payment, assuming no detrimental reliance by Bill?

    (A) Bill is entitled to sue Star only to enforce the payment.

    (B) Bill is entitled to sue Jane only to enforce the payment.

    (C) Bill is entitled to sue either Star or Jane to enforce the payment.

    (D) Bill may sue neither Star nor Jane to enforce the payment because it is a gift from Jane.

3. For this question only, assume Bill enrolled in college after learning of the Jane–Star agreement. Bill did so because he was counting on the payment from Star to pay his tuition for his freshman year. Also assume that two months after delivering the necklace, after Bill had enrolled in

college, but before the payment from Star was due or had been made, Jane suffered an unexpected illness and needed the money herself. Accordingly, she directed Star to pay her instead of Bill. Star paid Jane the $30,000 when it was due.

Which of the following statements best describes Bill's rights for breach of the Jane–Star contract only, in a jurisdiction that follows the rules of the Restatement 2d of Contracts?

(A) Bill is entitled to sue Star only.

(B) Bill is entitled to sue Jane only.

(C) Bill is entitled to sue either Star or Jane, but may only collect $30,000 total.

(D) Bill is not entitled to sue either Star or Jane because they modified their agreement before performance was due.

Fact Variation for Questions 4 and 5 (Variation of the Facts for Questions 1-3)

For Questions 4 and 5, assume that Bill had lent Jane $30,000, and the loan was due to be repaid in three months at the time of the Jane–Star contract. Hence, the selling of the necklace to Star, with payment to be delivered in three months to Bill, was to settle the Bill–Jane debt.

4. Under the Restatement 2d of Contracts, what is the best categorization of Bill?

(A) A donee-like intended beneficiary.

(B) A creditor-like intended beneficiary.

(C) An incidental beneficiary.

(D) Not a third party beneficiary at all.

5. Jane delivers the necklace to Star who is delighted with it. However, neither Star nor Jane pays Bill in three months when payment was due. Who may Bill successfully sue for $30,000 under any theory?

(A) Bill is entitled to sue Star only.

(B) Bill is entitled to sue Jane only.

(C) Bill is entitled to sue either Star or Jane.

(D) Bill is not entitled to sue either Star or Jane.

Facts for Question 6

Donna, a movie star, owed Hairstylist $500 for styling work Hairstylist had done at Hairstylist's posh Beverly Hills salon in preparation for a huge audition for a leading role in a Hollywood film.

When one of Donna's friends, Rhonda, subsequently made an offer to buy a painting from Donna for $750, Donna accepted. Donna and Rhonda agreed that Rhonda would pay the money directly to Hairstylist by June 1. Donna figured that the $750 would cover the $500 hairstyling debt, and also make for a $250 tip because she looked so good in her audition that she landed the role. In mid-June however, Donna received a surprise call from Hairstylist informing her that Rhonda had not paid any part of the $750, despite the fact that Rhonda had already taken possession of the painting.

6. If Hairstylist brings suit against Rhonda, how much can Hairstylist recover from her?

(A) $750.

(B) $500.

(C) $250.

(D) Nothing.

Facts for Question 7

Moneybags owned several thousand acres as part of his vast estate. In order to maintain the property, he struck a deal with Gardner to take care of all of the landscaping on the property. In order to do the job competently, Gardner told Moneybags that he would need to buy a new, large-model lawnmower-tractor. Moneybags told Gardner to pick out whatever model of tractor he wanted from whatever store he wanted to buy it from, and Moneybags would reimburse Gardner for it and let Gardner keep the tractor.

Gardner went to all of the major retailers and finally settled on an exceptional model at a great price from Home Depot. The Home Depot store he went to did not have the model Gardner wanted in stock, but would have one by the following Wednesday, five days later. Gardner said, "fair enough. I will buy it next Wednesday when you have one."

On Tuesday, the day before Gardner was going to pick up the tractor, Moneybags suffered a huge stock loss and told Gardner that he would have to let him go, and would not purchase the tractor. Home Depot had the tractor waiting the next day

7. In an action by Home Depot against Moneybags, Home Depot will:

(A) <u>Lose</u>, because it is only an incidental beneficiary of the Moneybags–Gardner contract.

(B) <u>Prevail</u>, because of reliance.

(C) <u>Prevail</u>, as a third-party intended beneficiary of the Moneybags–Gardner contract.

(D) <u>Prevail</u>, because Gardner was an agent of Moneybags.

Facts for Questions 8

City promises in its Charter that one if its obligations is to keep the roads in good repair for its citizens. Its citizens, in turn, are obligated to pay a city tax to pay for all required City services mentioned in the City's Charter.

City contracts with Contractor to build a new roadway in a newly developed part of City to benefit the public. The workmanship and quality of the road are horrendous and the roadway ends up with potholes, misidentified lanes, and a number of other problems.

8. In an action by a tax-paying citizen of City against Contractor for breach of the City–Contractor agreement, the citizen should:

(A) <u>Prevail</u>, because citizen is a creditor-like intended beneficiary of the City–Contractor agreement by virtue of paying taxes.

(B) <u>Prevail</u>, because citizen is a donee-like intended beneficiary of the City–Contractor agreement.

(C) <u>Prevail</u>, if the suit is brought as a class action on behalf of all effected tax-paying citizens of City.

(D) <u>Lose</u>, because citizen is an incidental beneficiary of the City–Contractor agreement.

Facts for Questions 9 and 10

Brother contracts to sell his Picasso sketch to Buyer for $25,000. Brother tells Buyer to pay Sister the $25,000, which he intends to be a gift which Sister could use to take a vacation. Brother delivers the painting, but Buyer later learns that it is an imitation, and not a real Picasso. The imitation painting is worth only $100 instead of $25,000. Buyer refuses to pay Sister and seeks to rescind the contract. Assume that Brother reasonably believed that the Picasso was genuine when he sold it to Buyer.

Sister sues Buyer for $25,000.

9.   What is the likely outcome?

(A) Judgment for Buyer, because of a misrepresentation defense.

(B) Judgment for Buyer, because Sister is an incidental beneficiary.

(C) Judgment for Sister, because Buyer may only assert a misrepresentation defense in a suit brought by Brother.

(D) Judgment for Sister, but only if the misrepresentation was fraudulent, and not either innocent or negligent.

10. Assume for this question only that the painting is real, but that Buyer refuses to pay any money to Sister.

In a suit by <u>Brother</u> against Buyer to enforce payment to Sister, what result?

(A) Judgment for Buyer, because only Sister may enforce the promise.

(B) Judgment for Buyer, because Sister was an incidental beneficiary.

(C) Judgment for Brother for the full price, which he may keep as promisee, because the payment was only a gift to Sister.

(D) Judgment for Brother, but the amount recovered must be given to Sister.

Facts for Questions 11 and 12

Seller wanted to sell his home, Blackacre, for $100,000. Buyer agreed to the $100,000 price and that Buyer would pay $25,000 of the price to Creditor for a debt that Seller owed to Creditor. Seller's secretary was to put the contract in writing but when she did, the term regarding paying $25,000 to Creditor was omitted. Yet when Buyer and Seller later signed the agreement, they failed to note the absence of the provision and neither party paid careful attention to the contract's terms. Buyer never paid Creditor any of the $25,000, even though title to Blackacre was exchanged.

11. In an action by Creditor against Buyer for the $25,000, assume Buyer prevails in a jurisdiction controlled by the Restatement 2d of Contracts. Which of the following would best explain that result?

(A) Creditor never gave notice on his own to either Buyer or Seller that it agreed to accept payment from Buyer, and thus was not an intended beneficiary under the agreement until such notice was given.

(B) The day after the written agreement was signed, before Creditor heard of any agreement, Seller told Buyer that he had changed his mind and the money should be paid directly to him instead.

(C) There was no consideration given by Creditor with regard to the promise by Buyer to pay him $25,000.

(D) Creditor was prevented by the Statute of Frauds from suing Seller on the original obligation.

12. Assume for this question that the original written contract for the sale of Seller's land called for Buyer to pay the entire $100,000 to Seller.

Later, a few weeks after the original Buyer–Seller agreement was completed, Seller makes a separate agreement with Buyer calling for Buyer to pay Creditor $25,000 instead of paying Seller the full amount of the purchase, so as to settle a $25,000 debt Seller owed Creditor.

What are the roles of the parties of the second agreement?

(A) Buyer is the Promisor; Seller is the Promisee; and Creditor is a Donee-like Intended Beneficiary.

(B) Buyer is the Promisor; Seller is the Promisee; and Creditor is a Creditor-like Intended Beneficiary.

(C) Buyer is the Obligor; Seller is the Assignor; and Creditor is the Assignee.

(D) Buyer is the Obligor; Seller is the Delegator; and Creditor is a Delegate.

CHAPTER 18
ASSIGNMENTS

QUESTIONS

Facts for Question 1

Sandy and Tom enter into a contractual agreement whereby Tom agrees to sell Sandy his old laptop for $800. Two days later, Tom decides his sister, Liz, needs the money more and instructs Sandy to pay the $800 for his laptop directly to Liz.

1. Identify the parties above:

   (A) Liz is an intended third party beneficiary to the contract between Sandy and Tom; Sandy is the promisor and Tom is the promisee.

   (B) Tom is the assignor, Sandy is the obligor, and Liz is the assignee.

   (C) Liz is the assignor, Tom is the obligor, and Sandy is the assignee.

   (D) Sandy is the delegating party, Tom is the obligee, and Liz is the delegatee.

Facts for Question 2

Amy would like to give her niece, Brenda, $5,000 to help her with the cost of attending law school. Carly owes Amy $5,000 from a preexisting loan obligation. Amy follows proper procedures in transferring to Brenda her right to receive the $5,000 from Carly. Brenda gave no consideration for anything to either Carly or Amy.

2. This situation is:

   (A) A gratuitous assignment.

   (B) An assignment for value.

(C) An ineffective assignment, because Brenda did not give Amy consideration for the $5,000, therefore the transfer is unenforceable.

(D) An ineffective assignment, because Brenda did not give Carly consideration for the $5000, therefore the transfer is unenforceable.

Facts for Question 3

Peter and Paul are in a contract whereby Paul is to clean Peter's 3,000 square foot home for $300. Peter decides he wants to do something nice for his wealthy mother, Mary, who lives in a 17,000 square foot mansion and has trouble cleaning it herself. He then assigns the right to have his home cleaned by Paul to Mary, so that she does not have to worry about cleaning her oversized home.

3.   Has there been a valid assignment?

(A) No, because Paul, the obligor, has not agreed to the assignment as is required for the effectiveness of any assignment.

(B) No, because Mary's home is so large.

(C) Yes, unless Mary objects to the assignment.

(D) Yes, because Peter has manifested an intention to assign the contractual right.

Facts for Question 4

Whistling Winery, a new winery, entered into a written contract with Fruity Farms to buy all of its monthly requirements of a certain grape from Fruity Farms for a period of two years at a specified unit price. The two also agreed to the delivery and payment terms, and included the following clause in the contract:

The parties covenant not to assign this contract.

Immediately following the signing of the contract, Fruity made an "assignment of the contract" to Big Bucks Bank for a $75,000 loan. Whistling Winery then ordered, took delivery of, and paid Fruity Farms the agreed price for Whistling's requirement of grapes for the first month of operations.

4. What is the most likely legal effect of the covenant not to assign the contract under modern contract law?

    (A) The covenant made the assignment to Big Bucks Bank ineffective.

    (B) The covenant did not have a legal effect.

    (C) Though Fruity's assignment to Big Bucks Bank was an effective transfer of Fruity's rights, it constituted a breach of contract between Fruity and Whistling Winery.

    (D) A covenant against assignments in a sale-of-goods contract applies only to the buyer and it does not apply to the seller.

Facts for Question 5

Rita owes Sasha $2,000, due on April 19. Sasha owes Timothy $1,500, due on April 14. On April 10, Timothy tells Sasha he is worried that she will not pay on April 14.

Sasha responds by promising that if she does not pay Timothy the $1,500 on April 14, on April 18 she will assign him the right to Rita's $2,000 payment, so if she (Sasha) breaches, Timothy will get a $500 bonus. Timothy agrees to the proposal.

5. As of April 11, is there an enforceable assignment between Sasha and Timothy?

    (A) Yes, because Sasha has manifested an intention to transfer the right to Timothy.

    (B) Yes, unless Sasha pays Timothy the money on April 14.

    (C) No, because Rita has not yet assented to the assignment.

    (D) No, because Sasha promised she would assign the right in the future.

Facts for Question 6

Ashley and Barry both own retail clothing stores. Barry has been so kind to Ashley over the years and Ashley would like to do something nice for Barry. Ashley was set to receive $700 worth of extra-small leggings in two weeks from Stretch, Inc., a clothing manufacturer. In order to give Barry a gift, Ashley told Stretch she assigned her right to the leggings to Barry. Assume no other communication relevant to this problem was exchanged between, or given by, any of the parties.

6. What more must be done, if anything, to make the assignment effective?

   (A) Nothing.

   (B) Stretch, Inc. must manifest its acceptance of the assignment.

   (C) Barry must manifest his acceptance to the assignment.

   (D) Both (B) and (C) are correct.

Facts for Question 7

Larry owes David $1,500. Mary contracts with David whereby she will paint David's master bedroom if David will assign his right to receive the $1,500 to Mary's daughter Frieda. David agrees to and assigns his right to Frieda.

7. When is the assignment effective?

   (A) As soon as David manifests his intent to assign the payment to Frieda.

   (B) Once Mary's mother paints David's bedroom.

   (C) Once Frieda manifests her acceptance of the assignment.

   (D) Once Larry manifests his acceptance to the assignment.

Facts for Question 8

Amy has a Lotto ticket with five of the six numbers on it in last week's drawing. It is worth $1,500. Amy wants to assign the right to collect the money to her sister, Dianne. Amy gives Dianne the ticket and says, "I know you have a big payment due next week and are struggling, so I'd like you to have these lottery winnings." For purposes of this problem, assume Dianne has not yet said anything in response to Amy's offer.

8. Has an effective assignment taken place?

   (A) No, because Dianne has not yet manifested her acceptance to the assignment.

   (B) No, unless the lottery commission assents to the assignment.

   (C) Yes, unless the lottery commission objects to the assignment.

   (D) Yes, because the purported assignment is accompanied by a writing.

Facts for Question 9

Elizabeth bought a washing machine set from Tom's Appliance Emporium on credit on January 10. Tom's told her the appliance was "in perfect shape" and "did not have any problems at all." As part of the purchase, Elizabeth signed a contract that stated she would make monthly payments of $50 over the next twelve months, the first of which was due on February 1. Tom's then assigned the right to receive Elizabeth's payments to Bank in return for an immediate payment by Bank of $900. Tom's and Bank notified Elizabeth of the assignment before she made her first payment.

The washing machine was delivered on January 15 and it did not work. Elizabeth learned that Tom knew that the washing machine was inoperative when he sold it to Elizabeth. Elizabeth refused to make any payments for the broken washing machine.

9. In a suit by Bank against Elizabeth for the missed payments, may Elizabeth validly assert a misrepresentation defense against the Bank?

   (A) No, because no one from the Bank made any misrepresentation to her.

   (B) No, but only because the assignment to the Bank was an assignment for value.

   (C) Yes, but only if Bank was aware of the misrepresentation.

   (D) Yes, because Bank is subject to any defense Elizabeth could use in a suit brought by Tom's.

Facts for Question 10

Author's Note:

Questions 10 and 11 deal with a rather specialized branch of assignment law known as the "holder in due course" doctrine. Many first year contracts classes do not cover this area, and if yours is among them, you may want to skip these questions. After all assignments are difficult enough without having to "borrow" issues that your class does not cover,

Fred's Computers purchases 200 laptops and computers from Manufacturer. In order to finance the transaction, Fred's executes a negotiable promissory note, promising to pay Manufacturer $2,000 a month for two years. Manufacturer then assigns for value its right to receive Fred's payments under the promissory note to Big Bank for an immediate payment of $37,000. Big Bank purchased the note for value, in good faith, and had no knowledge of any defenses against the Manufacturer when it bought the note.

Once Fred's gets the computers, none of them work. Fred's is furious and refuses to pay on the note. Big Bank sues Fred's for the missed payments.

10. In a suit against Fred's, Big Bank will:

   (A) <u>Prevail</u>, because it is a holder in due course of the negotiable promissory note.

   (B) <u>Prevail</u>, because Big Bank did not make any representations about the computers to Fred's.

   (C) <u>Lose</u>, because Fred's can assert any defenses it had against Manufacturer against Big Bank.

   (D) <u>Lose</u>, if Fred's objected to the assignment.

Facts for Question 11

Ann, an individual, purchased a car from Bob, an individual. In order to finance the purchase, Ann executes a negotiable promissory note, promising to pay Bob $100 a month for five years. Bob then assigns for value his right to receive Ann's payments on the car to Big Bank. Big Bank purchases the note for value and in good faith and without any knowledge as to the car or what was said in the transaction between Ann and Bob.

When Ann goes to drive the car, however, she finds that the car doesn't even run. Ann then refuses to make any of the payments on the car, and Big Bank responds by suing Ann.

11. In a suit against Ann, Big Bank will:

   (A) <u>Prevail</u>, so long as Big Bank had no knowledge of any defenses that could be asserted against Bob when it purchased the promissory note.

   (B) <u>Prevail</u>, because it is a holder in due course of a negotiable instrument.

   (C) <u>Lose</u>, because Ann can assert any defenses it had against Bob against Big Bank.

   (D) <u>Lose</u>, unless Big Bank can prove it did not make any misrepresentations to Ann about the car.

Facts for Question 12

Diamond Dealers, Inc. ("DD") sells Andrew a jewel set in a ring, claiming that the jewel is a 24-carat diamond. Andrew signs a contract whereby Andrew is to pay DD $200 a month for two years. DD assigns for value the right to receive the payments to First Bank for an immediate payment of $3,500.

The "diamond" was nothing more than cubic zirconium, which Andrew discovered when he used it to propose to his jewel-expert girlfriend, and she refused to wear it. Andrew then refused to make any payments on the ring, and First Bank sued Andrew.

12. In the suit by First Bank for lack of payment, may Andrew assert the fraud defense?

(A) Yes, Andrew may assert the defense.

(B) Yes, but only if First Bank knew about the fraud.

(C) No, because First Bank had nothing to do with the fraud Diamond Dealers committed.

(D) No, because this was an assignment for value.

Facts for Questions 13 and 14

Bob buys a refrigerator from Al's Electronics. Bob signs a promissory note in order to finance the purchase. In the note, Bob promises to pay $75 per month for the next three years. Al's then assigns for value its right to receive Bob's payment to Credit Bank for an immediate payment.

13. Bob then refuses to make payments, without reason. Credit Bank is upset and sues Al's Electronics for assigning them the contract of a "bum like Bob" who won't pay his bills. In the suit between Credit Bank and Al's Electronics, Credit Bank will likely:

(A) Lose, because Al's made no implied warranty as to Bob's solvency or willingness to pay.

(B) Lose, because Al's can assert any defenses against Credit Bank that Bob could have asserted against it.

(C) Prevail, because this was an assignment for value.

(D) Prevail, because Al's cannot assert the defenses that Bob has against Credit Bank.

14. For purposes of this question, assume that the reason Bob has not made payments is because the refrigerator does not work, a fact that Al's knew before it sold the refrigerator to Bob and assigned the contract to Credit Bank.

In <u>Credit Bank v. Al's</u>, Credit Bank should:

(A) <u>Lose</u>, because Al's made no implied warranty as to the value of the assignment.

(B) <u>Lose</u>, because Al's can assert any defenses against Credit Bank that Bob could have asserted against it.

(C) <u>Prevail</u>, because this was an assignment for value.

(D) <u>Prevail</u>, because Al's cannot assert the defenses that Bob has against Credit Bank.

Facts for Question 15

Jack owes Alex $500. Alex wants to give Dan a gift. Accordingly, Alex writes a letter to both Dan and Jack explaining that he is assigning his contractual right to receive the $500 from Jack to his friend Dan.

The next day, before the payment is due, Alex calls Jack and they agree to cancel the assignment. As such, Jack paid Alex, not Dan, the $500 when it was due.

15. Can Alex and Jack validly cancel the assignment to Dan's disadvantage?

(A) Yes, because it was a gratuitous assignment.

(B) Yes, unless Dan has materially relied on the assignment.

(C) No, because Alex made the assignment in a writing.

(D) No, because Dan must assent to the modification.

Facts for Question 16

Jason owes Lilly $2,000 under a contract. Jason is obligated to pay Lilly the money on November 8. On October 1, Lilly assigns for value the right to collect the $2,000 from Jason to Karl. Karl does not notify Jason of the assignment

On October 31, Lilly again assigns for value the same right to collect the payment of $2,000 from Jason, this time to Mary. Mary immediately notifies Jason of the assignment and Jason pays Mary the $2,000.

To the extent relevant, assume that Mary acted in good faith and was without reason to know of the prior assignment to Karl.

16. Under the Massachusetts/Restatement 2d rule, who has the first priority to the $2,000 by assignment, Karl or Mary?

(A) Mary, because she was the first to notify Jason, the obligor.

(B) Mary, because she was the first to receive satisfaction of the obligation from Jason.

(C) Karl, because he was the first assignee and "first in time means first in right."

(D) Karl, unless Mary was the first to file a financing statement with the Secretary of State.

Facts for Question 17

Sally owes Bank $2500 due to a loan. To get Bank's collections department off her back, she executes a written assignment of 50% of her monthly paycheck to Bank until the loan is paid off. Bank gives written notice of the assignment to Sally's employer.

17. What is the most accurate statement?

(A) Bank is entitled to 50% of Sally's paycheck paid by Sally's employer until the loan is repaid once it gave written notice to Sally's employer.

(B) Bank is entitled to 50% of Sally's paycheck paid by Sally's employer until the loan is repaid, but only because Sally made the assignment in writing.

(C) Bank is entitled to 50% of Sally's paycheck paid by Sally's employer until the loan is repaid, but only because it is an assignment for value, and not a gratuitous assignment.

(D) Bank is not entitled to 50% of Sally's paycheck paid by Sally's employer.

CHAPTER 19
DELEGATIONS

QUESTIONS

Facts for Question 1 and 2

Brett likes to travel, but only on a budget. He sought out his usual travel agent, Nick's Adventures to see if it had a vacation package to Prague, but Nick's did not have any "deals" to Prague. Nick's suggested that Brett try Tom's Travel instead.

Tom's had relationships with the Prague government and had deals with an airline and hotels in Prague. Tom's put together a package to provide Brett round trip plane tickets to Prague and accommodations at the Prague Hilton for a week for $1400. Brett signed a contract for that deal.

Tom, the owner of Tom's, realized his agency may have booked more trips than it had slots for under its deal with the Prague government. Accordingly, it contacted a competitor, Super Vacations, who also put together Prague trips and asked if it had the capacity to handle Brett's trip. Super Vacations said it could do so and so Tom "assigned the [Brett] contract" to Super Vacations.

Assume there are no other facts or communications relevant to this situation.

1. Which of the following statements are correct?

    (A) Tom's has effectively assigned the rights, and has effectively delegated the duties, under its contract with Brett to Super Vacations.

    (B) Tom's attempted delegation of its rights under its contract with Brett is invalid until Brett consents to having Super Vacations handle the trip.

(C) Tom's can neither effectively assign the rights nor effectively delegate the duties under the Brett contract to Super Vacations because it is a personal services contract.

(D) Tom's has effectively assigned the rights, but has not effectively delegated the duties, under its contract with Brett to Super Vacations.

2.   Consider the following statements:

>   I.   Nick's is the delegating party.
>
>   II.   Super Vacations is the delegate.
>
>   III.   Tom's is the delegating party.
>
>   IV.   Tom's is the delegate.
>
>   V.   Brett is the obligee.

Which of these statements is correct?

(A) V only.

(B) I, IV, and V only.

(C) II, III, and V only.

(D) II and III only.

Facts for Question 3

Paul has a contract with Ted's Tickets to secure him box seats to the upcoming Dodgers game for $1,000. Ted's then "assigns the contract" to another ticket agency, Sport's Tickets. Ted's Tickets deals mainly with concerts and Sport's deals mainly with tickets to sporting events, so the two frequently exchange contracts that the other specializes in.

Assume no other facts would be relevant to the described situation.

3.   Which of the following statements about the agreement is most correct?

(A) Ted's has effectively delegated the obligation to provide Paul with a ticket.

(B) Ted's has effectively assigned the right to receive payment under the contract.

    (C) Both an attempted assignment and an attempted delegation have taken place, but neither are effective.

    (D) Both (A) and (B) are correct.

Facts for Question 4

Pat contracts with "Wild Things," a famous rock band, to perform at an event Pat was planning in Los Angeles. As the concert neared, the band became very busy and did not want to travel to Los Angeles, so "Wild Things" delegated the obligation to play to a local hip-hop group where the brother of one of the "Wild Things" members was the front man.

Pat was not pleased to hear of the change and wants to challenge the validity of the purported delegation.

4.   In <u>Pat v. Wild Things</u> over the validity of the delegation, a court should rule that the delegation is:

    (A) Effective, because the delegating party retains control over the delegate.

    (B) Ineffective, because Pat had a "substantial interest" in having the Wild Things perform.

    (C) Effective, because Pat, as the obligee, does not need to assent to, or even know of the delegation for it to be effective.

    (D) Ineffective, unless Wild Things can show a substantial interest in having the hip-hop group perform.

Facts for Questions 5 and 6

Gardener has a contract to do the landscaping at Owner's home for $2,500 per year. Gardener delegates the obligation to do the work to Landscaper. Gardener does not possess any special talents making his landscaping services different from any others, and Landscaper is known for doing good work.

5.   Assuming a court would find the delegation enforceable, which of the following statements is most accurate?

    (A) Both Landscaper and Gardener have the right and the obligation to landscape Owner's home.

    (B) Landscaper only has the duty to landscape Owner's home, but both Gardener and Landscaper have the right to landscape Owner's home.

(C) Gardener only has the duty to landscape Owner's home, but both Gardener and Landscaper have the right to landscape Owner's home.

(D) Landscaper can only acquire the right to landscape Owner's home upon Owner's approval of the delegation.

6. Assume there is a valid anti-delegation clause in the agreement between Owner and Gardener. Which of the following is the most accurate statement?

(A) The attempted delegation between Gardener and Landscaper would be unenforceable.

(B) The attempted delegation between Gardener and Landscaper would be enforceable, but Gardener would be liable to Owner for breach of contract.

(C) The attempted delegation between Gardener and Landscaper would be enforceable, because anti-delegation clauses are usually interpreted as just prohibiting assignments, not delegations.

(D) The attempted delegation between Gardener and landscaper would be enforceable if Landscaper was objectively suitable to do the landscaping work at Owner's home.

Facts for Question 7

On March 1, Preston contracted with Dan to do all of the yard work on his (Preston's) house for $2,000. Dan's services were much in demand, and so he required Preston to prepay for the work. Preston paid Dan. Performance by Dan was to take place on March 20.

It turns out that Dan was owed $2,000 by Jerry from an independent loan. Jerry did not have the cash to repay Dan, but offered to perform the landscaping work for Dan at Preston's house. Dan was okay with that, but said he would only go forward if Preston released Dan from any obligation under the landscaping contract.

Dan and Jerry approached Preston with the deal. Preston knew that Jerry is a very well-known landscaper and rarely takes jobs, so he accepted the offer, releasing Dan from the contract.

On March 20 neither Dan nor Jerry showed up to do the work.

7. Which of the following statements is true?

(A) Preston can bring suit against Jerry only.

(B) Preston can bring suit against Dan only.

(C) Preston can bring suit against Dan or Jerry.

(D) Preston can bring suit against Jerry only if Dan is insolvent.

Facts for Question 8

Thomas contractually owes John $10,000 from a previous transaction between the two. Later, Thomas contracts with Dillon whereby Dillon is to pay John $10,000 in exchange for Thomas doing a renovation on Dillon's kitchen.

Consider the following statements:

I. John may enforce the promise to pay $10,000 against Thomas.

II. John may enforce the promise to pay $10,000 against Dillon.

III. Thomas may enforce the promise to pay $10,000 against Dillon.

IV. There is an enforceable third party beneficiary contract and a delegation.

8. Which of the above statements is (are) correct?

(A) I only is correct.

(B) I, II, III, IV are all correct.

(C) I, II, IV only are correct.

(D) II, III only are correct.

Facts for Question 9

The President of the United States makes a statement on the televised State of the Union Address whereby he delegates to the viewing audience the right to pay his American Express bill every month while he is in office.

9.   Which of the following is accurate?

(A) The delegation is not enforceable because it is not in writing.

(B) American Express can accept payment of the President's bill from anyone in the viewing audience who sends it in, but is not obligated to do so.

(C) American Express is obligated to accept payment of the President's bill from anyone in the viewing audience who sends it in.

(D) American Express has the right to sue anyone in the viewing audience, as well as the President, for non-payment if the bill does not get paid.

CHAPTER 20
REMEDIES

QUESTIONS

Facts for Question 1

In June, Buyer, a local market owner, enters into a valid contract with Seller, an apple farmer, whereby Seller is to sell his entire crop of apples to Buyer for $5,000. There are no special characteristics about the Seller's apples differentiating them from all other apples of that type. Later, an apple cider manufacturer approaches Seller and offers him $6,500 for his entire apple crop in order to meet the manufacturer's increased demands for apple cider around the Fourth of July. Although he already promised the crop to Buyer, Seller found the deal too good to pass up and accepted the cider manufacturer's offer.

Buyer discovered this arrangement and sued for specific performance, while the apples were still in the Seller's possession. Buyer was able to schedule an expedited hearing on his specific performance request and the matter was promptly heard.

1. At the hearing seeking specific performance the Buyer should:

   (A) <u>Prevail</u>, because specific performance is generally more available under the UCC than at common law.

   (B) <u>Prevail</u>, because future contracts are subject to specific performance under the UCC.

   (C) <u>Lose</u>, because Buyer can be adequately compensated by cover or market differential damages.

   (D) <u>Lose</u>, because specific performance is not available in anticipatory repudiation situations.

Facts for Question 2

Mega Mall ("MM") contracted to lease space in the mall for ten years to Super Sports ("SS"), a sporting goods store. The lease contained a "no competition" clause where MM could not lease space in the mall to another sporting goods store.

Despite the no competition clause, MM wanted to lease to Outdoor Emporium ("OE"). OE sells a large variety of items, but has a large section of its store dedicated to sporting goods. MM conceded that it was breaching by leasing to OE. SS was obviously upset about MM adding another sporting goods retailer to the mall and brought suit for a prohibitory injunction.

2.   In the suit seeking an injunction, the injunction should be:

   (A) Denied, because monetary damages are sufficient to compensate SS for the breach.

   (B) Granted, because an equitable injunction is always used in breaches of lease contacts because real estate is considered unique.

   (C) Denied, because imposing an injunction would pose too great a burden on the court which would outweigh any benefits realized by the non-breaching party.

   (D) Granted, because money damages are inadequate and calculating actual damages is too speculative.

Facts for Question 3

Seller owned a valuable guitar that Jimi Hendrix signed during *The Cry of Love Tour*. In March, Buyer agreed to purchase Seller's guitar for $35,000. Buyer paid a $1,000 deposit and the contract called for him to take delivery of the guitar, and pay the balance due in two weeks.

Because *The Cry of Love Tour* was Hendrix's last, guitars signed from the tour are very rare, making Seller's one of only forty in existence, and the only such guitar currently being advertised for sale. After making the deal, the Seller had second thoughts and decided that his emotional attachment to the guitar was too great to give it up.

Buyer was furious when he learned Seller planned not to transfer ownership of the guitar, in part because only one of such signed guitars comes up for sale every few years.

Buyer has not sought to purchase another guitar from a third party, nor has he advertised to purchase a replacement.

Buyer has brought suit for specific performance to compel the Seller to complete the deal he made with Buyer.

3. In the suit seeking specific performance the Buyer would:

(A) <u>Prevail</u>, because specific performance is the typical remedy used by the courts for breach of contract disputes.

(B) <u>Prevail</u>, because the Buyer would experience undue difficulty in procuring a replacement.

(C) <u>Lose</u>, because money damages are the typical remedy used by the courts.

(D) <u>Lose</u>, because specific performance is not available unless Buyer first seeks, and is unable to effect, cover.

Facts for Question 4

Andrew is a famous actor in Hollywood and contracts with Producer to give Producer his exclusive services for the next four months to film a new movie. Andrew was to be the featured star of the film. Just a few days after signing that contract, Andrew signs a contract to make another movie during part of the four-month period. In order to do both, he will have to divert much of his attention from Producer's movie to the new project.

Producer brings suit for specific performance to compel Andrew to exclusively make his movie.

4. In the suit for specific performance requiring Actor to use his best efforts to work for Producer and make Producer's film during the relevant four-month period, Producer will likely:

(A) <u>Prevail</u>, because Producer contracted for Andrew's specific acting talents, which cannot be replaced by a grant of money damages.

(B) <u>Lose</u>, because the contract calls for personal services.

(C) <u>Lose</u>, because Andrew can still complete both projects.

(D) <u>Prevail</u>, because equity requires Andrew complete the contract he originally made.

Facts for Question 5

John was employed as a specialized dentist at Specialist Dental Office ("SDO") in Los Angeles. SDO's entire business is replacing teeth in patients with cleft palates. John learned of the details of the unique teeth replacement procedures for patients with cleft palates while working at SDO as the specialized procedure is not taught in dental school.

John's employment contract contained a covenant not to complete, providing that after leaving SDO, he may not practice dentistry on the West Coast for eighteen months. The contract was freely negotiated and John knowingly and voluntarily entered the agreement.

John ultimately left SDO and opened a general dentistry office of his own in Sacramento, about 400 miles away from SDO. As a general dentist, it is unlikely John will deal with replacing teeth in individuals with cleft palates.

5.   SDO brings suit for a prohibitory injunction to stop John from practicing dentistry based on the covenant not to compete. In the suit, SDO should:

   (A) Lose, because the covenant not to compete is too broad.

   (B) Prevail, because under the covenant not to compete John agreed not to practice dentistry on the West Coast for eighteen months after leaving SDO.

   (C) Prevail, because the covenant was freely negotiated and both knowingly and voluntarily entered into by John.

   (D) Lose, because a covenant not to compete is only enforceable if former employees abuse the knowledge of trade secrets they acquire to the detriment of the employer.

Facts for Question 6

Seller owns a very successful sandwich shop in Town. He contracted to sell the shop to Buyer. A large part of what the Buyer purchased was the reputation, success and goodwill of Seller's shop. In order to protect the customer base the shop has, the contract contained a covenant not to compete where Seller could never open another sandwich shop in Town or in any area within ten miles of Town.

A few years later, Seller, deciding he missed operating a sandwich shop, opened a new shop in a separate city six miles away from Town.

Buyer has brought suit for a prohibitory injunction to enforce the covenant not to compete against Seller and stop him from operating the new shop.

6.   In the suit for prohibitory injunction, Seller should:

   (A) Lose, because the covenant not to compete is sufficiently limited to the same geographic market.

(B) <u>Lose</u>, because non-enforcement of the covenant would not give the Buyer everything he bargained for when he purchased the shop.

(C) <u>Prevail</u>, because the covenant not to compete is not sufficiently limited.

(D) <u>Lose</u>, because Seller opened a competing sandwich shop within 10 miles of Town.

Facts for Question 7 and 8

Peter contracted with Driver to give Driver a license to cut and harvest timber on Peter's unbuildable swamp land. A fully negotiated point of the contract called for Driver to pull all the tree stumps it created from the swamp when it was done ("Tree Stump clause") . Indeed, Peter actually took less per linear foot of tree from Driver than his neighbors were getting from similar deals because he wanted to ensure the stumps were removed. The Tree Stump clause was important to Peter.

When Driver had finished harvesting the timber, Driver left the stumps as they were and refused to remove them after determining it would be extremely expensive to take them out.. There were estimates that it could cost $40,000 to remove all the stumps. Experts have determined the stumps being left behind only reduce the value of Peter's swamp property by $500. Peter has made no attempt to get estimates of his own and hire a third party to remove the stumps.

Peter has brought suit for specific performance to compel Driver to remove the stumps.

7. In the suit for specific performance Peter should:

(A) <u>Prevail</u>, because removal of the stumps was fully negotiated and freely bargained for.

(B) <u>Prevail</u>, because money damages are insufficient to put Peter in the same position he would be as if the contract had been completed.

(C) <u>Lose</u>, unless Peter attempts to cover the breach by hiring a third party to handle the removal of the stumps.

(D) <u>Lose</u>, because ordering specific performance would cause an unreasonable hardship or loss to Driver.

8.   Which of the following is (are) true?

(A) The goal of expectation damages is to put the non-breaching party in the position it was in before the contract had been entered into.

(B) The goal of expectation damages is to put the non-breaching party in the position it would have been if the contract had been performed.

(C) The non-breaching party must make reasonable efforts to mitigate damage or it will not be awarded any expectation damages.

(D) Both (B) and (C) are true.

Facts for Questions 9–12

Developer hires Contractor to construct a mall shopping center for $10 million. In the middle of construction, Developer unjustifiably breaches. Contractor was expensive for the area, and most contractors would have bid the job at $8 million.

At the time of the breach, other reasonable builders in the area would have spent $2 million in labor and materials. Contractor, however, spent $2.5 million, using his own internal costs for labor. Contractor competently estimates that he would have spent another $6 million in labor and materials to finish the construction, meaning he would have made a profit of $1.5 million on the project, i.e., $10 million contract price, less the $2.5 million he has already spent, less the $6 million he would have had to spend to complete performance.

At the beginning of the contract, Developer's land was worth $5 million. The value of the land with a partially completed structure on it is $6.8 million.

9.   The value of Contractor's expectation interest is:

(A) ($10 million) – ($8.5 million).

(B) ($8 million) + ($2.5 million).

(C) ($1.5 million) + ($2.5 million).

(D) ($10 million) – ($6 million) + ($2.5 million).

10. The value of Contractor's reliance interest is:

(A) $8 million.

(B) $2.5 million.

(C) $2 million.

(D) ($6 million) – ($2.5 million).

11. The value of Contractor's restitution interest as measured under the "Net Benefit" method is:

(A) ($10 million) ⊢ ($5 million).

(B) ($6.8 million) – ($5 million).

(C) $2.5 million.

(D) $2 million.

12. The value of Contractor's restitution interest as measured under the "Cost Avoided" method is:

(A) ($10 million) ⊢ ($5 million).

(B) ($6.8 million) ⊢ ($5 million).

(C) $2.5 million.

(D) $2 million.

Facts for Questions 13–16

David hires Paul to construct a mansion for $1 million. In the middle of construction, David materially and totally breaches. At the time of the breach, Paul has spent $500,000 in labor and materials. Paul was new to the area and felt he needed to discount his prices a bit to get established. Hence, he had priced himself a bit under market, as the market value of Paul's services if another reasonable contractor in the area had performed them would be $600,000.

Paul competently estimates that he would have spent another $300,000 in labor and materials to finish construction, meaning he would have made a profit of $200,000 on the project, i.e., $1,000,000 contract price, less the $500,000 he had already spent, less the $300,000 he would have to spend to complete performance.

David had already paid Paul $100,000 in progress payments at the time of David's breach. At the beginning of the contract, David's land was worth $400,000. The value of the land with a partially completed structure on it is $750,000. The market value of the partially completed structure is $150,000.

13. In an action by Paul against David for breach of contract, the amount of an expectation damages award Paul would be entitled to recover from David after a verdict in his favor *at trial* would be:

(A) ($200,000) – ($100,000).

(B) ($500,000) + ($200,000) – ($100,000).

(C) ($500,000) + ($200,000) – ($100,000) – ($300,000).

(D) ($500,000) + ($200,000).

14. In an action by Paul against David for breach of contract, the amount of a reliance damages Paul would be entitled to recover from David after a verdict in his favor *at trial* would be:

(A) $600,000.

(B) $500,000.

(C) ($500,000) – ($100,000).

(D) ($500,000) – ($300,000).

15. In an action by Paul against David for breach of contract, the amount of a restitution award as valued under the "Net Benefit" theory Paul would be entitled to recover from David after a verdict in his favor *at trial* would be:

(A) ($750,000) – ($400,000) – ($100,000).

(B) ($750,000) – ($400,000).

(C) ($600,000) – ($100,000).

(D) $600,000.

16. In an action by Paul against David for breach of contract, the amount of a restitution award as valued under the "Cost Avoided" theory Paul would be entitled to recover from David after a verdict in his favor *at trial* would be:

(A) ($600,000) – ($100,000).

(B) ($500,000) – ($100,000).

(C) ($600,000) – ($150,000) – ($100,000).

(D) ($600,000) + ($100,000).

Facts for Question 17

Pam contracted with Daredevil Adventures whereby Pam was to construct a commercial water park for Daredevil for $4,000,000. After finishing the foundations at a cost of $600,000, Pam was notified by Daredevil that due to a drop in interest in water parks, it was going to abandon the project. The President of Daredevil ordered Pam to stop building and leave the premises.

Pam decided she would keep building and spent an additional $500,000 until finally leaving the site. Pam would have made a profit of $400,000 on the completed project, and after spending the "extra" $500,000 it still would have cost her an additional $2,500,000 to complete the water park.

17. In an action by Pam against Daredevil for breach of contract the amount of expectation damages Pam would recover is:

(A) ($600,000) + ($400,000).

(B) ($600,000) + ($400,000) + ($500,000).

(C) ($600,000) + ($400,000) – ($500,000).

(D) $600,000.

Facts for Question 18

Dan contracts with Paula to build an addition onto Paula's house for $20,000. Just before beginning construction Dan breaches and walks away from the job. Paula contacted five other contractors in the area to bid for the job. She selected the cheapest of the five to replace Dan at $23,000. The average bid price was $25,000 and the highest was $28,000. Paula then brought suit against Dan for the breach. The $23,000 contractor competently completed the job and Paula paid him the $23,000 contract price.

At trial, Dan wants to offer testimony by Terry, another contractor in the area, that if Paula had contacted him he would have bid the job for $20,000. Terry was not one of the five contractors contacted by Paula. As such, Dan wants to assert he owes Paula nothing because the additional costs could have been avoided by calling Terry.

18. In an action by Paula against Dan for breach of contract, Paula will recover:

(A) $0.

(B) ($25,000) – ($23,000).

(C) ($25,000) – ($20,000).

(D) ($23,000) – ($20,000).

Facts for Question 19

Dawn's Publishing makes a contract with Pattie to publish a novel she is writing. This is Pattie's first published book and Dawn's is paying her exclusively on a royalty basis under the contract, i.e., she will only be paid a percentage of each book sold.

Dawn's breaches as it unjustifiably refuses to publish the book. Pattie unsuccessfully, yet reasonably, attempted to find another publisher willing to publish the book.

Pattie now brings suit for the breach, seeking lost profits.

19. In Pattie's action for lost profits, Pattie should:

(A) Prevail, because Pattie reasonably sought to cover by seeking alternative third party publishers to replace Dawn's.

(B) Prevail, because the breach resulted in lost profits to Pattie, for which she is entitled to recover.

(C) Lose, because the lost profits are too uncertain to be recovered.

(D) Lose, because Dawn's could not foresee, or have reason to foresee, lost profits as a consequential loss resulting from the breach.

Facts for Question 20

Parts Plus ("Parts") produces expensive custom auto parts. Parts's top seller, which is back ordered due to its popularity, is the X80 21-inch chrome wheels. Recently a part on the machine that produces X80's broke and was not repairable, and so Parts needed to order a new part from a third party that manufactures replacement parts for their machine.

An employee of Parts went to the replacement manufacturer's plant 500 miles away and inspected the part. Satisfied that it would work, he packaged the part in a crate and took it to Delivery Direct, a common carrier, to have it sent by expedited service for a part this size, which was promised not to exceed two days. The cost for "regular" shipping was $50; the cost of the expedited shipping was $200. Delivery Direct did not know what was in the crate and was not made aware of any specific requirements of Parts other than Parts paid to get the replacement part to its factory on an expedited basis.

As a result of a negligent mistake on the part of Delivery Direct, the part did not leave for Parts Plus manufacturing plant on schedule, and even then was sent via "regular" shipping. As such, the part did not arrive until seven days later, rather than the two days promised. As a result of the delay Parts suffered $10,000 in lost profits due to the five day delay in manufacturing, i.e. the difference between the two day shipping it was promised and the seven day shipping it actually experienced. Parts has brought suit for damages including consequential damages for lost profits.

20. In Parts's action for breach of contract against Delivery Direct seeking lost profits, Parts should:

(A) <u>Prevail</u>, because Parts' contract with Delivery was for the part to arrive within two days, and the lost profits from the delay were directly caused by the breach.

(B) <u>Lose</u>, because the lost profits were not foreseeable.

(C) <u>Prevail</u>, because these are direct damages, and as such are collectable as consequential loss.

(D) <u>Lose</u>, because awarding the lost profits would be inequitable.

Facts for Question 21

Dover Builders contracted to build an office for Paper Productions, a new company that Dover knew intended to produce unique greeting cards. Dover was contractually obligated to complete the project on January 1, but did not actually finish construction until April 15. As a result of the delay, Paper could not produce any cards to attempt to sell to retailers for over four months. After reasonable efforts, Paper was unable to find temporary replacement offices during the delay. Paper has brought suit for lost profits from the delay in opening its company's operations.

21. In Paper's action for breach of contract seeking the lost profits, Paper should:

(A) <u>Prevail</u>, because the lost profits are the foreseeable result of the delay in construction.

(B) <u>Lose</u>, because lost profits are not available as a result of breach of a construction contract.

(C) <u>Prevail</u>, but only because Paper reasonably attempted to "cover" by seeking alternative arrangements during the delay.

(D) <u>Lose</u>, because the lost profits depend on the uncertain tastes and preferences of the public.

Facts for Question 22

Peter's supermarket has been in operation for 10 years, and has decided to undergo an extensive and complicated renovation on its building to make a more pleasant shopping experience. Peter contracts with Dale's construction to do the renovation project. Under the contract Dale was to finish the renovation on May 1, but Dale does not finish until July 1. The reason for the delay was that the time to do some of the work was underestimated by Dale's, but other contractors would likely have made the same mistake and Dale's was not negligent in believing it could finish by May 1.

Peter, upset that he was delayed in reopening the supermarket by two months, has brought suit for consequential lost profits as a result of the breach. Peter has based his damage calculations on the average profits Peter's has made during May and June over the past 10 years.

22. In Peter's action for breach of contract seeking the lost profits, Peter should:

(A) <u>Prevail</u>, because the lost profits can be determined with reasonable certainty.

(B) <u>Prevail</u>, because lost profits must always be granted when suffered in order to give the non-breaching party the benefit of the bargain.

(C) <u>Lose</u>, because Dale's was not negligent in causing the delay.

(D) <u>Lose</u>, because the profits cannot be determined with sufficient certainty.

Facts for Question 23

Patrick contracted with Douglas whereby Douglas was to build Patrick a brand new two-story home. In the contract it specified Douglas was to use concrete manufactured by Johnson Company in building the foundation. When construction was just about complete it was discovered that Douglas mistakenly used concrete manufactured by Rock-Solid Concrete. Rock-Solid concrete is of the same quality as Johnson concrete.

The difference in the fair market value of the house based on the use of Rock-solid versus Johnson concrete is about $500 because saying a home was made with Johnson Concrete has a big enough impact on the market that it affects the home's selling price. Johnson concrete is slightly more expensive, and the difference in the costs of the two types of concrete for the amount used in Patrick's home was $1,100.

To take out the foundation made with Rock-Solid and re-pour it with Johnson concrete at the point in time when the mistake was discovered would cost $200,000.

23. In an action by Patrick against Douglas for breach of contract, Patrick should recover:

(A) $200,000.

(B) $1,100.

(C) $500.

(D) $0, because there was no actionable breach since the quality of the two types of concrete are equal.

Facts for Questions 24 and 25

Buyer contracted with Seller to purchase a piece of property for $100,000. This was a good deal for Buyer because competent evidence can establish that the fair market value of the property at the time of contracting was $120,000.

At the time he signed the contract Buyer paid $10,000 as a down payment, and later incurred expenses of $2,000 for title insurance reports, termite inspections, etc. Just after Buyer had made those expenditures, Seller breached and announces she was refusing to transfer the deed to Buyer. Buyer brings suit for breach of contract.

24. In a jurisdiction that applies the "American Rule," the proper valuation of Buyer's damages is:

  (A) ($120,000) – ($100,000) + ($10,000) + ($2,000).

  (B) ($2,000) + ($10,000).

  (C) ($120,000) – ($100,000) + ($10,000).

  (D) ($120,000) – ($100,000).

25. In a jurisdiction that applies the "English Rule," the proper valuation of Buyer's damages is:

  (A) ($120,000) – ($100,000) + ($10,000) + ($2,000).

  (B) ($2,000) + ($10,000).

  (C) ($120,000) – ($100,000) + ($10,000).

  (D) ($120,000) – ($100,000).

Facts for Question 26

Merchant Buyer contracts with Seller for the purchase of thirty cars to stock his lot for a highly advertised big sale at the dealership. This is the biggest event Buyer has ever hosted, and his reputation hinges on having a fully stocked lot for his customers to shop from. At the last minute, Seller breaches and refuses to deliver the cars.

Buyer is able to cover and purchase a replacement inventory from another dealership, but suffered severe emotional distress as a result of Seller's breach. Buyer has brought suit for breach of contract, seeking cover and emotional distress damages.

26. With regard to Buyer's emotional distress damages, Buyer should:

  (A) <u>Prevail</u>, if Buyer can prove his damages with sufficient certainty.

  (B) <u>Lose</u>, because emotional distress damages are typically not collectable for breach of contract.

  (C) <u>Prevail</u>, because emotional distress is a foreseeable result of Seller's breach.

  (D) <u>Lose</u>, because Buyer was able to cover by purchasing replacement inventory before the event.

Facts for Question 27

Pauline contracted with Doctor Darren to perform plastic surgery on her face. Doctor Darren was a licensed physician authorized to perform the procedure, but this was only the second such procedure he had performed. The first had resulted in a medical malpractice action against him.

Doctor Darren "guaranteed" that the surgery would make Pauline more beautiful and enhance her appearance. As a result of the surgery Pauline became disfigured and suffered severe emotional distress from injuries she sustained. There were other doctors in the area with better records of success in facial plastic surgery whom Pauline could have had perform the procedure.

Pauline brought suit for breach of contract, and sought damages for emotional distress.

27. Regarding the part of her suit for breach of contract in which she sought emotional distress damages, Pauline should:

    (A) Prevail, because emotional distress is part of the expectation interest under contract law.

    (B) Lose, because typically emotional distress damages are not awarded in breach of contract cases.

    (C) Prevail, but whatever damages she can otherwise collect will be offset by the contributory negligence attributed to her in selecting her doctor and not going to a different doctor with a better history of successful procedures.

    (D) Prevail, because the breach of contract was associated with physical injury.

Facts for Question 28

Buyer, a manufacturer of steel columns, contracts with Seller to buy ten tons of raw steel to be delivered at Buyer's manufacturing plant for $30,000. Buyer is low on raw steel material and made it clear how important the delivery was to its business.

Just after making the contract, Seller was offered $40,000 for the same ten tons of steel, but it does not have enough steel to complete both contracts. Seller accepted the second offer for $40,000 and breached with the original Buyer.

Buyer experienced delays in his production and was furious because Seller knew how important the steel delivery was to his plant and knew that it would negatively impact his ability to produce steel columns.

Buyer brings suit for damages, including a claim for punitive damages.

28. Regarding Buyer's claim for punitive damages, Buyer should:

   (A) <u>Prevail</u>, because punitive damages are awarded in "bad faith" breaches such as this one.

   (B) <u>Lose</u>, because generally punitive damages are not awarded in a breach of contract case.

   (C) <u>Lose</u> under the modern rule of denying punitive damages in contract claims, but likely prevail under the common law rules regarding punitive damages and intentional breaches.

   (D) <u>Prevail</u>, but any recovery is capped at the $10,000 additional purchase price Seller received from the breach.

Facts for Question 29

Husband and wife took out a life insurance policy on his wife's life for $150,000 and paid premiums on the policy on time for twenty-five years. When the wife died, the insurance company did not pay out the value of the policy to her husband. They claimed, on very tenuous evidence, that the wife committed suicide, which was excluded from the policy.

Husband sued for breach of contract. When confronted at a hearing in the case, the insurance company representative told Husband's attorney that the insurance company often does this, knowing that the surviving spouse typically will settle for less than face value of the policy instead of fighting a lengthy legal battle.

Thereafter Husband amends his complaint to sue for punitive damages as well.

29. In Husband's action for punitive damages, Husband should:

   (A) <u>Lose</u>, because punitive damages are generally not awarded in breach of contract cases.

   (B) <u>Lose</u>, because Insurance Company breached to obtain a cheaper outcome making it an "efficient breach."

    (C) <u>Prevail</u>, because the insurance company intentionally breached the contract.

    (D) <u>Prevail</u>, because of the "bad faith" involved in the breach.

Facts for Question 30

Patti was hired by Derek to landscape his house for $20,000, plus the cost of materials. The job was supposed to start on January 10. Two weeks before the job was to begin, and before Patti had obtained any necessary materials, Derek called Patti and told her he had changed his mind and decided against landscaping the home. Patti diligently tried but could not find any other work for the time period that she was supposed to be working on Derek's home.

Patti filed suit on February 5, and received a judgment against Derek that was entered on November 1. Derek has not paid any of the judgment.

30. Which of the following statements is (are) correct:

      I.   Patti is entitled to pre-judgment interest for the period from January 10 to November 1.

      II.   Patti is entitled to post-judgment interest from February 5 to November 1.

      III.   Patti is entitling to post-judgment interest beginning November 1 until the judgment is satisfied by Derek.

      IV.   Patti is not entitled to pre-judgment interest.

    (A) II and IV only.

    (B) I and II only.

    (C) III and IV only.

    (D) I and III only.

Facts for Question 31

Penny purchased a weed whacker from Daniel, a merchant retailer of landscaping supplies. She injured her foot when some defective parts on the weed whacker failed. Daniel paid for her medical treatment, but refused to pay for any emotional distress resulting from the accident.

Penny sued for breach of warranty, and was awarded $20,000 for emotional distress by a jury. The judgment was officially entered on September 15.

31. Which of the following is the most accurate statement?

    (A) Pre-judgment interest on the $20,000 judgment is proper because $20,000 is a finite sum.

    (B) Penny will only receive pre-judgment interest on the $20,000 award if she can show emotional distress was a foreseeable result of the breach.

    (C) Pre-judgment interest on the $20,000 award will be awarded beginning on September 15 until the judgment is satisfied.

    (D) Penny cannot collect pre-judgment interest on the $20,000 award.

Facts for Question 32

Seller contractually agrees to sell his business to Buyer in exchange for a promised payment of $100,000/year for the next ten years. Buyer immediately repudiates his payment obligations and says he will be making no payments under the contract. Seller quickly gets a judgment in his favor, before the first payment was to be made.

32. Which of the following is the most accurate statement regarding Seller's award of damages in the breach of contract action?

    (A) Seller will receive a judgment for $1,000,000.

    (B) Seller will receive a judgment requiring Buyer to pay $100,000 a year for the next ten years.

    (C) Seller will receive a judgment amount based on the $1,000,000 total contract price, reduced to present value.

    (D) Buyer is entitled to an order of specific performance requiring payment of the $1,000,000 value of Seller's performance.

Facts for Question 33

Pristine TV's placed an order with Darren's electronics for 100 television sets with thirty-two-inch screens at $200/set ($20,000 total contract price). Darren was supposed to make the sets available for pickup by Pristine on July 1, in time for its summer sale on July 15. Darren knew of the importance of timely delivery as Pristine told Darren that it was out of inventory for the sale. Under their agreement, Pristine would have to travel 150 miles at a cost of $300 to pick up the sets on July 1.

On the scheduled day of delivery, Darren's notified Pristine that it was unable to timely provide the sets under the contract. Pristine was forced to find replacement sets. After diligent search, Pristine could not find any thirty-two-inch sets, but did fins and purchase thirty-six-inch sets at $210/set ($21,000 total contract price). In order to get the sets as soon as possible (which was July 17), Pristine had to pay $400 for express shipping.

Pristine lost two sales because of the delay in receiving the sets, costing it $250 in lost profits.

33. In an action by Pristine against Darren, how much are Pristine's cover damages (assuming Pristine acted in good faith throughout):

(A) ($21,000) – ($20,000).

(B) ($21,000) – ($20,000) + ($400) + ($250) – ($300).

(C) ($21,000) – ($20,000) + ($400) – ($300).

(D) ($21,000) – ($20,000) + ($400).

Facts Common to Questions 34–36

The wholesale price of lemons is listed daily on the national lemon exchange, which is easily accessed via the Internet and major publications. For this problem assume there is an abundance of lemons and a wholesale buyer can obtain almost any amount at any time on the exchange. The prices vary from market to market, but all are listed on the exchange.

Buyer is a manufacturer and retailer of lemonade. On January 10 Buyer entered into a contract with Seller, a farmer, for delivery of 1,000 lbs. of Seller's lemons on May 1 for $600, with tender of delivery to be at Seller's farm. There is no characteristic that would differentiate Seller's lemons from any other lemons available on the exchange.

The following prices were listed on the exchange for 1,000 pounds of lemons on each date indicated:

	Price in Buyer's Market	Price in Seller's Market
January 10:	$625	$627
February 28:	$615	$617
March 15:	$615	$615
May 1:	$640	$625
December 1:	$602	$604
December 2:	$598	$599

34. On February 28, Seller anticipatorily repudiates and tells Buyer he will not deliver the lemons. Buyer did not cover and has brought suit for market differential damages. Trial was held on December 1, and the next day, December 2, the judge entered judgment in favor of Buyer.

Buyer's damages should be:

(A) ($617) – ($600).

(B) ($640) – ($600).

(C) ($602) – ($600).

(D) ($615) – ($600).

35. Buyer and Seller did not communicate after the contract was entered into until May 1, when Seller refused to deliver any lemons. Assume Buyer again did not cover and the same trial and dates as set forth in Question Thirty-Four occurred.

The correct amount of Buyer's damages should be:

(A) ($615) – ($600).

(B) ($640) – ($600).

(C) ($602) – ($600).

(D) ($625) – ($600).

36. The lemons were timely delivered in a truck hired by Buyer on May 1 and delivered to Buyer that day. When the lemons arrived Buyer discovered for the first time that the lemons were rotten and immediately rejected them. Assume buyer again did not cover and the same trial and dates occurred.

The correct amount of Buyer's market differential damages should be:

(A) ($615) – ($600).

(B) ($640) – ($600).

(C) ($602) – ($600).

(D) ($625) – ($600).

Facts for Question 37

A computer salesman at Dream Computers told Peter that the video card in the computer he was interested in could play every game on the market, including *Planet of War*, the most graphic-intensive game in the world. Satisfied, Peter buys the computer for $2,000.

When he gets home, Peter discovers the computer cannot even play the most basic games. Peter does some research and learns a computer that can play *Planet of War* well would cost at least $10,000. In addition, most computer companies would not charge more than $1,500 for a computer with the capabilities identical to the one Peter bought from Dream Computers.

Peter has decided to keep the computer but wants to bring suit for damages.

37. In an action by Peter against Dream for breach of contract, what types of remedies are available to Peter?

(A) Cover damages.

(B) Market differential damages.

(C) Warranty damages.

(D) Peter may elect from all three types of damages.

Facts for Question 38

Buyer contracted with Seller to make Buyer a custom six foot statue of himself made of marble and gold for $25,000. Seller skillfully made the statue exactly as Buyer requested. The materials to build the statue cost $10,000 and Seller's labor to craft the statue is $9,000. Upon delivery Buyer acknowledged the statue was perfect, but refused to accept it, as he no longer wished to have a statue in his house. Seller did not attempt to cover and sell the statute to someone else.

Seller has brought suit against Buyer for breach of contract.

38. Seller will most likely be entitled to:

(A) ($25,000) − ($9,000) − ($10,000).

(B) Nothing because Seller made no attempt to cover.

(C) ($9,000) + ($10,000).

(D) $25,000.

Facts for Question 39

Seller contracted with Buyer to sell 100 laptops at $800/unit. Seller timely delivered conforming laptops on the date set in the contract, but Buyer nevertheless wrongfully rejects them. Seller pays $300 to have the goods shipped back to its warehouse.

Had Buyer accepted the goods, Buyer would have had to pay $200 for storage of the inventory. After calling ten other retailers, Seller finds another buyer willing to pay $750/unit for the 100 laptops, which is a commercially reasonable price under the circumstances. Seller sent Buyer an e-mail to let Buyer know of his plans to re-sell the computers and giving Buyer a chance to buy them at the $750 price. Buyer did not respond to the e-mail.

As such, Seller sold the laptops to the retailer, for $50 less per unit, thus earning $5,000 less ($50 × 100 laptops) than it would have made on the sales of the computers under the original contract.

Seller brings suit against Buyer for breach of contract. At trial, Buyer calls the President of Top Dollar Electronics, another retailer much further away, who testifies that her company would have bought the laptops for $800 per unit had Seller contacted her.

Seller first became aware of Top Dollar at trial when its President testified.

39. In Seller's action for breach of contract, Seller's damages would be:

    (A) Nothing, because Seller could have sold the laptops to Top Dollar for $800 per unit.

    (B) ($5000) + ($300).

    (C) $5000.

    (D) ($5000) + ($300) − ($200).

Facts for Question 40

Seller is a manufacturer of bottles in Oregon and contracts to sell 50,000 bottles at $0.25/bottle to Buyer, a California company. Under the contract, tender of the bottles was to take place in Oregon on June 1, with delivery expected in California on June 5. Buyer was to pick up the bottles.

On June 1 Seller was ready to tender the bottles, but Buyer breached by not sending anyone to pick them up, and refuses to do so thereafter.

The fair market value of the bottles on June 1 was $0.22.bottle in California and $0.20/bottle in Oregon. On June 5 the fair market value of the bottles was $0.21/bottle in California and $0.19/bottle in Oregon. Seller brings suit against Buyer for breach seeking market differential damages.

40. In Seller's action for breach of contract, the proper valuation of Seller's market differential damages is:

(A) ($0.25 – $0.22) × 50,000.

(B) ($0.25 – $0.20) × 50,000.

(C) ($0.25 – $0.21) × 50,000.

(D) ($0.25 – $0.19) × 50,000.

Facts for Question 41

Consumer Buyer contracts with Merchant Seller, a furniture distributor, to purchase a couch from Seller's inventory for $500. Seller has a large inventory of that model on hand.

After making the deal, Buyer breaches and contacts Seller to tell him not to deliver the couch. The next week Seller is able to sell the very same couch it had set aside for Buyer to a new customer for the same $500 price. The acquisition cost to Seller (including overhead) is $400, meaning the profit to Seller from the sale of the couch was $100: [$500 (purchase price) – $400 (acquisition cost)].

Seller brings suit against Buyer for the breach of contract.

41. In Seller's action, Seller is entitled to recover:

(A) Nothing, because it sold the couch to the second buyer for $500, and buyer is a consumer, not a merchant.

(B) $500, the purchase price of the couch.

(C) $400, the acquisition cost of the couch.

(D) $100, the profit from the sale of couch.

Facts for Question 42

Buyer entered into a contract with Seller whereby Seller was to build a custom cabinet for Buyer made out of mahogany for $5,000. Seller would earn a $500 profit from the manufacture and sale of the cabinet.

Buyer repudiated when Seller had spent $2,500 towards production of the cabinet. However, part of the $2,500 Seller spent is $700 worth of mahogany which has not been cut for the cabinet, and which can be used by Seller in other projects.

Seller brings suit against Buyer for breach of contract.

42. In Seller's action, Seller's damages would be:

   (A) ($500) + ($2,500) – ($700).

   (B) $500.

   (C) ($2,500) – ($700).

   (D) ($500) + ($2,500).

Facts for Question 43

Pierre contracted with Daphne to perform legal services for her, and in consideration for the work done, Daphne agreed in the contract to transfer her house to Pierre in ten years. At the time of contracting the house was in a desolate area and its fair market value was $20,000. Nevertheless, the two parties agreed if Daphne breached the agreement and didn't turn over the house when due, she would owe Pierre $250,000. ("$250K Clause")

As it turned out, during the ten years, a massive city was built around the house appreciating its fair market value. Various appraises have estimated its value to be between $220,000 and $280,000 at the end of the ten-year period. Daphne refuses to transfer the property and Pierre brings suit, seeking to enforce the $250K Clause.

43. Which of the following statements is most accurate in a jurisdiction following the Restatement 2d of Contracts?

   (A) The $250K Clause is unenforceable because the damages amount is unreasonable in light of the anticipated harm at the time the contract was entered into.

   (B) The $250K Clause is enforceable because the damages amount is reasonable in light of the actual harm caused by the breach.

   (C) The $250K Clause is not enforceable because the damages amount is unreasonable in light of the actual harm caused by the breach.

   (D) The $250K Clause is only enforceable if Pierre can prove his services were worth at least $250,000.

Facts for Question 44

Phillip contracted with Dante whereby Dante was to build a solar power system on Phillip's property for $50,000, of which $2,500 was profit. A system this size produces sufficient power so that Phillip would not have to purchase any power from the local utility.

The contract called for a project completion date of March 1. Additionally, there was a liquidated damages clause where for every day late the project finished, Dante would have to pay $200 to Philip.

Dante in fact did complete the project late, ultimately finishing on April 1. The utility company bills its customers monthly.

Phillip has brought suit for damages, seeking $6,200 ($200/day for thirty-one days between March1 and April 1) based on the liquidated damages clause.

44. In Phillip's action for breach of contract seeking damages based on the liquidated damages clause, Phillip should:

    (A) <u>Prevail</u>, because the clause is reasonable in light of the actual damages and the anticipated damages at the time the contract was entered into.

    (B) <u>Lose</u>, because the clause is unreasonable in light of the actual damages and the anticipated damages at the time the contract was entered into.

    (C) <u>Prevail</u>, but only up to the value of the $2,500 profit expected under the contract.

    (D) <u>Lose</u>, because the actual damages from late completion are easy to prove.

Facts for Question 45

Buyer contracts with Seller for the purchase of helium gas on an annual basis. The contract ran for ten years, but provided, "Buyer's obligations under this contract are either: (a) to purchase $200,000 worth of helium each calendar year under this agreement; or (b) pay Seller $45,000 on December 31 of the first year it does not order $200,000 worth of helium."

As the contract performance date nears, Seller is concerned that Buyer is going to back out of the deal.

45. Which of the following statements is most accurate regarding the quoted clause:

(A) The clause is enforceable as an alternative performance clause.

(B) The clause is not enforceable because the liquidated amount is not reasonable in light of the anticipated or actual harm.

(C) The clause is not enforceable because the actual damages can be calculated.

(D) The clause is an enforceable liquidated damages clause.

CHAPTER 21
DISCHARGE BY SUBSEQUENT AGREEMENT

QUESTIONS

Facts for Question 1

Terry takes his car, which had been making a funny "knocking" sound and generally running very poorly to Gil's garage, where Gil examined it thoroughly and offered to fix it for $600.

Two days later, Gil called Terry and told him that he wouldn't be able to fix the car for less than $750. Terry told Gil "I really need the car as soon as possible, but you're really doing me a disservice with that price. But go ahead and fix it." The next day, Terry picked up the car, but paid only $600.

1. To the extent relevant, Gil did not change any position as a result of Terry's promise and there was nothing supporting Gil's increased price other than his desire to make more money.

In an action by Gil to recover the additional $150, who will prevail?

(A) Gil, because Terry's promise to pay $750 was a valid accord and satisfaction.

(B) Gil, because Gil relied on Terry's promise to pay the increased amount to his detriment.

(C) Terry, because Gil was under a pre-existing duty to fix the car for $600.

(D) Terry, because the modification was not in writing.

Facts for Question 2

Contractor agrees to install doors on a new home for Buyer for $2,500. Due to delivery delays, Contractor is unable to install the doors on time, which costs Buyer a substantial, but hard to calculate, amount.

When Contractor tries to collect on the full balance, Buyer states that he does not believe he owes the entire $2,500. Buyer repeats his

189

claim that he has been damaged and says, "Once I subtract the damage, I think I only owe you about $500." Contractor says, "I need more than that!" and the parties cease their negotiations.

A few days later, Buyer mails a check to Contractor for $500 and writes in the memo line "for full payment on door installation job." Contractor crosses out the language, writes that he is endorsing the check "under protest and with reservation of all rights," endorses, and cashes the check. The check is "good" and the money is put in Contractor's account. Once he knows the $500 is safely in his account, Contractor demands the remaining $2,000 from Buyer.

Assume the "for full payment on door installation job" clause on the memo line described the offer to settle in sufficient detail and was sufficiently prominent under applicable rules.

2. In a jurisdiction that has adopted the UCC, in an action by Contractor to recover the remaining balance, who will prevail?

(A) Contractor, because $2500 is the amount of the contract.

(B) Buyer, because the final payment was an effective settlement.

(C) Contractor, by crossing out "for full payment on door installation job," and writing "under protest and with reservation of all rights," he retained his right to full payment.

(D) Contractor, because he acted in good faith in performing the contract.

Facts for Question 3

Thomas is a rural doctor who recently treated Serena for high blood pressure. Thomas reasonably billed Serena $200, which was in accordance with their agreement, but Serena complains that she does not have all of the money right now. Thomas responds with "Well, if you deliver five of your famous blueberry pies to my home next Friday, I will accept that in lieu of the bill."

Serena then delivers five blueberry pies to Thomas the following Friday in accordance with Thomas's offer. However, the day after receiving the pies, Thomas is in a car accident and needs cash to fix his car. He calls Serena and demands that she pay him the $200 minus the reasonable value of the pies she delivered. Serena refuses, saying "a deal is a deal."

3. If Thomas sues to recover the $200 less the value of the pies from Serena, who will prevail?

(A) Thomas, because the modification of their doctor–patient agreement was not supported by consideration.

(B) Thomas, because he retained the right to collect under the original agreement by operation of law.

(C) Serena, because Thomas "waived" his right to payment when he told Serena she could deliver the pies instead.

(D) Serena, because her obligation to pay was "discharged" when she delivered the pies.

Facts for Questions 4–6

Vanessa loaned Alex $1,000 in August to buy a new computer for college. Alex was to repay the debt by February 1. When the date to pay neared, Alex realized he would not be able to pay. Knowing that Vanessa badly wanted to go to an upcoming concert that Alex had tickets for, Alex told Vanessa "If I promise to leave my two front row tickets to the concert for you at the will-call booth, will you agree to accept that instead of payment for my debt?" Vanessa immediately accepted. However, when the date of the concert came, Alex forgot to leave the tickets at will-call and Vanessa missed the concert.

4. In an action by Vanessa against Alex for breach of contract, she should:

(A) Prevail, and is entitled to recover $1,000 under the original loan.

(B) Prevail, but will be limited in her suit to recovery of the value of the concert tickets.

(C) Prevail, and is entitled to recover $1,000 plus the value of the concert tickets.

(D) Lose, because the modification of the original agreement was not supported by consideration.

5. For the purposes of this question only, assume that instead of Alex offering to give Vanessa concert tickets, Alex met her along with his cousin Zack and said to Vanessa, "Well, I know your car needs fixing that would cost you around what I owe, so if my cousin Zack will fix your car, will you take that in exchange for forgiving my debt?" She asks Zack, "Are you okay with this?" Zack says, "Sure. I am a good mechanic and am happy to help Alex." Vanessa immediately accepts. However, Zack never fixes Vanessa's car. Assume no fraud on anyone's part.

Vanessa will be able to:

(A) Recover from Zack only for the value of the repairs to the car.

(B) Recover from Alex only for the value of the repairs to the car.

(C) Recover from either Alex or Zack for the value of the repairs to the car.

(D) Recover from Alex only, and only for the original debt.

6. For purposes of this question, again assume Vanessa, Alex, and Zack met. Alex said, "Well, I know your car needs fixing that would cost you around what I owe, so if my cousin Zack will fix your car, will you take that in exchange for forgiving my debt?" She asks Zack, "Are you okay with this?" Zack says, "Sure. I am a good mechanic and am happy to help Alex." Vanessa says, "Well . . . if Zack really fixes the car, I'd be okay with it, but you have disappointed me before, Alex. So if you actually finish the repairs, I will accept the repairs in lieu of the $1,000 debt. But if the car is not fixed, the original debt stays in place." Zack and Alex then agreed to the deal as proposed by Vanessa.

Zack never fixes Vanessa's car. Assume no fraud on anyone's part. Vanessa will be able to:

(A) Recover from Zack for the value of the repairs to the car.

(B) Recover from Alex for the original debt.

(C) Vanessa can choose whether to pursue (A) or (B).

(D) Recover from Alex only, but can sue him for either the value of the repairs to the car or for the original debt.

Facts for Questions 7 and 8

Brett and Michael are good friends and huge fans of Billy Idol. Michael had a signed album that Brett had always wanted. For years, Brett had been asking Michael to sell it to him, but Michael always refused. Finally, after years of asking, Michael had a change of heart and agreed to sell the album for $400. The agreement was made on a Wednesday and both parties agreed they would meet the following Friday to exchange the money for the album.

On Thursday, the day before Brett and Michael were to meet, Brett called Michael and explained that his wife was pregnant and that he should not be spending money on old rock and roll albums. Michael said "Congratulations! I completely agree, we can call off the deal."

Later that day, Michael gets into a fender bender. He discovers that it will cost hundreds of dollars to fix his car and calls Brett to force Brett to go through with the deal. Brett refuses to go through the deal and stands his ground.

7. In an action by Michael against Brett for breach of contract, Michael will:

(A) Prevail, because Brett's renunciation was oral.

(B) Prevail, because the renunciation was not supported by consideration.

(C) Lose, because the original contract was not in writing.

(D) Lose, because the contract was rescinded.

8. Assume for this question only that Brett and Michael did not talk on Thursday and they met on the Friday as agreed upon. Michael gave Brett the album, but when Brett told Michael he did not have the $400, Michael said "That's okay, you can pay me later." On Brett's birthday the following week, Michael got a card for Brett and wrote in it: "For your birthday, you do not have to pay me for the Billy Idol album, Happy Birthday!" In a jurisdiction that follows the Restatement 2d of Contracts, can Michael later change his mind and demand the $400?

(A) No, because Michael renounced his right to payment.

(B) Yes, because his "gift" promise is unenforceable for lack of consideration.

(C) Yes, because Brett will be unjustly enriched if Michael cannot demand payment.

(D) No, because the original agreement was not in writing.

CHAPTER 22
APPLICABILITY OF ARTICLE 2 OF THE UCC

QUESTIONS

Facts for Question 1

Seller offers his watch for sale for $500. Seller's friend, Buyer, has always admired Seller's watch and accepts his friend's offer of $500, and they agree on delivery the following Friday. Seller and Buyer are individuals, not merchants.

1. Which of the following statements is correct?

    (A) Article 2 of the UCC will govern the transaction.

    (B) Article 2 of the UCC will not apply because at least one party must be a merchant for the UCC to apply.

    (C) Article 2 of the UCC will not apply because both parties must be merchants for the UCC to apply.

    (D) Article 2 of the UCC will not initially apply because the watch is a "future good," but will apply once the performance and payment obligations become enforceable.

Facts for Question 2

Paul leases a car from Dimwit Rentals ("Dimwit"), a rental car company. Later that day Paul gets into an accident in the car he leased. He believes that the accident was caused by defective maintenance on the part of Dimwit. Paul wants to bring suit for breach of warranty and collect the damages resulting from the accident.

2. Which of the following statements is most correct?

    (A) Article 2 of the UCC will govern the transaction.

    (B) Common law rules will govern the transaction.

(C) Article 2A of the UCC will govern the transaction.

(D) The rules of the Restatement (Second) of Contracts will govern the transaction.

Facts for Question 3

Seller offers his RV for sale in a local advertising periodical for $50,000. The trailer has its own engine. Buyer sees the ad and contacts Seller to purchase the RV. Seller plans to take the RV on a trip across the United States and use it as his primary residence. After some negotiation the two parties agree on a price.

3.   Which of the following statements is correct?

(A) Article 2 of the UCC will not apply since the RV is not a "good."

(B) Article 2 of the UCC will not apply because the RV will be used as a residence.

(C) Article 2 will apply regardless whether the RV is classified as a "good."

(D) Article 2 will apply because the RV is a "good."

Facts for Question 4

Buyer purchases a new stereo from Amazon.com. Under the agreement delivery is to take place in one week. Buyer paid for the stereo by PayPal when she ordered. At the time of the order, no particular stereo was set aside for Buyer. The next week, someone in Amazon's delivery department selects a particular stereo to deliver to Buyer from the inventory in the warehouse, and delivery is timely accomplished.

4.   Which of the following is most correct?

(A) Article 2 applies since the stereo was movable when purchased.

(B) Article 2 applies since the stereo was movable at the time of identification to the contract.

(C) Article 2 does not apply since the stereo was not "identified" to the contract at the time of purchase.

(D) Article 2 does not apply since a stereo is not a "good" within the definition of Article 2.

Facts for Questions 5 and 6

Buyer purchases a brand new dishwasher from merchant Seller for $400, and paid an extra $200 to have it delivered and installed. The unit was installed timely, but three weeks after the installation, the dishwasher malfunctions and floods Buyer's house.

Subsequent investigation established that the problem was caused by Seller's negligent installation of the dishwasher by improperly tightening a water hose.

5.   In a jurisdiction which follows the "Predominant Purpose" test, which of the following is correct?

(A) Article 2 will govern the contract because this is a contract for goods.

(B) Article 2 will not govern because this is a contract for services.

(C) Article 2 will govern because the breach occurred when the "good" malfunctioned.

(D) Article 2 will not govern because the breach occurred as a result of negligent installation.

6.   In a jurisdiction which follows the "Gravamen" test, which of the following is correct?

(A) Article 2 will govern the contract because this is a contract for goods.

(B) Article 2 will not govern because this is a contract for services.

(C) Article 2 will govern because the breach occurred when the "good" malfunctioned.

(D) Article 2 will not govern because the breach occurred as a result of negligent installation.

Facts for Question 7

Seller recently discovered he has struck it rich by finding oil beneath the surface of his property. He advertises the newfound oil for sale at $200 per barrel. Buyer, an owner of several gas stations, saw the advertisement, but offered Seller $180 per barrel. Seller reluctantly agreed, but said, "Only if you pay for and perform all of the harvesting of the oil yourself." This was included into their final written contract. Buyer erected some oil rigs on the property and began pumping out the barrels of oil.

7. Which of the following statements is correct?

    (A) Article 2 will govern the transaction regardless of who harvests the oil.

    (B) Article 2 will govern because Buyer is harvesting the oil.

    (C) Article 2 will not govern because Buyer is harvesting the oil.

    (D) Article 2 will not govern because this is a transaction for real property.

CHAPTER 23
WARRANTIES

QUESTIONS

Facts Common to Questions 1 and 2

Brianna Buyer is running an extreme marathon in South Africa in several months. She has been training very hard, and feels more than ready for the seven day, 155-mile race. Brianna goes to a running store, Shady Sellers, to get the perfect pair of shoes to get her through the grueling physical feat.

Fact Variation for Question 1

Brianna talks with an employee at Shady's and says she is looking for him to provide her with a shoe that can last for many miles, is good on rough terrain, and can breathe well in the extreme heat. Shady's employee does not pay much attention to what Brianna is telling him and gives her a cloth running shoe with no special features which would make it long lasting, good on rocks, or wick away the heat. When Brianna travels to South Africa to compete, she sprains her ankle within the first three miles of the race and is forced to stop running the extreme marathon.

1.   Assume that the cloth shoes would have been adequate for ordinary running shoes. Does Brianna have any warranty claims against Shady Sellers?

   (A) Yes, Brianna has an express warranty claim because Shady's employee represented to her that the shoe would be acceptable.

   (B) Yes, Brianna has an implied warranty of merchantability claim against Shady's because the cloth shoe was not of average quality for ultra-marathoners.

   (C) Yes, Brianna has an implied warranty of fitness for a particular purpose claim because she told Shady's employee what she needed, relied on Shady's employee to give her a shoe to meet those requirements, and Shady's employee sold her the shoe.

(D) No, Brianna has no warranty claims against Shady Sellers because Shady Sellers did not make any representations to Brianna.

Fact Variation for Question 2

Brianna goes to Shady Seller, except instead of discussing her needs with an employee, she grabs the first pair of shoes she finds. Brianna buys the same cloth shoe described in Question 1. She sprains her ankle within the first three miles of the race and has to stop running.

2. Assume that the cloth shoes would have been adequate for ordinary running use. Does Brianna have any warranty claims against Shady Sellers?

(A) Yes, Brianna has an express warranty claim because Shady's represented to her that the shoe would be acceptable.

(B) Yes, Brianna has an implied warranty of merchantability claim against Shady's because the cloth shoe was not of average quality.

(C) Yes, Brianna has an implied warranty of fitness claim because a Shady's employee sold her the shoe.

(D) No, Brianna has no warranty claims against Shady Sellers.

Facts for Question 3

Bianca, a historian at a rock and roll museum, contacted Sasha, the owner of the document on which John Lennon wrote the lyrics for "All You Need is Love," and had the following conversation on September 1:

B: Are you sure that that document really contains the lyrics on which John Lennon personally wrote "All You Need is Love?"

S: Yes, they are. I bought this at an auction from Mary's Music Auction House a year ago, and I have a letter from Mary's authenticating it. I wouldn't be asking $ 1.5 million for it if it were not authentic.

B: That's important to me, because this is going to be our big attraction at the museum. We plan to advertise all over town and draw people in with this memorabilia. Everyone loves The Beatles. But it would be very damaging to our reputation if it turned out that this was not authentic.

S: I understand. However, I would not have bought it from Mary's if I wasn't certain that these were the real lyrics.

B: Well, OK, I'll take it. Can you deliver it on December 1?

S: That sounds great. Will do.

On December 1, Sasha tendered the document with the lyrics, and Bianca tendered a $1.5 million check. However, on January 1, the man who had sold Mary's the document with the lyrics on it admitted that it was fake and that he had perpetrated fraud. The authentic document with the lyrics was actually owned by an avid rock and roll memorabilia collector in Great Britain. Subsequent investigation revealed that neither Mary's, nor Sasha knew that the document with the lyrics on it that was sold by Sasha was not authentic.

3.   Assuming that Article 2 applied to this transaction, which of the following warranties, if any, has Sasha breached?

   I.   Express Warranty

   II.   Warranty of Merchantability

(A) I and II.

(B) I only.

(C) II only.

(D) Sasha has breached neither of the listed warranties.

Facts for Question 4

Seller is a restaurant kitchen supply store and Buyer is a chef that is in the process of opening a new restaurant. Buyer goes to Seller's store to look for knives and Seller shows Buyer a set of ceramic knives. Seller explains to Buyer that these are the best knives in the business, that they can cut through any type of food, and that they are self-sharpening, so they last much longer than stainless steel knives. Buyer is so impressed with Seller's description that he buys four sets of the knives at $1,000 a set. However, when Buyer gets them to the restaurant and tests them, he is very disappointed to find that they will not cut through much of anything, not even a head of lettuce, and they are very dull. Buyer is furious and sues Seller.

Assume Seller knew that Buyer had relied on his statements regarding the knives when making the purchase.

4. Does Buyer have a claim for breach of express warranty against Seller?

(A) No, because Seller did not promise anything to Buyer.

(B) No, because Buyer did not test the knives before leaving the store.

(C) Yes, based on Seller's description of the goods.

(D) Yes, but only if Seller signed something guaranteeing that the knives would cut through any type of food.

Facts for Question 5

Buyer is a stay at home dad with five children under the age of ten. His home is rather chaotic, and requires a great deal of cleaning. Buyer goes to Seller, a home store, with the intention of purchasing a new vacuum cleaner. The store is running a video produced by the manufacturer demonstrating the Spick-and-Span 2000, an expensive vacuum cleaner. The store has turned off the sound on the video, which runs on a continuing loop.

Buyer watches the video and is very impressed when he sees that it picks up glass, mud, pet hair, and food without any trouble. Based on the video, Buyer purchases the vacuum on the spot and rushes home to clean his house from top to bottom. However, the suction on the vacuum cleaner is so weak that it fails to pick up any of the dirt in the first room Buyer attempts to clean.

5. Does Buyer have an actionable express warranty claim against Seller?

(A) Yes, Buyer has an actionable express warranty claim against the Seller, but only if Seller had some writing enclosed in the packaging guaranteeing that the vacuum would pick up the dirt in Buyer's home.

(B) Yes, Buyer has an actionable express warranty claim against Seller, based on the video of the Spick-and-Span 2000 that Buyer watched.

(C) No, Buyer does not have an actionable express warranty claim against Seller because Seller did not promise Buyer anything, but does have an express warranty claim against the manufacturer, who produced the video.

    (D) No, Buyer does not have an actionable express warranty claim against Seller because Buyer did not rely on any representations from Seller.

Facts for Question 6

Buyer went to Box Store, an electronics merchant seller. Buyer wanted to purchase a computer. Because he was a gamer, he wanted a computer that would run *World of Warcraft* effortlessly. Box Store's sales representative assured Buyer in their conversation leading up to the purchase that the Model X-100 computer Buyer was looking at would easily run the program.

In purchasing the computer, Buyer signed a "Bill of Sale" which contained the following language:

> Box Store makes no representation regarding the compatibility of its computers to run any software.

> This Bill of Sale consists of the complete agreement between Buyer and Box Store and all other oral and/or previous agreements are merged herein.

The computer cannot not run *World of Warcraft*.

6. If Buyer sued Box Store for breach of express warranty regarding the ability of the computer to run *World of Warcraft* and <u>lost</u>, what would be the most likely reason?

    (A) An express warranty is inoperative whenever the seller disclaims it.

    (B) An oral express warranty is inoperative in light of a written warranty disclaimer.

    (C) The warranty was never introduced into evidence under the parol evidence rule.

    (D) Buyer was not reasonable in relying on a warranty made during negotiation.

Facts for Question 7

Buyer goes to Seller, an electronics retailer, to purchase a new television set. Buyer selects a 52-inch TV and pays Seller $1,500 for it. However, when Buyer takes the television home and attempts to use it, he finds that it does not turn on.

7.   At this time, does Buyer have any warranty claims against Seller?

(A) Yes, Buyer has a claim for breach of the implied warranty of merchantability.

(B) Yes, Buyer has a claim for breach of the implied warranty of fitness for a particular purpose against Seller.

(C) No, Buyer has no warranty claims against Seller.

(D) No, Buyer does not have any warranty claims against Seller, unless Seller expressly warranted to Buyer that the television would work.

Facts for Questions 8–10

Barry Buyer contacts Sarah Seller about an ad she placed in the paper to sell her Honda Accord for $12,000. Barry and Sarah work out the details and on Saturday, July 5, Sarah tenders the keys and title to the car, and Barry tenders payment. When Barry tries to drive the car home it won't even start. Both Barry and Sara are individuals, Sarah said nothing whatsoever about the attributes of the car, and she has no expertise in cars.

8.   Does Barry have a breach of warranty claim against Sarah?

(A) Yes, Barry has a claim for breach of the implied warranty of merchantability.

(B) Yes, Barry has a claim for breach of an express warranty.

(C) Yes, Barry has a claim for breach of an implied warranty of fitness.

(D) No, Barry has no warranty claims against Sarah.

9.   For this question assume Sara is a merchant seller and that she has placed a prominent notice that the Honda is being sold "as is." Once again the car does not start after Barry bought it.

Does Barry have a breach of warranty claim against Sarah?

(A) Yes, Barry has a claim for breach of the implied warranty of merchantability.

(B) Yes, Barry has a claim for breach of an express warranty.

(C) Yes, Barry has a claim for breach of an implied warranty of fitness.

(D) No, Barry has no warranty claims against Sarah.

10. For this question again assume that Sarah is a merchant seller. This time, she has posted a prominent sign on the Honda providing, "There are no warranties which extend beyond the description on the face hereof." Once again, the car does not run after Barry bought it.

Does Barry have a breach of warranty claim against Sarah?

(A) Yes, Barry has a claim for breach of the implied warranty of merchantability.

(B) Yes, Barry has a claim for breach of an express warranty.

(C) Yes, Barry has a claim for breach of an implied warranty of fitness.

(D) No, Barry has no warranty claims against Sarah.

Facts for Question 11

Buyer, a farmer, contacts Seller, a farm supplier. Buyer orders fifty bushels of grain, and Seller accepts the order, with delivery set for August 1. However, when the bushels arrive, Buyer decides they are not up to the quality he is used to from other suppliers. Buyer sues Seller for breach of the implied warranty of merchantability.

11. Assume that the bushels of grain were of average quality. Does Buyer have a warranty claim against Seller?

(A) Yes, because they are not of the quality Buyer is used to.

(B) Yes, because Buyer had a particular purpose for the grain (to farm it) and he cannot use the grain for this purpose because he is not satisfied with it.

(C) No, because the grain is of average quality.

(D) No, because there is no implied warranty of merchantability for fungible goods.

Question 12

12. Which of the following, if any, are appropriate modes of disclaiming an implied warranty of merchantability?

(A) "Seller makes no representations regarding the quality of goods, and disclaims all warranties, including the warranty of merchantability."

(B) "Goods are sold as is."

(C) "Seller makes no representations regarding the quality of the goods."

(D) Both (A) and (B) are appropriate and effective modes of disclaiming the implied warranty of merchantability.

Facts for Question 13

Buyer is an electronics store and orders 100 laptops from Seller, an electronics manufacturer. The laptops arrive on time and Buyer accepts and tenders payment. However, the next day Buyer tests the laptops and finds that none of the computers are operable and returns them to Seller with a note that says, "These computers stink."

Eight months later, Buyer sues Seller for breach of the implied warranty of merchantability. There were no communications between Buyer and Seller between the return of the computer and the filing of the suit.

13. Might Seller have a procedural defense against Buyer?

(A) Yes, Buyer must notify Seller of the breach of warranty within a reasonable time after the breach was discovered and particularize the defects to make an effective rejection.

(B) No, because a court would likely find the commencing of litigation as sufficient to give Seller notice of the warranty claim and a sufficient particularization of the defects.

(C) No, because Seller was the one that breached, so Buyer has no duty to notify Seller of the breach.

(D) No, because notice requirements among merchants are found unconscionable.

Facts for Question 14

Buyer purchases a powerful wood chipper from Seller. There is a guard over the blades on the machine that has a fixed a decal providing, "DO NOT REMOVE! IMPORTANT SAFETY PROTECTION! BLADES ARE VERY POWERFUL!"

Buyer was clearing trees on his property and some of the branches would not fit with the guard in place. He told his wife that he knew it was dangerous, but he had to clear all the trees, so he removed the guard and ended up injuring his arm, getting it entangled with the blades.

14. Does Buyer have a breach of warranty claim against Seller?

(A) Yes, Buyer has a breach of the implied warranty of merchantability claim, as well as a breach of implied warranty of fitness for a particular purpose.

(B) Yes, but Buyer only has a claim for breach of the implied warranty of merchantability.

(C) No, in a jurisdiction that recognizes assumption of the risk as a complete defense in a warranty action.

(D) Yes, but the damages would be reduced due to comparative negligence.

Facts Common to Questions 15 and 16

Paula purchased an antique revolver from the civil war era from Dennis for $2,000 on May 5. On August 13, Paula received a letter from Anne, stating that she was suing Paula for the antique revolver because it had actually belonged to Anne's family, and was lost during the war. Paula and Anne go to court and Anne loses because she cannot prove the gun actually belonged to her family.

Fact Variation for Question 15

When Paula purchased the revolver from Dennis, Dennis explained to her that the gun was an antique, and he couldn't guarantee that there were no competing claims to the revolver. Despite this warning, Paula is furious and sues Dennis for breach of warranty of title.

15. Assume that Anne's claim was a colorable claim. In <u>Paula v. Dennis</u>, what is the likely result?

(A) Paula will prevail because Anne had a colorable claim of title. Paula will be awarded attorney's fees Paula expended in defending the suit brought by Anne only.

(B) Paula will prevail because Anne had a colorable claim of title. Paula will be entitled to both attorney's fees she spent defending the suit brought by Anne, and the $2,000 she paid for the revolver.

(C) Dennis will prevail because he disclosed to Paula that there might have been a competing claim to the title.

(D) Dennis will prevail because Paula won the suit against Anne.

Fact Variation for Question 16

When Paula purchases the revolver, Dennis makes no mention of the fact that there may be competing claims to the revolver. Anne sued as before, because she had colorable evidence the pistol belonged in her family. Even though Paula prevailed against Anne in the claim to the revolver because the court felt Anne could not establish her claim beyond a preponderance of the evidence, Paula still sues Dennis for breach of the warranty of title.

16. In <u>Paula v. Dennis</u>, what is the likely result?

(A) Paula will prevail because Anne had a colorable claim of title. Paula will be awarded the attorney's fees she expended in the suit against Anne only.

(B) Paula will prevail because Anne had a colorable claim of title. Paula will be entitled to the attorney's fees she expended in the suit against Anne, and the $2,000 she paid for the revolver.

(C) Dennis will prevail because Paula should have known that there would be another claim to the revolver.

(D) Dennis will prevail because Paula won the suit against Anne.

Facts for Question 17

Paul bought a cell phone at Dan's Electronics. Paul subsequently receives notification from Alfred that Alfred is suing Paul for the cell phone because he believes it is his. The only theory Alfred pled supporting his suit is that because he saw the cell phone before Paul in the store, it belonged to him.

Paul and Alfred go to trial, and Alfred loses because he has no evidence that the phone was his, nor any reason to believe it was his. Paul then sues Dan's for breach of the warranty of title.

17. In <u>Paul v. Dan</u> for breach of the warranty of title, what is the likely outcome?

(A) Paul will prevail because Alfred had a colorable claim to the cell phone. Paul will receive attorney's fees only.

(B) Paul will prevail because Alfred had a colorable claim to the cell phone. Paul will receive attorney's fees expended in the suit brought by Alfred and will be refunded the purchase price of the cell phone.

(C) Dan's will prevail because Paul won in the suit against Alfred.

(D) Dan's will prevail because Alfred did not have a colorable claim to the cell phone.

PART 2
ANSWERS

CHAPTER 1
OFFER, ACCEPTANCE, AND MUTUALITY

ANSWERS

Answer to Question 1

(D) is the correct answer.

(D) is correct because there is a presumption that contracts between domiciliary family members, and in certain other social situations like dating, are not enforceable. *See Balfour v. Balfour*, 2 K.B. 571 (1919). Therefore, unless the court found that the presumption would be overcome by facts and circumstances indicating that the parties actually intended to make a legal commitment, the agreement is unenforceable.

(A) is incorrect.

(A) is incorrect because even if there is consideration given for the promise, there is still a presumption that husbands and wives do not intend to enter into legally binding agreements when making promises to one another. Therefore, the legal benefit or detriment would be irrelevant.

(B) is incorrect.

(B) is incorrect because even if there is a moral obligation, promises in social and inter-familial situations among family members living in the same home are presumed unenforceable. Therefore, any moral consideration grounds would be irrelevant.

(C) is incorrect.

(C) is incorrect because a legal benefit would only be relevant, if at all, regarding consideration. It is irrelevant to the question of whether social and inter-familial promises should be enforced.

Answer to Question 2

(D) is the correct answer.

(B) is correct because Sally has only made a statement of future intention; she has not made an offer. Restatement 2d § 26 provides that a "manifestation of willingness to enter into a bargain is not an offer," if the person to whom it is addressed knows or should know that the person making it does not intend to conclude the bargain without further manifestation of assent. Because Sally only said that she "had decided . . . to sell," rather than she was "*offering* to sell," her motorcycle, she had not made an offer under Restatement 2d § 24. In other words there were no "words of commitment" by Sally sufficient to make an offer.

(C) is also correct because, in contracts language, Sally entered into a "preliminary negotiation" whereby she solicited an offer from Brian, and it was Brian who made an effective revocable offer for the bike when he said, "I will buy your motorcycle for $800." Sally thus became the offeree and was empowered to accept the offer and conclude the deal without a further manifestation of assent, or she could reject the offer.

(A) is incorrect.

(A) is incorrect because Sally did not make an enforceable offer, so Brian could not have accepted. At this time, Brian is the one who has made an enforceable offer, and Sally has not yet accepted it.

Answer to Question 3

(B) is the correct answer.

Restatement 2d § 26 states that a manifestation of willingness to enter into a bargain is not an offer if the person to whom it is made has reason to know that the person making it does not intend to conclude the bargain until he or she has made a further manifestation of assent; rather, it is only a "preliminary negotiation." Over time, there are certain, oft-repeated fact situations which the courts have held are presumptively "preliminary negotiations" and not "offers." One of those is price quotes. As such, Store's price quote of $2/linear foot for the fencing was not an offer, but rather a preliminary negotiation/solicitation of an offer from Homeowner. Hence, it was Homeowner who made the offer to purchase 200 linear feet of the fencing at $2/linear foot under Restatement 2d § 24.

The reason price quotes are usually not offers is illustrated here. Store quoted a price for the fence, but it might not have 200 feet in inventory. If its price list was considered an offer to sell, and it did not have the requisite fencing in stock, any customer could put it in breach by ordering more than it had. Hence, contract law dictates that Store solicits the offer by means of the price quote, and that it, absent an "exception," is the customer who actually makes the offer when he or she comes to the store and brings the material to the checkout stand. *See* Restatement 2d § 26, Cmt. c.

(A) is incorrect.

(A) is incorrect because Store made a price quote which was a preliminary negotiation, and not an offer. Homeowner's statement therefore constituted an offer that Store could later accept if Homeowner came to the Store.

(C) and (D) are incorrect.

(C) and (D) are incorrect for the same reason that (A) is incorrect.

Answer to Question 4

(D) is the correct answer.

Over time contract law has established certain phrases which have been held to be preliminary negotiations or solicitations to make an offer under Restatement 2d § 26, rather than an offer itself under Restatement 2d § 24. One of these is the phrase, "I wouldn't consider selling for less than . . ." Hence, rather than making an offer to Buyer to sell his home for $75,000 with sufficient words of commitment, Seller is engaging in preliminary negotiations. Seller's statement that he wouldn't consider selling is also likely not certain enough to constitute an acceptable offer under Restatement 2d § 33. Under this rule, terms of a contract must be reasonably certain to provide a basis for establishing breach and providing an appropriate remedy. Here, Sam has not given a definite price, and has not mentioned how payment should be made, or when the sale would take place. Thus, this manifestation of intention was not certain enough to be effectively accepted. Instead, if anyone made an enforceable offer, it was Barry when he said he would buy Sam's property for $75,000, although there are indefiniteness concerns in considering that conversation an offer as well.

(A) is incorrect.

(A) is incorrect because Seller did not make an offer to Buyer, as explained above.

(B) is incorrect.

(B) is incorrect because Seller did not do anything that would allow an acceptance to be implied by his conduct. Instead, Buyer has made an offer if anyone has, and Sam has failed to accept the offer.

(C) is incorrect.

(C) is incorrect because it is irrelevant whether the fair market value is $60,000. The parties are free to contract for whatever price they want, so long as it is freely negotiated, and a "fair" price will not constitute a contract if there is no offer and acceptance.

Answer to Question 5

(B) is the correct answer.

This problem is based on *Lonergan v. Scolnick*, 276 P.2d 8 (Cal. Ct. App. 1954), where the court found that the language of commitment necessary to find an enforceable offer was not present in any communication between the buyer and seller. Based on Restatement 2d § 26, these were only preliminary negotiations that required further manifestation of assent to form a contract. The fact that Seller told Buyer he had other offers strongly supports the finding that a further manifestation of assent was needed before a bargain could be concluded and an offer found under Restatement 2d § 24.

(A) is incorrect.

(A) is incorrect because Seller had not yet made an offer to Buyer. Instead, the two were engaged in preliminary negotiations, based on Restatement 2d § 26. Therefore, Seller could not have revoked an offer since no enforceable offer existed.

(C) is incorrect.

(C) is incorrect because there was no language of commitment in Seller's statements. Seller had thus not made an offer to Buyer yet, because Seller was still considering selling to other buyers. Further, there are also no facts to support a finding that Buyer had made an offer and Seller had accepted it.

(D) is incorrect.

(D) is incorrect because Seller had not made an offer, as described above. Reliance, as manifested by a material change of position (the opening of escrow), is insufficient to find a contract when there has been no offer and acceptance.

Answer to Question 6

(D) is the correct answer.

(D) is correct because, while Restatement 2d § 26, Cmt. b, says that advertisements are presumptively not intended or understood as offers to sell, that presumption can be overcome if there is some language of commitment, or an invitation to take action without further communication in the advertisement. Here, the advertisement meets all the criteria for an enforceable offer via advertisement: the time to accept, the place to accept, the price, and the terms of acceptance, i.e., first-come-first served. This rule was applied in *Lefkowitz v. Great Minn. Surplus Store*, 86 N.W.2d 689 (Minn. 1957).

(A) is incorrect.

(A) correctly states the general rule that advertisements are solicitations for offers, and not offers. However, that rule is only presumptive. Advertisements can be offers if they show language of commitment. Here, because the advertisement names the price, time, place and first-come-first-served basis, it is specific enough to constitute an offer.

(B) is incorrect.

(B) is incorrect because whether the ad is an offer is subject to the same analysis under the UCC and common law. This comes from UCC § 1–103(b), which states that unless displaced by specific provisions of the UCC, the principles of common law control and there is no specific provision in the UCC regarding the effectiveness of advertisements as offers.

(C) is incorrect.

(C) is incorrect for the same reason that (B) is incorrect. Whether an ad is an offer is subject to the same analysis under the UCC and common law.

Answer to Question 7

(C) is the correct answer.

(C) is correct because Restatement 2d § 26, Cmt. b explains that ads are generally not offers. Rather, ads are an invitation to the public to come and make an offer to purchase. If the ad had further words of commitment, such as "first come first serve," it may have been enough to constitute an offer, but this ad did not.

One of the reasons for the general rule is shown by the facts of this problem, namely inventory concerns. That is, if a store runs out of inventory, the law does not want to allow customers to come in and demand goods the store does not have, thereby putting the store in breach. Instead, the general rule is that the customer is the offeror in response to the ad, and the store, as offeree, can choose to accept the offer (if it has the goods in inventory) or to reject the offer (if it is out of inventory).

(A) is incorrect.

(A) is not correct because this ad was not specific enough to constitute an offer, i.e., there were no terms regarding how many jeans were for sale, whether it was first-come-first served, etc. Rather, it was an invitation to the public to come and make an offer to Sally Seller.

(B) is incorrect.

(B) is not correct because there is no obligation for a seller to offer a "rain check" to a customer who wants to purchase a good which the store has run out of. This is because, e.g., it may be that the only reason a store is offering goods on hand at that price is because it got a good deal on that amount of inventory on hand. If replacing those goods would cost more, courts do not want to force stores to have to sell these replacement goods at an advertised price. Some stores may offer a "rain check" to foster customer relations, and a few states require rain checks in certain situations under special consumer protection legislation, but there is no requirement under common law contract principles to do so.

(D) is incorrect.

(D) is not correct because Sally has not made an offer for the reasons stated under (C) and (A) above. Thus, Betty could not tender performance in order to accept, because there was no offer to accept.

Answer to Question 8

(B) is the correct answer.

(B) is correct because Restatement 2d § 26, Cmt. b explains that advertisements and catalogues are generally, and presumptively, not offers. For example, your law school did not make you an offer when it put out its catalogue. Rather, you made the offer when you sent in your application, and your offer was accepted when the school offered you enrollment. However, contract law views the circumstances such that when you made your offer, you impliedly made it on the terms set forth in the catalogue, and when the law school accepted your offer, it became bound by the terms in its catalogue, which were impliedly incorporated into your offer.

Here, Pam was the offeror when she applied for a job. However, implied in her offer were the terms of the ad, e.g., she was offering her services to work under the terms described in the advertisement. Thus, when she was hired, Tar–Mart was bound by the terms of the ad, one of which "guaranteed" a 5% pay raise every six months on the job.

Certainly Tar–Mart could have made the 5% pay raise contingent on "good performance" or an absence of complaints in its ad. But it did not, and so is bound by the "guarantee" in the advertisement.

Note also that if Tar–Mart had said nothing in its ad about pay increases, but had a clause in its employer manual calling for pay raises being contingent on an absence of customer complaints, both Pam and Tar–Mart could well have been subject to that provision if it was definite enough to be an offer and the employee knew of its terms when he or she began or continued work.

(A) is incorrect.

(A) is incorrect because Tar–Mart did not make an offer when it placed the ad. This is because ads are generally not offers, and Tar–Mart's ad did not have sufficient words of commitment. Restatement 2d § 26.

(C) is incorrect.

(C) is incorrect for two reasons. First, while ads are *generally* not offers and only solicitations for offers, they can be offers if they are specific enough. Second, (C) is also incorrect because the ad was not an offer, but it did set forth the terms of the offer that Pam made when she applied for the job.

(D) is incorrect.

(D) is incorrect because while Tar–Mart could have made the 5% raise contingent on good performance, it stated in the ad that the pay raise was "guaranteed." Thus, Tar–Mart is obligated to provide the raise for the reasons stated under (B) above, regardless of its good faith.

Answer to Question 9

(A) is the correct answer.

Based on the objective theory of contracts, the question becomes whether a reasonable person in the position of the party who seeks to enforce the contract would conclude that an enforceable offer was made and thus a valid contract has been formed. Here, Danny made the offer boastfully, while he was still upset and tipsy, and offered to pay one hundred times what the bottle of wine was really worth. It is unlikely that a reasonable person in Pearl's position would believe that Danny really intended to make such an offer for the return of the wine seriously, especially when he could have purchased a replacement at the wine store for $2,500 such as Pearl did.

(B) is incorrect.

(B) is incorrect because the offer is invalid. This is because Danny never intended to make an enforceable offer under the objective theory of contracts, not because the wine bottle is gone.

(C) and (D) are not the best choices.

(C) and (D) are not the best choices because it seems as though Danny made this offer in jest/anger after being upset about losing the bottle of wine. Under the objective theory of contracts it does not seem like a valid offer for the reasons stated under (A) above.

Answer to Question 10

(A) is the correct answer.

(A) correctly states the result under the objective theory of contracts. The objective theory of contracts provides that there is a contract where a reasonable person in the position of the party who seeks to enforce the contract would conclude that a contract had been formed. Here, the parties negotiated the price, the price was fair market value, they wrote the contract down and signed it, added Dean's wife, and decided when payment would be made. Because it would seem to Dean that a contract had been formed, this would likely be enough.

Restatement 2d § 16 provides that a contract is voidable if the person entering into the contract is intoxicated and the other party has reason to know that by reason of intoxication the person is unable to understand the consequences of the transaction or unable to act in a reasonable manner in relation to the transaction. Here, the facts say that Dean was unaware that Peter was feeling intoxicated, so this contract would not be voidable on the basis of Restatement 2d § 16. This fact scenario is loosely based on *Lucy v. Zemer*, 196 Va. 493 (1954), where the court held that there was an enforceable contract under like circumstances.

(B) and (C) are incorrect.

(B) and (C) are incorrect because the subjective intention of the parties is not what matters here. Rather, the objective understanding is what is important under modern mutuality principles.

(D) is incorrect.

(D) is incorrect because an adequate signed writing can satisfy the statute of frauds, and the fact that it is on a napkin is not determinative. Restatement 2d §§ 131–134.

Answer to Question 11

(B) is the correct answer.

Pam's offer is known as an "indifferent" or "ambiguous" offer because it gives Bill the choice of either accepting by performance (painting the salon), or accepting by promise (promising to paint the salon). In other words, by its very terms, Pam is "indifferent" as to whether Bill can accept by promise or action. Acceptance of indifferent offers by performance is governed by Restatement 2d § 62, which provides that beginning or tendering performance in response to an indifferent offer should be treated the same as a promissory acceptance. That is, once Bill began painting, such act is to be treated as if Bill promised to paint. The significance of treating that act as a promissory acceptance is that, upon acceptance, both the offeror and offeree are bound and neither can fail to perform completely without being in breach. This is in contrast to acceptance under a unilateral contract offer under Restatement 2d § 45, which is described in the explanation of (C).

(A) is incorrect.

(A) is incorrect because Bill's beginning to paint the salon constituted an acceptance of Pam's offer and a promise to complete the performance. Restatement 2d § 62. Thus, Pam could not revoke her offer thereafter because a contract was already formed.

(C) is incorrect.

(C) is incorrect because this choice explains the rule if the situation were governed by Restatement 2d § 45, which it is not. Section 45 provides that when the offeror makes an unambiguous offer for a unilateral contract, i.e., when the offer makes it clear that the only way it can be accepted is by performing an act, then beginning or tendering performance by the offeree establishes a unilateral option contract. Under such a contract, once the offeree begins performance, he or she must be given a chance to complete it, meaning that the offeror is bound to keep the offer open for a reasonable time allowing the offeree the opportunity to fully complete the act or acts called for by the offer. However, the option contract is unilateral, because the offeree is free to stop performance without consequence at any time.

Think of a reward offer where a bank offers a reward for information leading to the apprehension and conviction of an individual who robbed the bank. This is a situation where the offer is unambiguously one for a unilateral contract, i.e., the only way an offeree can accept the offer and the contract is by actually performing the act called for—providing information which leads to the apprehension and conviction of the robber. As such, it is governed by Restatement 2d § 45.

If the offeree starts looking for such information, a unilateral option contract is formed whereby the bank must give the offeree a reasonable time to complete performance, but the offeree may quit looking for the robber at any time without consequence.

In Question 11, however, Bill began performance in response to an indifferent offer, which is governed under Restatement 2d § 62, meaning that both Pam *and* Bill are bound under the contract once Bill began painting the salon.

(D) is incorrect.

(D) is incorrect because Bill has accepted Pam's offer, and thus is entitled to full contract damages, not just what he has earned for whatever painting he has done before Pam breached and ordered him off her property.

Answer to Question 12

(C) is the correct answer.

This kind of offer is known as a "general" offer, i.e., an offer that is directed to a potentially unlimited number of offerees. The offer presented in this question is a special kind of general offer known as a reward offer.

There is a presumption in general offers that only the first person who performs the acts called for in the offer can accept it. Restatement 2d § 29, Cmt. b. That presumption can be overcome by facts and circumstances to the contrary, e.g., in *Carlill v. Carbolic Smoke Ball*, 1 Q.B. 256 (1893), the ad made it clear the general reward was offered to any and all people who used the smoke ball and caught the flu.

However, there is no indication based on these facts that Paul intended to pay more than one person. Therefore, while anyone who knew about the offer could accept it, once the first person performed the acts and accepted (Ann), this terminated the power of acceptance for everyone else.

(A) is incorrect.

(A) is incorrect because the facts do not mention Paul attempting to revoke the reward offer. Rather, the question deals with the termination of acceptance of a reward offer once the first person accepts.

(B) is incorrect.

(B) is incorrect because there is a presumption that only the first person can accept reward offers. Therefore, even though Dana knew about the reward and intended to accept it, her power of acceptance terminated once Ann accepted the reward offer.

(D) is incorrect.

While ads generally are not offers, reward offers have "words of commitment," and are effective, enforceable offers. Restatement 2d §§ 24, 26.

Answer to Question 13

(C) is the correct answer.

Therese cannot recover because she did not know of the offer when she accepted it. Although Camille's ad constitutes an enforceable reward offer, and even though Therese did the acts called for by the offer, an offeree cannot effectively accept an offer to enter into a unilateral contract if he or she does not know about it. Restatement 2d § 51. The idea is that the reward offer must induce action to be accepted and so if the putative offeree was going to do the act anyway (which was true here of Therese), the offer did not motivate the acts and therefore did not constitute acceptance of it.

(A) and (B) are incorrect.

(A) and (B) are incorrect because they reach the wrong result under Restatement 2d § 51. There is no contract with Therese because she did not know about the offer before she gave the information.

(D) is incorrect.

(D) states the rationale incorrectly; Therese loses because she did not accept the offer since she didn't know about it, not because of a defect in Camille's offer itself. This general reward ad was sufficiently detailed to constitute an effective offer.

Answer to Question 14

(A) is the correct answer.

Randy should win because Camille's offer was not effectively revoked before Randy did the requested act (providing the information), which amounted to acceptance. Where an offer is made generally to the public, as in an online ad, it may be revoked by a notice given equal publicity when there is no better means of communication reasonably available (known as the "equal publicity rule"). Restatement 2d § 46. When the offer was already communicated to the public, a revocation must be communicated to be effective. Here the attempted revocation by Camille was not communicated until after Randy gave his tip.

(B) is not the best choice.

Randy will win on a breach of contract theory, as explained above, so the detrimental reliance theory is not the best choice.

(C) is incorrect.

(C) is incorrect because Therese's information was not in response to the ad. There is a general presumption that only the first person who accepts a reward offer may collect the reward. Restatement 2d § 29, Cmt. b. However, since Therese did not effectively accept the offer set forth in the ad, Randy was still able to accept it as the power of acceptance had not yet been terminated.

(D) is incorrect.

(D) is irrelevant because the offer did not say that the tip had to lead to a purchase, only that Camille would pay the reward if given the tip as to the availability of the record, which is what Randy did. While the original offer could have said that the reward would be paid only for "information leading to the *purchase* of the record," it did not state this and Camille is bound by the language of the ad she authored.

Answer to Question 15

(B) is the correct answer.

(B) is the correct choice because in this situation, Drug's, Inc.'s ad was an offer to enter into a unilateral contract, therefore once Piper started performing knowing of, and in response to, it, a unilateral option contract was deemed created, and the offer could not be withdrawn for a reasonable time—enough time to allow Piper to do the acts necessary for acceptance. Restatement 2d § 45. While Drugs, Inc. could not revoke the offer to Piper, the retraction ad was effective against anyone who had not yet began using the product, even if they did not see the retraction ad under the "equal publicity rule." Restatement 2d § 46.

(A) is incorrect.

(A) is incorrect because it is irrelevant whether Piper learned of the revocation. Piper had already begun performance and had the irrevocable option to finish. Restatement 2d § 45. Drugs, Inc. could therefore not revoke the reward offer for a reasonable time as to her or to anyone else who had already started using the product intending to accept the offer if they got sick.

(C) is incorrect.

(C) is incorrect based on Restatement § 54(1), which states that in general no notification is necessary when an offer invites an offeree to accept by rendering performance. Here, the offer did not request notification, and invited acceptance by performance, so Piper was not required to notify Drugs, Inc. when she started taking the drug and "began performance" in response to the offer. This problem is similar to *Carlill v. Carbolic Smoke Ball Co.*, 1 Q.B. 256 (1893), where the court said the nature of the offer implied that no notification was necessary before Ms. Carlill started using defendant's "smoke ball" to avoid the flu.

(D) is incorrect.

(D) is incorrect because an offeror cannot revoke a reward offer at any time. Reward offers cannot be revoked against an offeree who has already begun performance for a reasonable period of time necessary to complete performance. Restatement 2d § 45.

Answer to Question 16

(D) is the correct answer.

While there is a presumption that only the first person can accept a reward offer, this presumption is rebutted when the nature or language of the offer is such that more than one person may accept the offer. This situation is similar to *Carlill v. Carbolic Smoke Ball*, 1 Q.B. 256 (1893) where the court found that the nature of the wording in the ad made it manifest that the offer could be accepted by any person who did the acts and otherwise met the criteria set forth in the offer. Restatement 2d § 54, Cmt. b.

(A) is incorrect.

(A) is not the best choice for the reasons stated above. While there is a presumption that only the first person can accept a reward offer, in situations such as this a reasonable person would find that anyone who uses Sick–Me–Not as directed and gets sick may accept.

(B) is incorrect.

(B) is incorrect because generally reward offers do not require notification to the offeror before beginning performance in response to the offer, unless the offeror expressly or impliedly requests the notification in the offer itself. Restatement 2d § 54(1).

(C) is incorrect.

(C) is incorrect because Piper can collect on a breach of contract theory, and is not limited to a promissory estoppel recovery.

Answer to Question 17

(A) is the correct answer.

(A) is correct because Restatement §§ 51, 53 provide that an offeree who learns of an offer after he or she has rendered part of the performance requested by the offer may accept by completing the requested performance and indicating his or her intention to accept. Therefore, even though Paula did not know of the offer until after she had begun performing, because she knew of the offer before she completed performance, she can effectively accept the reward offer. Her intention to accept the offer is evidenced by her demanding the $200. Thus, Darla is obligated to pay Paula the reward.

(B) is incorrect.

(B) is incorrect because the issue here is whether Paula must know of the reward when she begins performing. Under Restatement §§ 51, 53 she does not; she only has to know about the reward before she *completes* performance. Additionally, because Paula began driving before she learned of the reward, the facts do not support a finding that she materially relied on the offer when she drove the wallet to Darla.

(C) is incorrect.

(C) is incorrect because Restatement § 51 states that so long as the offeree learns of the offer before completing performance, he or she can effectively accept the offer. Thus, it does not matter that Paula did not know of the reward when she began driving to Darla's home, because she learned of the offer before she completed performance.

(D) is incorrect.

(D) is incorrect because it does not matter that Paula did not learn of the reward from Darla's blog, so long as she learned of the reward from any source before completing performance.

Answer to Question 18

(D) is the correct answer.

(D) is correct because to have a valid acceptance of a reward offer, the offeree must manifest an intention to accept it at the time the acts called for in the offer are completed. Restatement 2d § 53(3). Here, when

Paula told both Adam and Darla that she would not take her money, this is evidence that Paula did not intend to accept the offer, and instead intended for her actions to be an unenforceable gift. Once such choice is made, the purported offeree cannot change his or her mind.

(A) and (B) are incorrect.

(A) and (B) are incorrect for the reasons stated above. In telling Darla she would not accept the reward, Paula manifested an intention not to accept the offer. Therefore, Paula did not effectively accept the reward offer.

(C) is incorrect.

(C) is incorrect because it misstates the law of reward offers. Paula did not have to know of the reward before she began returning the wallet. Paula would only have to learn of the offer before she completed performance, i.e., before she returned the wallet, to validly accept it.

Answer to Question 19

(A) is the correct answer.

(A) is correct because an offer can be accepted only by a person to whom it is made. Restatement 2d § 52. Thus, because Buyer made the offer to Factory A, Factory B cannot accept the offer. Note that *if* the contract had already been performed, the question of whether Factory B could perform becomes one of delegation. But here what was transferred was not a contractual right to make the clips, but the power to accept an offer to make the clips.

(B) is incorrect.

(B) is incorrect because there are no facts to support a finding that the "generic" clips were specially made goods. But even if they were, it is irrelevant. The issue here is that Buyer made the offer to Factory A, and therefore only Factory A, and not Factory B, may accept the offer.

(C) is incorrect.

(C) is incorrect because an offeree cannot transfer a power of acceptance under a revocable offer.

(D) is incorrect.

(D) is incorrect because only the person to whom an offer is made may accept an offer under Restatement 2d § 52. Thus, Factory B may not validly accept the offer. By manufacturing and sending the clips, it is making an offer to sell the clips to Buyer.

Answer to Question 20

(A) is the correct answer.

Here Buyer made a counteroffer, i.e., "an offer relating to the same matter as the original offer and proposing a substituted bargain differing from that proposed offer." Restatement 2d § 39(1). Typically, a counteroffer acts as a rejection and terminated the power of acceptance in the counter-offeree. Restatement 2d § 39(2). However, that rule is subject to exceptions. One exception is when the original offeror, here Seller, *revived* the original offer by stating that the offer remains open, even after the counteroffer was made, and extended the power of acceptance until the next day Hence the power to accept remained with Buyer at the time Buyer accepted.

(B) is incorrect.

(B) is incorrect, because a merchant's firm offer under UCC § 2–205 can only be made by a merchant and then usually only by means of a signed writing. Seller's offer was a revocable one.

(C) is incorrect.

(C) is incorrect because Buyer's counteroffer did not terminate the power of acceptance because Seller revived and extended the offer.

(D) is incorrect.

There is a general presumption that in a face-to-face conversation, the offer lapses once the conversation ends. Restatement 2d § Cmt. d. However, because Seller expressly said that the offer would remain open until the next day, the facts and circumstances rebut the presumption.

Answer to Question 21

(A) is the correct answer.

The rule is that the power of acceptance terminates upon a counteroffer. Restatement 2d §§ 36(1)(a), 39(2). The question is whether Buyer's statement is a counteroffer. It is not. Restatement 2d § 39, Cmt. b explains that a "mere inquiry" requesting a better offer is ordinarily not a counteroffer. Buyer made a mere inquiry when he asked if Seller would consider selling for less. A counteroffer, on the other hand, is when the acceptance is made to depend on the offeror's assent to the changed/added terms. Here, Buyer did not make his acceptance dependent on the cheaper price, so the power of acceptance had not terminated, and Buyer effectively accepted the offer.

(B) is incorrect.

(B) is incorrect because the power of acceptance never terminated because Buyer made a "mere inquiry" and not a counteroffer.

(C) is incorrect.

(C) is incorrect because the power of acceptance had not terminated when Buyer asked Seller to consider selling for less. While it is true that Buyer had a power, and not a right, to accept, because this was a revocable offer (as opposed to an irrevocable offer which creates a "right" of acceptance), the power of acceptance was still in existence after Buyer's inquiry. Therefore, Buyer could and did effectively accept.

(D) is incorrect.

(D) is incorrect because Buyer did not make a counteroffer to Seller; rather he made a "mere inquiry," as explained above. Therefore the power of acceptance had not terminated, and Buyer effectively accepted the offer.

Answer to Question 22

(D) is the correct answer.

Painter's statement that he couldn't do the job for less than $3,500 was a rejection of the original offer and counteroffer. Restatement 2d §§ 38, 39. As such, it terminated his power to accept Homeowner's office. Restatement 2d §§ 36(1), 38(1), 39(2). Therefore, Painter's second telephone message that attempted to accept the original offer was invalid as an acceptance of the original offer, because the power to accept that original offer had been immediately terminated by the rejection and counteroffer. Instead, it actually was an offer by Painter to paint the house for $2,000. The offer was not accepted by Homeowner, and thus Painter cannot recover anything on a breach of contract theory.

(A) is incorrect.

Painter made a rejection of the original offer and a counteroffer in his first phone message. Therefore, it is irrelevant whether Homeowner detrimentally relied on the message, because the power to accept the original offer was automatically terminated by the rejection counteroffer. Restatement 2d §§ 38(1), 39(2). The fact that Homeowner did not materially change position in reliance on Painter's first message does not allow Painter to revive the original offer by attempting to accept it later.

(B) is incorrect.

(B) is not the best choice because it implies that painter should recover the reasonable value of his services, not the contractual amount, which could be different. Since the call of the question excludes any theory of recover not based on breach of contract, and as there was no enforceable contract, any choice which permits painter to recover is incorrect. Thus, even if painter was due a restitutionary recovery under the circumstances, (B) is an incorrect choice under a breach of contract theory.

(C) is incorrect.

(C) is incorrect because Painter cannot make Homeowner contractually obligated merely by stating his intention to do something that would benefit Homeowner. For example, the owner of the local clothing store cannot make a stranger obligated to him by saying, "Stranger, I'm going to drop by your home on Wednesday and drop off a pair of pants, and send you a bill at the end of the month." Painter made an offer to paint the home, but that offer was not accepted by Homeowner. There is no valid acceptance by silence or inaction in this situation as none of the provisions of Restatement 2d § 69 apply.

Answer to Question 23

(D) is the correct answer.

(D) is the correct choice because Buyer said he planned to keep Seller's offer under further advisement. Restatement 2d § 38(2) provides that a manifestation of intention not to accept an offer is a rejection, *"unless* the offeree manifests an intention to take it under further advisement" (emphasis added). Because this is exactly what Buyer did, there was no rejection and so Seller's offer remained viable, i.e., the power of acceptance remained in Buyer. Buyer thereafter accepted Seller's offer when he said he would buy the ticket for $200.

(A) is incorrect.

(A) is incorrect because, while Buyer did ask Seller to consider a lower price, this was not a rejection or a counteroffer because Buyer made it clear he was still considering the $200 offer. Restatement 2d § 38(2).

(B) is incorrect.

(B) is incorrect because while there is a presumption in face-to-face conversations that the power of acceptance lapses at the end of the conversation, the conversation did not end in the fact situation for the question. Therefore, the power of acceptance never terminated in the facts described.

(C) is incorrect.

(C) is incorrect because Buyer's power to accept Seller's offer had not yet terminated. Restatement 2d § 38(2). Therefore, Buyer validly accepted Seller's offer when Buyer said "I'll take it for $200," rather than making an offer of his own.

Answer to Question 24

(C) is the correct answer.

An option contract is a contract, the subject matter of which is the right to accept an offer in an underlying contract. Restatement 2d § 25. Here, an option contract was formed between Elizabeth and Thomas for there was an offer, acceptance, and consideration exchanged for a contract the subject matter of which was the right to accept an offer in the underlying puppy sale contract.

Under the mail box rule generally, acceptances *are* effective on dispatch. Restatement 2d § 63(a). However, there is an exception under the Restatement for option contracts. Under Restatement 2d § 63(b), "an acceptance under an option contract is not operative until received by the offeror." Here, the letter with the check in it was not received by Elizabeth on or before April 8, and so at that point she was contractually free to sell the puppy to another, which she did when she sold it to Amanda.

(A) is incorrect.

Thomas does not own the puppy because acceptance of an option contract is effective only when it is <u>received</u> by the offeror, not upon proper dispatch. Restatement 2d § 63(b). Here, Elizabeth did not receive Thomas's acceptance until it was too late (after April 8).

(B) is incorrect.

(B) is incorrect because an option contract can be formed orally, so long as there is an offer, acceptance and consideration exchanged, as occurred here. Restatement 2d § 25, Cmt. c.

(D) is incorrect.

If a contact subject to the Statute of Frauds does not satisfy the Statute, it is *voidable*, not void. In other words, the parties can go forward with the contract if they wish. So, while the puppy contract would be a contract that is subject to the Statute of Frauds set forth in

UCC § 2–201 since it is for a sale of goods in excess of $500, and while the contract was oral and thus did not satisfy the Statute, the parties can still enforce the agreement if the party with the defense, here the buyer, wishes to do so. Here, Amanda tendered the payment, which was accepted by Elizabeth and Elizabeth told Amanda the puppy was hers.

Answer to Question 25

(A) is the correct answer.

(A) is the best answer because there is a common law presumption in face-to-face and telephone conversations that the reasonable time to accept is before the conversation ends. *See* Restatement 2d § 41, Cmt. d. Therefore, when Buyer failed to accept when they were at dinner (when the face-to-face conversation was still occurring), there was a lapse of time and the power of acceptance terminated. Restatement 2d §§ 36(1)(b), 41.

(B) is incorrect.

(B) is not the best answer because using the common law presumption regarding face-to-face conversations, the power of acceptance lapsed (was terminated) when the face-to-face conversation ended. Hence, it is therefore irrelevant whether the terms of the contract were sufficiently definite. Besides, in a simple agreement such as a watch exchanged for money, the agreement probably was definite enough to be enforced.

(C) is incorrect.

(C) is incorrect because there is a common law presumption that the power of acceptance terminates at the close of a face-to-face conversation, so Buyer could not accept the offer three days later. Restatement 2d § 41, Cmt. 41.

(D) is incorrect.

(D) is incorrect because Buyer could not accept the offer, as explained above, so no contract was ever formed. Additionally, the Statute of Frauds defense would not be available here, because the Statute of Frauds applies to the sale of goods over $500 under UCC § 2–201, and here the watch was to be sold for only $50.

Answer to Question 26

(B) is the correct answer.

The power of acceptance under a revocable offer is terminated upon the offeror's revocation of the offer, and revocable offers can be revoked at any time by the original offeror. Restatement 2d §§ 36(1)(c), 42. This is true even if the offeror says he or she will keep the offer open for a specified period of time.

A revocation is a "manifestation [by the offeror] of an intention not to enter into the proposed contract." Restatement 2d § 42. Here the offeror, Seller, revoked her offer when she said she changed her mind and would keep the table, thus terminating Buyer's power to accept the offer and form a contract. When Buyer said "I'll take it," it is Buyer who is making a new offer to purchase the table which can be accepted or rejected by Seller.

(A) is incorrect.

(A) is incorrect because Buyer did not reject the offer. A rejection is a "manifestation of intention not to accept the offer." Restatement 2d § 38. Buyer did not manifest an intention not to accept the offer. All he said is that he didn't know right then whether he wanted to accept it or not, and asked for additional time to consider the offer.

The issue is that the Seller thereafter revoked his offer, and that is when the power of acceptance terminated.

(C) is incorrect.

(C) is incorrect because, although the Seller made an offer originally, that offer was later revoked. Therefore, Buyer was unable to accept the original offer and no contract was formed. Even if Buyer had validly accepted, the statute of frauds does not apply to this transaction, because UCC § 2–201 applies for the sale of goods more than $500. Therefore, the fact that the contract was oral would not have made the contract voidable by Buyer.

(D) is incorrect.

No option contract was formed because there was no consideration given to create an option contract. Restatement 2d § 25. Seller merely was giving Buyer time to think about the offer, but Seller was free to revoke the offer at any time since it was a revocable offer.

Answer to Question 27

(A) is the correct answer.

When an offeror takes action inconsistent with a continued intent to enter into the promised contract, and this becomes known to the offeree by means of a reputable source, an effective "indirect revocation," has taken place. Restatement 2d § 43. An indirect revocation terminates the offeree's power of acceptance. Restatement 2d §§ 36(1)(c), 43. This was also the holding of *Dickenson v. Dodds*, 2 Ch. D. 463 (Eng. 1876). Here, Buyer learned from Seller's reliable co-worker that Seller had sold the exercise bike to another employee. Thus, there was an indirect revocation.

(B) is incorrect.

(B) is incorrect because Seller's offer was revocable, not irrevocable. Just because the offeror promises to hold the offer open does not make it irrevocable. To be irrevocable, there must either be an option contract (Restatement 2d § 25), a merchant's firm offer (UCC § 2–205), or one of the situations where an option contract is implied (Restatement §§ 45, 87(2)).

(C) and (D) are incorrect.

(C) and (D) are incorrect because a reputable third party can indirectly, even if not directly, revoke an offer by conveying to the offeree the actions of the offeror which make performance of the offer impossible. Restatement 2d § 43.

Answer to Question 28

(B) is the correct answer.

This rule states that upon the death of the offeror, the offer is terminated immediately, regardless of whether the offeree knows, or even should know, of the death. If the offeree does not know of the offeror's death and is reasonable in not knowing, to a reasonable person in the offeree's shoes (the objective theory), the offer appears as though it can still be effectively accepted. Because the offer cannot still be effectively accepted, this rule seems more consistent with the subjective theory of contracts (i.e. consistent with the idea that there can be no subjective meeting of the minds between the two contracting parties because one has perished), and not the objective theory.

(A) is incorrect.

(A) is incorrect because if, following the offeror's death, a reasonable person believed that the offer could still be effectively accepted, under the objective theory of contracts the offer could still be accepted.

(C) is incorrect.

(C) is incorrect for the same reason that (A) is incorrect.

(D) is incorrect.

(D) is incorrect because the rule following the death of the offeror is more consistent with the subjective theory of contracts (that there can be no subjective meeting of the minds).

Answer to Question 29

(B) is the correct answer.

No contract was formed between Seller and Buyer Jr. because an offeree's power of acceptance is terminated by the death of the offeree. Restatement 2d § 36(1)(d). Thus, once Buyer died, the power of acceptance of the original offer was terminated. If Buyer had accepted the offer, his estate would have been responsible for performing it, and paying for the car. But since the offer had not yet been accepted, the power of acceptance terminated and Buyer's estate cannot accept on his behalf.

Note that Buyer Jr. cannot accept the offer on his own behalf either because an offer can only be accepted by a person to whom it was made. Restatement 2d § 52. Thus, only Buyer, and not Buyer Jr. was entitled to accept this offer.

(A) is incorrect.

Acceptance by e-mail would have been an effective mode of acceptance, since it is a routine mode of business communication and was sent within the time provided in the revocable offer by Seller. The issue here is that the power of acceptance terminated when Buyer died.

(C) is incorrect.

(C) is incorrect because the estate did not have power to accept the offer. Reliance can sometimes be used as a "substitute" for consideration, but it cannot be used to create a power of acceptance in someone who never received a viable offer.

(D) is incorrect.

The power of acceptance had terminated when Buyer died. Therefore, the estate could not effectively accept the offer.

Answer to Question 30

(D) is the correct answer.

Here there has been a non-occurrence of an implied condition of the offer, which terminated Seller's power to accept the offer. Restatement 2d § 36(2). An implied condition of acceptance under the terms of the offer is that the subject matter of the agreement will continue to exist and continue to be legal. The power of acceptance is terminated upon the supervening illegality of the contract after the offer is made. Restatement 2d § 36, Cmt. c. Therefore, once the EPA outlawed the pesticide Seller could no longer accept Buyer's offer.

(A) is incorrect.

(A) is incorrect because it is irrelevant when the offer was made. If the subject matter of the offer becomes illegal or is destroyed before the offer is accepted, the power to accept the offer is terminated. Restatement 2d § 36(2).

(B) is incorrect.

(B) is incorrect because, again, it is irrelevant whether the acceptance was made within a reasonable time. The power of acceptance had terminated when the subject matter of the offer became illegal. Thus, Buyer can no longer accept the offer.

(C) is incorrect.

(C) is incorrect because there are no facts to support a finding that the offer was terminated by a lapse of time. Rather, the offer was terminated by the non-occurrence of an implied condition of the offer.

Answer to Question 31

(C) is the correct answer.

(C) is the correct answer because the power of acceptance is terminated by the non-occurrence of any condition of acceptance under the terms of the offer. Restatement 2d § 36(2). Sarah made an express condition of acceptance when she said she would sell the book—namely she would only sell the book on the condition that (or if) Angela won the singing competition. As soon as Angela lost, the condition of acceptance could not occur and the power of acceptance was terminated.

(A) is incorrect.

(A) is incorrect because Sarah placed a condition on the acceptance when she made the offer. When the condition did not occur, the power of acceptance was terminated.

(B) is incorrect.

(B) is incorrect because Sarah is the "master of the offer" and can place any legal condition on acceptance of the offer, regardless whether it is related to the subject matter of the contract. Therefore, the condition was valid and the power of acceptance terminated when Angela did not win the competition.

(D) is incorrect.

(D) is incorrect because Sarah did not revoke her offer. The power of acceptance terminated when the express condition did not occur.

Answer to Question 32

(C) is the correct answer.

Betty's offer is an express "indifferent" offer, meaning that it could be accepted by promise (calling her back), or performance (showing up and building the fence). When the offeree accepts an indifferent offer by beginning or tendering performance, it is treated as a promissory acceptance under Restatement 2d § 62. That is, as soon as performance started, a contract is formed and both parties are bound; it is treated the same as if Sam had said, "I accept your offer." Since Sam accepted by beginning performance, at that point both parties are bound and Betty cannot revoke. Note that most "indifferent" or "ambiguous" offers, which can be accepted either by a promise or performance at the discretion of the offeree, are implied from the circumstances, not express.

(A) is incorrect.

(A) is incorrect because Sam accepted the offer. Restatement 2d § 62 provides an ambiguous offer can be accepted by performance if the offeree begins the invited performance. Here, Sam accepted by performance by beginning to build the fence. Betty can therefore no longer revoke the offer.

(B) is incorrect.

(B) is incorrect because Betty made an effective ambiguous offer when she asked Sam to build her a fence, and told him he could either accept by promise (by calling her back), or performance (by showing up and building the fence).

(D) is incorrect.

(D) is incorrect because Betty made an ambiguous offer and under Restatement § 62, when Sam accepted by performance (by beginning to build the fence), the two entered into a contract. Under Restatement § 62, once Sam began performance, both parties were bound and Sam could not stop performance without legal consequence. This is in contrast to formation under Restatement 2d § 45. Under Restatement § 45, when there is an unambiguous offer for a unilateral contract and the offeree begins performing, the offeror and offeree are treated as if they had entered into a unilateral option contract, where the offeror can no longer revoke the offer, but the offeree can discontinue performance without consequence.

The current situation is governed by Restatement 2d § 62, and so Sam is obligated to complete performance. If it had been governed by Restatement 2d § 45, Sam would not have been obligated to complete performance.

Answer to Question 33

(C) is the correct answer.

(C) is correct because under Restatement 2d § 45, beginning performance in response to an unambiguous offer to enter into a unilateral contract creates a unilateral option contract exercisable by the offeree. Here, Alex began performance by beginning to work on the roof. This created a unilateral option contract. Owner's offer became irrevocable for a reasonable period of time which would allow Alex to finish; but the option contract is unilateral only, meaning that Alex could walk off the job without consequence.

(A) is incorrect.

(A) is not correct because, while Alex has a duty to notify Owner within a reasonable time *after* beginning performance, Restatement 2d § 54, Alex has no duty to notify Owner before beginning performance.

(B) is incorrect.

(B) is not correct because acceptance by promise is not a valid acceptance in response to an unambiguous offer to enter into a unilateral contract.

(D) is incorrect.

(D) is not correct because under Restatement 2d § 45, the option contract is unilateral only, and beginning performance does not obligate Alex to finish the job.

Answer to Question 34

(C) is the correct answer.

(C) is correct because Restatement 2d § 62 controls when there is a beginning (or tender) of performance in response to an ambiguous offer. When an offer invites acceptance by promise or performance at the offeree's discretion, i.e., is an "indifferent" or "ambiguous" offer, Restatement 2d § 62 provides that the beginning (or tender) of performance constitutes a valid acceptance, and constitutes an enforceable contractual promise to complete the performance. Therefore, once Alex began working, both Alex and Owner were bound by the contract.

(A) is incorrect.

(A) is incorrect because Alex cannot cease work without breach. Under Restatement 2d § 62 once Alex began performance in response to an ambiguous offer, she was bound to the agreement and could not stop without being in breach.

(B) is incorrect.

(B) is incorrect because once Alex began performance, Alex and Owner were in a binding contract. Thus, Owner cannot revoke his offer anymore.

(D) is incorrect.

(D) is incorrect because Restatement 2d § 62 provides that where an offer invited the offeree to choose whether to accept by promise or performance, and the offeree begins performance, such act is treated as a promissory acceptance and constitutes a valid acceptance. Therefore, once Alex began on the roof, the two were in an enforceable contract.

Answer to Question 35

(C) is the correct answer.

(C) is correct because the parties are in a contract. The offer was ambiguous, meaning it could be accepted either by Buyer's promise to ship or by Buyer's beginning performance. Once Seller picked and tagged the vases as belonging to Buyer, it began performance. At that point, the contract was formed and neither party can terminate or back out without consequence.

(A) is incorrect.

(A) is incorrect because Seller began performance in response to an ambiguous offer, thereby accepting the offer and forming the contract. Hence Seller may not revoke without legal consequence.

(B) is incorrect.

(B) is incorrect because under Restatement 2d § 62, once Seller tendered and/or began performance, that act operated as a promise to render complete performance. Therefore, Seller cannot revoke without legal consequence.

(D) is incorrect.

(D) is incorrect for the same reason that (A) is incorrect. By identifying the goods as belonging to Buyer and tagging them as such, Seller had begun performance, and a contract was thereby formed. There was no requirement that the goods reach the Buyer before a contract was formed. As such, Buyer could not revoke without legal consequence.

Answer to Question 36

(B) is the correct answer.

Because this scenario involves the sale of goods (television sets), this situation is governed by the UCC. This was an ambiguous offer, meaning it could be validly accepted by beginning performance. UCC § 2–206. (Note that the UCC does not specifically use the term "ambiguous" or "indifferent" offer. However, UCC § 2–206 permits the offeree to choose between promising shipment of the goods, actual shipment of the goods, or beginning manufacture of the goods, as a valid means of acceptance in this type of situation, making it an "ambiguous" offer.) So when Seller began manufacturing sets, it had effectively accepted the contract.

Under UCC § 2–206(2) however, where the beginning of a requested performance is a proper manner of acceptance, the seller must notify the buyer that it is beginning to perform. If it does not, the offeror "may treat the offer as having lapsed before acceptance." Therefore, (B) is correct as it sets forth the appropriate consequence.

(A) is incorrect.

Seller's offer was ambiguous, inviting the beginning of performance as a proper acceptance. If notice was communicated to Buyer within a reasonable time, the resulting contract would be enforceable under UCC § 2–206(2). However, since no such notice was given, Buyer can treat the agreement as having lapsed.

(B) is incorrect.

Even though Seller's manufacture of the televisions acted as a valid acceptance of the offer, Buyer is not obligated to accept the televisions because it had not received notice that Seller was beginning performance within a reasonable time after it ordered the goods. Instead, under UCC § 2–206(2), the Buyer may treat the offer as having lapsed.

(D) is incorrect.

(D) is not the best choice because it sets forth the standard under a contract governed by the Restatement and not the UCC under similar fact situations. Under Restatement 2d § 54(2), where the offeree does not notify the offeror within a reasonable time of the beginning performance in a situation where the offeror would not have reason to know performance had begun, "the contractual duty of the offeror is discharged." Because this scenario deals with the sale of goods, it is governed by the "may treat the offer as having lapsed before acceptance" standard under UCC § 2–206(2) and not the "discharge" standard of Restatement 2d § 54(2). While the ultimate effects of applying the Restatement and UCC rules are similar, it is important to know the different standards.

Answer to Question 37

(B) is the correct answer.

At common law, if an offeree sent non-conforming goods in response to a unilateral contract offer, there was no acceptance of the offer. That is, if the offeror made it clear that it would only pay if it receives a banana, and the seller sends an apple, the seller has not accepted the unilateral contract offer. Instead, it has made a counteroffer to sell an apple.

While the rule makes sense in a face-to-face transaction, over time abuse arose in a situation like the following: a seller places an order for, e.g., 60-inch flat screens on a unilateral contract basis. However, the manufacturer is out of 60-inch flat screens but it has a bunch of the less popular 42-inch televisions in stock. So it would send the 42-inch screens in the hopes that the buyer will, albeit reluctantly, try to sell the 42-inch screens rather than have to go through the hassle of finding another source for the 60-inch flat screens. There was no recourse for the buyer because it was like the banana/apple scenario above—legally the seller would just be making a counteroffer for the 42-inch sets. This was known as the "unilateral contract trick."

The UCC changed this situation. In UCC § 2–206(1)(b), a seller who sends non-conforming goods in response to an offer is deemed to have simultaneously accepted the offer and breached the contract. That way, if the 42-inch flat screens come, at least the buyer can sue the seller for breach of contract and take advantage of the remedies set forth in the Code, like cover.

However, the UCC also recognizes in UCC § 2–206(1)(b) that there are certain situations in which the buyer who is out of inventory of the good ordered is really acting in good faith when it sends non-conforming goods. For example, where the buyer really believes that what it is sending would serve the buyer's needs because other buyers have liked it, etc. The UCC allows for that to occur via an "accommodation" shipment—where the seller sends some type of communication that acknowledges it is not sending conforming goods but is sending the non-conforming goods as an accommodation to the buyer. In that case, what the seller sends is merely a counteroffer, which can be accepted or not by the buyer.

Here, Manufacturer made an accommodation shipment. That is, it made a counteroffer and did not simultaneously accept the offer and breach the contract under UCC § 2–206. Retailer rejected the counteroffer when it sent the semi-widgets back. Hence there was never a contract between them and, while Retailer is entitled to reject the counteroffer, it has no right to sue Manufacturer for breach of contract.

(A), (C), and (D) are incorrect.

These are not the correct choices for the reasons set forth in the explanation of (B) above.

Answer to Question 38

(A) is the correct answer.

(A) is correct because Owner's offer was an indifferent offer, so Painter could accept by performance or promise. However, Restatement 2d § 54 provides that if an offeree who accepts by performance has reason to know that the offeror has no adequate means of learning of the acceptance, "the contractual duty of the offeror is discharged," unless the offeree uses reasonable diligence to notify owner of the acceptance, the offeror waives notice, or the offeror otherwise learns of the acceptance. Because Owner does not visit the vacation home at the time Painter will accept, Painter has a duty to notify the Owner that he is beginning to paint, or Owner's contractual duty is discharged.

(B) is incorrect.

(B) is incorrect for the reasons stated above. Restatement 2d § 54 states that an offeree must notify the offeror within a reasonable time after beginning performance if the offeree has reason to know the offeror has no means to learn of the performance.

(C) and (D) are incorrect.

(C) and (D) are also incorrect because Owner's offer was indifferent. It did not require Painter to accept by promise or by performance only.

Answer to Question 39

(B) is the correct answer.

Generally, silence in the face of an offer will not be interpreted as acceptance. However, here Barry's promise to pay for baking lessons can be inferred from his conduct in showing up at the time and place for the baking lessons and participating in them. Thus, his assent by conduct formed an implied-in-fact contract, and he is obligated to pay $550.

(A) is incorrect.

This would be the measure of Francis French–Fry's recovery under a quasi-contract theory, which is sometimes called an implied-in-*law* contract. Implied-in-fact contracts are different from implied-in-law or quasi contracts. This fact pattern involved a true contract that was based on Barry's intent to enter into the contract inferred from his conduct. Quasi contracts are not contracts at all, but rather situations in which contract law implies an obligation.

(C) is incorrect.

Given the structured nature of the cooking lessons and the application, this transaction appears to be an arms-length business transaction. For example, Barry was told that the lessons were $550. Hence, there is nothing in the facts from which a gratuitous intent may legitimately be inferred.

(D) is incorrect.

This choice <u>would be</u> correct if the correct response applied the Statute of Frauds rule that states that contracts for $500 or more must be in writing. However, that rule applies only to UCC transactions involving the sale of goods under UCC § 2–201, and this contract involved a service—cooking lessons. Services contracts must be in writing only when they cannot by their terms be performed within one year of their making. Restatement 2d § 130. The one-year-rule does not apply here because the baking lessons took less than one year from the date of the making of the contract to perform.

Answer to Question 40

(C) is the correct answer.

Under Restatement 2d § 69(1)(b), where the offeree has given the offeror reason to believe that assent to the offer may be manifested by silence or inaction, the silence or inaction of the offeree will be deemed an effective acceptance. Here, in their contract, Musician agreed to be automatically billed for a month's worth of service without any affirmative act on his part. This falls under Restatement 2d § 69(b), and Musician is stuck with the charge.

(A) is incorrect.

(A) is incorrect because to support a finding of unconscionability there must be both substantive and procedural unconscionability. Procedural unconscionability is generally an absence of meaningful choice, but here Musician could have gone with Spotify if he wanted to avoid the thirty day cancellation provision, and thus had a meaningful choice in the alternative. Substantive unconscionability requires an unfairness in the terms, and here the monthly fee was the same as Spotify and a thirty day cancellation was standard in the industry. Hence, there is no basis for finding unconscionability.

(B) is incorrect.

(B) is incorrect for the reason that (C) is correct as explained under (C) above.

(D) is incorrect.

(D) is incorrect because by means of their contract, there was a bargained-for exchange. Just because one party decides not to use the goods or services provided does not mean there was not an enforceable contract.

Answer to Question 41

(D) is the correct answer.

(D) is correct because, while Restatement 2d § 69(1)(a) provides that if an offeree takes the benefit of offered services and has reason to know that they were offered with the expectation of compensation there is an effective acceptance by silence, that rule is subject to the requirement that the offeree have opportunity to reject the offered services first. Here, Contractor built the home while Owner was in Europe. Therefore, there was no opportunity to reject the offered services, so there was no effective acceptance by silence, and thus no contract which would support a breach action.

(A) is incorrect.

(A) is incorrect because Owner did not have a reasonable opportunity to reject the services, so there was no acceptance by silence in this instance. Restatement 2d § 69.

(B) is incorrect.

(B) is incorrect because this situation would not allow a quasi-contract recovery. Quasi-contracts describe situations in which the law implies an obligation that otherwise does not exist to avoid unjust enrichment. This situation usually occurs when medical professionals render aid to persons that are unable to accept the aid. Here, Contractor knew that the property was Owner's and chose to build the home without entering into a contract to do so. Therefore, while Owner may be enriched by Contractor's actions, he is not <u>unjustly</u> enriched, and thus no quasi-contract action will prevail. Contractor is deemed to have made a gift of the home under contracts law.

(C) is incorrect.

(C) is incorrect because the price is not the issue here. The issue is that Restatement 2d § 69(1)(a) cannot apply because Owner had no reasonable opportunity to reject the services because he had no way to know of the project.

Answer to Question 42

(D) is the correct answer.

Under the "mailbox rule" an acceptance is generally valid on dispatch if it is properly dispatched and is an authorized method of acceptance. Restatement 2d §§ 63, 66, 68. An exception to this rule occurs if: (a) there is an acceptance followed by rejection; (b) the rejection is received first; and (c) the offeror relies on the rejection.

Here, the acceptance was mailed first and was an effective acceptance. The express mail rejection arrived first, however. If Sam had relied on the rejection, for example if Sam had taken another job during the same time he had offered to work for Ashley such that he could not have done both jobs, then the rejection would have become the operative response from the offeree. However, the facts do not support a finding that Sam relied on the rejection in any way. Indeed, Sam said he wanted to do the job. Therefore, Sam will prevail because the first letter (the acceptance) had legal effect when it was sent.

(A) is incorrect.

(A) is incorrect because the only way the express mail letter (the rejection) would become operative is if Sam relied on the rejection as set forth in the explanation to (D). Here, there are no facts to show Sam relied on the rejection, so the acceptance (the first mailed letter) remains effective.

(B) is incorrect.

(B) is incorrect because the acceptance letter (the first mailed letter) was effective on dispatch, so long as the rejection letter was not received first, and Sam (the offeror) did not rely on it. Again, Sam did not rely on the rejection, so the acceptance remained operative.

(C) is incorrect.

(C) is incorrect because the second letter (the rejection letter) would only have legal effect if it was received first, and Sam relied on it. Though it was received first, Sam did not rely on it, so the letter sent by express mail did not have legal effect at all.

Answer to Question 43

(A) is the correct answer.

Under the "mailbox rule," when a rejection is followed by an acceptance, the first to arrive becomes the operative response. Restatement 2d § 63. Betty's June 24 letter is a counteroffer, which serves as a rejection. Her June 25 letter (the letter sent by express mail) is an acceptance. The June 24 letter arrived first, so it is the operative document. Thus, (A) is correct and Sam will lose because the rejection was received first and is therefore the operative response.

(B) is incorrect.

(B) is incorrect because under the "mailbox rule" rejection letters are never operative on dispatch. The rejection letter is only operative in this instance because it arrived before the acceptance letter, not because it was the first to be mailed.

(C) is incorrect.

(C) is incorrect because in order for the acceptance letter to be operative, it would have had to be received first. Here, the rejection letter was received first, so it is operative.

(D) is incorrect.

(D) is incorrect for the same reason (C) is incorrect, the rejection letter was received first, so it is the operative response.

Answer to Question 44

(C) is the correct answer.

Under the "mailbox rule," where an offeree sends a rejection followed by an acceptance, the first response to arrive is operative. Here, the June 25 express mail acceptance arrived first, so the contract was made at that point. Once an offer has been effectively accepted, it can no longer be rejected, and thus Sam's receipt of the June 25 counteroffer/rejection sent by express mail has no effect.

(A) is incorrect.

(A) is incorrect because for Sam to lose, he would have had to receive the counteroffer/rejection first. Here, he received the acceptance first, so a contract was formed.

(B) is incorrect.

(B) is incorrect for the same reason that (A) is incorrect. Sam will prevail because he received the acceptance before he received the counteroffer/rejection.

(D) is incorrect.

(D) is incorrect because under the "mailbox rule," a rejection is operative when it is received, not when it is sent.

Answer to Question 45

(C) is the correct answer.

Absent facts and circumstances to the contrary, an estimate is not considered an offer, but rather a solicitation for an offer. Restatement 2d § 26, Cmts. b and c. Therefore, there is as yet no contract, and Owner has made an enforceable offer which can be accepted or rejected by Plumber.

(A), (B), and (D) are incorrect.

These choices are all incorrect for the reason that (C) is correct.

Answer to Question 46

(A) is the correct answer.

Once Plumber began work, she accepted the offer of Owner, and they were in an enforceable bilateral contract. As such, it is irrelevant what others in the area would have charged, because the terms of *this* contract were $60/hour.

The question then becomes whether the correct charge is $240 or $270. The general rule is that when work is done on the basis of an estimate, a person in the position of the Owner is agreeing to pay for the actual value of the work, and not the estimated price, so long as the work was done in good faith. If Owner wanted a fixed price, he needed to negotiate a fixed price contract, and not gone forward on the basis of an estimated time commitment.

(B) is incorrect.

(B) is incorrect because the contract was based on an estimate, not a fixed price. To get a fixed price, the Owner and Plumber would have had to enter into further negotiations so that Plumber agreed to accept the risk that she might spend more time than she estimated and was willing to commit to a price. (Of course, if she spent less time than she estimated, she would still be entitled to $240 under a fixed price contract). The convention is that when contracting by means of an estimate, the risk is on the person in the position of Owner that the work might take longer than estimated, and that individual has agreed to pay for the time actually expended, again assuming good faith. On the other hand, if the work took less than the four hour estimate, the person in the position of the Owner is entitled to the benefit of that shorter time expenditure, and would only be obligated for the actual time spent performing the job.

(C) and (D) are incorrect.

As explained above in the explanation to (A), once Plumber began work, she entered into an enforceable contract for $60/hour with Owner, and thus it is irrelevant what other plumbers would charge for the work.

Answer to Question 47

(B) is the correct answer.

The fact situation described is a quintessential example of a situation allowing for quasi-contractual recovery. "Quasi-contract" is also known as "implied-in-law" contract. It describes situations in which there is no contract formed at all, but where law and society had decided that compensation is nonetheless due and thus imply an obligation as a matter of law. Often it applies to a situation in which a heath care professional provides services to an unconscious individual. The theory is that, had the individual been conscious, he or she almost certainly would have accepted an offer of assistance. Dr. Brown is entitled to recovery even though the victim died because the victim was benefited by her efforts.

Quasi-contract is actually a species of restitutionary recovery whereby the law seeks to avoid unjust enrichment. The idea is the injured victim was *enriched* by Dr. Brown's services and it would be *unjust* for him to retain those benefits without paying for them. In restitution, the amount of the enrichment is judged by the average value of those services within the community. So Dr. Brown is not entitled to whatever she generally charges ($2,000), but what the average trauma doctor charges in the community ($400). In restitution language, quasi-contractual recovery is based on the "cost avoided" basis of recovery in restitution, which values the services at the average amount charged in the community for the services that the enriched party avoided having to pay in obtaining the benefit. Restatement 2d § 371(a).

(A) is incorrect.

As explained above, recovery in quasi-contract is based on the average value for the services in the community, not the rate at which Dr. Brown charges.

(C) is incorrect.

(C) is incorrect because the estate is liable for the contractual obligations, including quasi-contractual obligations, of the deceased. So while the estate cannot accept an (heretofore unaccepted) offer that has been made to the deceased before his or her passing under Restatement 2d § 36(1)(d), the estate is obligated for contractual obligations (where the deceased had entered into a contract or incurred a quasi-contractual obligation) before passing.

(D) is incorrect.

(D) is incorrect because this is a situation in which Dr. Brown is entitled to quasi-contractual recovery, as described above.

CHAPTER 2
UCC § 2–207

ANSWERS

Answer to Question 1

(D) is the correct answer.

This is a quintessential UCC § 2–207 case. At common law, there would have been no contract between Daycare and Company because of the discrepancy in the shipping terms. This was known as the common law "mirror image rule" and it provided that if the offer and acceptance were not mirror images of each other, no contract was formed.

Under UCC § 2–207, discrepancies between the offer and acceptance usually do not result in there being no contract. (The instances where such discrepancies will still result in no contract being formed are illustrated in other questions in this chapter).

The way to analyze a UCC § 2–207 case is to start by asking whether a contract was formed by the exchange of the writings or forms under UCC § 2–207(1). If the purported acceptance was a "definite and seasonable expression of acceptance," and the acceptance was not "expressly made conditional" on the offeror's assent to the additional or different terms in the acceptance, a contract has been formed, even if there are some differences between the two writings.

Here, Company's acceptance was definite because it involved the same subject matter, quantity, and price as the Purchase Order. The acceptance was seasonable because upon receiving the Purchase Order, Company immediately sent its Acceptance of Purchase Order. Therefore, the two are in a contract based on UCC § 2–207(1) and when Company did not deliver the food on the promised date, it breached the contract.

(A) is incorrect.

(A) is incorrect because this states the rule under common law's "mirror image" rule. It is because of the unfairness to the buyer in this situation—Daycare would not be alone in only checking to ensure the type of food, price, quantity, and delivery date were correct and then not reading all the pre-printed prolix of the acceptance and expecting that the food would be delivered on time—that the drafters of the UCC decided UCC § 2–207 was needed.

(B) is incorrect.

(B) is incorrect because Daycare did not have to assent to the different term to form a contract under UCC § 2–207(1).

(C) is incorrect.

(C) is incorrect because a contract had formed between Daycare and Company based on Daycare's Purchase Order and Company's Acceptance of Purchase Order, for the reasons stated above. Therefore, it is irrelevant whether Daycare materially relied on Company sending the dog food.

Answer to Question 2

(A) is the correct answer.

(A) is correct because under UCC § 2–207 Contractor and Supplier had a contract for windowpanes of stainable quality.

The first step is to determine whether the parties had a contract based on the exchange of their forms under UCC § 2–207(1). They did. Supplier's Acceptance of Purchase Order was an acceptance because it is a "definite and seasonable expression of acceptance." UCC § 2–207(1). The acceptance was seasonable in that Supplier immediately sent the acceptance, and it was definite because it dealt with the same terms of Contractor's offer (with the exceptions of the Limitation Clause and the provision regarding the stainable quality of the windows).

The next step is to determine what terms became part of that contract. When a contract is formed by exchange of forms under UCC § 2–207(1), the terms of the agreement are determined under UCC § 2–207(2). Under UCC § 2–207(2)(a), the different term of the acceptance does not become a part of the contract if the offeror included a clause in his or her form limiting acceptance to the terms of the offer, which occurred here. Thus, the terms of the contract were those in Contractor's Purchase Order, which called for stainable quality windows. Since that's not what Contractor was sent, Supplier breached.

(B) and (D) are incorrect.

These results would be correct under common law, which would judge this scenario under the "last shot doctrine," which provides that when the parties perform, the last document exchanged between the parties becomes the operative document. In other words, under the last shot doctrine, Supplier's Acceptance would be deemed a counter-offer, and that counter-offer would be deemed accepted by conduct when Contractor accepted the windows. In that case, the contract would be for paintable quality windows only.

(C) is incorrect.

(C) is incorrect because, as explained above, the contract was for stainable quality windowpanes.

Answer to Question 3

(C) is the correct answer.

(C) is correct because this problem illustrates one of the exceptions to the general rule under UCC § 2–207 that the exchange of forms usually results in an enforceable contract.

Under UCC § 2–207(1), an acceptance that has additional or different terms operates as an acceptance if it is "a definite and seasonable expression of acceptance." Here, the "confirmation" is not a definite and seasonable expression of acceptance because the terms are too different from the offer. That is, an offer to buy 500 pounds of grapes at $3 per pound is not accepted by a promise to sell 500 pounds of bananas at $18 per pound. These are two different transactions.

In the language of UCC § 2–207(1), Buyer's form was not a "definite . . . expression of acceptance." The legal effect of an acceptance that is so far different than the offer is that the purported acceptance is treated as a counter-offer. So the status of the parties is that Seller had made an offer of 500 pounds of grapes at $3 per pound, and Buyer made a counteroffer to sell 500 pounds of bananas at $18 per pound. As the counteroffer was never accepted, no contract was formed between the parties, making Choice (C) correct.

(A) and (B) are incorrect.

(A) and (B) are incorrect because the Purchase Order form and the "confirmation" were too different for the "confirmation" to constitute an acceptance. Therefore, Buyer and Seller have no contract at all.

(D) is incorrect.

(D) is incorrect because it does not matter whether Seller ships 500 pounds of bananas, Buyer would have no duty to accept the bananas because Buyer and Seller are not in a contract. If Seller shipped the bananas and Buyer accepted, however, the two would be in a contract based on their actions, but the sending of the bananas, by itself, does not make a contract.

Answer to Question 4

(D) is the correct answer.

This question illustrates another example of a situation in which a purported acceptance with additional or different terms does not result in an enforceable contract.

UCC § 2–207(1) states that if a purported acceptance makes acceptance "expressly . . . conditional on assent to the additional or different terms" found in the purported acceptance, then the acceptance/acknowledgment is treated as a counter-offer. Here, Seller's Acknowledgment form states: "Seller's acceptance is hereby expressly made conditional on Buyer's assent to the additional and different terms of this Acknowledgment." Thus, Seller has made a counteroffer, and the counteroffer was not accepted. As such, there is no enforceable contract between them, making Choice (D) the correct choice.

(A), (B), and (C) are incorrect.

(A), (B), and (C) are incorrect for the reasons Choice (D) is correct. When Seller stated that acceptance was "expressly conditioned" on Buyer's assent to the additional or different terms found in the Acknowledgement, Seller made a counter-offer, rather than an acceptance under UCC § 2–207(1).

Answer to Question 5

(C) is the correct answer.

The way UCC § 2–207 is structured is that if there is no contract formed by the exchange of forms under UCC § 2–207(1), the only way a contract *might* thereafter be formed is by conduct. As provided in UCC § 2–207(3), "Conduct by both parties which recognizes the existence of a contract is sufficient to establish a contract for sale although the writings of the parties do not otherwise establish a contract." Here, Seller sent the laptops and Buyer accepted them. As such their actions established a contract.

The next issue is what the terms of that contract are. UCC § 2–207(3) continues, "In such case [where there is a contract by conduct] the terms of the particular contract consist of those terms on which the writings of the parties agree . . ." This is known as the "knock out rule," whereby the terms both parties have in their forms become part of the contract, and those terms in which only one party has in its form is knocked out. As a consequence, the correct warranty claims period is neither the one year period provided by Buyer in the Purchase Order nor the ninety day period provided by Seller in the Acknowledgement, but rather whatever the law would otherwise provide if neither party had anything about a warranty claims period in its forms (which would be four years, under UCC § 2–725).

(A), (B), and (D) are incorrect.

These choices are incorrect under the "knock out" rule of UCC § 2–207(3) as explained above.

Answer to Question 6

(C) is the correct answer.

The issue here is whether the "subject to" clause is equivalent to the "acceptance is expressly made conditional on assent to the additional or different terms" language of UCC § 2–207(1). The reason this is an issue is that a purported acceptance which has the "acceptance is expressly made conditional ..." language is treated as a counter-offer. If the purported acceptance is really a counter-offer, then there was no contract based on an exchange of the writings, and both contract formation and the terms of any resulting contract would be judged under UCC § 2–207(3).

This exact issue was addressed in *Dorton v. Collins & Aikman Corp.*, 453 F.2d 1161 (6th Cir. 1972). There, the court held that the "subject to" clause was very different from the "acceptance is expressly made conditional on assent to additional or different terms" clause in UCC § 2–207(1). The reason is that in the latter, by definition the offeror must affirmatively assent to the additional or different term(s), or else no contract is formed by the writings.

But the *Dorton* court said that by using the phrase "subject to," the offeree was trying to "slip in" its terms by silence. That is, by saying, in essence, "my acceptance is subject to my arbitration clause and if you don't object, my terms become operative," the offeree is trying to gain an unbargained for advantage by silence. The court would not allow such a stealthy insertion of a term to occur.

Accordingly, by not requiring an affirmative assent by the offeror, Seller's form here was not a counteroffer, but rather an acceptance, with different terms. Since the parties have a contract based on the exchange of writings, the terms of that contract are judged under UCC § 2–207(2). That provision states that, between merchants, the additional terms in the acceptance become part of the contract *unless* one of the conditions in UCC § 2–207(2)(a)–(c) exist. One of those conditions is where the offeror expressly limited acceptance of its offer to the terms of the offer/purchase order, as occurred here. UCC § 2–207(2)(a). As such, the arbitration clause does not become part of the contract, and the court should not order the case to arbitration.

(A) is incorrect.

(A) is incorrect because the "subject to" language does not make Seller's purported acceptance into a counter-offer. It is a valid acceptance and under UCC § 2–207(2)(a), the arbitration clause does not become operable, and hence (A) is not correct. This problem is based on *Dorton v. Collins & Aikman Corp.*, 453 F.2d 1161 (6th Cir. 1972), where the court held that this exact language (the "subject to" clause) was insufficient to transform the acceptance into a counter-offer.

(B) is incorrect.

(B) is incorrect because Buyer's knowledge of the clause is neither relevant nor determinative. Whether the arbitration clause becomes part of the contract is determined under UCC § 2–207(2), and since the offer limited acceptance only to the terms of the offer, the arbitration clause cannot become part of the contract. UCC § 2–207(2)(a).

(D) is incorrect.

(D) is incorrect because the "knock out" rule is only applicable in situations in which UCC § 2–207(3) controls formation, which is itself only applicable when the parties fail to have a contract formed by the exchange of their writings and the question is whether they have a contract by conduct. Here, the contract is established by the exchange of forms under UCC § 2–207(1) and thus the terms are determined under UCC § 2–207(2). As such, UCC § 2–207(3) and its "knock out" rule plays no role in the resolution of this problem.

Answer to Question 7

(D) is the correct answer.

Once a contract is found based on the exchange of the writings under UCC § 2–207(1), the next step in the UCC § 2–207 analysis is to go to UCC § 2–207(2) to determine what terms are part of that contract.

Under UCC § 2–207(2), if the contact is between merchants, any additional terms in the acceptance become part of the contract *unless* one of the situations described in UCC § 2–207(2)(a)–(c) applies. Under UCC § 2–207(2)(b), one of those exceptions where the additional terms of the acceptance do <u>not</u> become part of the contract is when the additional terms of the acceptance "materially alter" the deal.

UCC § 2–207, Cmt. 4 provides that clauses which "materially alter" the contract are those that "result in surprise or hardship if incorporated without express awareness by the other party." In other words, they are terms which the other party would be surprised once he or she was aware that they were "slipped" into the contract. Comment 4 then goes on to list several of such common clauses, one of which is "a clause negating . . . standard warranties." Therefore, the additional term here, the warranty disclaimer, will not become a part of the contract. (If you are wondering what kinds of clauses would not cause the other party to be surprised to find it "slipped" into to the contract, *see* UCC § 2–207, Cmt. 5).

(A) is incorrect.

(A) is incorrect because Buyer does not have to object to the term to keep it out. Because it materially alters the deal, the warranty disclaimer does not become part of the contract, regardless of the action of Buyer. In other words, the word "unless" makes (A) incorrect because the same result would occur even if Buyer failed to object to the term.

(B) is incorrect.

(B) is incorrect because, while UCC § 2–207(2) states that additional terms in the offeree's acceptance become part of the contract when two merchants are involved, there are three exceptions when that does not occur. This problem demonstrates the exception set forth in UCC § 2–207(2)(b), that additional terms do not become a part of the contract if they materially alter the deal. Here, a disclaimer of all warranties materially alters the deal, as described in UCC § 2–207, Cmt. 4, and so the additional term will not become a part of the contract.

(C) is incorrect.

(C) is incorrect because while a clause by the offeror (here Buyer) limiting acceptance to the terms of the offer would mean that the warranty disclaimer would not become part of the contract under UCC § 2–207(2)(a), that is not the only way nor the only reason such a clause would not be incorporated. Because a warranty disclaimer also materially alters the deal, it does not become part of the contract under UCC § 2–207(2)(b) as well.

Answer to Question 8

(D) is the correct answer.

The analysis of this problem is the same as Question 7. The question then becomes whether the clause allowing the seller to cancel the contract "materially alters" the deal. Under UCC § 2–207, Cmt. 4, "a clause reserving to the seller the power to cancel upon the buyer's failure to meet any invoice when due" is a clause which materially alters the contract. As such, Choice (D) is the correct answer.

Typically professors do not like to force students to make a call such as whether a particular clause "materially" alters the contract, unless there is some objective basis such as a case or comments to a statute that say so. With that said, it might well be prudent to memorize the examples of clauses given in Comments 4 and 5 to UCC § 2–207.

(A), (B), and (C) are incorrect.

These choices are incorrect for the same reasons explained in the choices of Question 7.

Answer to Question 9

(B) is the correct answer.

The structure of the analysis of this question is the same as for Questions 7 and 8. The different result stems from the fact that UCC § 2–207, Cmt. 5 provides that "a clause providing for interest on overdue invoices" is not a clause which materially alters the deal, as it is one of a number of "examples of clauses which involve no element of unreasonable surprise and which therefore are to be incorporated in the contract . . ."

(A), (C), and (D) are incorrect.

These choices are incorrect for the reasons explained in Question 7, and set forth in the explanation of (B) above.

Answer to Question 10

(A) is the correct answer.

The first step in the UCC § 2–207 analysis is to determine whether a contract is formed by exchange of the writings under UCC § 2–207(1). Here, Seller's Acknowledgement was sent timely and was a definite expression of acceptance. There was no "acceptance is expressly made conditional . . ." language in the acceptance. As such, the parties have a contract based on the exchange of their forms.

Once a contract is found based on the exchange of the writings under UCC § 2–207(1), analysis goes to UCC § 2–207(2) to determine what terms are part of that contract. Under UCC § 2–207(2), if the contract is between merchants, any additional terms in the acceptance become part of the contract *unless* one of the situations described in UCC § 2–207(2)(a)–(c) applies. Under UCC § 2–207(2)(a), one of those situations where the additional terms of the acceptance do <u>not</u> become part of the contract occurs when notification of objection to them . . . is given within a reasonable time after notice of them is received."

Here Buyer objected to the arbitration clause within a reasonable time after receiving the acceptance (she read the form and immediately called Buyer), and thus the arbitration provision will not become part of the contract.

(B) is incorrect.

(B) is incorrect because it does not matter whether Buyer expressly limited acceptance to the terms of the offer, because Buyer notified Seller that she objected to the arbitration clause. Therefore, under UCC § 2–207(2)(c), the arbitration clause is not a part of the contract.

(C) is incorrect.

(C) is incorrect for the reasons stated above. The arbitration clause did not become a part of the contract because Buyer notified Seller of her objection within a reasonable time. UCC § 2–207(2)(c).

(D) is incorrect.

(D) is incorrect because, while the arbitration clause would also not become part of the contract if the court found it materially alters the contract under UCC § 2–207(2)(b), the clause also does not become part of the contract because Buyer objected to it, pursuant to UCC § 2–207(2)(c).

The reason this choice is incorrect is the word "unless." The way it is structured states that if the court does not find that the arbitration clause materially alters the deal, it will become part of the contract. As explained above, that is not true because regardless of its materially altering characteristic, it will be excluded from the contract because Buyer objected to the arbitration clause under UCC § 2–207(2)(c).

Answer to Question 11

(D) is the correct answer.

Once a contract is found based on the exchange of the writings under UCC § 2–207(1), the next step in a UCC § 2–207 analysis is to go to UCC § 2–207(2) to determine what terms are part of the contract.

Under UCC § 2–207(2), where either one of the parties is a non-merchant, then "the additional terms [found in the acceptance] are construed as proposals for addition to the contract." Because Buyer is an individual, any different term found in Rip–Off's Acceptance would only be a proposal made to Buyer which he could accept or reject as he saw fit. Only if Buyer affirmatively accepted the arbitration clause would it become part of the contract.

(A), (B), and (C) are incorrect.

These choices are incorrect because when a non-merchant is involved, any different term found in the acceptance is only a proposal that is made to the offeror, which the offeror would have to affirmatively accept to make it part of the contract. Hence it is irrelevant whether the term materially alters the contract or objection is made to it, etc. The term simply never becomes part of the deal unless the offeror affirmatively accepts it.

Answer to Question 12

(C) is the correct answer.

Choice I is false because the situation described <u>is</u> decided by UCC § 2–207. UCC § 2–207(1) provides, "A definite and seasonable expression of acceptance *or a written confirmation which is sent within a reasonable time* operates as an acceptance." Similarly, UCC § 2–207, Cmt. 1 provides, "This section is intended to deal with two typical situations. <u>The one is the written confirmation, where an agreement has been reached orally</u> . . ." (Emphasis added).

What happens in this situation is that the oral agreement of the parties is viewed as the "offer" and it is compared to the terms of the confirmation, which is then examined for additional or different terms, as if it was the acceptance in a more typical exchange of forms situation.

Choice III is false because UCC § 2–207, Cmt 5 provides, "a clause fixing a reasonable time for complaints within customary limits" is a clause that does not "materially alter" the deal.

Choice II is true. If either of the parties were a non-merchant, any arbitration clause in the acceptance would only be a proposal for addition to the contract, and would have to be specifically agreed to by the buyer/offeror to be effective under the first sentence of UCC § 2–207(2). If both parties were merchants, the buyer's previous objection to arbitration would mean it would not become part of the deal (unless the buyer changed its mind) under UCC § 2–207(2)(a) and/or (2)(c).

(A), (B), and (D) are incorrect.

These choices are incorrect for the reasons that Choice (C) is correct.

Answer to Question 13

(D) is the correct answer.

This question is presented to illustrate a rather sophisticated issue under UCC § 2–207. If you examine UCC § 2–207(1) you will see that a purported acceptance can be effective even if it "states terms additional to or different from those" in the offer. But when you examine UCC § 2–207(2) to determine whether those additional or different terms become part of the contract, you will see that the word "different" is left out. It states only, "The additional terms are to be construed as proposals . . ." The issue is then what happens to terms in the purported acceptance that are "different" from those in the offer. UCC § 2–207(2).

As Choice (D) suggests, different courts have adopted different approaches to deal with the issue. There are three such approaches. The first theory is that "different" terms should be treated the same as "additional" terms. This theory is supported by UCC § 2–207, Cmt. 3, which provides, "whether or not additional *or different* terms will become part of the agreement depends upon the provisions of subsection (2)." (Emphasis added). UCC § 2–207, Cmt. 3. This treats the omission of "different" terms from the text of UCC § 2–207(2) as essentially a typo.

The second theory is known as the "literalist" approach, which states that the "different" terms never become a part of the contract unless the offeror specifically and separately agrees to them. This treats the omission of "different" from UCC § 2–207(2) as deliberate, meaning "different" terms never become part of the contract, even if some "additional" terms can become part of the deal, at least when the contracting parties are merchants. It is known as the "literalist" approach because it applies the words of the statute literally.

The third and final approach is known as the "Cmt. 6" approach, which states that because the offer and acceptance forms conflict, it can be assumed that each party objects to the "different" terms in the other's form. Therefore, under the "knock out rule," each clause will be knocked out of the other's form, and there is either no term on this issue, or either a "gap filler," or the law that would apply if nothing was mentioned about these terms in either form is used to provide the operative term under the contract. It is known as the "Cmt. 6" approach because there is some support for the idea of a mutual implied objection in Cmt. 6, but in truth, the approach stretches the language of the comment and is really a policy choice to make a situation work which is not dealt with in the text of UCC § 2–207 itself.

(A), (B), and (C) are incorrect.

(A), (B), and (C) are incorrect for the reasons stated above.

Answer to Question 14

(B) is the correct answer.

Author's Note:

For this and all the remaining questions in this chapter, note that we are dealing with a "different" term in the purported acceptance. It is a "different" term because Buyer has indicated a delivery date of October 1 and Seller has indicated a "different" delivery date of October 5.

(B) is correct because under the first approach to "different" terms, which finds support in UCC § 2–207, Cmt. 3, different terms are treated the same as if they were additional terms under UCC § 2–207(2). Because Seller's Acknowledgment form states the same quantity and price of notebooks as Buyer's Purchase Order and was made in a timely manner, the Acknowledgment is a definite and seasonable expression of acceptance under UCC § 2–207(1). Thus, UCC § 2–207(2) determines whether the different term (October 5 delivery date) becomes a part of the contract.

Under UCC § 2–207(2), because the contract is between merchants, the different term in the acceptance (October 5) becomes operative unless it materially alters the deal, as prescribed in UCC § 2–207(2)(b).

(A) is incorrect.

(A) is incorrect because October 1 was the delivery date stated in the offer. Thus, only if the delivery date materially alters the offer would the date be October 1. If it materially altered the offer, it would fall into one of the exceptions under UCC § 2–207(2), and the different delivery date in the acceptance would not become a part of the contract.

(C) is incorrect.

(C) is incorrect because this would be the result under the literalist approach. Under the literalist approach, different terms cannot be a part of the contract unless specifically agreed to by the offeror.

(D) is incorrect.

(D) is incorrect because this would be the result under the "Cmt. 6" approach. Under the "Cmt. 6" approach, the different terms will "knock each other out" and either there will be no term on that issue, or a gap filler will be used to establish a term.

Answer to Question 15

(C) is the correct answer.

(C) is the correct answer because under the literalist approach, the different term in the acceptance will never be a part of the contract unless the offeror specifically and separately agrees to it. Thus, unless Buyer specifically agrees to an October 5 delivery date, October 1 (the date on the offer) will be the delivery date.

(A) is incorrect.

(A) is incorrect because October 1 is the date specified in the offer. October 1 will automatically be the delivery date, unless Buyer agrees to change the date to October 5 under this theory.

(B) is incorrect.

(B) is incorrect because it states the result under the "different" terms theory that finds support under UCC § 2–207, Cmt. 3, as explained in Question 14.

(D) is incorrect.

(D) is incorrect because it states the result which would be true under the "Cmt. 6" theory, as explained in Question 16 below.

Answer to Question 16

(D) is the correct answer.

(D) is correct because under the "Cmt. 6" theory, if the offer and acceptance forms conflict, it is assumed that each party objects to the clause in the other's form. Therefore, the "knock out rule" applies and each clause will be knocked out of the other's form. There will thus either be no term on the issue (and the law that normally applies in the absence of a term will become operative), or a gap filler is used to provide the term. Here, the delivery term would be knocked out, and the time for delivery would be a "reasonable time" under the UCC gap filler regarding the time of delivery. UCC § 2–309.

(A) is incorrect.

(A) is incorrect because under the "Cmt. 6" rule, both the October 1 and October 5 delivery date are "knocked out." The delivery date will be a reasonable time under the UCC gap filler, as explained in Choice (D).

(B) is incorrect.

(B) is incorrect because it states the result that would be true under the "different" terms theory that finds support under UCC § 2–207, Cmt. 3, as explained in Question 14.

(C) is incorrect.

(C) is incorrect because this would be the result under the literalist approach. Under the literalist approach different terms cannot be a part of the contract unless specifically agreed to by the offeror. Under the "Cmt. 6" approach, however, the different terms are both knocked out and a gap filler is used to establish the term.

CHAPTER 3
INDEFINITENESS AND GAP FILLERS

ANSWERS

Answer to Question 1

(C) is the correct answer.

The indefiniteness doctrine regulates the enforceability of contracts when a court cannot determine the agreement's essential or material terms, or cannot, with sufficient precision, fashion an appropriate remedy for its breach. Both offers themselves (Restatement 2d § 33(1)), and the resulting entire agreement (Restatement 2d § 33(2)) must be sufficiently definite to be enforceable. In situations involving indefiniteness as to the entire agreement, the agreement is not enforceable unless "[it] provide(s) a basis for determining the existence of a breach and for giving an appropriate remedy." Restatement 2d § 33(2).

There are four main reasons as to why a court will not enforce a contract when it cannot ascertain essential terms with sufficient certainty:

(1) if a court does not know what a term to a contract is, the court cannot tell whether that term was breached;

(2) if a court does not know what a term to a contract is, it cannot fashion an appropriate remedy for the breach of that term;

(3) courts have traditionally expressed a reluctance to rewrite a contract for the parties, which they would have to do in order to enforce an indefinite agreement; and

(4) there was a suspicion by early common law courts that if the parties had not reached agreement on an essential or material term like price, they probably did not reach a final agreement as to the deal, and were still in the process of negotiating. Hence, allowing a claim for breach of contract would not be effectuating the intent of the parties.

Under a strict application of the common law indefiniteness doctrine, Priscilla would prevail because the agreement would be unenforceable because: (1) the court cannot tell when construction is due, so it cannot tell whether the contract has been breached; (2) even if the court could tell that the contract has been breached, it cannot fashion an appropriate remedy, for it is impossible to tell on what date damages began to run; and (3) to make the contract definite, the court would have to rewrite the contract and insert a construction date, something courts, at common law at least, were generally unwilling to do. Also, (4) there would be suspicion that the parties were still negotiating.

Although the parties have "agreed to agree" on the construction beginning and end date, the facts indicate that they have not made good on that agreement to determine the term at a later date.

Note that under Restatement § 204, a court is empowered to supply essential terms in certain situations, as explained in Question 2 below.

(A) is incorrect.

As discussed in the explanation of Choice (C) above, Sarah will lose because the contract is unenforceable due to indefiniteness.

(B) is incorrect.

(B) is incorrect because a writing would not, by itself, make the contract enforceable. The problem with the agreement is not that it is within the Statute of Frauds and requires a writing under Restatement 2d § 110, but rather it fails to be enforceable due to indefiniteness. Restatement 2d § 33(2).

(D) is incorrect.

(D) is incorrect for the same reasons (B) is incorrect, i.e., because the problem with the enforceability of the agreement is indefiniteness, not whether there was a writing.

Answer to Question 2

(A) is the correct answer.

Under a strict application of the early common law, the parties to a contract had to manifest understandable agreement about the following essential or material terms: (1) the subject matter of the contract; (2) the quantity to be purchased; (3) the price; (4) the time of performance; (5) the place of performance; and (6) payment terms. If the agreement did not contain these terms the contract was deemed unenforceable because it was too indefinite. Sometimes a court would be flexible as to overlook the absence of certain of these terms, but English common law courts routinely refused to enforce agreements without one of the terms listed above for the reasons given in the answer to Question 1 above.

However, modern contract law has relaxed the indefiniteness rule, but not eliminated it. Under both the Restatement 2d and the UCC, a contract will still fail for indefiniteness if the court cannot find a reasonably certain basis to determine the existence of a breach or fashion an appropriate remedy. Restatement 2d § 33(2); UCC § 2–204(3). However, modern contract law has relaxed the indefiniteness rule by applying it differently and by granting a court the authority to insert certain terms into the agreement when the parties have failed to do so. It has done so in two ways.

First, in situations in which the parties have agreed to a term but that term seems ambiguous on its face, courts are now more willing to examine the circumstances surrounding a transaction so as to <u>interpret</u> the language in a way to give definite effect to an ambiguous term.

Second, as is the case here, are situations in which the parties have not reached an agreement as to a particular term. Modern courts are far more willing to examine the circumstances surrounding a transaction so as to <u>imply</u> a reasonable term that may fill in the "gaps" left by the parties. Restatement 2d § 204.

This question is based on *Shayeb v. Holland*, 73 N.E.2d 731 (Mass. 1947). There the court implied a "reasonable price" term, as determined by an appraisal, as the price to be applied when the tenant exercised the option to purchase the property.

There are several notes which must be understood to appreciate the scope of this rule. First, note that a court will not "gap fill" for either the subject matter or the quantity under the contract. If there is no demonstrable agreement on these terms, a contract will still be unenforceable due to indefiniteness,

Second, note that this problem does not present an "agree to agree" case. That is, the lease does not specifically provide that if the tenant gives proper notice, the tenant can purchase the property at a price to be agreed upon by the parties. If it did, even under modern Restatement law, a court would not insert a reasonable price term. The reasoning is that the parties themselves have made an express condition to the sale (that they reach agreement on price). So if they don't reach such an agreement, a court will not impose a deal on a party who said the price had to be agreed upon before the deal was enforceable. But where the parties say nothing about the mechanism for reaching a price, a court will assume that the parties "likely" meant the sale would be at a "reasonable" price and use some objective third party measure to determine that price.

Third, note also that the result of this question would be the same if governed by the UCC as § 2–305 provides that if price is not stated, and the parties fail to later agree, the price will be that of "reasonable price at time of delivery." The one difference between how Restatement 2d § 204 and UCC § 2–305 are applied is that the latter will apply even when there is an "agree to agree" clause as to price, whereas, for the reasons set forth above, such "agree to agree" clauses are not typically enforced under the Restatement.

(B) is incorrect.

Although this choice correctly states that Tenant would likely win, it uses the wrong manner to determine the missing term. Tenant, as winner, would not be able to unilaterally set the price term; rather, the court will <u>imply</u> a reasonable price term by examining the circumstances surrounding the transaction on the assumption that the parties' probably meant that the price would be a reasonable price pending ten years after lease formation.

(C) is incorrect.

(C) is incorrect for the reasons set forth in the explanation of Choice (A) above. Modern contract law and the Restatement 2d have relaxed the common law rule on indefiniteness and under the Restatement 2d, if the parties have sufficiently agreed upon a bargain such that it can be defined as a contract, and have not agreed with respect to an essential term, a term which is reasonable in the circumstances can be supplied by the court. Restatement 2d § 204.

(D) is incorrect.

(D) is incorrect for reasons set forth in the explanation of Choice (A) above. The agreement to exercise the option was enforceable with the court implying an objectively reasonable price term.

Answer to Question 3

(D) is the correct answer.

Although the contract may well be too indefinite, on its face, to be enforced due to the ambiguity concerning which home is covered under the agreement, contract law has developed rules which help make indefinite contracts enforceable. One of these rules provides that an ambiguity in an agreement can be removed through part performance. Restatement 2d § 34(2). Part performance removes the uncertainty and establishes "that a contract enforceable as a bargain has been formed."

Restatement 2d § 34(2). Here, when Mrs. Smith allowed Paul to landscape the Huntington Beach property, that part performance removed the uncertainty as to the location for Paul to perform his landscaping duties under the agreement, and Paul would be entitled to the full $150 contract price.

Further, a court could easily determine whether the contract had been breached because Mr. and Mrs. Smith have failed to pay and can fashion a remedy by using the price term of the contract to award damages pursuant to Restatement 2d § 33.

(A) is incorrect.

(A) is incorrect for the reasons (D) is correct. Although the term regarding which home is to be landscaped is potentially so ambiguous as to make the agreement unenforceable on indefiniteness grounds, the conduct (part performance) by the Smiths removes the uncertainty and the contract would be enforceable as requiring performance at the Huntington Beach home. Restatement 2d § 34(2). As such, Paul is entitled to the contracted for price, not just the fair market value of his services.

(B) is incorrect.

(B) erroneously assumes that the lack of a writing would make the contract unenforceable. But the Statute of Frauds would not be an issue with this problem as it does not fall within those instances specified in Restatement 2d § 110. So the contract is enforceable and, as such, Paul can recover for the contract price of $150.

(C) is incorrect.

(C) is correct in stating that the contract is enforceable, but gives the wrong reason for it being so. The contract, on its face, is likely not sufficiently definite to be enforces, and it is the part performance of Paul landscaping the Huntington Beach home that removes the uncertainty that makes the contract enforceable. Restatement 2d § 34(2).

Answer to Question 4

(D) is the correct answer.

The UCC approaches indefiniteness by including provisions that become operative if the parties have not reached a final agreement on certain terms under their contract. That is, when the parties have left "gaps" in their agreement, the UCC has rules that provide for "gap fillers" that give the courts a basis to decide whether a party is in breach and how to fashion a remedy to deal with that breach. That is, if there is sufficient evidence that the parties have actually reached an agreement to buy and sell a good, with demonstrable quantity and subject matter terms, a court will "gap fill" the missing terms from the provisions set forth in the Code.

This question is an instance in which the time of delivery is left out. There is a "gap filler" for this "gap" in the agreement, set forth in UCC § 2–309. That provision states that if no time for shipment or delivery is agreed upon, *the seller must tender the goods within "a reasonable time."* What a reasonable time is depends on all the circumstances, e.g., how complicated the good is to make, past dealings of the parties, practice within the industry, etc. The facts here do not give an indication as to the surrounding circumstances, but the answer choice provides that a court considers two weeks was a reasonable time.

(A) is incorrect.

This choice is incorrect because the parties have entered into a valid agreement even though terms that would be essential or material at common law were left out. The UCC provides "gap fillers" to supply these missing terms, which were designed as the drafter's best guess as to what the parties probably would agree to had they turned to that term. Here, the drafters picked a "reasonable time" as the gap filled time of performance when the parties fail to reach agreement on that term. UCC § 2–309.

(B) and (C) are incorrect.

Both of these choices are incorrect because they misstate the law. Neither the Buyer nor the Seller can unilaterally fill the gap left by both parties after an agreement has been made. Rather, as set forth in the explanation of (D) above, the UCC provides that performance must take place after a reasonable time if the parties have not indicated a time of performance in their contract. UCC § 2–309.

Answer to Question 5

(B) is the correct answer.

As explained in the answer to Question 4, the UCC approaches indefiniteness by including provisions called "gap fillers" which the court is entitled to insert into the agreement if the parties have not reached a final agreement on certain terms under their contract. So long as there is enough evidence to show an agreement has been reached, and there is an indication of the subject matter and quantity, the UCC authorizes the court to insert statutory gap fillers into the contract to ensure the transaction will be enforceable.

This question deals with gaps left in regards to place of delivery and time of payment. These terms are governed by UCC §§ 2–308 (place of delivery) and 2–310(a) (time of payment).

UCC § 2–308 states that, as a general rule, if the place of delivery is not agreed upon by the parties, that delivery is to take place at the <u>seller's</u> place of business or residence. However, for specific goods located somewhere else, e.g., a racehorse at a particular breeder's farm, delivery is to take place at the location of the specified goods if the parties know of the place at the time of contracting. UCC § 2–308. Applied here, there is no indication that these are specific goods located somewhere that the parties are aware of that would require delivery at another location. Therefore, delivery would occur at <u>Seller's</u> place of business. The reason for having the default "gap filler" be the Seller's place of business (or where the good is presently located) is that it assumes no shipping charges were included in the contract price. If the Seller had to send the goods to the Buyer's place of business or residence (or move them from where they currently reside), which might be more convenient for the Buyer, a shipping charge would have to be included in every contract, which the drafters of the UCC decided not to do.

UCC § 2–310 provides that in the absence of an agreement as to payment terms, payment is due *at the time and place at which the buyer is to receive the goods*. UCC § 2–310(a). Thus, Buyer would be required to pay for the widgets when they are delivered to Buyer at Seller's place of business.

(A) is incorrect.

(A) is incorrect because the parties have entered into a valid agreement as the UCC specifies agreements can still be enforceable even without agreement as to various specific terms. As set forth in the explanation to Choice (B) above, the UCC provides that the place of delivery and time of payment would be Seller's place of business with payment upon delivery and receipt. UCC §§ 2–308, 2–310(a). Thus, the contract would be enforceable with the "gap fillers" provided by the UCC.

(C) and (D) are incorrect.

Both of these answer choices incorrectly state the UCC rule as explained under Choice (B) above. Choice (C) erroneously states the rule regarding time of payment while Choice (D) erroneously states both the rule regarding place of delivery and time of payment.

Answer to Question 6

(C) is the correct answer.

This question deals with the "mode of delivery" gap filler, which is governed by UCC § 2–307. As a general rule, in the absence of an agreement by the parties, a buyer is entitled to demand delivery of all goods called for in a single contract in one lot; similarly the seller is entitled to deliver them in one lot. UCC § 2–307. However, where circumstances make it <u>reasonable</u> either to make or accept the delivery in several lots and, in good <u>faith</u>, the other party would not be <u>harmed</u> by such action, delivery or acceptance in multiple lots is required. UCC § 2–307, Cmt. 3.

For example, suppose a car dealer ordered 100 cars from the manufacturer. If it is reasonable to do so and it does so in good faith, e.g., it only has fifteen empty spaces on the lot, it can demand that the manufacturer deliver in lots so long as the manufacturer would not be harmed by such multiple lot delivery. Similarly, if the manufacturer routinely delivered 100 cars in multiple lots, it could demand such delivery if it would not harm the buyer to do so.

(A) and (B) are incorrect.

These choices incorrectly state the rule of UCC § 2–307 by ignoring circumstances that may alter the general rule as outlined under Choice (C) above. Namely, a party is not <u>always</u> required to deliver in either a single or multiple lots, but rather delivery in a single lot is the general rule, but that may be altered due to circumstances, good faith, and convenience.

(D) is incorrect.

(D) incorrectly states that Buyer has the unfettered discretion to demand delivery in multiple lots, as explained in (C), Seller and Buyer's good faith fetter the discretion of the Buyer to demand delivery in multiple lots.

Answer to Question 7

(D) is the correct answer.

When appropriate, a properly proven usage of trade, course of dealing, or course of performance can be used to "cure" an indefinite contract. UCC § 1–303; Restatement 2d § 222. Usage of trade is a practice or method of dealing involved in a vocation or trade that is common amongst those in the vocation or trade, the existence and scope of which must be proved as facts. Or in other words, there is a meaning of the term understood in the trade or industry. UCC § 1–303(c).

Course of dealing refers to the conduct concerning the past transactions between the parties in question which serves to establish a common basis of understanding for interpreting terms of the agreement. In other words, the parties have affixed a meaning of the present same or similar term used in previous contracts between the same parties. UCC § 1–303(b).

Course of performance refers to the sequence of conduct between the parties to a specific transaction. In other words, the parties have affixed a meaning of a term under the specific contract through their previous actions. UCC § 1–303(a).

Here, (A) is an example where usage of trade that could be used as a gap filler. Choice (B) is an example where course of dealing can be used as a gap filler. Choice (C) is an example where the course of performance between Contractor and Supplier can be used as a gap filler.

(A), (B), and (C) are incorrect.

These answer choices are incorrect because each would be a correct statement.

Answer to Question 8

(C) is the correct answer.

This question tests the student's knowledge of the definitions of usage of trade, course of dealing and course of performance, along with the hierarchy of which applies when they are in conflict.

The problem states that the parties have performed previously under a one month delivery agreement. This makes one month the time for delivery under their "course of dealing." UCC § 1–303(b). The problem also indicates that the usage of trade is a two week delivery. UCC § 1–303(c). (Note there is no course of performance here because this was the only delivery and order under the current contract, UCC § 1–303(a)).

Accordingly, the issue now becomes which controls when the course of dealing conflicts with the usage of trade. UCC § 1–303(e) sets forth the required hierarchy in which certain types of gap fillers supersede others when the methods of term interpretation are inconsistent. At the top of the hierarchy are the express terms of the agreement, which prevail over course of performance, course of dealing, and usage of trade. UCC § 1–103(e)(1). Next, course of performance prevails over course of dealing and usage of trade. UCC § 1–103(e)(2). Lastly, course of dealing prevails over usage of trade. UCC § 1–103(e)(3). Although the UCC does not state it explicitly, there is universal agreement that course of performance, course of dealing and usage of trade all take precedence over any of the traditional gap fillers found in UCC §§ 2–305 *et. seq.*

Applied here, there is no express term that would dictate when delivery would be set, thus, next in the hierarchy would be course of dealing, which prevails over the usage of trade, making Choice (C) the correct answer. The delivery in a "reasonable time" gap filler of UCC § 2–307 is subordinated to the delivery date established by the course of performance.

(A) is incorrect.

(A) erroneously provides that the usage of trade would be the correct gap filler. When they are in conflict, course of dealing prevails over the usage of trade. UCC § 1–303(e).

(B) is incorrect.

(B) is incorrect because there is no "course of performance" under these facts as the shipment discussed in the problem was the only shipment under the current contract, UCC § 1–303(a).

(D) is incorrect.

(D) is incorrect because the course of dealing between the parties would supply the correct "gap filler" as to the delivery dates in the absence of the agreement of the parties, and thus "save" the contract from indefiniteness.

CHAPTER 4
CONSIDERATION AND
PROMISSORY ESTOPPEL

ANSWERS

Answer to Question 1

(C) is the correct answer.

This example is loosely based on *Hamer v. Sidway*, 27 N.E. 256 (N.Y. 1891). This was an offer to enter into a unilateral contract, i.e., David was bargaining for the acts of Paul. Under a unilateral contract, the consideration supporting the offeror's promise must consist of one of the following elements: an act, a forbearance, or the creation, modification, or destruction of a legal relationship. Restatement 2d § 71(2),(3). Here, Paul gave up a legal right to engage in the activities that David wanted him to refrain from doing. In bargaining for the forbearance, David's promise is supported by adequate consideration.

(A) is incorrect.

(A) is incorrect because David bargained for Paul's refraining from playing football, and hence he received a legally enforceable benefit by having another forbear from doing a legal activity as part of the bargain. As such, there is sufficient consideration to support the promise.

(B) is incorrect.

Generally contracts which, by their very terms, cannot be completely performed within a year must be in writing to be enforceable. Restatement 2d § 130. This was such a contract, since Paul was only 14 and could not perform completely under the deal until he turned 21. However, the Restatement and a majority of courts find that there is a "reliance" exception which makes enforceable promises which would otherwise be unenforceable under the Statute of Frauds when, "the promisor should reasonably expect to induce action or forbearance on the part of the promisee ... and which does induce the action or forbearance." Restatement 2d § 139. Here, Uncle David should reasonably expect his promise to induce forbearance by Paul, and Paul did refrain from playing football, so the promise is enforceable, even though oral.

(D) is incorrect.

There is a presumption that promises among certain classes of family members are not enforceable, e.g., the promise of the husband to take the kids to school this week if the wife takes out the trash could not be sued upon in court. However, the presumption does not extend to extended family and in any event it can be overcome by the facts and circumstances. Here, the facts indicate that David is serious about the promise to Paul (making the promise in front of 100 guests at his birthday party), and given their relationship, the presumption is overcome.

Answer to Question 2

(A) is the correct answer.

The main difference between this and the previous question is the legal status of the actions constituting the forbearance. In Question 1, Paul had a legal right to play football in college and high school. However, in this question, Bill is refraining from the use of a drug which he is already under a legal obligation to forbear using, since cocaine is illegal. As such, Bill had a pre-existing duty not to engage in such illegal activity, and hence his forbearance is not a legal detriment which would make the acts adequate consideration.

(B) is incorrect.

As explained in answer choice (B) to Question 1 above, it is not the fact that the promise is oral that makes it unenforceable. Here, it is unenforceable because there is no consideration to support the promise.

(C) is incorrect.

This answer choice is incorrect for the reasons that (A) is correct, namely, that Bill's actions in this case are not adequate consideration because he has no legal right to use cocaine; thus he is not forbearing an activity he has a legal right to partake in.

(D) is incorrect.

As explained in answer choice (D) to Question 1 above, there is a presumption that promises among certain classes of family members are not enforceable. However, as explained under (A) to this question above, the problem with this question is not the fact that it is a promise between family members.

Answer to Question 3

(C) is the correct answer.

This contract is completely enforceable. Donald made an offer that Patty accepted. The consideration in this case was a "bargained-for exchange" in which both parties were given incentive to enter into the bargain by the prospect of receiving a benefit from the other ($5,000 for Donald, a car for Patty). Restatement 2d § 71.

(A) is incorrect.

(A) is incorrect because as mentioned under (C), Patty's payment of $5,000 is adequate consideration. Typically, courts will not inquire into the adequacy of one party's consideration, even if its economic value seems disproportionate to the economic value of what the other party received in return. Restatement 2d § 79(b). The reason is that courts will let parties make their own judgments as to how much a return promise or performance is worth and will not try to impose any objective economic proportionality standards regarding the validity of consideration. Thus, a "peppercorn," or (today) a dollar, etc., can generally serve as valid consideration for a promise, no matter how extravagant, so long as the promise was freely bargained for and freely given in exchange for the peppercorn, dollar, etc.

(B) is incorrect.

The parties could have effectively structured the deal so that it was not final until Patty took delivery of the car or title officially changed hands, but there is nothing in the facts to suggest that was the deal they made here. In fact, it is the opposite, the deal was done and the contract formed when Donald accepted the check. A party cannot simply renege on a contract once it is formed. Note that title is a concept that affects third parties; it is not instrumental to whether the buyer and seller formed an enforceable contract.

(D) is incorrect.

(D) is incorrect because here the contract is supported on "normal" bargained-for consideration grounds under Restatement 2d § 71. Moral consideration is synonymous with "past" considerations and refers to those sets of promises the law will enforce even though the act that induced the promise took place before the promise was made under Restatement 2d § 86. The Restatement calls these "promises for benefit [already] received." Here, Donald's desire to "help" his niece is not a type of moral obligation to her, as his promise to sell her the car was part of a contemporaneous bargained-for exchange.

Answer to Question 4

(B) is the correct answer.

This would be considered an implied-in-law contract, or quasi-contract. That is, it is a situation in which it would be unjust for a party to receive benefits from another without paying for them. Peter was benefitted by Dr. Jones's efforts and it is considered unjust for him to retain those services without paying for them, such an obligation transfers to his estate. That is, the fact that Dr. Jones's efforts were ultimately unsuccessful in saving Peter's life is irrelevant to the question of whether Peter's estate is responsible in restitution for Dr. Jones's services.

(A) is incorrect.

(A) is incorrect for two reasons. First, Smith cannot be liable on a contract theory to Dr. Jones because he never entered into a contract with Dr. Jones. Second, Smith cannot be liable in restitution under quasi-contract because Dr. Jones did not perform any services that benefitted Smith.

(C) is incorrect.

This answer choice is incorrect for the same reasons that (A) above is incorrect, because Smith cannot be liable to Dr. Jones.

(D) is incorrect.

This answer choice is incorrect for the same reasons that (B) above is correct.

Answer to Question 5

(D) is the correct answer.

The Restatement 2d has relaxed the common law rules relating to the adequacy of "past" or "moral" consideration to be effective consideration. Under Restatement 2d § 86, a promise based on past consideration will be enforceable to the extent necessary to avoid injustice unless: a) the promisee intended the benefit received by the promisor as a gift, or b) the value of the promise is disproportionate to the benefits received. Here, the students intended to make a gift of the dog wash and groom and Smith promised them $20 each *because of* their acts, but *not in exchange* for them, so it is not a bargained-for exchange, but a gratuitous promise.

(A) is incorrect.

This answer choice is incorrect because it assumes Smith made an enforceable promise, which he did not.

(B) is incorrect.

(B) is incorrect because it assumes Smith had an enforceable obligation of some sort to the students. *However,* he did not.

(C) is incorrect.

(C) is incorrect because it inaccurately states the Restatement 2d § 86 rule regarding past or moral consideration.

Answer to Question 6

(A) is the correct answer.

Smith's promise to pay Peter's widow is only a gift promise and thus unenforceable for reasons explained below.

(B) is incorrect.

Although (B) accurately states one part of the rule of Restatement 2d § 86 (*see* Answer to Question 4, above), § 86 cannot be used to enforce Smith's promise since Peter's widow provided no benefit to Jones as is required under that provision.

(C) is incorrect.

On these facts, there is no evidence that Peter's widow relied on Smith's promise such that the doctrine of promissory estoppel may apply.

(D) is incorrect.

Even if Jones obtained some peace of mind, that benefit in itself is not "bargained for" as the term is used in the Restatement 2d's formulation of consideration: a performance is bargained for if: 1) it is sought by the promisor in exchange for his or her promise; and 2) it is given by the promisee in exchange for that promise. Restatement 2d § 71(2).

Answer to Question 7

(A) is the correct answer.

Carlos's statement to Brittany was a gratuitous promise to pay for her losses. Carlos was not going to receive anything from Brittany and she was not promising to forbear any action or claim she may have in exchange for Carlos's promise. Therefore, absent any consideration, there is no enforceable contract between Carlos and Brittany.

If Brittany had threatened to sue Carlos and Carlos made the promise to get her to forbear her suit, then there might be consideration. The Restatement 2d provides that forbearance to assert a claim or the surrender of a claim or defense which proves to be invalid is not consideration unless: 1) the claim or defense is in fact doubtful because of uncertainty as to the facts or the law or 2) the forbearing/surrendering party believes at the time promises are made that the claim or defense may be fairly determined to be valid. Restatement 2d § 74. In other words, if Brittany agreed to forgo a suit against Carlos in return for a promised payment, that would be adequate consideration because Carlos and Brittany believed that the claim may be fairly determined to be valid at the time they had agreed to the settlement. But again, that is not the case as Brittany had no thoughts of suing Carlos, and it was not part of the promise for Brittany to forgo that right.

(B), (C), and (D) are incorrect.

Mistake of fact, the statute of frauds, and the indefiniteness of Carlos's promise are all inapplicable to Carlos's promise. Because the promise lacked adequate consideration, no contract was formed to which the defenses listed may be applicable.

Answer to Question 8

(D) is the correct answer.

The Restatement 2d sets forth three situations in which past or moral obligations stemming from gift promises made in recognition of past acts can serve as valid consideration to enforce a promise: when a promise is made in recognition of a benefit previously conferred on the *promisor* (subject to other requirements of Restatement 2d § 86), or promises to pay debts made unenforceable under the statute of limitations or by bankruptcy under Restatement 2d §§ 82 and 83.

Cornelius could not enforce Brett's promise because the benefit conferred by Cornelius was not received by the *promisor*, Brett, which is required under Restatement 2d § 86, but rather by Alex, Brett's adult son. Restatement 2d § 86, Cmt. a, Ill. 1. This question is loosely based on *Mills v. Wyman*, 3 Pick. 207 (Mass. 1825).

(A) is incorrect

Choice (A) is incorrect because Brett's promise was made after the benefit had already been conferred by Cornelius, and is not in exchange for anything in the future from Cornelius. It is a gratuitous promise for past services, not part of a bargained-for exchange which could constitute consideration.

(B) and (C) are incorrect.

These answers are incorrect for the reason (D) is correct, namely that the promise made here does not fit into one of the situations in which past or moral consideration can become enforceable under the Restatement 2d.

Answer to Question 9

(A) is the correct answer.

A valid obligation owing under a contract can become unenforceable because, among other things, the statute of limitations governing the claim has run, or because the debtor has discharged the obligation in bankruptcy. At common law, a promise to pay such an unenforceable debt would be deemed a gift promise and thus unenforceable.

However, the Restatement 2d has special rules governing these situations. Restatement 2d § 82 governs the statute of limitations and provides that if a debtor acknowledges that he or she still owes a debt, which is only made unenforceable due to the running of the statute of limitations, or if debtor promises not to assert the statute as a defense in a subsequent collection suit, such promises are enforceable against the debtor. Restatement 2d § 83 governs bankruptcy and provides that if a debtor expressly promises to pay all or part of a contractual debt that is either discharged in bankruptcy, or is dischargeable in bankruptcy proceedings begun before the promise was made, that promise is binding against the debtor.

Note, however, that only the <u>actual promise</u> made after the running of the statute of limitations or post-bankruptcy is enforceable; not the original debt. Here the promise was to repay $7,500, not $10,000, and thus only the former is an enforceable promise.

Note also that many bankruptcy experts state that Restatement 2d § 83 likely is in conflict with the bankruptcy code and may not be enforceable in a bankruptcy court.

(B) is incorrect.

As mentioned in the explanation for choice (A), it is the value of the post-running of the statute of limitation promise of $7,500 which is made enforceable and thus, the original debt for $10,000 would continue to be unenforceable because of the running of the statute of limitations.

(C) is incorrect.

As mentioned, Restatement 2d § 82 covers debts made unenforceable from the running of the statute of limitations. This section acts as an exception to the general rule making "past" consideration inadequate, and thus the promise here would not be unenforceable for lack of consideration.

(D) is incorrect.

Choice (D) is incorrect for the same reasons answer (A) is correct, namely, the promise is enforceable under the Restatement 2d § 82.

Answer to Question 10

(B) is the correct answer.

An exclusive dealing contract is one in which one party promises to give the other the exclusive rights to sell his, her, or its goods or services. UCC § 2–306(2). Arguably such agreements are illusory because the supplying party is bound to supply goods or services while the other party is often not contractually obligated to sell (or even try to sell) the goods or services. However, contract law makes these kinds of agreements enforceable by implying a duty of good faith on the selling party. Most courts require only a duty of "reasonable efforts," that is, the party must make a reasonable effort to market the goods or services supplied. However, UCC § 2–306(2) states the seller must use its "best efforts" to promote the sale of the product or services. Therefore, Best Buy's obligation under the exclusive dealing contract would best be described as one of "best efforts" to sell Dell computers. However, that requirement does not include a continuing obligation to purchase more as the parties have stipulated to the first agreement with later agreements to be conditioned on mutual agreement.

(A) is incorrect.

Although the agreement on its face may not state that Best Buy is obligated to do anything regarding Dell computers, contract law and UCC § 2–206 require Best Buy to at least use good faith (and likely to use its "best efforts") to market and sell the computers.

(C) and (D) are incorrect.

Best Buy's obligation is one of best efforts under UCC § 2–206. (C) and (D) both inject arbitrary limits and continuing obligations that were not in the original agreement.

Answer to Question 11

(D) is the correct answer.

A requirements contract is one in which a buyer agrees to purchase all of a particular good or service it requires from one seller, and an output contract is one in which a seller agrees to sell all its output of a particular good or service to one buyer. UCC § 2–306(1). This contract would be a requirements one.

Like exclusive dealings, contract law and the UCC impose a good faith requirement that makes these kinds of contracts enforceable and not illusory. The argument that they are illusory is that, e.g., in a requirements contract, a party is obligated to order all it wants from one supplier, but is not obligated to order anything if, in good faith, it does not need it. So it is as if the purchaser is saying, "I'll order if I feel like it." What saves it from being invalidated for lack of consideration is the good faith requirement, i.e., it is obligated to purchase its needs from the supplier if it has any good faith needs, and thus it is obligating itself to do something it did not otherwise legally have to do absent the agreement–order from the supplier if it has a good faith need for it.

UCC § 2–306(1) states that the parties have bargained for "such actual output or requirements as may occur in good faith," but that one cannot be compelled to deliver a "quantity unreasonably disproportionate to any stated estimate," if the parties went to the trouble of setting forth an estimate in their agreement.

Here, the 500% increase from the estimate, especially since the course of performance had been around the stated estimate, is a quantity unreasonably disproportionate to the estimate and is not enforceable.

(A) is incorrect.

(A) is incorrect because requirements contracts are recognized as being valid under UCC § 2–306 and the consideration, as mentioned in (D) above, is the obligation of good faith.

(B) is incorrect.

(B) is incorrect because Carl and Sammy had an enforceable contract, not a standing offer, and under UCC § 2–309(3), Sammy must give reasonable notice before he can terminate the contract.

(C) is incorrect.

Although Carl is acting in good faith in ordering 1,000 pounds, as is required under the UCC, the supplier need not supply any amount that is not reasonably proportionate to any stated estimate. Here, the amount ordered is 5 times the stated estimate.

Answer to Question 12

(A) is the correct answer.

Under the terms of the agreement, Carl is entitled to order the estimated amount under the requirements contract, and the lack of expected profit is not an excuse for failing to perform.

(B) is incorrect.

Choice (B) is incorrect because under a requirements contract, the concern is whether the person with requirements (here, Carl) is acting in good faith. Thus it is Carl's behavior and good faith that are at issue for the purposes of this question, not Sammy's bad faith. Moreover, making a decision based on losing money is not necessarily bad faith. However, it is still a breach.

(C) is incorrect.

Choice (C) is incorrect because losing a few cents per pound under the contract is not enough to trigger the commercial impracticability defense. Courts speak of costs rising 6–10 times before the defense kicks in. Going from making a few cents per pound to losing a few cents per pound would not qualify.

(D) is incorrect.

Requirements contracts are not illusory under UCC § 2–306 because of the imposition of good faith, thus the contract is enforceable.

Answer to Question 13

(B) is the correct answer.

Restatement 2d § 89 sets forth three situations in which a modification of a contract is enforceable even without new consideration, i.e., three situations which are exceptions to the pre-existing duty rule: (i) if the modification is fair and equitable in view of circumstances not anticipated by the parties when the contract was made; (ii) to the extent provided by statute; or (iii) to the extent justice requires enforcement in view of material change of position in reliance on the promise. Here, the price of gas has unexpectedly and suddenly risen, making the promise based on circumstances not anticipated when the contract was made.

Note that if Tony had not agreed to pay the increased fee per truckload, Larry would not be entitled to the extra compensation. But the question focuses on whether a modification, agreed to by both parties, is enforceable without new consideration.

(A) and (C) are incorrect.

Both of these choices are incorrect because as mentioned in (A), Restatement 2d § 89 acts as an exception to the pre-existing duty rule.

(D) is incorrect.

As explained in (B) above, there are only a few instances in which a modification under common law does not need consideration. This is contrasted with UCC § 2–209(1), which provides that modifications under the UCC does not require consideration for a modification to be binding.

Answer to Question 14

(B) is the correct answer.

The doctrine of Promissory Estoppel is set forth in Restatement 2d § 90, which states that a promise is binding if: (i) in making the promise, the promisor should reasonably expect to induce action or forbearance on the part of the promisee; (ii) the promise does in fact induce foreseeable action or forbearance by the promisee; and (iii) injustice can be avoided only by enforcement of the promise.

Here, it was foreseeable that Uncle's promise would cause Nephew to rely, and Nephew did, in fact, rely on the promise. If a court thus found the third requirement, Nephew would have a valid claim on a promissory theory, at least for the expenses Nephew incurred in taking off work and the long trip, and possibly for the watch itself. Note that it is possible that Nephew could not obtain the watch if the court determines that the trip was a necessary, but incidental, requisite to accept the gift.

(A) is incorrect.

Uncle's promise was a gift promise, and was not part of a bargained-for exchange. However, as mentioned under (B) above, the promise may still be enforceable despite a lack of consideration under a promissory estoppel theory.

(C) is incorrect.

Choice (C) is incorrect because there is no evidence that the Uncle was bargaining for anything, e.g., for Nephew's company as Uncle did not like Nephew. Rather, the trip to pick up the watch was simply an incidental act, necessary to effectuate the gift promise. Uncle did not intend to make the trip as a benefit he would receive as part of a bargained-for exchange.

(D) is incorrect.

Promises to family members can be made enforceable. There is a general (but rebuttable) presumption against contracts between family members but there is no such presumption against a promissory estoppel theory of recovery.

Answer for Question 15

(D) is the correct answer.

When a party makes a promise to the other without sufficient consideration, but the other party changes position in reliance upon the promise, the first party will be estopped from denying the enforceability of the promise. Restatement 2d § 90. Here, Pauline could show that her detrimental reliance on her grandmother's promise in spending the money to go on her trip thinking that she would be reimbursed makes the promise enforceable to the extent necessary to prevent injustice. However, under promissory estoppel, the promise is only enforceable to the extent justice requires. Here, Pauline only relied on the promise in expending $1,000, and thus justice would require that the promise only be enforced to that extent, and not to the full amount promised.

(A) is incorrect.

The general rule is that past consideration is insufficient to render a party's promise enforceable. However, here there was no past promise or performance by Pauline to induce Daniella to make the promise. Therefore, past consideration is not an issue for this problem.

(B) is incorrect.

Daniella's promise was a gift promise, but even gift promises can become enforceable under promissory estoppel principles, so long as the reliance is foreseeable, actually completed, and justice will be served by enforcing the promise. Restatement 2d § 90.

(C) is incorrect.

As explained in (B) above, the promise was only enforceable to the extent justice requires, i.e., to the extent it was actually relied upon, which means it is only enforceable to $1,000, and not to the full amount of the original promise.

Answer for Question 16

(B) is the correct answer.

Under Restatement 2d § 90(2), a charitable subscription is binding without proof that the promise induced action or forbearance.

(A), (C), and (D) are incorrect.

Restatement 2d § 90(2) makes promises to donate to a charity enforceable even in the absence of a showing of reliance by the charity, and even if the charitable donor acts in bad faith.

Without Restatement 2d § 90(2), the charity would have to prove foreseeable and actual reliance under Restatement 2d § 90(1) in order to enforce the promise. However, Restatement 2d § 90(2) gets rid of this requirement.

CHAPTER 5
STATUTE OF FRAUDS

ANSWERS

Answer to Question 1

(C) is the correct answer.

Contracts which cannot be completely performed within a year are said to be "within the Statute of Frauds (the "Statute" or "SOF") Restatement 2d § 130, meaning they must be in writing, signed by "the party to be charged" and have all essential terms set forth in the writing to be enforceable. Restatement 2d § 131. To be within the Statute , however, it must truly be factually <u>impossible</u> under the terms of the contract itself for the agreement to be completed within a year of its making. For example, a contract calling for someone to begin working as a teacher six months from now, with the contract to run for a nine-month school year, cannot be completed within a year of its making, and thus is unenforceable unless in writing under Restatement 2d § 130 (unless some other exception applies).

Here, while it is factually unlikely that such a large project could be completed in less than a year, there is nothing in the contract itself that makes the completion of performance <u>impossible</u> within a year, and therefore the Statute does not apply. Thus, the contract can be enforced, even if oral.

(A) is incorrect.

(A) is incorrect because there is no "factually unlikely" doctrine that alters the "impossible to complete within a year" rule of Restatement 2d § 130. As an exam note, watch out when professors put phrases in quotes. Sometimes, of course, they do so because that is the right answer. But often it serves as a distracter, misleading the student to choose the wrong answer because it "sounds legal."

(B) is incorrect.

(B) is factually incorrect. There is nothing in the agreement which makes it objectively impossible for the contract to be fully completed within a year.

(D) is incorrect.

(D) is incorrect because it sets forth a legally incorrect statement. Any contract, regardless of the subject matter, must be in writing to be enforceable if it cannot be completely performed within a year of its making, unless some other exception applies.

Answer to Question 2

(B) is the correct answer.

The Statute applies to contracts for the sale of land. In general, any contract for the transfer of an interest in land, other than a license, must be in writing to be enforceable. Restatement 2d § 125. Because an easement is an interest in land, the agreement for the sale of an easement would be within the Statute and there are no facts indicating there was a writing or any other exception that would satisfy the Statute of Frauds.

(A) is incorrect.

Although this agreement is not for the sale of an entire parcel of land, an easement is still a type of "interest" in land as set forth in the explanation of Choice (B) above, and thus its sale must be in a signed writing to be enforceable. Restatement 2d § 125.

(C) is incorrect.

Buyer is asserting the Statute as a defense, and so is the party to be charged. Buyer *could* waive the defense and go along with the sale if Seller wanted to as well. But Buyer is not waiving the defense—Buyer is the one asserting it in the litigation.

(D) is incorrect.

As discussed in the explanation of (B) above, the statute of frauds would apply here, making (B) correct and (D) incorrect.

Answer to Question 3

(D) is the correct answer.

Statement I is incorrect because Buyer is not agreeing to act as a guarantor or a surety. A suretyship agreement occurs when one party, the surety, agrees to pay a debt, but only if the primarily liable party, the principal, defaults. Here Buyer has a primary obligation to pay the purchase price for Blackacre, regardless of who Seller designates to receive the money. Restatement 2d § 112.

Statement II is incorrect because Buyer's oral agreement to pay part of the sale price to Lender would be regarded as collateral to the land sales contract. In other words, the Lender–Buyer agreement is for the repayment of a loan, which, by itself, does not call for a transfer of an interest of land, and is therefore not within the Statute of Frauds and does not require a writing.

(A), (B), and (C) are incorrect.

These choices are all incorrect for the reason that (D) is correct.

Answer to Question 4

(D) is the correct answer.

Once the Statute of Frauds has been satisfied by a writing, either party can freely testify as to the "correct" terms of the contract. That is, once there is an appropriate signed writing, the Statute is satisfied. Once satisfied, the parties are not estopped to testify that the terms of the agreement are different than those set forth in the signed writing. The reason is that the purpose of the Statute is to give the court a belief that the testimony rests on a real transaction. Once a court believes that, the parties can freely testify (under the Statute) as to what the terms of the transactions actually were.

(A), (B), and (C) are incorrect.

Each of these choices is incorrect for the reasons that (D) is correct.

Answer to Question 5

(C) is the correct answer.

The general rule is that transfers of an interest in real property must be in writing to be enforceable. Restatement 2d § 125. However, under Restatement 2d § 129, "A contract for the transfer of an interest in land may be specifically enforced notwithstanding failure to comply with the Statute of Frauds if it is established that the party seeking enforcement, in reasonable reliance on the contract . . . has so changed his position that injustice can be avoided only by specific enforcement." This is known as the "estoppel" exception.

Here, Granddaughter and Beau meet the criteria. They reasonably relied on the contract and changed their positions in life such that only enforcement of the promise would be just.

(A) is incorrect.

(A) is incorrect because, while it sets forth the general rule for the transfer of an interest in land under the Statute of Frauds, it does not take into account the "estoppel" exception of Restatement 2d § 129.

(B) is incorrect.

Even if "work the land" term is a little indefinite, certainly the 10% of the revenues is not. Furthermore, "work the land" must mean something, and all the work that Granddaughter and Beau did to work the property over the fifteen years with Grandfather's knowledge saves the contract from indefiniteness due to part performance. Restatement 2d § 34(2).

(D) is incorrect.

(D) is incorrect because regardless of whether Grandfather fraudulently induced Granddaughter and Beau to move onto the property, they can still enforce the oral contract under Restatement 2d § 129.

Answer to Question 6

(D) is the correct answer.

The "equal dignities rule" involves situations in which there are principals and agents. The rule provides that if a contract would have to be in writing if signed by the principal to be enforceable, then the agreement by which the agent becomes authorized to act for the principal must also be in writing to become enforceable. That is, the "agent-authorizing" document has an "equal dignity" as far as the writing requirement goes, with the actual contract document itself.

Here, Seller has no problem since both the authorizing and the land sales agreement were in writing. However, the Buyer's authorizing agreement was oral. As such, Broker was not sufficiently authorized to sign the written land sale contract on Buyer's behalf and Broker's signature on the land sale document is thus not an effective signature.

(A) is incorrect.

(A) would be correct in a state that did not adopt the equal dignities rule since the land sale contract itself was in writing, and the principal/agent relationship was disclosed on that agreement.

(B) is incorrect.

The equal dignities rule provides that if a contract must be in writing in order to satisfy the Statute of Frauds, then the authority of an agent to enter into such a contract must also be in writing. Although Seller's agency contract with Agent was in writing, as pointed out in the explanation for (D), the agency contract between Buyer and Broker was oral and thus would not satisfy the Statute.

(C) is incorrect.

Ordinarily Agent would have the authority to sign for Seller on his behalf, but as mentioned in the above answer choices, the contract would not be enforceable in an "equal dignity" jurisdiction.

Answer to Question 7

(C) is the correct answer.

This contract is for the sale of goods, and thus governed by the UCC. The UCC's Statute must be satisfied if the contract is for $500 or more for the agreement to be enforceable. UCC § 2–201.

Under UCC § 2–201(1) there must be a writing, signed by the party who is asserting the SOF defense (the "party to be charged" in contracts vernacular), and containing some quantity in order for the Statute to be satisfied. Here, there is no writing signed by Donna (the party asserting the SOF defense) which contains a quantity term, and thus the SOF is not satisfied under UCC § 2–201(1).

However, the Statute can also be satisfied by the "Merchant's Confirmatory Memorandum" under UCC § 2–201(2). Under that provision, a party who has not signed anything may still lose his or her SOF defense if the requirements of § 2–201(2) have been met. These requirements are:

(a) the contract is between merchants;

(b) the party who asserts the enforceability of the contract sends a signed writing with a quantity term in it confirming an oral contract between the parties (the "Confirmatory Memo");

(c) the party who was sent the Confirmatory Memo actually receives it, and it is sent to an address whereby that party would have reason to know of its contents, (i.e., it is not sent to the Istanbul office of the company when the correspondent is located in Miami); and

(d) no objection is made to the confirmatory memo within ten days.

If all of these elements are met, then the party who receives the confirmatory memo has no SOF defense, even though that party has not signed anything—or indeed has done nothing other than receive the memorandum.

Here, Fact Statement I would help Phil in overcoming Donna's assertion of the Statute as a defense because Donna's objection to Phil's Confirmatory Memo would be untimely. To be effective, such objection would have to be sent within ten days of its receipt, and sending the objection on May 16 would be <u>twelve</u> days after its receipt,

Fact Statement III would also be helpful to Phil in overcoming the Statute defense. In order for the Statute even to apply, the contract must be in excess of $500. So any oral contract under the UCC is enforceable if it is for $500 or less.

Fact Statement II would not help Phil, because if the contract was for a $2000 television, then the Statute would have to be satisfied. Thus, Donna's objection, if sent within ten days of its receipt, would mean she preserved her SOF defense.

(A), (B), and (D) are incorrect.

These choices are incorrect for the reasons that Choice (C) is correct.

Answer to Question 8

(C) is the correct answer.

Statement II is true because Phil is the "party to be charged" (the one asserting the SOF defense) and he sent an adequate Confirmatory Memorandum under UCC § 2–201(2), which was not objected to by Donna within ten days. Note that while he did not "sign" the memorandum with his full name, his initials are a sufficient "signature" for Statute of Frauds purposes under UCC § 1–201(37).

Statement I is incorrect because the party seeking to assert the SOF defense is Phil, not Donna, so Phil is the "party to be charged."

Statement III is incorrect because all the requirements of UCC § 2–201(2) were satisfied by Phil's letter.

(A), (B), and (D) are incorrect.

These choices are incorrect for the reasons that (C) is correct.

Answer to Question 9

(B) is the correct answer.

UCC § 2–201(1) requires that a contract for a sale of goods for $500 or more must be in writing, be signed by the party to be charged, and have a quantity term to be enforceable. However, there are exceptions to that rule, i.e., situations in which the Statute can be satisfied in other ways. One of these is the merchants confirmatory memo exception set forth in UCC § 2–201(2).

Three more exceptions are set forth in UCC § 2–201(3)(a)–(c). These include:

(a) where the goods are "specially manufactured goods;"

(b) where the party against whom enforcement is sought makes an evidentiary admission that a contract, or its elements exist (an evidentiary admission is one made under oath in a court or arbitration proceeding); and

(c) where there are "goods for which payment has been made and accepted or which have been received and accepted."

Here, only one machine has been accepted, so Manufacturer can only successfully enforce the agreement for the price of one machine, or $10,000. As set forth in UCC § 2–201, Cmt. 2, " 'Partial performance' as a substitute for the memorandum can validate the contract only for the goods which have been accepted."

Note that if the parties were in a jurisdiction which recognized the estoppel exception to the Statute, then Manufacturer's reliance on the deal in making the second machine might allow it to enforce the agreement for both machines on reliance grounds.

(A) is incorrect.

This choice is incorrect because the partial performance exception in UCC § 2–201(3)(c) would only allow the agreement to be enforced for the one machine accepted by Buyer, or $10,000.

(C) and (D) are incorrect.

As discussed in the explanation of (B) above, the agreement can only be enforced under the "part performance" exception up to the one machine accepted by Buyer.

If the pressing machines were "specially manufactured goods," the Statute defense would be lost for the entire agreement and it could be enforced for $20,000. However, the pressing machines are not specially manufactured goods within the meaning of the UCC. A specially manufactured good is one that is "not suitable for sale to others in the ordinary course of seller's business." UCC § 2–201(3)(a). Here, there was nothing distinctive about the machines that made them tailored to Buyer specifically, and the problem provides that they could be used by any other dry cleaner.

Answer to Question 10

(D) is the correct answer.

This question combines Statute of Frauds and remedies issues.

When the goods involved in a UCC contract are specially manufactured goods, i.e. goods which are "not suitable for sale to others in the ordinary course of seller's business," a contract is fully enforceable even if oral. UCC § 2–201(3)(a). In this question, the machines are specially manufactured goods which are tailored to Buyer's business. Hence, there is no restriction in seeking to enforce the contract for two pressing machines.

The next question is how much Manufacturer is entitled to since it can establish a breach of contract by Buyer as to both machines. It is entitled to $10,000 for the first machine, because once the good is accepted, the buyer is responsible for the purchase price. UCC §§ 2–607(1), 2–709(1)(a). It is also entitled to the full purchase price as to the second machine as attempted resale of the machine to another dry cleaner would be "unavailing" given that it was made especially for Buyer. UCC § 2–709(1)(b).

(A), (B), and (C) are incorrect.

These choices are incorrect for the reasons that (D) is correct.

Answer to Question 11

(D) is the correct answer.

Under UCC § 2–201(3)(a), a buyer has no Statute of Frauds defense if the subject matter of the contract involves specially manufactured goods, i.e., goods "not suitable for sale to others in the ordinary course of the seller's business." Here the key chains are specially manufactured goods because no one other than Harvard will likely buy them.

The fact that Harvard has no SOF defense does not mean, however, that it will lose a lawsuit brought by Ace. There was no order for the key chains after all, and, as plaintiff, Ace would have the burden of proof to show that the non-existent contract was made, which will be difficult to do. Hence, all the sending of the specially made key chains does is remove one defense in the lawsuit—the Statute—from Harvard's arsenal. But it does not mean Harvard will lose the case.

(A) is incorrect.

(A) is incorrect because Harvard will not become liable for a contract it did not enter into regardless whether it objected to the invoice or not. Harvard cannot be deemed to have accepted the key chains by silence and inaction. Restatement 2d § 69. It might look better if Harvard objected, but liability will not be imposed on Harvard for failing to object.

(B) is incorrect.

(B) is incorrect because a party in the position of the buyer loses its SOF defense under the UCC when the subject matter of the contract is, as here, specially manufactured goods under UCC § 2–201(3)(a).

(C) is incorrect.

(C) is incorrect because both Choice (A) and Choice (B) are incorrect.

Answer to Question 12

(D) is the correct answer.

This question tests knowledge of a mix of Restatement and UCC rules. It is a UCC contract because it involves the sale of goods, but where the UCC does not have a specific rule to the contrary, common law/Restatement rules specifically apply. UCC § 1–103(b).

At the time of its making, the oral contract would not be enforceable because Buyer's obligations cannot be fully completed within a year from the making of the contract. Restatement 2d § 130. However, where one party has completely performed his or her obligations under a contract, the Statute *is* satisfied. UCC § 2–201(3)(c). That provision states that a contract is enforceable "with respect to goods for which . . . have been received and accepted."

Here, once Seller fully performed, the Statute would be satisfied and Seller would be able to enforce the contract for the full amount of the contract price. Once again, the idea is that if one party has completely performed—delivering firewood to another—there is enough for a court to believe that the testimony of the oral contract rests on a real transaction as set forth in UCC § 2–201, Cmt. 1. Thus, once goods are accepted and it seems as if a contract has been formed, there is more of a chance the buyer will get away with fraud if the Statute applies and no evidence of the making of the contract is admitted, than if the Seller is allowed to explain what the transaction was.

(A) is incorrect.

This choice is incorrect because installment contracts that cannot be performed within a year are within the Statute and cannot be enforced unless in writing, absent any other exception applying.

(B) is incorrect.

The fact that Buyer cannot perform within a year became moot (for SOF purposes) when Seller fully performed his obligations. UCC § 2–201(3)(c). Therefore, Seller's defense that the contract is still within the Statute of Frauds would fail.

(C) is incorrect.

Buyer loses the "one year" Statute defense provided by Restatement 2d § 130 once she accepted delivery of the wood. UCC § 2–201(3)(c).

Answer to Question 13

(B) is the correct answer.

Because this is a contract for the sale of goods for $500 or more, the transaction will not be enforceable unless the UCC's SOF is satisfied. Here, it is Owner who is the "party to be charged" for she is the one against whom enforcement of the contract is sought.

Statement II is correct because the Statute is satisfied by the check under the "part performance" exception set forth in UCC § 2–201(3)(c). The check "afford[s] a basis for believing that the offered ... evidence rests on a real transaction." UCC § 2–201, Cmt. 1. That is, people don't go around handing each other checks for $20,000 with statements on it like "For DEPP's Ferrari" unless they probably have a deal of some sort. Yes, it *could* be a loan, or a gift, or something else, but the fact that one party gave the other $20,000, and Owner accepted the check and cashed it is sufficient to show some sort of transaction exists between them.

Under the part performance exception, the rule is that the transaction can be enforced only up to the amount of the goods received or the amount of the payment accepted. But it would make no sense to enforce it only up to 1/10 of a $200,000 car. So the courts have taken the position that acceptance of a check for the down payment on anything means that the contract can be enforced up to one item. That is, suppose the transaction were for two Johnny Depp cars, at $100,000 per car. Acceptance of the check by Owner would allow the deal to be enforced as to one of the cars, not both, because only part payment had been made.

As such, the SOF defense will fail because of the part performance exception, and Owner has no defense in the breach of contract action.

Statement I is incorrect because the part performance exception will cause the Statute of Frauds defense to <u>fail</u>.

Statement III is incorrect because it is Advertiser who is trying to enforce the contract and Owner who is asserting the SOF defense. Hence, the signature by <u>Advertiser</u> on the check does not lose the SOF defense for Owner. It is Owner's *acceptance and cashing* of the check that costs her the defense.

(A), (C), and (D) are incorrect.

Each of these choices is incorrect for the reasons that (B) is correct.

Answer to Question 14

(D) is the correct answer.

One part of the common law Statute of Frauds deals with contracts made upon consideration of marriage. Restatement 2d § 124. The key to applying it is to remember that it was designed to apply in older times when a party (usually the bride's father) actually bargained with the groom to get the groom to propose, promising him a dowry or some other compensation if he married the father's daughter. As discordant as it sounds to modern ears, it was, to some extent, a commercial transaction, and so contract law had rules for it, one of which was the Statute as exemplified in Restatement 2d § 124.

Restatement 2d § 124 provides that a bargain in which "all or part of the consideration is either marriage or a promise to marry is within the Statute ..." Hence, if the promise at issue was made in consideration of marriage, i.e., as part of a bargain in which one party wanted to induce the other to marry, or to promise to marry, it is within the Statute and must be in writing to be enforceable. On the other hand, if the promise was made only in contemplation of marriage, like a pre-nuptial agreement, the Statute does not apply.

Here, the agreement was not entered into with one party's agreement of marriage being part of the bargained-for exchange because the parties had already agreed to be married before they started negotiating the pre-nuptial agreement. Rather, it was made in contemplation of marriage, i.e., with marriage on the horizon, and thus its enforceability is not subject to the Statute.

(A) and (C) are incorrect.

Usually pre-nuptial agreements are not within the Statute as they are not made as part of an exchange in which the marriage itself is bargained for, but rather are made in contemplation of marriage, after the engagement. Only in the former case is the promise subject to Restatement 2d § 124.

(B) is incorrect.

Even if Fred entered the pre-nuptial agreement under fraudulent circumstances, there was no promise in the agreement itself that made a proposal, or marriage itself, part of the deal. As such, the agreement is not within the Statute.

Answer to Question 15

(B) is the correct answer.

The "suretyship" provision of the Statute of Frauds requires that a promise to answer for the debt of another (a surety or guaranty contract) must be in writing. Restatement 2d § 112. Uncle's obligation is a surety because he is not primarily liable for the debt, but only agreed to pay if Grandfather did not.

Author's Note:

Note many contracts professors do not cover surety contracts when covering the Statute of Frauds, so if this seems like new information to you, you may not need to review the rules of Restatement 2d §§ 112 et. seq.

(A) is incorrect.

The contract between Niece and Uncle was not illusory because each undertook a legal obligation which they would not have had otherwise in a bargained-for exchange. Niece, who was under no obligation to accept Grandfather's offer for a unilateral contract, agreed to accept it. Uncle, who was under no obligation to pay for Niece's tuition or for any "A" grades earned, promised to make payment for the same if Grandfather defaulted. The agreement between Niece and Uncle is enforceable as far as consideration is concerned (Restatement 2d § 113); it is the lack of a writing that makes the agreement unenforceable by Niece.

(C) is incorrect.

As mentioned in the explanation of (A), the consideration to Uncle is that Niece would render the performance required under the unilateral contract issued by Grandfather. Niece was under no preexisting duty to render the performance, and the fact that the same performance would provide consideration for both Uncle and Grandfather does not alter its legal sufficiency. In other words, the same consideration that made the agreement enforceable against Grandfather makes the surety promise enforceable against Uncle. Restatement 2d § 113. Again, it is the lack of a writing that makes the promise unenforceable by Niece.

(D) is incorrect.

There is a presumption that promises among certain classes of family members are not enforceable (e.g., Husband will take the kids to school this week if Wife takes out the trash), but the presumption does not extend to extended family and in any event it can be overcome by evidence of contrary intentions of the parties. Here, the facts indicate that Uncle is serious about enforcing Grandfather's promise, and given that their relationship is one of extended family (Niece/Uncle as opposed to Husband/Wife), the presumption was overcome.

Answer to Question 16

(C) is the correct answer.

The answer to this question turns on an exception to the suretyship provision of the Statute.

Saul was acting as a surety for Deacon's promise. That is, Saul would only be liable if Deacon, the principal, did not pay. If that were all we knew, the promise would have to be in writing to be enforceable under the suretyship provision of Restatement 2d § 112.

However, under Restatement 2d § 116, if the reason for which the surety makes the promise is "mainly for his own economic advantage, rather than to benefit the third person," then the promise is not within the Statute and can be enforced even if oral. This is known as the "main purpose" or "leading object" exception.

Here, the "main purpose" of Saul's promise was to benefit himself (the surety) financially, and not Priscilla (the third party), and so his oral suretyship promise is enforceable even if oral.

(A) is incorrect.

Although suretyship agreements generally require a writing to be enforceable because they are within the Statute of Frauds (Restatement 2d § 112), Saul's promise fits into the "main purpose" exception to that rule (Restatement 2d § 116), and thus is outside the Statute and enforceable even though oral.

(B) is incorrect.

Deacon is principally liable for the debt, but Saul has made himself liable as well as a surety if Deacon fails to pay the debt.

(D) is incorrect.

Priscilla may be able to enforce Saul's promise on promissory estoppel grounds if she can show reasonable reliance. However, Saul's promise is also enforceable on suretyship grounds and so the words, "but only" in the choice make this answer incorrect.

CHAPTER 6
CAPACITY

ANSWERS

Answer to Question 1

(A) is the correct answer.

In order to enter into an enforceable contract, a party must have sufficient judgment to decide whether to bind himself or herself to an enforceable promise. Restatement 2d § 12(1). As it relates to age, the rule is that until a person reaches the age of majority (in all states, eighteen years of age), any contract entered into by that person is voidable at the option of the minor. Restatement 2d §§ 12(2)(b), 14. (Although note that Restatement 2d § 14 provides that the last day on which the contract is freely voidable is "the beginning of the day before the person's eighteenth birthday.")

The test is not whether the particular minor that entered into the contract is sufficiently mature to understand the nature of entering into a legal bargain; the rule rests solely on the age of the individual.

Statement I is correct and Statement IV is incorrect because Teresa need not wait until she turns eighteen before beginning disaffirmance proceedings. She is entitled to disaffirm the contract while a minor.

Statement V is correct, and Statements II and III are incorrect because of the rule on "restitution" adopted by the Restatement 2d, i.e., the rule regarding whether the minor can just turn over the purchased good "as is" upon disaffirmance or whether the minor must pay for the reasonable use and/or damage caused during the use of the item as a minor. Restatement 2d § 14, Cmt. c provides, "[an infant's] disaffirmance revests in the other party the title to any property received by the infant under the contract. If the consideration received by the infant has been dissipated by him, *the other party is without remedy* . . ." Hence, under the Restatement's rule, Teresa can turn over the car in whatever condition it is in, and need not pay for its use—Seller "*is without remedy*" once the contract is avoided.

Note that even under the Restatement 2d, there are a few situations in which the minor must pay restitution (as discussed in the answer to Question 3), but in situations like the one described in this question, no restitution is required.

Note also that other jurisdictions have different rules regarding payment for restitution by a minor. Even the Restatement recognizes this, as the comment quoted above continues, "But some states, by statute or decision, have restricted the power of disaffirmance . . . by requiring restoration of consideration received." Restatement 2d § 14, Cmt. c.

(B), (C), and (D) are incorrect.

These choices are incorrect for the reasons set forth in the explanation to (A).

Answer to Question 2

(D) is the correct answer.

The ability of a minor to disaffirm the contract does not last forever. It lasts throughout the period of minority, but once the minor turns eighteen, things begin to change. If the buyer takes some sort of act (or even some sort of inaction) which indicates that the former minor wants to continue with the contract as an adult, then the contract will thereafter be enforceable. The process by which the new adult indicates he or she wishes to continue with the contract is known as "ratification."

Generally there are three ways that a former minor/new adult can ratify the contract, each of which is described in Choices (A), (B), and (C). Restatement 2d § 85.

Choice (A) describes the process of "express" ratification. That is, Teresa's statement, "I will continue to pay for the car," was an express affirmation of her desire to continue with the contract, and such ratification made the contract enforceable from that point forward.

Choice (B) describes the process of "implied-in-fact" ratification. If the new adult takes action that indicates he or she wishes to continue with the contract, the agreement is thereby ratified. Here, Teresa's continuing to use the car and make payments on it for a year after she turns an adult is an example of implied-in-fact ratification.

Choice (C) describes the most commonly used form of ratification: ratification by silence and inaction. The rule is that a minor is given a reasonable time to disaffirm the contract after reaching the age of majority, and if the contract is not disaffirmed within that reasonable time, ratification will be implied. While facts of a contract are important to determine what is a reasonable time, in general, the more benefits the minor has received under the contract, the less amount of time will be given to disaffirm after obtaining majority. Here, Teresa kept the car for over a year, which is more than a reasonable time given that she was allowed to use the car in the interim.

(A), (B), and (C) are incorrect.

These answer choices are incorrect when taken individually as set forth in the explanation to (D) above.

Answer to Question 3

(B) is the correct answer.

The majority and Restatement 2d rule regarding treatment of the economic benefit received by the minor while in possession of the goods is that there is no restitutionary recovery for any loss in value for the non-minor in credit sales. Restatement 2d § 14, Cmt. c. This rule is subject to several exceptions, some of which are adopted in various states (i.e., the exact rules in any one state can vary):

(1) cash sales, e.g., where a minor buys a candy bar from a grocery store for $1 and eats it, the minor can disaffirm the contract, but is liable in restitution for the value of the harm to the good or $1;

(2) contracts for "necessities," where the minor buys, whether for cash or on credit, something like food, bedding, etc. that the court determines is a "necessity;" and

(3) where the benefit procured by the minor was via misrepresentation of age, e.g., where a minor takes affirmative steps to convince the seller that he or she is an adult at the time of contracting, such as a fake ID or even just a statement of adulthood.

None of these exceptions are present in this question. Therefore, Sally is entitled to recover what she has put into the contract, and that amount is not subject to any restitution to the other party or offset due to any loss in value.

(A) and (D) are incorrect.

These answer choices are incorrect for the reasons set forth in the explanation to Choice (B) above, namely they ignore or misapply the rule of the Restatement 2d.

(C) is incorrect.

This answer choice would be correct under the minority view regarding restitution of the non-minor in a disaffirmance. This so-called "New Hampshire" rule states that the non-minor is entitled to restitutionary (fair value) recovery upon the disaffirmance of <u>any</u> credit sale by a minor so long as the minor would be unjustly enriched from the use of the goods without having to pay for such use. However, as discussed under Choice (B) above, the question calls for the majority rule which is embodied in the Restatement 2d.

Answer to Question 4

(B) is the correct answer.

If a guardian has been appointed for an individual due to a mental illness, Restatement 2d § 13 provides that the individual has no capacity to contract and any contract entered into by the individual under guardianship is voidable by the guardian. However, the general rule regarding the requirement of the person subject to a guardianship to pay restitution is that restitution is required for the use of the good or service by such an individual if either: (a) the contract was for "necessities," or (b) the non-incapacitated person neither knew or should have known of the individual's incapacity at the time of contracting. Applied here, the facts indicate that the salesperson was unaware of Ben's incapacity, and thus restitution would be due for Ben's usage of the television (including depreciation), but the contract itself would be voidable.

Note that the contract is voidable by the guardian, not void. So if Ben's mother wanted to go ahead with the purchase, she could do so and ratify the transaction.

Note also that if Ben were somehow to get a court to dissolve the guardianship, then he too could ratify the contract, either expressly or by implication. Restatement 2d § 85.

(A) is incorrect.

Although this answer choice correctly points out that the contract is voidable by Ben's guardian, it incorrectly points out the consequences if the contract is disaffirmed. As set forth in the explanation to Choice (B) above, the retail store is entitled to restitution because the salesperson did not know or have any reason to know of Ben's mental illness.

(C) is incorrect.

(C) is incorrect because it is not the awareness of the particular person making the contract that is controlling; rather it is the fact that a guardian had been appointed over the financial affairs of an individual. Hence, even though Ben may have had a lucid moment in which he comprehended what he purchased, that is not determinative. The key is that Ben suffers from a mental infirmity that prevents him from having the capacity to contract, which a court has recognized by appointing a guardian.

(D) is incorrect.

(D) is incorrect because the fact that the salesperson might not have had any reason to know of Ben's mental infirmity does not mean the transaction is not voidable by the guardian. Once a guardian is appointed, then the individual subject to the guardianship has no capacity to enter into a contract that his or her guardian does not wish to ratify.

However, the fact that the sales representative did not have any reason to know of Ben's infirmity <u>does</u> mean that the store can recover in restitution for the reasonable use of the item until the contract is disaffirmed.

Answer to Question 5

(B) is the correct answer.

The rules regarding the capacity of a mentally ill person, who does not have a guardian appointed, to enter into enforceable agreements are set forth in Restatement 2d § 15. That section describes two separate tests (assuming the incapacity is not due to temporary intoxication and/or drug use): the "cognition" test under Restatement 2d § 15(1); and the "acts" test under Restatement 2d § 15(2). Some jurisdictions adopt one or the other test; some adopt either, meaning the plaintiff gets to choose which theory he or she wants to use to avoid the contract.

This question asks about the cognition rule, which provides that an individual incurs voidable contractual duties if he or she entered into a contract "unable to understand in a reasonable manner the nature and consequences of the transaction." Restatement 2d § 15(1). Applied here, the key fact is that Terry was not completely aware of the decision's ramifications, and the words of the test were incorporated into this answer choice. As such, the contract would be voidable.

(A) is incorrect.

(A) is incorrect because it assumes that a contract entered into by anyone suffering a mental illness is voidable. This is not true, so long as the individual does not have a guardian appointed. Thus, the answer is too broad and not a correct statement of law because an individual with a mental illness, but with sufficient acuity to understand the nature and consequences of a particular transaction, can enter into an enforceable agreement for that transaction under the "cognition" test.

(C) is incorrect.

(C) is incorrect because, although the awareness of the non-incapacitated party has relevance under the "acts" test, it is not a part of the cognition test.

(D) is incorrect.

(D) is incorrect because the answer incorrectly provides that if Terry did not understand the consequences of entering into the agreement, the contract would be enforceable. This is the opposite of the correct answer as set forth in the explanation of (B) above.

Answer to Question 6

(C) is the correct answer.

A contract is voidable under the "volition" or "acts" test when the individual is "unable to act in a reasonable manner in relation to the transaction and the other party has reason to know of his [or her] condition." Restatement 2d § 15(1)(b). Under this test, avoidability is thus dependent on a showing: (1) the individual does not have the mental ability to control his or her actions in a reasonable manner; and (2) the other party has reason to know of the mental infirmity.

Here, the facts indicate that Terry loved her husband and that she was not aware of the decision's ramifications, indicating that she was not in control of her actions in a reasonable manner. In addition, the school district was aware of the mental illness based on the reasons for Terry's leave of absence. As such, the contract would be voidable under the test. Note that this problem is based on *Ortelere v. Teacher's Retirement Board*, 25 N.Y.2d 196 (1969) (holding the teacher's choice was voidable under the "acts" test).

(A) is incorrect.

(A) is incorrect because the answer is overly broad and an incorrect statement of law. A contract entered into by someone suffering a mental illness is enforceable if both elements of the "acts" test are not met.

(B) is incorrect.

(B) is incorrect because, while this answer sets forth the correct answer under the cognition test, it is the "acts" test which is the subject of this question.

(D) is incorrect.

Although Terry may be acting willfully, that does not override the elements of the "volition" or "acts" test, which asks not whether she was acting willfully, but rather whether the individual can control her actions in a reasonable manner.

Answer to Question 7

(D) is the correct answer.

The avoidability of a transaction when one party is temporarily mentally infirm due to intoxication or other drug use is governed by Restatement 2d § 16. That section provides, "[a] person incurs only voidable duties by entering into a transaction if the other party has reason to know that by reason of the intoxication: (a) he is unable to understand in a reasonable manner the nature and consequences of the transaction [the "cognition" test] or (b) he is unable to act in a reasonable manner in relation to the transaction [the "volition" or "acts" test].

Here, the facts indicate that Lucille is aware of B.B.'s intoxication and Choice (A) sets forth the correct rule of voidability of the contract under the "volition" or "acts" test, while Choice (C) sets forth the correct rule of voidability of the contact under the cognition test. Thus both answer choices are correct, making Choice (D) the best answer.

(A) and (C) are incorrect.

As set forth in the explanation of Choice (D) above, since both provide reasons to make the contract voidable, making (D) the correct answer.

(B) is incorrect.

Most states provide that a party found incompetent under the cognitive test due to intoxication at the time of making a contract is entitled to disaffirm the contract regardless whether the intoxication is voluntary or involuntary, and regardless whether the underlying transaction is fair.

Answer to Question 8

(C) is the correct answer.

Although the contract is voidable due to B.B.'s intoxication, Lucille's awareness of it, and his inability to control his actions in a reasonable manner (Restatement 2d § 16(b)), the affected party has the option to disaffirm or ratify the contract once the incapacity no longer affects the individual. Restatement 2d § 85. Thus, once B.B. is no longer intoxicated, and affirms or ratifies the deal, it becomes enforceable.

(A) and (B) are incorrect.

These choices are incorrect because a contract made while a party was under temporary incapacity due to intoxication is not void, only voidable (and only then if the other elements of Restatement 2d § 16 are satisfied). Accordingly, the agreement can be effectively ratified by B.B. after the intoxication fades. Restatement 2d § 85.

(D) is incorrect.

This answer choice is incorrect because it ignores the fact that the contract was voidable by B.B. before he ratified it. Restatement 2d § 16(1).

Answer to Question 9

(A) is the correct answer.

Although the Restatement 2d has a requirement that the non-incapacitated party must know of the other party's temporary incapacity before a contract is voidable (Restatement 2d § 16), the majority rule followed by most states is that a party rendered incompetent under the cognitive test (unable to understand the nature and consequences of the transaction) due to alcohol or drug use at the time of the making of the contract is entitled to disaffirm the contract to the same extent as all other classes of mental incompetents, regardless of the other party's knowledge of the incapacity. This is true regardless of whether the intoxication is voluntary or involuntary.

Thus, Mike, in disaffirming the contract only a couple days after it was made and when the medication is no longer affecting him, is entitled to avoid the transaction under common law rules.

(B) is incorrect.

(B) is incorrect because this answer allows for the contract to be voidable with Mike being aware of the nature and consequences of the transaction. This is not true. If the incapacity does not affect the individual's cognition, the contract is enforceable.

(C) is incorrect.

Isa's not knowing of Mike's condition would be helpful if the jurisdiction followed the Restatement 2d § 16 (as set forth in the explanation of Choice (A) above), but the call of the question states that the question is testing the rules under the common law.

(D) is incorrect.

(D) is incorrect because the answer sets forth an incorrect statement of contract law. Incapacity due to drug use can make a contract voidable as explained under Choice (A) above.

CHAPTER 7
MISTAKE AND
MISUNDERSTANDING

ANSWERS

Answer to Question 1

(C) is the correct answer.

Under contract law, a "mistake" is a belief that is not in accord with the facts at the time the contract was entered into. Restatement 2d § 151. Mistake can be "mutual," where both parties are mistaken as to the same fact, or "unilateral," where only one party is mistaken. When the elements of either type of mistake are met, the contract can be avoided, and thus mistake is treated as a "defense" to formation, and is usually asserted by a party who either does not want to go forward with the deal or who, after performing, discovers the "mistake" and seeks to rescind or avoid the agreement. This question deals with mutual mistake.

Mutual mistake occurs when both parties to a contract are under substantially the same erroneous belief as to a true, material fact present at the time of the transaction. Restatement 2d § 152. Under the Restatement 2d § 152, the elements of mutual mistake are:

(1) the mistake of both parties must be to a basic assumption on which the contract was made;

(2) the mistake must have a material effect on the agreed exchange of performances; and

(3) the party seeking to avoid the contract must not bear the risk of that mistake.

It is the last element where many mistake claims fail, so it must always be analyzed with some care. Under Restatement 2d § 154, a party in a mistake case assumes the risk of the mistake's occurrence when:

(a) the risk was allocated to that party by express agreement of the parties;

    (b) the party is aware at the time the contract is made, that he or she has only a limited knowledge of the true facts, but treats that limited knowledge as sufficient (known as "conscious ignorance"); *or*

    (c) as a matter of law the court finds it reasonable to place the risk on that party.

Applied here, the difference between a sterile and a fertile bull may well be a change in the "essential nature" of the contract (the buyer received something totally different than what he thought he was buying). Also, the seller would receive more than eight times the value of the bull he is selling, which is a substantial windfall, while the buyer pays more than eight times than he should and gets less than half of what he thought he would receive. However, the buyer's mistake defense fails when it comes to the assumption of the risk.

As the facts indicate, it is common knowledge that the bull may turn out to be sterile and the buyer proceeded anyway, essentially "gambling" with the deal, which would make it reasonable for the buyer to bear the risk of mistake. As such, the mistake doctrine would not provide a defense to buyer.

Note that this problem is a factual variant of the famous case of *Sherwood v. Walker*, 33 N.W. 919 (Mich. 1897).

(A) is incorrect.

The reason that mistake would not be available here is not because of a price disproportionate to the actual value of the bull, but rather because the buyer knew of the *risk* of the sterility of the bull and proceeded anyway, thereby assuming the risk of the mistake.

(B) is incorrect.

(B) is incorrect because although buyer did not know at the time of sale that the bull would be sterile, he nevertheless assumed the risk that it may turn out to be sterile as set forth in the explanation to Choice (C) above. Restatement 2d § 154.

(D) is incorrect.

(D) is incorrect because the contract was enforceable when the cattlemen agreed to buy/sell the bull (the time of contracting).

Answer to Question 2

(A) is the correct answer.

The main difference between this question and the previous is that the teacher did not enter the contract knowing of the risk that the bull could be sterile. However, under Restatement 2d § 154(b), a party can still be deemed to assume the risk of the mistake if, "he is aware, at the time the contract is made, that he has only limited knowledge with respect to the facts to which the mistake relates but treats his limited knowledge as sufficient." As indicated above, a party fulfilling this prong of the test is said to have assumed the risk of the mistake through "conscious ignorance."

Here, the teacher consciously took the risk that the bull might turn out to be sterile when he relied on his limited knowledge about the situation and proceeded anyway. Since he did so, he is deemed to have borne the *risk* of the calf not being as valuable as he hoped and cannot use the mistake doctrine to avoid the transaction because he was not acting reasonable in assuming there was no appreciable risk that he was under a mistaken belief. Restatement 2d § 154, Cmt. b. Note that this problem is loosely based on *Backus v. MacLaury*, 106 N.Y.S.2d 401 (1951).

(B) is incorrect.

(B) is incorrect because the contract did not become enforceable at the time the teacher took delivery of the bull; rather, it was enforceable when the cattleman and the teacher contracted to buy/sell the bull.

(C) is incorrect.

Although the teacher was unaware that the bull may be sterile, as set forth in the explanation to (A) above, the teacher still assumed the risk by treating his limited knowledge regarding the risks as sufficient and proceeding with the deal anyway.

(D) is incorrect.

The price being disproportionate to the actual value of the bull might be relevant to establish that the mistake was as to a basic assumption under the contract. But it has no effect on the real problem here—the fact that the teacher assumed the risk under the conscious ignorance doctrine. Restatement 2d § 154(b).

Answer to Question 3

(D) is the correct answer.

This question deals with "unilateral" mistake, and the elements of the doctrine are set forth in Restatement 2d § 153. Under that provision, the party seeking to avoid a contract under the doctrine of unilateral mistake must show:

(1) that he or she did not bear the risk of the mistake for any of the reasons set forth in Restatement 2d § 154 (which are set forth in the answer to Question 1 above) <u>plus either</u>:

    (a) the effect of the mistake is such that enforcement against the mistaken party would be unconscionable or;

    (b) the non-mistaken party either had reason to know of the mistake or caused the mistake.

Applied here, even though franchisee's actions may be negligent, the elements of unilateral mistake are present. Franchisee did not expressly or impliedly assume the risk because he entered into the agreement for a stated rent ($600). In a similar case involving McDonald's, the court provided that paying double the agreed amount of the lease for the entire term of a ten-year lease would be unconscionable, i.e., the franchisee would lose so much money on the deal that in good conscience a court could not force him to bear that loss. Restatement 2d § 153(a). Further, the landlord's knowledge of the error would also be a reason, under Restatement 2d § 153(b), to allow the mistaken party to avoid the double payments using unilateral mistake. *McDonald's Corp. v. Moore*, 237 F. Supp. 874 (W.D.S.C. 1965).

(A) is incorrect.

As set forth in the explanation of Choice (D) above, even if the accountant was negligent, the elements of unilateral mistake are still present and would allow the franchisee to recover the excess payments.

(B) is incorrect.

(B) is incorrect because: (1) the franchisee did not expressly assume the risk by asking the accountant to handle the rent payments, and (2) the franchisee did not impliedly assume the risk under any of the reasons set forth in Restatement 2d § 154. This is not an instance where the franchisee is "gambling" or assuming that he is getting into a bargain in which a different outcome may arise. Rather, the term of rent is explicitly set and it was a mistake made in the process of making payments that the franchisee has not assumed the risk for.

(C) is incorrect.

It is not the fact that franchisee did not know of the mistaken payments that would allow him to prevail in a suit to recover the excess payments; rather, it is because the elements of unilateral mistake are met. Restatement 2d § 153.

Answer to Question 4

(A) is the correct answer.

This is an example of a valid case for asserting unilateral mistake. As set forth in Restatement 2d § 153, Cmt. b, "The most common sorts of such mistakes [unilateral mistakes] occur in bids on construction contracts and clerical errors in the computation of price or in the omission of component items." To establish an actionable unilateral mistake defense, the mistaken party needs to show that he or she did not bear the risk of the error under Restatement 2d § 154 (which was the case here), and either that enforcement would be unconscionable or that the other party "had reason to know of the mistake," or caused it. Here, this choice assumes that Contractor would have reason to know of the mistake, which is reasonable given that the amount of Sub 3's bid was less than half that of the other bids.

(B) is incorrect.

(B) is incorrect for the reasons that Choice (A) is correct.

(C) is incorrect.

(C) is incorrect because negligence is not the test for unilateral mistake. As set forth in Restatement 2d § 153, the elements are that the party asserting the defense must not have assumed the risk of the mistake for any of the reasons set forth in Restatement 2d § 154, and either that enforcement would be unconscionable, or the non-mistaken party either had reason to know of the mistake or caused it.

(D) is incorrect.

Under Restatement 2d § 153, unilateral mistake can be established *either* when enforcement of the promise would be unconscionable (Restatement 2d § 153(a)), _or_ when the non-mistaken party knows of the mistake or caused it (Restatement 2d § 153(b)). Hence, the fact that enforcement would not be unconscionable is not determinative if it is found that Contractor had reason to know that the bid was mistaken.

Answer to Question 5

(D) is the correct answer.

Misunderstanding occurs when the parties ascribe a different meaning to the same material term of a contract. Restatement 2d § 20. The mistake doctrine, on the other hand, occurs when an agreement is made on the assumption of a fact which objectively turns out not to be true. Restatement 2d § 151. Here, there was no mistake as to any objective fact; rather, there was a misunderstanding as to the term "Dreamliner."

(A) is incorrect.

As set forth in the explanation of Choice (D) above, this would be a situation in which the doctrine of misunderstanding is applicable, not mistake. There is no mistaken belief not in accord with the facts, as defined under Restatement 2d § 151.

(B) is incorrect.

The problem here is not assumption of risk, but rather a "misunderstanding" of the term "Dreamliner."

(C) is incorrect.

The fact that the goods were delivered in accordance with Seller's understanding of the agreement is not important with regard to either the misunderstanding or the mistake doctrine.

Answer to Question 6

(A) is the correct answer.

As set forth in the explanation of Choice (D) in the previous question, the doctrine of misunderstanding would be applicable in this situation because both parties attached different meanings to a key term of the contract. If neither party knows or has reason to know of the meaning of the term attached by the other, then no contract is formed. Restatement 2d § 20(1)(a).

Similarly, note that if both parties know the other ascribes a different meaning to the term, no contract is formed in that instance as well. Restatement 2d § 20(1)(b).

Here, both parties had no reason to know of the other's meaning of the term "Dreamliner" and so no contract was ever formed since there was no mutual manifestation of agreement to go forward on the same material terms, as is necessary for contract formation.

Note that this question is loosely based on the famous case of *Raffles v. Wichelhaus*, 159 Eng. Rep. 375 (1864), a case about two ships called *Peerless*.

(B) is incorrect.

(B) is incorrect because the answer incorrectly states the law. Under Restatement 2d § 20(2), if one party knows of the misunderstanding and the other does not, a contract is formed and the meaning attached to the term is the one of the party who did not know of the misunderstanding.

(C) is incorrect.

The fact that the goods were delivered in accordance with Seller's understanding of the agreement is not important with regard to applicability of the misunderstanding doctrine. Because the elements of Restatement 2d § 20(1) are met, there is no contract and hence no duty of Buyer to accept the lumber.

(D) is incorrect.

(D) is incorrect because the misunderstanding of the parties means that there is no contract, and hence there is nothing to "breach."

CHAPTER 8
DURESS

ANSWERS

Answer to Question 1

(B) is the correct answer.

In our legal system, contracts are enforced when they are freely and voluntarily entered into by those with capacity to do so. When one party is under duress caused by some sort of threat, however, the freedom to contract is imperiled. This chapter contains problems that demonstrate when duress will provide a defense to a party who does not perform. Contract law provides that duress is a defense to formation, meaning that when its elements are met, the contract is voidable (in most instances) under Restatement 2d § 175 or void (in a few cases) under Restatement 2d § 174.

The basic rule is that where one party's agreement to the contract is induced by an "improper threat" of the other, the contract is voidable. Restatement 2d § 175(1). What constitutes an "improper threat" differs depending on whether the terms of the resulting deal are "fair" or not. That is, contract law views it differently if a party comes into court and says, "I sold my $1,000 watch for $1,000, but I really didn't want to sell it" versus a party who says, "I sold my $1,000 watch for $10 and I didn't want to sell it." In the former case, contract law is much more worried about a claim of duress being fabricated to cover seller's remorse; hence the different rules for "fair" and "unfair" transactions.

This question deals with a situation in which the resulting deal was fair, i.e., the contract was to sell the tickets for face and market value. Under the Restatement 2d § 176(1), a threat made to induce a party to enter a contract where the terms of the contract are fair is "improper," thus making the agreement voidable, if:

(a) what is threatened is a crime or tort;

(b) what is threatened is criminal prosecution;

(c) what is threatened is the bad faith use of the civil process, or

(d) the threat is a breach of the duty of good faith and fair dealing.

Choice (B) is thus correct because Portia may disaffirm the contract based on duress by improper threat because Dawn has threatened both a crime and a tort in threatening to poison Portia's husband Albert. Restatement 2d § 176(1)(a). Thus, the contract is voidable due to duress by improper threat.

(A) is incorrect.

Contracts are "void" (as opposed to voidable) under a duress theory only if a party enters into the contract because he or she has been threatened with imminent physical force. Restatement 2d § 174. Here, Dawn has threatened *Albert*, and not Portia. Therefore, the contract is *voidable* because Portia was compelled to enter into the contract due to a threat that Dawn would commit a crime or tort. Restatement 2d § 176(1)(a).

(C) is incorrect.

(C) is incorrect for the reason Choice (B) is correct.

(D) is incorrect.

(D) is incorrect because the issue here is that the contract is voidable due to duress by improper threat, as set forth in the explanation to Choice (B). It is true there was no reasonable alternative for Portia, and so arguably the procedural unconscionability requirement for a finding of unconscionability is present. However, the deal was on fair terms, so there was no substantive unconscionability.

Answer to Question 2

(C) is the correct answer.

Penelope may avoid the contract because a threat of criminal prosecution is an improper threat under contract law. Restatement 2d § 176(1)(b). Penelope may avoid the contract whether or not she embezzled the money because the issue here is that Penelope did not enter the agreement to "repay" the money of her own free will and voluntary decision making. When a contract is formed under duress, freedom of contract is put at risk because the party entering into the contract does not have free choice and the ability to voluntarily make a decision. Thus, these contracts are unenforceable.

Note that if the "repayment" agreement had been reached as part of a settlement of a civil suit brought against Penelope by the bank, it would likely be enforceable, so long as the bank had credible evidence that Penelope had committed embezzlement.

Note also that the agreement is voidable by Penelope, not void. She certainly can decide to go forward with it if she continues to believe that it is worth repaying the money rather than having her employer go to the police and having the police start an investigation. But the point is that if she wants to, she can avoid the contract since her agreement to it was induced by an "improper threat" by the bank employee. (A list of the "improper threats" where the deal was fair are provided in the explanation of Question 1). If she decides to avoid the contract, the agreement of the bank to keep the matter quiet is avoided as well, and the bank is thereafter free to report the suspected crime to the authorities.

(A) is incorrect.

(A) is incorrect because duress by improper threat renders a resulting agreement *voidable*, and not *void*. Restatement 2d § 175.

(B) is incorrect.

(B) is incorrect for the reasons stated in the explanation of (C). It does not matter whether Penelope actually embezzled money; what matters is that Penelope's agreement to the contract was induced by what contract law views as an "improper threat." Restatement 2d § 176(1). The contract is therefore voidable, regardless of whether Penelope was guilty of embezzlement.

(D) is incorrect.

(D) is incorrect because the contract is voidable for the reasons stated in the explanation of (C). It is irrelevant whether Damon was reasonable in believing Penelope embezzled money because his threat to induce Penelope to sign the contract was "improper" under contract law. Restatement 2d § 176(1)(a).

Answer to Question 3

(D) is the correct answer.

(D) is correct because Dane has threatened the bad faith use of the civil process in threatening to sue Parker for breach of warranty, without grounds for doing so, unless Parker agrees to paint the inside of Dane's home. Therefore, the contract is voidable due to duress by improper threat. Restatement 2d § 176(1)(c).

Note that if Dane really believed he had a breach of warranty claim against Parker, his threat would not be in bad faith. Thus, if Parker offered to paint the inside of Dane's home to settle the valid dispute, the promise would be enforceable.

Again, the contract is only voidable by Parker, so if she wants to do the job and enforce the contract, she can. The point is she does not have to go through with the contract because the threat that was used to induce her agreement was "improper" under contract law. Restatement 2d § 176(c).

(A) is incorrect.

(A) is incorrect because the contract is *voidable* due to duress by improper threat, not *void*. Restatement 2d § 175.

(B) and (C) are incorrect.

(B) and (C) are incorrect because the contract is voidable for the reasons stated in the explanation of (D). First, it is irrelevant whether Dane is paying Parker a fair price, because Dane threatened Parker with the bad faith use of the civil process, so the contract is voidable. Restatement 2d § 176(1)(c). Thus, Choice (B) is incorrect. Second, Parker did not have a free choice to paint the interior of Dane's home because she was induced to do so by improper threat, so Choice (C) is incorrect.

Answer to Question 4

(C) is the correct answer.

Peter may avoid this contract because he entered into it under duress by improper threat. Doreen's threat not to finish the first job unless Peter hired her for another was a breach of her duty of good faith and fair dealing, and was therefore "improper" under Restatement 2d § 176(1)(d).

(A), (B), and (D) are incorrect.

(A), (B), and (D) are incorrect for the reason (C) is correct. Doreen's threat was a breach of her duty of good faith and fair dealing, and thus Peter did not have free choice and voluntary decision making in deciding whether or not to hire her to landscape his vacation home. Thus, the contract is voidable, not void, by Peter, regardless of whether Doreen charges a reasonable price. Further, while Peter could always "fire" Doreen, if they have a valid contract, he cannot do so without legal consequence, and would be liable to her for her profit if they had an enforceable agreement. Restatement 2d § 176(1)(d).

Answer to Question 5

(B) is the correct answer.

This question deals with a situation in which the agreement which results from the improper threat is not "fair." The rules governing this kind of problem are in Restatement 2d § 176(2), which provides that a threat that induces an agreement which is not on fair terms is "improper" if:

(a) the threatened act would harm the recipient and not significantly benefit the party making the threat;

(b) the effectiveness of the threat is significantly increased by prior dealing between the parties; or

(c) what is threatened is a use of power for an illegitimate ends.

Here, David's threat to expose Phoebe's extramarital affair would harm Phoebe but would not significantly benefit David. Thus, Phoebe may avoid the agreement. Restatement § 2d 176(2)(a).

(A) is incorrect.

(A) is incorrect because the price of the watch being so low is not the "only" reason Phoebe can avoid the contract. The disparity between the price and the value of the watch is relevant, but not determinative. The disparity is relevant because it means that the rules of Restatement 2d § 176(2) should be applied, rather than the rules of Restatement 2d § 176(1), which apply when the underlying transaction is on "fair" terms. But if there was no improper threat that induced her agreement, e.g., if Phoebe really needed the money and David's offer was the best she could get at the time, the agreement would be enforceable regardless of the disparity between the price for the watch and its value. This would be a modern day example of the "peppercorn" theory of consideration, where courts will not avoid an agreement based on the "equivalence of the values exchanged." Restatement 2d § 79(b).

(C) and (D) are incorrect.

(C) and (D) are incorrect for the reasons set forth in the explanations of Choices (A) and (B) above. That is, a court will not upset a transaction just because one party seemed to get a good bargain. Restatement 2d § 79(b) provides that "If the requirement of consideration is met, there is no additional requirement of equivalence in the values exchanged." However, in Comments d and e to that provision, the drafters state, "Disparity in value . . . sometimes indicates that the purported consideration was not in fact bargained for but was a mere formality . . . Inadequacy may also help to justify rescission on the grounds of . . . duress or undue influence." Hence, while a court will enforce a bargain where a party gets a good deal, i.e., a lot of value for a small price, if the agreement was voluntarily entered into, the disparity between price and value justifies a court to examine the transaction for duress or some other contract defense, such as occurred here.

Answer to Question 6

(C) is the correct answer.

Under Restatement 2d § 176(2)(b), if a threat induces agreement to a contract with unfair terms, the threat is deemed "improper" and the agreement is rendered voidable if prior dealing between the parties significantly increases the effectiveness of the threat.

Here, the terms of the agreement are unfair because Paula is paying $1,000 for $90 worth of cinnamon rolls. Further, the prior dealing between Betty and Paula (i.e. the five year business relationship, and the fact that the cinnamon rolls made Paula's famous) significantly increased the effectiveness of Betty's threat. Betty knew Paula needed the cinnamon rolls for the big meeting and would likely be willing to pay the absurd amount. Thus, the agreement is voidable by Paula due to duress by improper threat.

(A) is incorrect.

A contract induced by duress by improper threat is *voidable*, not *void*. Restatement 2d § 175.

(B) is incorrect.

Breach of the duty of good faith is one of the reasons that a threat would be improper *if the underlying agreement was fair*. Restatement 2d § 176(1). Here, however, the terms of the deal were unfair—$1,000 for $90 worth of cinnamon rolls. Thus, this scenario is governed by the reasons making a threat "unfair" given in Restatement 2d § 176(2). Under § 176(2), there is nothing about the breach of the duty of good faith making the threat "unfair," making Choice (B) incorrect.

(D) is incorrect.

(D) is incorrect for the reasons stated in Choice (C). It is true that Paula did not <u>have</u> to buy the pastries for the meeting. However, that is not the test under the duress defense. The question is whether her agreement to pay the $1,000 was induced by an "improper threat," and under the circumstances, the threat was improper under Restatement 2d § 176(2)(b).

Answer to Question 7

(A) is the correct answer.

If a party is compelled to enter into a contract by use of physical force, the contract is void. Restatement 2d § 174. This means there is no agreement and neither party can enforce the terms of the agreement.

Thus, because Phyllis entered into the contract because David threatened to stab her, this contract is void, not voidable.

It is important to note that with contracts made void by duress by physical compulsion, the threat of physical harm must be imminent to make the contract void. Thus, if David had said "sign this contract to sell me your bike for $200, or I will stab you with this knife, *someday*," the threat would not be imminent and the scenario would be analyzed under duress by improper threat.

(B), (C), and (D) are incorrect.

(B), (C), and (D) are incorrect for the reason (A) is correct. A "void" agreement is a bit of an oxymoron, but it is important to realize that there is no enforceable contract between the parties, so there is nothing for Phyllis to "ratify" later.

Answer to Question 8

(C) is the correct answer.

If a victim of a contract entered into under duress avoids the contract, he or she is entitled to restitution. Therefore, Patricia would be entitled to the return of her car because that is the benefit she has conferred on Darren.

However, under the rules of "mutual restitution" a party seeking restitution must return whatever benefits he or she has received from the other party. Restatement 2d § 384. Contract law colloquially describes this obligation by stating that, "to get restitution a party must do restitution."

The question then is how much does Patricia have to return? If she returned the entire $6,000, Darren would be unjustly enriched because he would have had use of the car for free during the period of time he was in possession of it. Another way of looking at it is that Patricia may have given Darren a $6,000 car when they signed the contract, but that is not what she is getting back. She is getting back a $6,000 car that has been reduced in value by Darren's possession and use. Restitution is an equitable remedy and it would not be fair for her to bear the loss from the depreciation, damage, and wear and tear caused to the car while in Darren's possession when Darren was the party who improperly threatened Patricia. As such, she can withhold a reasonable amount from the $6,000 she must return to Darren.

(A) is incorrect.

(A) is incorrect because Patricia would be unjustly enriched if she got her car and got to keep the entire $6,000 payment. Restatement 2d § 384.

(B) and (D) are incorrect.

(B) is incorrect because Patricia is entitled to compensation for the use of the car by Darren in restitution. She is entitled to withhold that amount from the payment she otherwise must return. (D) is incorrect because Patricia gets to withhold that money at the outset, and need not bring a separate lawsuit to enforce her rights after paying Darren the full $6,000. If Darren thinks she withheld too much, it is up to him to sue her for unjust enrichment, not the other way around.

CHAPTER 9
UNDUE INFLUENCE

ANSWERS

Answer to Question 1

(A) is the correct answer.

When the elements of "undue influence" are met, a party can avoid the contract. The elements of "undue influence" are given in Restatement 2d § 177:

(1) The victim "by virtue of the relation between [the victim and the other party] is justified in assuming that the [other party] will not act in a manner inconsistent with his welfare"; and

(2) the advantaged party engages in "unfair persuasion."

In a case with similar facts, *Methodist Mission Home v. N.A.B.*, 451 S.W.2d 539 (Tex. Civ. App. 1970), the court found that a mother who recently gave birth in a home for unwed mothers could assert the defense of undue influence because: (1) the mother was justified in assuming that the counselor would not act in a manner inconsistent with her interests and welfare; and (2) the counselor engaged in "unfair persuasion" because she knew the mother who had "just given birth is usually emotionally distraught and particularly vulnerable to efforts . . . to persuade her to give up her child."

Thus, in this fact pattern there was a sufficient "special relationship" between Paula and the counselor, because Paula was staying at the maternity home and being counseled by the employee that convinced her to give her child up for adoption.

Further, many of the attributes that are looked to as evidence of "unfair persuasion" are present here, i.e. (1) Paula was particularly susceptible to persuasion; (2) Darla's employee told Paula the decision was urgent; (3) Paula was given no time to seek outside advice; and (4) the discussion and consummation of the transaction was in an "unusual place." Therefore, Paula would be able to avoid the contract on undue influence grounds.

(B) is incorrect.

(B) is incorrect because Darla's made no threat to Paula that caused her to agree to give her baby up for adoption, as is required to use a defense of duress. Restatement 2d § 175. Therefore, Paula would not be able to assert the defense of duress, but instead may assert undue influence as the reason to avoid the contract.

(C) is incorrect.

(C) is incorrect because it does not matter whether the counselor acted in good faith or not. The focus is on: (1) the relationship between the counselor and Paula and (2) whether the counselor had engaged in "unfair persuasion." Here there was unfair persuasion because the counselor did not give Paula sufficient time for reflection and did not allow her to seek outside advice.

(D) is incorrect.

The relationship between the dominant party and the victim necessary to trigger undue influence does not need to be a "fiduciary" relationship, which is often defined as "someone in whom a party is reasonable in reposing trust and confidence." The definition of the relationship necessary for undue influence is given in Restatement 2d § 177(1): "by virtue of the relation between [the victim and the other party] is justified in assuming that the [other party] will not act in a manner inconsistent with his welfare." Contracts scholars believe this definition to cast a wider net than just those who are in a fiduciary duty, which is justified by the language in Comment a to Restatement 2d § 177, which states, "Relations that often fall within the rule include those of parent and child, husband and wife, clergyman and parishioner and physician and patient. In each case it is a question of fact whether the relation is such as to give undue weight to the other's attempts at persuasion."

Answer to Question 2

(D) is the correct answer.

(D) is correct because the insurance adjuster's tactics involved unfair persuasion (an unfair bargain, no opportunity to seek independent advice, and Pearl was particularly susceptible because she had just been in an accident and was in pain). The insurance adjuster's tactics also involved domination because Pearl could not leave her hospital room. Therefore, Pearl likely will be able to avoid this contract based on undue influence. This fact pattern is based on *Weger v. Rocha*, 138 Cal. App. 109 (1934), where the court found that the release was disaffirmed on the basis of undue influence.

Note that an insurance adjuster is not someone typically that an injured party "is justified in assuming ... will not act in a manner inconsistent with his welfare," Restatement 2d § 177(1). But this problem shows that the definition given above must be interpreted liberally. In Restatement 2d § 177, Cmt. a, the relationship is more broadly described as whether "the relation is such as to give undue weight to the other's attempts at persuasion." Here, Pearl found herself in a situation where the insurer's attempts at persuasion, especially in promising immediate payment, gave him undue weight in trying to persuade her.

(A) is incorrect.

(A) is incorrect because it does not matter whether Pearl understood the terms of the contract. The issue is whether Pearl was improperly pressured into signing the release by someone with whom she was in a "special relationship."

(B) and (C) are incorrect.

(B) and (C) are incorrect because they deal with the elements of duress. This fact scenario raises the issue of undue influence, not duress, because no "improper threats" were made by the adjuster as defined in Restatement 2d § 176.

Answer to Question 3

(D) is the correct answer.

The commercial law scholars White & Summers have identified the following factors as those which argue for a finding of improper persuasion, necessary for a finding of undue influence:

(1) discussion of the transaction in an unusual place or at an unusual time;

(2) consummation of the transaction in an unusual place or at an unusual time;

(3) insistent demand that the transaction close quickly and extreme emphasis on untoward consequences of delay;

(4) use of multiple persuaders by the advantaged party;

(5) absence of third party advisors for the victim;

(6) unfair resulting bargain; and

(7) susceptibility of the disadvantaged party.

Therefore, Choice (D) is the correct answer, as Choice (A), (B), and (C) all list factors implicating undue influence.

(A), (B), and (C) are incorrect.

(A), (B), and (C) are individually correct, hence Choice (D) is the best answer.

Answer to Question 4

(B) is the correct answer.

Restatement 2d § 177(3) provides that if a party's manifestation of assent is induced by undue influence by one who is not a party to the transaction, "the contract is voidable by the victim unless the other party to the transaction in good faith and without reason to know of the undue influence either gives value or materially relies on the transaction." Therefore, Choice (B) is correct because it states this rule.

An example of a situation where a third party might exercise undue influence is where parents unfairly persuade their only daughter to go to college X by not giving the daughter enough time for reflection, the chance to talk to college counselors at her high school, etc. At the point when the acceptance is set, daughter likely could immediately avoid the transaction, even though the college, the other contracting party, is innocent and acting in good faith, on undue influence grounds. However, if the college materially relies on the transaction after receiving daughter's letter, e.g., by turning down other students and reserving a place in the small entering class for daughter, the contract becomes enforceable at that point because of the innocence and good faith of the college, the other contracting party.

(A), (C), and (D) are incorrect.

(A), (C), and (D) are incorrect for the reasons Choice (B) is correct.

CHAPTER 10
FRAUD & MISREPRESENTATION

ANSWERS

Answer to Question 1

(B) is the correct answer.

A misrepresentation in contract law is any assertion that is not in accord with the facts. Restatement 2d § 159. A misrepresentation can be made with three different mental states: (1) innocent (when the speaker did not know, and was not at fault for not knowing, that the statement was wrong); (2) negligent (where the speaker believed what he or she was saying was true, but was careless in making that statement, e.g., if in the problem Debbie would have negligently measured the parcel as fifty acres); or (3) with "scienter." Scienter itself is made up of three different mental states: (a) when the speaker knows he or she is lying; (b) when the speaker knows that he or she had no idea whether the assertion was correct (if Debbie had not had a survey done and just said it was fifty acres without having any idea on the matter); and (c) when the speaker is "reckless" in making the statement. When the assertion is made with scienter, there is "fraud."

Identifying the mental state can be important to ascertain whether misrepresentation can be asserted in a breach of contract case. Under Restatement 2d § 164, misrepresentation can be alleged successfully in a breach of contract action if the following can be established:

(1) A misrepresentation of an existing fact;

(2) The misrepresentation was either fraudulent *or* material;

(3) The misrepresentation was actually relied upon; and

(4) Such reliance was reasonable.

One of the big differences between using misrepresentation in tort and contract is that in tort, the innocent party is entitled to money damages. In contract, it only acts to allow the innocent party to avoid the transaction. Restatement 2d § 164.

A contract entered into because of misrepresentation is voidable, not void, meaning the innocent party can choose to go forward with the transaction if he or she wishes to do so. (Note that, as explained in Question 2 below, where there has been "fraud *in the factum*," and not "fraud in the inducement," the contract is <u>void</u>, not voidable. But the number of fraud *in the factum* cases is small.)

Here, Statement II is correct because Debbie was reasonable, but wrong, in asserting the property was 50+ acres. That makes the statement an innocent misrepresentation.

Statement V is correct because all the elements for invoking the misrepresentation doctrine set forth above are met. The statement that the property was 50+ acres was a misrepresentation; it was material (meaning the true facts would make a difference to a reasonable person in deciding whether to enter into the transaction); Paula relied on it in making her purchase, and her reliance was reasonable.

Statement I is incorrect because Debbie does not have the right to avoid the transaction since she was the party who made the misrepresentation. Recall that the innocent party has the right to go forward with the deal, so if Debbie wanted to avoid the transaction but Paula did not, Paula would prevail.

Statement III is incorrect because the sole remedy for the claim of misrepresentation in a breach of contract case is to avoid the transaction, not damages. It is only in tort where damages are awarded.

Statement IV is incorrect because the statement was made by Debbie innocently; not with scienter.

(A), (C), and (D) are incorrect.

These choices are incorrect for the reason (B) is correct, as explained above.

Answer to Question 2

(A) is the correct answer.

When a party misrepresents the very nature of the contract itself, there is *fraud in the factum*. In such a situation, the contract is void and never enforceable. Restatement 2d § 163. This differs from where there is just misrepresentation in inducement to enter the contract where the contract is then voidable by the innocent party. Here, Paul represented that what Dwayne was signing was just an autograph for a fan; Dwayne had no idea it was any form of contract. As such it was fraud *in the factum* as the very nature of the document itself was misrepresented to Dwayne, and was void from its inception.

(B) is incorrect.

(B) represents the outcome if there had been merely misrepresentation in inducement to enter into the contract rather than *in the factum*, e.g., if Paul had induced Dwayne to buy a refrigerator from him by telling him it had a freezer in it, when Paul knew it did not. Had the facts misrepresented by Paul only induced Dwayne to enter the agreement, rather than misrepresent the existence or nature of an agreement at all, Choice (B) would be proper.

(C) is incorrect.

(C) is incorrect for two reasons. First, the contract is void, not voidable, since there was fraud *in the factum*. But even had there been fraud in the inducement, the party making the misrepresentation does not have the right to avoid the transaction.

(D) is incorrect.

(D) is incorrect for the reasons (A) is correct. The contract is not enforceable due to misrepresentation and is void because the misrepresentation was fraud *in the factum*.

Answer to Question 3

(C) is the correct answer.

Normally using words like "in my opinion" and "pretty good" express a belief without certainty as to quality, and they are not actionable as an opinion. Restatement 2d § 168(1). In other words, such statements are not "statements of fact" which are necessary to establish a misrepresentation defense. Restatement 2d § 164.

However, in every opinion there is at least one fact: that the opinion expressed is the party's true opinion. Restatement 2d § 168(2). Here we know that Drew was aware that his work was neither of good quality nor speedy. He has thus misrepresented "the fact" of what his true opinion is to Patricia. Thus the contract is voidable by Patricia on misrepresentation grounds.

(A) is incorrect.

(A) represents the outcome *if* Drew's misrepresentation constituted fraud *in the factum*. It was not because Patricia knew she was entering into a contract for painting. She was induced to enter that contract because of Drew's misrepresentation regarding the quality and speed of his work.

(B) is incorrect.

(B) is incorrect because the contract is not voidable by Drew. He is the party which has misrepresented an existing fact, giving <u>Patricia</u> the right to avoid the contract.

(D) is incorrect

As discussed in the explanation of Choice (A) above, the comment by Drew would not be classified as an unenforceable opinion. In order for the contract to be enforceable, Drew would have had to express only his true opinion during the negotiations.

Answer to Question 4

(A) is the correct answer.

As discussed in the answer to Question 3, an opinion is typically an unenforceable belief without any certainty. Restatement 2d § 168. "Trade talk" or "puffing" is seen as insufficiently "factual" statements to support a misrepresentation claim, and are merely opinions. Typical examples involve saying "this is the best" or "this is a superior product" and will not be a basis for a misrepresentation defense.

Here, Seller told Buyer that their jelly is the "best." This is unprovable trade talk or puffing about the product, and is not a factual claim about its product. Whether one type of jelly is the "best" is not determinable with certainty as it would depend on each person's tastes as to what they prefer in a jelly; whether the term meant best tasting, best value, best packaging, etc. Since the only assertion was trade talk or puffing, it is not actionable as misrepresentation, and Buyer could not avoid the contract based on any misrepresentation by Seller.

(B) is incorrect.

(B) is incorrect for the reasons discussed in (A). There is not a viable misrepresentation defense based on the trade talk and puffing language used by Seller.

(C) is incorrect.

(C) is incorrect because the answer wrongly assumes a valid misrepresentation defense existed for Buyer based on the language used. Further, his having sampled the jelly would not affect his ability to assert misrepresentation if it existed.

(D) is incorrect.

Merchant sellers will be held to the usage of trade within the industry. UCC § 1–303. Nevertheless, there is no "usage of trade" given in the facts which would transform an unactionable opinion or "puff," into an actionable statement of fact.

Answer to Question 5

(D) is the correct answer.

There are five situations where an actionable misrepresentation occurs even though a party is silent and makes no false affirmative statement of fact: (1) when affirmative action is taken to conceal a fact; (2) when a party learns of subsequent information which is necessary to disclose to prevent a previous assertion from misrepresenting a fact; (3) when a party knows disclosure is necessary to correct a mistake of the other party as to a basic assumption of the contract; (4) where a party knows that disclosure is necessary to correct a mistake of the other party as to the effect of a writing; and (5) where the other party is in a relation of trust or confidence with the silent party. Restatement 2d §§ 160, 161. When one of these situations is present, a party's silence will be taken as a misrepresentation of the true facts. In other words, it is treated as if the seller said the opposite of the true facts, i.e., here, it is as if the seller said "There are no holes in the walls."

Here, Seller took affirmative actions to conceal the fact that the walls of the house are riddled with holes. Since he took the affirmative acts of disguising the holes, he has misrepresented the fact of their existence to Buyer. Thus the contract is voidable by Buyer under a misrepresentation theory.

(A) is incorrect.

Buyer would not be entitled to the $210,000, which might be the fair market value of the property. Since Buyer is voiding the contract, he would have to be put in the same position he would have been in had the contract not been entered into, and thus is only entitled to the $200,000 he paid for the house.

(B) is incorrect.

As discussed in the explanation to (D), Seller's silence here is deemed a misrepresentation because he took affirmative steps to conceal the defect.

(C) is incorrect.

For the reasons discussed in the explanation of (D), Seller would not lose a claim to void the contract and would not be forced to keep the house and accept damages based on the holes.

Answer for Question 6

(A) is the correct answer.

When one party knows that the other party is mistaken as to a basic assumption on which the contract is based, the first party's silence will act as a misrepresentation. Restatement 2d § 161(b).

Here, Buyer was mistaken as to a basic assumption of the contract, i.e., he was assuming that when someone purchases a "refrigerator," the unit comes complete with the cooling system inside and even said something about the cooling system. As Seller was aware there was no cooling system, and Buyer was operating on the assumption the system was included, Seller was obligated to inform Buyer of his mistake. In other words, Seller had a "duty to speak" about the absence of the cooling system to inform a potential purchaser as to his or her mistake about the basic assumption. Thus, the contract is voidable by Buyer.

(B) is incorrect.

While this is another situation where silence may act as misrepresentation, nothing indicates Seller took any affirmative acts to conceal the fact the cooling system was missing. It was missing when he got it. He simply did not mention it to Buyer.

(C) is incorrect.

Just because Buyer did not ask about the cooling system does not mean Seller was relieved of his duty to speak up about the absence of the system. It was Seller who had an obligation to inform Buyer about his mistake as to a basic assumption under the contract as evidenced by Buyer's statement regarding the cooling system.

(D) is incorrect.

(D) is incorrect for the reasons discussed in the explanation to (A). This situation is an instance where Seller had an obligation to speak, and his silence will not prevent a misrepresentation claim.

Answer to Question 7

(B) is the correct answer.

Another example of when a party's silence acts as a misrepresentation of a fact is when the party is in a relationship of trust or confidence (such as a fiduciary relationship) with the other, "trusting" party. Restatement 2d § 161(d). When a party is in a special relationship with the other party, he or she has an obligation to speak about information of which the "trusting" party is unaware. Because the "trusting" party will presume all relevant information has been disclosed to them by a person in whom it is reasonable to repose trust and confidence, given the relationship, the "sharp" party's silence acts as a misrepresentation.

Here, Debbie has been an asset manager for Penny for many years, and they are in a fiduciary relationship. Penny was unaware there was an event occurring which made her property significantly more valuable, and Debbie, being aware of the event, was under a duty to disclose the true facts to Penny. Because Debbie did not disclose that information, the contract is voidable by Penny under a misrepresentation theory, even though Debbie said nothing one way or the other about the amusement park.

(A) is incorrect.

(A) represents the outcome if there had been misrepresentation of fraud *in the factum*, where a contract is void from its inception. That is not the case here as Penny knew she was entering into a land sale contract.

(C) is incorrect.

(C) is incorrect for the reasons given in the explanation of Choice (B). The contract is in fact voidable by Penny on misrepresentation grounds.

(D) is incorrect.

(D) incorrectly states Debbie could void the contract, but she cannot. Debbie is the party who misrepresented a material fact by her silence.

Answer to Question 8

(A) is the correct answer

Under Restatement 2d § 161(a), "a person's non-disclosure of a fact known to him is equivalent to an assertion that the fact does not exist . . . where he knows that disclosure of the fact is necessary to prevent some previous assertion from being a misrepresentation." In other words, when new information makes previous assertions false, remaining silent will act as a misrepresentation, even if the previous assertion was true when it was made. By not correcting to reflect the new information, it is as though the misrepresenting party is reasserting that their previous statements remain true.

Here, Derek was being truthful when he said he had not been diagnosed with cancer when he filled out the application. However, when he was then diagnosed with the disease prior to the acceptance by Pristine, he was under a duty to inform Pristine of the new diagnosis. Thus Derek's silence acted as a misrepresentation of an existing fact, namely, his status as a person diagnosed with cancer.

(B) is incorrect.

(B) is incorrect because Derek did not correct the assertion after subsequently learning new information which made the previous "no cancer diagnosis" incorrect.

(C) is incorrect.

Pristine was not under an obligation to inquire again, or condition its acceptance on, whether the previous assertion was still true. It was Derek who had a duty to correct the misapprehension.

(D) is incorrect.

One situation where misrepresentation may be based on silence is where a party learns of subsequent information that makes his or her previous assertion false, even where that previous assertion was true when it was made. Pristine does not need to prove there was any additional agreement to inform them of subsequent information.

Answer to Question 9

(B) is the correct answer.

The general rule is that in an arm's length transaction (a transaction between "strangers"), where none of the special circumstances and relationships set forth in Restatement 2d § 161 exist, a party need not disclose information which is legally available to both parties during the negotiations. Note that the party still may not mislead the other to conceal the facts, but simply remaining silent will not support an action for misrepresentation. This question is loosely based on *Laidlaw v. Organ,* 15 U.S. (2 Wheat.) 178 (1817).

Here, Reporter had no duty to disclose to Businessman what he learned at the public Commission meeting. Again, Reporter could not affirmatively mislead Businessman, but avoiding the question in an arm's length transaction is not actionable.

(A) is incorrect.

In an arm's length transaction such as the one described in this question, Seller was under no duty to disclose the facts legally available to either party during negotiations.

(C) is incorrect.

Whether Reporter can use for his personal benefit information he learned while working is an issue between Reporter and his employer. It does not make Reporter's silence actionable in an arm's length transaction with Businessman.

(D) is incorrect.

The reason Businessman will lose is because Reporter was not under an obligation to disclose the information about the road extension. Whether Businessman inquired is not relevant. Note if Businessman had inquired, and then Reporter actively misled Businessman as to the truth about the road, then a viable claim for misrepresentation would have existed.

Answer to Question 10

(D) is the correct answer.

One issue in this problem is the mental state of Seller when he spoke of the roof. This problem shows an example of a party who makes a misrepresentation with "scienter," i.e., one who knows that what he is saying is untrue. A misrepresentation made with scienter is known as fraud.

As set forth in the explanation to Question 1, for a viable claim of misrepresentation, the fact misrepresented must be either fraudulent or material. Here, Seller acted fraudulently in making the representation to Buyer. The statement was intended to deceive and induce Buyer into entering the contract, and Seller possessed scienter. In other words, Seller knew that the representation's he made were not true, and did so anyway. Thus, Buyer may bring a misrepresentation claim as Seller fraudulently misrepresented the state of the roof.

The second issue is how much inspection is required by the Buyer. This is an issue because not only must there be actual reliance to assert misrepresentation successfully, but that reliance must be justified, and if the misstatement is easy to discover, any reliance on it may not be justified.

As set forth in Restatement 2d § 172, "A recipient's fault in not knowing or discovering the facts before making the contract does not make his reliance unjustified unless it amounts to a failure to act in good faith and in accordance with reasonable standards of fair dealing." In other words, the buyer can pretty much take what the seller tells them at face value. It is only when discovering the misstatement is so obvious that failing to uncover it is "bad faith." For example, if a car salesman tells the potential buyer that the car has air conditioning, and the buyer test drives the car on a hot day for an hour, it likely would be a "bad faith" claim to assert he didn't know about the absence of an air conditioner in the car.

Here, it is difficult to get to the roof. As such, Buyer is not "guilty" of contributory negligence or otherwise at fault in relying on Seller's statements about the roof, no matter how easy it might be to spot if Buyer got to the roof. He has no duty to get up there himself. As such, Buyer can avoid the transaction based on the Seller's misrepresentation, making Choice (D) the correct answer.

(A) is incorrect.

(A) is incorrect because he misrepresentation would make the contract voidable only by Buyer, the innocent party. The contract would not be voidable by Seller.

(B) is incorrect.

For the reasons discussed in the explanation of (D), Buyer's reliance on Seller's representation about the roof is justified as he had no duty to climb on the roof and his failure to do so was not "bad faith." Restatement 2d § 172.

(C) is incorrect.

As discussed in the explanation of (D), a misrepresentation in contract law may be *either* fraudulent or material to support a misrepresentation claim. Since Seller acted fraudulently here, the absence of holes in the roof need not be material also.

CHAPTER 11
UNCONSIONABILITY

ANSWERS

Answer to Question 1

(D) is the correct answer.

Under UCC § 2–302(1) and Restatement 2d § 208, if a court finds a contract is unconscionable the court may: (1) refuse to enforce the entire contract, (2) enforce the remainder of the contract without the unconscionable clause or clauses, or (3) modify or limit application of any clause to avoid an unjust result. Therefore, (D) is correct.

Note that the unconscionability doctrine is thus an exception to the general rule that courts "interpret" contracts, rather than getting involved in rewriting them. Under the doctrine of unconscionability, a court is authorized to change the parties' duties and rewrite a contract to remove any unconscionable clauses or alter the effect of any unconscionable clauses.

Note also that unconscionability is a decision for the court, not the jury. A frequent question in this area focuses on who has the power to declare a clause, or an entire contract, unconscionable. The answer is the court only.

(A), (B), and (C) are incorrect.

(A), (B), and (C) are each individually correct, making (D) the best answer.

Answer to Question 2

(A) is the correct answer.

A finding of unconscionability requires that there be both procedural and substantive unconscionability.

Procedural unconscionability is generally defined as the absence of meaningful choice on the part of the aggrieved party. Typically procedural unconscionability is broken into two components: (1) oppression, which is defined as unequal bargaining power; and (2) surprise, which focuses on how "hidden" the unfair clause is in the prolix of the agreement.

Substantive unconscionability occurs when the terms of the agreement are unreasonably favorable to one party.

Note that while both procedural and substantive unconscionability are required for a finding of unconscionability, courts use a "sliding scale" test to determine if unconscionability exists. Under the "sliding scale" test, the greater the presence of one type of unconscionability, the less the presence of the other is necessary before a court will find a contract unconscionable.

(B), (C), and (D) are incorrect.

(B), (C), and (D) are incorrect for the reason (A) is correct. A conclusion that a clause of a contract, or the entire contract itself, is unconscionable requires a finding of <u>both</u> procedural and substantive unconscionability.

Answer to Question 3

(C) is the correct answer.

When a court examines an agreement for unconscionability it is only concerned with any substantive and procedural unconscionability which exist <u>at the time the parties enter into the contract</u>. Therefore, if the terms of the contract were substantively fair at the time of entering into the contract, i.e. there is no substantive unconscionability, then the contract may not be disaffirmed due to unconscionability.

(A) and (B) are incorrect.

(A) and (B) are incorrect for the reason (C) is correct. The terms of the contract are looked at as of the time of making the contract. Therefore, this contract may not be disaffirmed based on unconscionability now, even though there is an unfair interest term presently, because the interest term was fair at the time of making the contract.

(D) is incorrect.

(D) is incorrect because a finding of unconscionability requires both the presence of substantive and procedural unconscionability. Therefore, a court could not "forgive" the lack of substantive unconscionability.

Answer to Question 4

(D) is the correct answer.

While unconscionability is most commonly applied when a merchant seller sells to a consumer on unfair terms, the doctrine is not limited to consumer transactions. In fact, recently the doctrine of unconscionability has been applied with greater frequency to merchant-to-merchant business contracts, *see, e.g., A & M Produce v. FMC Corp.*, 186 Cal. Rptr. 114 (Cal. App. Ct. 1982), and can be applied to non-UCC transactions as well, as evidenced by Restatement 2d § 208.

Unconscionability will apply as long as both procedural and substantive unconscionability is found. Thus, the doctrine applies to merchant <u>or</u> consumer transactions.

(A), (B), and (C) are incorrect.

(A), (B), and (C) are incorrect for the reasons (D) is correct.

CHAPTER 12

"ILLEGALITY" AND CONTRACTS UNENFORCEABLE ON GROUNDS OF PUBLIC POLICY

ANSWERS

Answer to Question 1

(C) is the correct answer.

When an agreement calls for one of the parties to commit a criminal act, it is unenforceable due to public policy. Restatement 2d § 178. In other words, when the contract calls for acts that are illegal, it is unenforceable by either party and void. Contract law has determined enforcement of the performance duties under these types of contracts is outweighed by public policy against the prohibited acts.

Here, the agreement was for the murder of Preston's neighbor, clearly a criminal act. As such, Preston will not be able to enforce the obligation under the agreement for Dean to pay the remaining $7,000.

(A) and (B) are incorrect.

(A) and (B) are incorrect because the agreement is void since its subject matter calls for Preston to commit an illegal act. Restatement 2d § 178.

(D) is incorrect.

Preston will lose because the contract is void under Restatement 2d § 178. Hence there is no viable agreement to "breach," materially or immaterially.

Answer to Question 2

(A) is the correct answer.

When there has been partial or complete performance under an illegal contract, the court will "leave the parties as they find them." That is, there is no right to restitution by either party. So Dean is out the $3,000.

Note, the *in pari delicto* doctrine, when applicable, acts as an exception to the above rule, as explained in Choice (C) below. However, the doctrine does not apply to this situation.

(B) is incorrect.

The agreement between Dean and Preston is void. Restatement 2d § 178. As such, Preston cannot "earn" money under a non-existent or non-viable agreement. It does not matter what he does pursuant to it. Once it was formed with the obligation of committing an illegal act, that agreement was void.

(C) is incorrect.

When applicable, the *in pari delicto* (meaning "in equal fault") doctrine allows one party to recover in restitution for a payment made under a contract that is unenforceable due to public policy/illegality. The elements of *in pari delicto* are:

(1) The party seeking restitution was not guilty of an act of "serious moral turpitude," and

(2) the other party in the contract was more blameworthy.

Here, Dean contracted with Preston to murder his neighbor, an act of serious moral turpitude, so the doctrine cannot apply.

For an example of when *in pari delicto* <u>does</u> apply, *see Bateman Eichler v. Berner*, 472 U.S. 229 (1985), where the investors who were guilty of insider trading were allowed to recover their broker fees from the stockbrokers who gave them the insider tips.

(D) is incorrect.

When there has been performance under an illegal contract, courts leave the parties as they find them, and does not order repayment of any monies paid on an unjust enrichment or any other theory in the absence of an *in pari delicto* situation.

Answer to Question 3

(D) is the correct answer.

Contracts that include a payment of a bribe, or which are procured by a bribe, are void and unenforceable due to illegality. Restatement 2d § 178. The term illegal refers to acts that are *against public policy*, and a bribe falls in this category.

The contract between Peter and Dan calls for Dan to bribe the owner of the general contractor and, as such, would be unenforceable on illegality grounds.

(A) and (C) are incorrect.

(A) and (C) are individually true, making (D) the correct choice.

(B) is incorrect.

It does not matter that the bribe was never paid by Dan. The purpose of the agreement was illegal, even though only part of the payment went to the bribe, and that means the contract is void and unenforceable.

Answer to Question 4

(D) is the correct answer.

Another example of an "illegal" contract is one that is procured by a bribe, even if the bribe was actually paid by a third party—here Dan. As an illegal contract, it is unenforceable and void. Restatement 2d § 178.

(A), (B), and (C) are all incorrect.

The contract is not enforceable because it is an illegal contract procured by a bribe. Hence it is unenforceable by either party, and Peter is not entitled to recovery for its breach under any theory.

Answer to Question 5

(C) is the correct answer.

In agreements where a party should be licensed, but is not, whether the contract is enforceable depends on the purpose of the licensing requirement. Restatement 2d § 178. If the purpose of the licensing requirement is for a government agency to control the skill and moral quality of those participating in the occupation, such as for lawyers and doctors, the lack of a license makes the contract unenforceable. On the other hand, when the licensing requirement is primarily a revenue raising measure, the lack of a license will not make the contract unenforceable under contract law.

Here, the contract is for carpentry work in a municipality that requires all contractors to be licensed. The facts state the purpose of the licensing statute was to raise money (the $500 fee), and no other requirements of skill or quality were necessary to obtain a license. Since the statute is primarily a revenue raising measure, the contract is enforceable.

(A) is incorrect.

The contract is enforceable since the licensing requirement's primary purpose was to raise revenue, and not to screen for the competency of the licensee.

(B) is incorrect.

(B) is incorrect because the contract is enforceable regardless of whether Dave investigated the licensing status of Paula.

(D) is incorrect.

(D) is incorrect because the contract is enforceable regardless of whether Dave waives the license requirement.

Answer to Question 6

(C) is the correct answer.

Where a jurisdiction imposes a licensing requirement as a means for regulation of the competence and morals of the licensee, such as a licensing requirement for attorneys, a purported contract with an unlicensed practitioner is void and thus unenforceable. Restatement 2d § 178.

(A) and (B) are incorrect.

(A) and (B) are incorrect because a "contract" with an unlicensed attorney is unenforceable due to illegality/public policy. Restatement 2d § 178. This is true regardless of how competently the job was done by the unlicensed professional.

(D) is incorrect.

Patrick can recover nothing under the contract. He also would not be entitled to restitution for any work he had done under an unjust enrichment or any other theory. Under the rules of professional responsibility of most states, Patrick would also be required to refund any money he had been paid by Darlene in fees or costs.

Answer to Question 7

(D) is the correct answer.

When a statute makes a type of contract illegal for the protection of a particular class of persons, a party within that class has the option of avoiding or enforcing the contract. In these situations the contract is voidable, not void, by the party protected by the statute. Restatement 2d § 178.

Here, the statute was to protect consumers from interest rates on credit agreements in excess of 15%. Penny falls into the class of persons as a consumer shopping at Department Store. As such, the contract is voidable by Penny, meaning she has the option of avoiding the contract or enforcing it. Thus, both (A) and (B) are correct.

(A) and (B) are incorrect.

Both (A) and (B) are individually true, making (D) the correct answer.

(C) is incorrect.

Department Store does not have the option to enforce the contract; as to the Store, it is unenforceable as illegal and against public policy. However, Penny can waive the protection of the statute and choose to enforce the agreement since the reason the agreement is "illegal" is to protect individuals situated like Penny, and she is entitled to waive those protections in the voidable (by her) contract.

CHAPTER 13
PAROL EVIDENCE RULE AND INTERPRETATION

ANSWERS

Answer to Question 1

(D) is the correct answer.

The parol evidence rule regulates when a party can introduce "parol evidence," which is evidence of an agreement that one party claims was part of the final deal, but which does not appear in the final written agreement of the parties.

The rules regarding the extent of parol evidence that can be introduced depend on the level of "integration" of the final written document. Determining whether an agreement is integrated, and, if so, the extent of the integration, is thus the first step in a parol evidence analysis. The types of integration and the process for determining the level of integration are set forth below.

A writing is "integrated" if it contains at least one term *intended by the parties* to be their final expression of agreement as to that term, i.e., the term is no longer meant to be part of a preliminary draft or negotiation, but rather is the term to which both parties have agreed to be bound. Restatement 2d § 209(1).

A writing is "partially integrated" if the parties intended it to be the final expression of at least one term, but did not intend it to be a final expression of *all terms* of the agreement. Restatement 2d § 210(2). If a writing is partially integrated, some parol evidence is admissible to supplement the writing.

A writing is "totally integrated" if it is intended to be the *complete and exclusive* expression as to *all terms* of the agreement. Restatement 2d § 210(1). If a writing is totally integrated, *no evidence* of any parol term can be admitted. Restatement 2d §§ 210, 213, 215, 216. This makes sense because if a writing is found to be a wholly integrated contract, by definition, the parties have intended for it to be the complete statement of their final agreement and there is no term that was supposed to be part of the agreement that was not found in the written agreement.

The decision of integration is a decision for the <u>judge</u> to make *outside the presence of a jury*. Thus, it is considered a <u>question of law</u> and not a *question of fact*. Restatement 2d § 210(3). Under the Restatement 2d §§ 210 and 214, which is the prevalent view today, a party can introduce all relevant evidence to the judge in a hearing and/or briefing to establish the circumstances surrounding the making of the writing in order to show the writing might not be completely or totally integrated. Thus, Choice (D) is correct as it reflects the rules outlined in the Restatement 2d.

By way of illustration, if after a hearing the judge decided that the contract at issue in this question was totally integrated, Buyer would not be able to introduce the proffered parol evidence, i.e., evidence that the Seller said he would throw in the hot tub. So whether or not the Seller made such a statement, the jury would never hear about it if the judge ruled the agreement was completely integrated.

On the other hand, if the judge ruled that the agreement was only partially integrated after the hearing, then Buyer <u>might</u> be able to introduce evidence of the hot tub agreement to the jury. Whether he would or not depends on whether the judge also determines that the hot tub inclusion is a "consistent additional term." If it is a consistent additional term, then the Seller would be able to testify about the conversation regarding the hot tub, and a jury might or might not believe him.

If the judge rules that the hot tub agreement is not a consistent additional term, i.e., is a "contradictory" term then, once again, Buyer could not introduce evidence of the hot tub agreement. The tests for consistent and contrary additional terms are discussed later in this chapter, but the point here is that the determinations by the judge at the beginning of the parol evidence analytical process—whether the agreement is partially or totally integrated and whether that parol term is a consistent or an inconsistent additional term—are crucial to the rights of the parties to introduce evidence of a parol term thereafter. To summarize:

Judge Ruling on Contract	Judge Ruling on Term	Parol Evidence Admissibility
Totally Integrated	Contrary Additional Term	Parol Evidence is *not* admissible
Totally Integrated	Consistent Additional Term	Parol Evidence is *not* admissible
Partially Integrated	Contrary Additional Term	Parol Evidence is *not* admissible
Partially Integrated	Consistent Additional Term	Parol Evidence *is* admissible

(A), (B), and (C) are incorrect.

These answers are incorrect because they provide an erroneous statement of the Restatement 2d rules regarding integration and the parol evidence rule as described in the explanation of (D) above.

Answer to Question 2

(C) is the correct answer.

The rule regarding partially integrated agreements is that if the court rules that the agreement is partially integrated, *some parol evidence* is admissible to supplement the writing. The rule is that parol evidence is admissible if the alleged term agreed to is a *"consistent additional term."*

Under the Restatement 2d, a term is a "consistent additional term" if, under the circumstances, it is one that *"might naturally be omitted from the writing."* Restatement 2d § 216(2)(b). In other words, the question is, if the parties had really agreed to such a term (the "Shed Agreement"), is it is the kind of term which "might naturally" have been left out when the agreement was reduced to writing? If it is the kind of term which might naturally have been omitted, then it is a "consistent additional term" and it may be introduced to the jury. If it is not the kind of term which might naturally be omitted from the final writing, then it is an "inconsistent additional term" and it cannot be introduced to the jury.

You might ask, how could a term that the parties agreed to "might naturally be omitted" from the final written contract? Well, it is rare, but suppose the final written contract in this case was taken from the internet and had a few blanks in it for the address, price, etc., but nothing for unusual agreements, like removal of a shed. It only dealt with things like providing good title, paying with a cashier's check, etc. Alternatively, suppose the parties were friends and did not feel like they had to "document everything." In such a case, a clause calling for the removal of the shed "might naturally be omitted" from the final contract. If that is the case, then the Shed Agreement would be deemed a "consistent additional term" and Buyer would be permitted to testify about it to the jury. It would then be up to the jury to decide whether he is believable or not.

On the other hand, one could certainly argue that if the parties had really made the Shed Agreement, and it was important to the Buyer, the Buyer would probably double check to make sure the final writing had the Shed Agreement in it. If a court adopted that reasoning, then it would <u>not</u> be a case where such a term "might naturally be omitted" from the final writing, and a court would find that it is a "contradictory" additional term. Upon such a finding, Buyer would not be able to testify about the Shed Agreement to the jury.

This case is based on *Mitchell v. Lath*, 160 N.E. 646 (N.Y. 1928) in which the buyer of property argued that the seller orally agreed to remove an ice house from an adjacent piece of property the seller also owned that interfered with the view from the purchased piece of property. There, the N.Y. Court of Appeals split 4–3, with the majority holding that if the seller had really agreed to remove the ice house, it was the type of term that probably would have been included *somewhere* in the documents exchanged by the parties. As such, it was *not* the kind of term that "might naturally" be omitted from the writings. Hence, it was a "*contradictory*" term, and evidence of it could not be presented to the trier of fact, despite the contract being partially integrated.

The minority said land contracts dealt with issues like good title and payment terms, and so an ice house removal agreement was exactly the kind of term that might be omitted from the final writing and would have deemed it a "consistent additional term."

Finally, while up to this point all the discussion and citations have been to the Restatement 2d of Contracts, know that the parol evidence rule also exists in UCC § 2–202. It operates almost exactly the same as under the Restatement. The only substantive difference is the test for a "consistent additional term," and even then the difference is slight. As indicated above, the test under Restatement 2d § 216(2)(b) is whether the term "*might naturally be omitted* from the writing." Under the UCC the test is whether the term "*would certainly have been included*" in the final writing. UCC § 2–202, Cmt. 3. As applied to the facts of this question, if it were analyzed under the UCC test, the question would be whether the Shed Agreement, if it actually had been agreed to, would certainly have been included in the final writing under all the circumstances. If it would certainly have been included, then it is a contradictory term, and no evidence of its making can be proffered. If, however, the court determines that it would <u>not</u> certainly have been included in the final writing, then it is a consistent additional term, and the party will be entitled to introduce evidence to the jury if the court rules that the written agreement is only partially integrated.

(A) and (B) are incorrect.

These answers are incorrect as they misstate the law. It is not the case that parol evidence can *always* be introduced when the agreement is partially integrated nor is it the case that parol evidence can *never* be introduced in such a circumstance. If the parol term is judged a consistent additional term, it can be admitted; if it is a contradictory term, it cannot.

(D) is incorrect.

(D) is incorrect as it states a rule that is exactly the opposite of the parol evidence rule. If the Shed Agreement was a consistent additional term, it <u>could</u> be admitted to supplement a partially integrated contract.

Answer to Question 3

(A) is the correct answer.

Under the Restatement 2d, a term is a "consistent additional term" if, under the circumstances, it is one that *"might naturally be omitted* from the writing." Restatement 2d § 216(2)(b). In other words, the question is whether, if the parties had really agreed to such a term (the barter agreement), is it the kind of term which "might naturally" have been left out when the agreement was reduced to writing? If so, Matt can introduce evidence of its making to the jury. However, if it is a term that probably would have been included in the writings, i.e., it is the type of term that *naturally would <u>not</u> be omitted from a final writing,* then it is a "*contradictory*" term that <u>cannot be introduced</u> even to supplement a partially integrated writing.

This answer choice assumes the court would find that the barter agreement was the kind of term which "might naturally be omitted" from a contract for the sale of land, and so it would be admissible as a consistent additional term. The problem is adapted from Restatement 2d § 216, Cmt. d, Ill. 5.

(B) is incorrect.

(B) is incorrect because it states a rule that is exactly the opposite of the parol evidence rule, as set forth in the explanation of (A).

(C) is incorrect.

Avoidance of unjust enrichment would be an insufficient reason, in and of itself, to allow admission of the parol evidence. The barter agreement would only be admissible if a court determined it was a consistent additional term and the agreement partially integrated.

(D) is incorrect.

This choice has no basis in law. Although parties should be thorough in reviewing the writing to an agreement, there is no rule that it is either party's duty to ensure all favorable terms are reduced to writing such that parol evidence will not be barred because one party failed to do so.

Answer to Question 4

(B) is the correct answer.

The language in the block quote is known as a "merger" or "integration" clause (the terms are synonymous). Such clauses are usually found at or near the end of a written agreement and the idea is for these clauses to say that all terms on which the parties have reached agreement are integrated into (or have been "merged" into) the final written agreement.

The general rule is that such clauses have *persuasive*, but *not determinative*, effect on the question of whether the parties intended the agreement to be totally integrated. Sometimes they are just pre-printed clauses that no one reads at the bottom of long form agreements. Such clauses are not given much weight. On the other hand, sometimes such clauses are heavily negotiated clauses in fifty page contracts between Microsoft and IBM. In that case, they are given great weight. But in either event, their effect is that it makes it more likely that a court would find the agreement to be totally integrated with the clause than would be the case without it.

(A) is incorrect.

A merger or integration clause does not automatically mean the agreement is totally integrated; it only has persuasive effect.

(C) is incorrect.

(C) is incorrect because it sets forth an inaccurate rule. An integration clause makes it more likely that the agreement will be judged totally integrated by the court.

(D) is incorrect.

(D) is incorrect because it sets forth an inaccurate rule. The only effect of an integration clause is that it makes it more likely the agreement will be found totally integrated. If it is judged totally integrated, parol evidence will be excluded, not admitted, regardless of whether the parol term is a consistent additional term or a contradictory one.

Answer to Question 5

(D) is the correct answer.

Ordinarily, the parol evidence rule precludes admission of evidence of a contemporaneous or prior agreement to supplement or contradict the terms of a completely integrated writing.

However, there are recurring fact situations to which the parol evidence rule does not apply. Some call these "exceptions" to the parol evidence rule, but it is better to think of them simply as situations in which the parol evidence rule does not regulate, and in these situations, the proffered "parol" evidence is freely admissible. These situations are:

(1) Agreements made <u>after</u> the contract is made (these are "modifications" to the contract and the parol evidence rule has no effect on the admissibility of alleged oral modifications.) In other words, the parol evidence rule only regulates agreements made prior to, or contemporaneous with, the signing of the contract;

(2) Situations in which a party wants to show that no valid agreement ever existed (e.g., where one party wants to show that the agreement was a joke or it was only a draft and never agreed to);

(3) Where the alleged oral agreement is a condition precedent to the enforceability of the duties under the contract Restatement 2d § 271;

(4) Situations where the proffered evidence is to show the other party never paid the recited consideration, Restatement 2d § 218(1), e.g., where the contract said $5,000 had been paid and received, but where the seller wants to introduce evidence that he or she was never paid;

(5) Situations in which the evidence goes to show that the contract is voidable, e.g., evidence showing misrepresentation, duress, undue influence, etc. by the other;

(6) Situations in which the evidence speaks to the meaning of a term found in the written contract, e.g., if the written agreement says delivery shall be within "5 days" after the order, there would be no parol evidence rule issue if a party wanted to testify to an oral conversation between the parties that "5 days" means "5 business days"; and

(7) Situations in which usage of trade, course of dealing, or course of performance is used to explain the contract UCC § 2–202. Note that this is an explicit rule under the UCC, but is considered by most contract scholars to be true in contracts governed by common law and Restatement rules as well.

Here, the oral agreement to have Penske's approval before the contract went forward is a condition precedent to performance under the contract. Thus, the parol evidence rule would not prevent admission of evidence of the oral agreement. Restatement 2d § 217.

(A) is incorrect.

This is an accurate statement of law, but as set forth in the explanation of Choice (D) above, the rule does not apply to oral evidence of a condition precedent.

(B) and (C) are incorrect.

The reason the oral Penske-approval agreement is admissible is not because it contradicts the written agreement or involved a third party, but rather because the oral agreement constituted a condition precedent to the parties' obligations under the contract. Restatement 2d § 217.

Answer to Question 6

(D) is the correct answer.

Ordinarily, the parol evidence rule precludes admission of a contemporaneous or prior agreement which supplements or contradicts the terms of a completely integrated writing.

However, as indicated in the answer to the last problem, the parol evidence rule does not serve to block the introduction of usage of trade, course of performance, or course of dealing evidence offered to explain terms in the contract. UCC § 2–202(a).

(A) is incorrect.

This choice correctly states the general rule when an agreement is found to be completely integrated, but it ignores an "exception" to the rule as set forth in the explanation of (D) above.

(B) is incorrect.

(B) is incorrect because even a consistent additional term cannot be admitted when a court has determined the agreement is totally integrated.

(C) is incorrect.

(C) is incorrect because even though the answer correctly rests on the "would certainly" test for a consistent additional term under the UCC, UCC § 2–202, Cmt. 3, even consistent additional terms are not admissible under the parol evidence rule when the court finds the agreement completely integrated.

Answer to Question 7

(C) is the correct answer.

This question tests two aspects of the parol evidence rule: (1) whether an oral agreement made contemporaneous with the signing of the written contract is "parol evidence"; and (2) the "interpretation" exception to the parol evidence rule.

As to the first point, the UCC provides that parol evidence consists of "any prior agreement or of a contemporaneous oral agreement." UCC § 2–202. Hence, the contemporaneous oral side agreement is parol evidence under the rule.

Regarding the second point, as set forth in Question 5, there are several situations in which the parol evidence rule will not preclude proffered evidence. One of those situations is where the proffered evidence is introduced to explain a term in the written agreement. However, just because a party says his or her parol evidence is proffered to explain a term does not automatically mean it will be admitted. One more level of analysis must be undertaken, and there are two different rules which could govern the situation.

One test is the so-called "Williston" or "plain meaning" rule. That rule provides that if the terms of the agreement have a plain meaning, and can be effectively interpreted without reference to any extrinsic evidence, no such parol evidence as to the meaning of a term should be admitted. In other words, the evidence as to a meaning of a term in a written contract should only be allowed if the term in the contract is ambiguous.

The second approach, called the "Corbin" or "reasonably susceptible" test calls for a hearing before the judge at which the party proffering the evidence can introduce evidence to show his or her meaning of the term is "reasonably susceptible" to the contract under the circumstances. This approach has been adopted in Restatement 2d § 202(1).

Reference to the side oral agreement here would be admitted under either of the tests. The clause in the written agreement provides, "all natural ingredients are to be grown and purchased in accordance with the side oral agreement agreed to by the parties." It is ambiguous on its face because there is no way to know what the standards for all natural growth are without knowledge of the terms of the side agreement. As such, it would be admissible under the "plain meaning" test because a court would need to know those terms to assess whether Farmer breached.

A meaning that the standards for growth of the ingredients are those of the "Natural Ingredients Act" as agreed to in the side oral agreement is a "reasonably susceptible" interpretation given the circumstances. As such, evidence of the side agreement would also be admissible under the "reasonably susceptible" test.

The standards for both tests are given in this choice, making (C) the correct answer.

(A) is incorrect.

The evidence of the side oral agreement is parol evidence, but it is admissible to establish the meaning of a term under an "exception" to the parol evidence rule.

(B) is incorrect.

This choice is incorrect because the "interpretation" exception to the parol evidence rule would allow admission of the oral side agreement, regardless whether a court finds the written agreement totally or partially integrated.

(D) is incorrect.

Under UCC § 2–202, parol evidence consists of "any prior agreement or of a contemporaneous oral agreement." As explained in (C), the side oral agreement is parol evidence.

Answer to Question 8

(B) is the correct answer.

The "exceptions" to the parol evidence rule, i.e., the situations in which the parol evidence rule does not act to exclude evidence, were listed in the response to Question 5 above.

Situation I is an example of the exception when the evidence is introduced to establish that the agreement is voidable due to duress.

Situation II is an example of the exception when the proffered evidence is introduced to establish there was never a contract.

Situation IV is an example of the exception when the evidence is introduced to show the modification of an existing contract, and not to show a prior or contemporaneous agreement.

Statement III is a classic situation in which the parol evidence rule would apply. The terms of the contract are written and a party wishes to introduce oral, "parol" evidence that contradicts the writing. Note that if the buyer argued that the words "Blu-ray player" that were in the contract had a special meaning to the parties, i.e., here they meant a Blu-ray player *and* the stereo, the parol evidence rule would not apply and the evidence would be admitted under the exception allowing a party to introduce evidence about the meaning of a contractual term. However, here the question concerned Buyer's ability to introduce evidence of an oral agreement made before the written contract was signed.

(A), (C), and (D) are incorrect.

These answers are incorrect for the reasons given in the explanation of (B) above.

CHAPTER 14
CONDITIONS AND BREACH

ANSWERS

Answer to Question 1

(A) is the correct answer.

The clause makes Health Insurer's liability expressly conditioned on the presentation of the affidavit. That is, before the affidavit is presented the parties are in a valid contract, but the payment duties of Health Insurer under that contract are not enforceable by Patient until the condition is "fulfilled" or "satisfied."

The requirement of an affidavit is an <u>express</u> condition because the wording of the contract says that payment is made "on the condition that . . ." Other phrases that make duties conditional include "but only if" or "so long as."

The requirement of an affidavit is an express condition <u>precedent</u> because the affidavit must be submitted before Health Insurer's duty to pay becomes enforceable. In the language of the Restatement 2d, it is a condition precedent because it is: (a) an event not certain to occur (the doctor may or may not submit the affidavit), which (b) must occur before performance under the contract is enforceable (Health Insurer is not liable unless the affidavit is submitted), unless (c) performance is somehow excused. Restatement 2d § 224.

Author's Note:

Note that the Restatement 2d attempted to change the common law language of conditions. What was known as a "condition precedent" at common law is simply called a "condition" under Restatement 2d § 224, and what was known as a "condition subsequent" at common law is called "an event which terminates a duty" in Restatement 2d § 230. However, most courts continue with the modifiers "precedent" and "subsequent" and those terms will be used throughout this book.

(B) is incorrect.

(B) is incorrect because, as explained above, the affidavit requirement is a condition <u>precedent</u>. For it to be an express condition subsequent, the duties of Health Insurer would have to be enforceable *until* the condition was fulfilled, at which point the duties would become unenforceable. In the words of the Restatement 2d, the clause would have to be: (a) an event, the occurrence of which is not the result of a breach of the party's duty of good faith, which (b) terminates a party's duty to perform upon its occurrence, unless (c) its performance is excused. Restatement 2d § 230.

For example, suppose the clause provided, "Health Insurer will reimburse Patient for any health related cost unless a notice of fraudulent practice is filed by the State regarding that claim." That would be a condition subsequent because Health Insurer would be obligated under the contract until an event (the filing of the fraudulent practice notice) occurs, in which case liability would be cut off.

(C) is incorrect.

(C) is incorrect because the words "on the condition that," make the clause a condition, not a promise. The difference is that, as a condition, if the condition never occurs, no one is liable. On the other hand, a contractual promise is enforceable and if it is not performed, a breach occurs.

(D) is incorrect.

(D) is incorrect because there is nothing implied about the condition in this problem. The term, "on the condition that," makes the condition an express one.

Answer to Question 2

(C) is the correct answer.

This problem is based on *Audette v. L'Union St. Joseph*, 59 N.E. 668 (Mass. 1901) in which a court held that the religious objections of the doctor were irrelevant. What was crucial is that payment was conditioned upon receiving the required affidavit and it was not forthcoming.

Parties thus need to be careful in agreeing to express conditions as, except for a few exceptions, *see* Restatement 2d §§ 246 *et seq.*, they are strictly enforced. Hence, Health Insurer's duty to pay never became enforceable because the condition precedent was never fulfilled and the reason why is irrelevant.

(A) is incorrect.

(A) is incorrect because express conditions are subject to the "strict enforcement" rule and are not excused when there is a substantial equivalency.

(B) is incorrect.

(B) is incorrect because there is no "religious waiver" exception to the strict enforcement rule of express conditions, regardless of the credibility of the faith expressed.

(D) is incorrect.

This choice is incorrect because Health Insurer will prevail because of the strict construction rule for express conditions, regardless of whether the religious oath clause is unconscionable or not. In other words, the phrase "on the condition that" makes this choice incorrect.

Answer to Question 3

(B) is the correct answer.

The phrase "unless it rains on Monday" is an express condition subsequent. That is, Harvey has an enforceable obligation to purchase the stock unless something happens subsequent to the creation of the obligation (rain on Monday) which discharges the duty. Restatement 2d § 230. Note that the Restatement 2d would call the phrase "an event that terminates a duty" and not a condition subsequent, but most courts would stick with the "condition subsequent" vernacular. In the words of the Restatement 2d, it is an event that terminates a duty because rain falling on Monday is: (a) an event, the occurrence of which is not the result of a breach of the party's duty of good faith, which (b) terminates a party's duty to perform upon its occurrence, unless (c) its performance is excused. *Id.*

(A) is incorrect.

(A) is incorrect because the no-rain-on-Monday clause is a condition subsequent, not a condition precedent. A condition precedent is a clause whereby a duty under a contract does not become enforceable until the condition occurs, e.g., I will buy your house on the condition that I get a loan from the bank." There, the obligation to purchase the house does not become enforceable until the condition (getting the loan) occurs, i.e., the condition's occurrence must precede the enforceability of the duty. Here, however, the obligation to purchase the stock is in existence from the beginning of the contract, and it remains in existence unless and until it rains on Monday. As such, raining on Monday is a condition subsequent—an event occurring subsequent to the existence of the duty which terminates it.

(C) is incorrect.

As explained in (B) above, the clause at issue is an express condition subsequent, not an implied condition precedent.

An implied-in fact condition occurs when nothing explicit is said about the condition, but the parties' actions make it clear that a condition has been agreed to. For example, suppose Mary wants to buy an autographed Mickey Mantle rookie baseball card from Ted, but says, "Before I pay for it, I will require that the autograph be authenticated by Fred's Authenticating Co.," and Ted hands over the card. Ted has not explicitly agreed to the authentication condition by words, but his actions would lead a reasonable person in Mary's position to believe he had agreed to the authentication condition, so an implied-in-fact condition (in this case an implied-in-fact condition precedent) has been created.

(D) is incorrect.

Constructive or implied conditions are conditions that the parties have not expressly agreed upon, but which either contract law implies or constructs to help analyze the duties of the parties, or a condition the court implies to determine and carry out the parties' performance obligations. Restatement 2d § 226, Cmt. c. Here, the condition was expressly agreed to, making it an express condition subsequent.

Answer to Question 4

(D) is the correct answer.

One of the consequences of classifying express conditions as either conditions precedent or conditions subsequent is the allocation of the burden of proof to establish the occurrence of the condition. For conditions precedent, the party who is seeking to enforce the promise has the burden of proof to establish that the condition occurred. For example, if Mary contracts with Ted to "purchase Ted's house for $250,000 on the condition that Mary gets a loan from First Bank," it would be Ted, as the party who wants to enforce the obligation to purchase the house, who has the burden of proof to establish that Mary got the loan.

Where, as in this problem, there is a condition subsequent, the burden of proof is on the party who is asserting there is no longer an enforceable duty under the contract to establish that the condition occurred. Therefore, the burden of proof would be on Harvey to establish it was raining.

(A) is incorrect.

(A) is incorrect for two reasons. First, while the general rule is that a plaintiff in a lawsuit bears the burden of proof, that rule is not universal and is subject to exceptions. Second, where a condition subsequent is involved, the burden to establish that the condition occurred is on the person who used to owe the duty, but now claims that he or she does not, here Harvey.

(B) is incorrect.

(B) is incorrect because this problem involves a condition subsequent. This choice sets forth the correct allocation of the burden if it were a condition precedent.

(C) is incorrect.

(C) is incorrect because both (A) and (B) individually are incorrect.

Answer to Question 5

(C) is the correct answer.

Under the strict construction rule for express conditions, if the condition subsequent occurs, then the duty of the promisor (Harvey) is discharged unless excused. Restatement 2d § 230. In other words, courts do not care why the parties made the deal they did, or why they premised their obligations on the occurrence of a condition. All that matters is whether the condition occurred or not. If it did, and if it is a condition subsequent, then the duty is terminated.

(A) is incorrect.

There is no rule providing that parties cannot make their duties contingent on events outside of their control. Indeed, many conditional promises are contingent on such events, e.g., "I'll buy this Jaguar automobile if I win the lottery," is a perfectly proper and enforceable contractual promise if agreed to by the customer and Jaguar dealership in the course of a contractual negotiation.

(B) is incorrect.

An aleatory promise is one which turns largely on chance. Restatement 2d § 76, Cmt. c. The term "aleatory promise" has some relevance in consideration, but none in the enforcement of conditions. As noted in the explanation for (A) above, there is no prohibition against conditional promises made on events outside of the control of the parties.

(D) is not the best choice.

The result set forth in this choice is correct, but the reasoning is not as good as that in (C). In a condition subsequent situation, "that duty is discharged if the event occurs." Restatement 2d § 230. The right verb to describe what happens to the duty is thus "discharged," as set forth in Choice (C) and not "excused," as set forth in Choice (D).

Answer to Question 6

(D) is the correct answer.

This question turns on the proper interpretation of an ambiguous clause. There are different consequences depending on whether a clause is a promise, a condition, or both. For example, suppose a contract calls for a package to arrive at 3:00 p.m. on Wednesday. If the 3:00 p.m. delivery clause is an express condition precedent, the buyer does not have to accept it if the package arrives at 3:05 p.m. under the strict construction rule for express conditions. But the buyer would have no recourse against the seller for failing to delivery timely. All that happens is the condition precedent to accepting the good has not been fulfilled, but the seller has breached no enforceable promise.

If, however, the 3:00 p.m. delivery clause was a promise/duty under the contract, the buyer would likely be obligated to accept the package, but could sue the seller for breach for failing to deliver on time.

If it is both a condition and a duty, then the buyer could both reject the package <u>and</u> sue for breach if the package was not timely delivered.

The principal determinant in interpreting any contractual term is the intention of the parties. However, when the intent is unclear as to whether an obligation is intended to be a conditional promise, an unconditional duty, or both, contract law has adopted a few presumptions to govern a court's interpretation of such terms:

(1) An interpretation that a promise is an unconditional duty is favored when the event necessary to fulfill the condition is within the obligee's control, Restatement 2d § 227(2);

(2) An interpretation that reduces promisor's risk of forfeiture is preferred, Restatement 2d § 227(1);

(3) When in doubt, a promise should be interpreted as an unconditional duty; and

(4) An interpretation of a term as both a duty and condition is very unusual, and will require some special language such as, "Buyer's obligation to pay is expressly conditioned on arrival of the package by 3:00 p.m. on Wednesday, and Seller is obligated and will be liable in damages if the package is not delivered as specified."

This problem is an illustration of how an interpretation that a promise is an unconditional duty is favored over a conditional obligation when the event necessary to fulfill the condition is within the obligee's control. Restatement 2d § 227(2). In this situation, Steve's promise to purchase was conditioned on his choosing an A7 by July 1. Because it was completely under his (the obligee's) control to come to the dealership and choose a car, the clause will be interpreted as imposing an unconditional duty on Steve to buy a car, and so Al's would be able to successfully sue Steve for breach of contract.

(A) is incorrect.

As explained above, when a clause has a contingency in it, absent evidence to the contrary, it will be interpreted as a promise and not a condition when the contingency is in the complete control of one of the parties. Restatement 2d § 227.

(B) is not the best choice.

(B) would be a true statement if the clause were construed as a condition. That is, a party whose obligations are conditioned on an event somewhat in his or her control cannot hinder or frustrate the occurrence of that condition. Doing so is a violation of the duty of good faith and will result in the excuse of a condition. Restatement 2d § 245. An oft-used example is if John's obligation to buy Mary's house is contingent on his getting a loan from First Bank, if John never even applies for the loan, that "wrongful hindrance" of the condition will be seen as a breach of the duty of good faith, and the condition would be excused, meaning that John's obligation to purchase the house turns into an unconditional promise.

Here, because the picking of the car is entirely within Steve's control (as opposed to John's scenario where the occurrence of the condition is only partially within his control, the other part being whether the Bank would give him the loan if he did apply for it), the clause will be interpreted as an unconditional promise from the inception, and so the better answer is (D) since the clause is not a "condition" that is "excused."

(C) is incorrect.

(C) is incorrect for at least two reasons. First, as explained above, the clause will be interpreted as a promise and not a condition. Second, even if it was a condition, for Steve to waive the condition, it would mean he would say something like, "I waive my right to select the color of car—just send me any old A7." That did not occur.

Answer to Question 7

(C) is the correct answer.

Under virtually all modern decisions, and by statute in many states, a clause making a subcontractor's payment dependent upon payment to the general contractor is interpreted as setting forth an expected *time for payment* coupled with an <u>unconditional payment duty</u> by the general contractor, and <u>not</u> a condition to payment. In other words, the clause at issue in this problem means that General Contractor owed Carpenter $25,000 five days after Developer was <u>supposed to</u> pay General for the framing work. That obligation was unconditional, and so regardless whether General was paid or not, and regardless of the language of the promise, General owed Carpenter the money at the end of that time period.

This holding is a specific application of the rule providing that clauses should be interpreted, when possible, to reduce the promisor's forfeiture risk. Restatement 2d § 227(1). If payment of Carpenter was truly conditional on payment by Developer to General, Carpenter may be in a position where he or she did the work, but forfeited all payment for it, because the condition (Developer's payment to General) was never fulfilled. Therefore, a court would likely hold that General is liable to Carpenter for $25,000 under the contract.

(A) is incorrect.

(A) is incorrect for the reason (C) is correct. Such clauses are almost universally interpreted as being unconditional promises to pay, with an expected time for payment, rather than as conditional obligations.

(B) is incorrect.

(B) is incorrect because Carpenter is entitled under the contract to the contracted value of his services, regardless of their fair market value.

(D) is incorrect.

As the problem specifies, Developer has no right to condition payment on an inspection of Carpenter's work. But even if Developer did have such a right, General Contractor's obligation to Carpenter is still an unconditional duty, and the $25,000 was due five days after the expected date of the payment from Developer to General for the framing.

Answer to Question 8

(B) is the correct answer.

The clause providing, "the picture of Danielle on the announcements to be satisfactory to Diane or Diane shall have no obligation under this agreement" is known as a "personal satisfaction clause." Sometimes the personal satisfaction must be acknowledged by a party to the contract, and sometimes by a third party, e.g., Owner will pay the contractor a progress payment of $50,000 if an architect certifies that the framing is acceptable to architect and per the contract.

The standards for determining whether these clauses are breached differs depending on whether the clause was intended to measure an individual's "personal taste, fancy or judgment" or whether it is intended to measure more objective, market factors. Restatement 2d § 228. In the former case, it truly is a subjective standard; whereas the latter is measured by objective ones.

Here, the clause deals with a mother's approval of a graduation picture of her daughter. That is a prototypical "personal taste" clause and so Diane would be entitled to terminate all further obligations under the contract if she, honestly, if subjectively, did not like the picture. Restatement 2d § 228, Cmt. a; and Cmt. b, Ill. 4. This may seem unfair to Jack, but that is the deal he chose to make and it is an enforceable one.

(A) is incorrect.

(A) is incorrect because, as discussed above, the appropriate standard is subjective, not objective. An example of a personal satisfaction clause which would be judged under objective standards is a clause in a commercial lease that prohibits subletting without the personal approval of the landlord. Since it is commercial space, absent any indication from the parties' negotiations to the contrary, the landlord would be in breach if he, she, or it did not approve a proposed subtenant with good credit and a strong payment record, i.e., a subtenant who would objectively be acceptable. But such is not the case where personal satisfaction clauses turn on the personal taste or fancy of a party.

(C) is incorrect.

(C) is incorrect because the facts indicate that Diane had waived performance on the 15th when Jack informed her of the delay and she indicated for Jack to continue.

(D) is incorrect.

(D) is incorrect because the good faith requirement of Restatement 2d § 205 means there is sufficient restraint on the promisor to save the personal satisfaction clause from being illusory. That is, Diane must accept and pay for the announcements if she subjectively and in good faith likes the picture on the announcement.

Answer to Question 9

(D) is the correct answer.

The parties agreed that Jack would have to perform satisfactorily thirty days before Diane would have to pay. Hence acceptable performance by Jack is a condition precedent to Diane's performance obligations, as reflected by (D).

(A) is incorrect.

(A) is incorrect because, under the terms of the contract, the order is the opposite of that set forth in this choice—performance by Jack is the event that starts the thirty day clock on Diane's conditional payment obligations.

(B) is incorrect.

(B) is incorrect because it is contrary both to the facts of this problem and the applicable law. Together Restatement 2d §§ 238, 241(1) provide that, absent a contrary indication from the parties, when performance under a contract can be done simultaneously, e.g., exchange of a book for cash, there is a concurrent tender requirement, and both parties are obligated to tender performance at the same time.

Here, however, preparation of the announcements takes time and so this situation is governed by Restatement 2d § 234(2), which provides that accomplishment of the task that takes time (preparation of the announcements) is a condition to the requirement that does not (payment by Diane). Hence, this choice is wrong legally.

It is also wrong factually because the parties agreed in their contract that Jack had to perform first.

(C) is incorrect.

(C) is incorrect because: (a) factually Jack's performance is a condition to Diane's, just the opposite of what is indicated in this answer; and (b) Jack's satisfactory performance is a condition <u>precedent</u> to Diane's performance obligations, not a condition subsequent.

Answer to Question 10

(A) is the correct answer.

Contract law regulates the order of performance by using the constructive condition of tender. When executory (unperformed) performance duties under a bilateral contract can be performed simultaneously, both parties must establish a willingness and ability to perform, i.e., tender their performances before their performance duties are enforceable. Once tendered, their performances are due at the same time since the exchange of payment for goods can be done concurrently. Restatement 2d § 238.

If one party does not tender performance, he or she cannot enforce the duty of the other, e.g., where, as here, Costello refuses to demonstrate that he is willing and able to perform, the other party's (Abbott's) obligation to pay is not enforceable. That means that if Abbott does not pay, Costello has no right to sue him. In other words, Abbott's payment obligation never becomes enforceable because it is constructively conditioned on Costello's obligation to tender performance, and that did not occur.

On the other hand, when Abbott tendered performance (showed Costello the check and indicated he was willing to go forward), at that point Costello's duty to turn over the card became enforceable, and Abbott could sue him if he failed to part with the card.

(B), (C), and (D) are incorrect.

As explained in (A) above, this type of promise involving a bilateral contract with duties remaining on both sides that can be performed simultaneously is subject to a constructive condition of tender. Both parties are subject to the condition, thus these answers are incorrect.

Answer to Question 11

(D) is the correct answer.

As explained in the explanation to the previous question, the duties of both parties would be subject to the constructive condition of tender; hence, Costello's duty to perform is not enforceable until Abbott tenders performance which fulfills the constructive condition. In order to do so,

Abbott's actions must manifest a willingness and ability to perform. Restatement 2d § 238. Here, Abbott stated he was willing to proceed with the deal (willingness) and showed Costello the check (ability to perform), thus his tender fulfills the constructive condition, making Costello's performance enforceable. Therefore, when Costello leaves without handing over the card, he has breached the contract by failing to perform an enforceable promise, and Abbott has a viable breach of contract action against him.

(A) is incorrect.

(A) is incorrect because to fulfill his obligation to tender, Abbott need only manifest a willingness and ability to perform. He need not actually put the check into Costello's hand in order to do so.

(B) is incorrect.

(B) is incorrect because Costello did not tender performance. He may have had the card with him, but if he did not show it to Abbott and say he was willing to exchange it for the check, he has not tendered and thus is liable for breach.

(C) is incorrect.

This answer choice fails to apply the rule of constructive condition of tender. In a bilateral contract with executory duties remaining and where performance obligations are due simultaneously, at the time of making the contract, neither party's duties are enforceable. So Abbott and Costello were in a viable contract, but neither the duty to pay nor the duty to turn over the card became enforceable until the other party tenders performance.

Answer to Question 12

(C) is the correct answer.

In this scenario, both parties have tendered performance, thus both parties' duties have become enforceable. Once duties are enforceable, determining who is to perform first is governed by the "order of performance" rules of contract law. There is a different answer depending on whether: 1) performance of both parties can occur simultaneously, or 2) performance of one duty takes time and the other does not. Restatement 2d § 234.

The rule is if all or part of the performances to be exchanged under an exchange of promises can be rendered simultaneously, they are to that extent due simultaneously. Restatement 2d § 234(1). Here, both Abbott and Costello could make their exchanges simultaneously, i.e., the card and the check can be handed to the other simultaneously.

(A) is incorrect.

(A) sets forth a correct rule—a party whose performance takes time must perform first, at least where the other party's performance (usually payment by the buyer of services) does not take time. Restatement 2d § 234(2). However, the rule does not apply here because both parties can perform at the same time. For that reason, both are due simultaneously. Restatement 2d § 234(1).

Note that both of these rules apply as defaults—if the parties manifest a contrary intention, it is their intent that controls.

(B) is incorrect.

As explained in (C) above, the parties are obligated to perform at the same time. Restatement 2d § 234(1).

(D) is incorrect.

Just because Abbott tendered performance first does not mean he has to perform first. Once tender by both parties has occurred, contract law requires both parties to perform simultaneously. Restatement 2d § 234.

Answer to Question 13

(C) is the correct answer.

Restatement 2d § 234(2) provides, "where the performance of only one party ... requires a period of time, his performance is due at an earlier time than that of the other party." Hence, unless the parties or some other doctrine such as usage of trade dictates otherwise, Stylist must complete performance before Customer's payment obligation is due, because Stylist's performance "requires a period of time" to complete.

(A) is incorrect.

(A) is incorrect because the rule of Restatement 2d § 234(2) provides that Stylist, as the party whose performance will take time to complete, must complete it before Customer's payment obligation is enforceable. As such, it is irrelevant to the _order_ of performance that Stylist tendered performance.

(B) is incorrect.

(B) is incorrect for it states the rule opposite to that of Restatement 2d § 234(2). Note that some commentators have stated that the rule set forth in (B) should be the rule for the reason given in the answer, and there is no reason for the rule to be structured as it is in Restatement 2d § 234(2). Nevertheless, right now the rule is that the party whose performance takes time to complete must complete the performance before the payment obligation of the other party becomes enforceable.

(D) is incorrect.

(D) is incorrect for the reason (C) is correct, i.e., it is contrary to the rule of Restatement 2d § 234(2).

Answer to Question 14

(A) is the correct answer.

This question tests knowledge of material breach—both when it occurs and its consequence. Colloquially, a material breach is a "serious" breach. However, the Restatement 2d has a more technical definition: a material breach is "an uncured material failure to render a performance due at an earlier time." Restatement 2d § 237. In order to determine whether the party's "failure to render performance" is "material," Restatement 2d § 241 outlines several factors which need to be weighed:

(a) the extent to which the non-breaching party will be deprived of the reasonably expected benefit of his or her bargain;

(b) the extent to which the non-breaching party can be fully compensated for the breach if made to stay in the contract and complete performance;

(c) the extent to which the breaching party will suffer a forfeiture if the breach is declared material and the non-breaching party need not perform under the contract;

(d) the likelihood the breaching party will cure his or her failure; and

(e) the extent to which the breaching party performed within the standards of good faith and fair dealing.

Using these factors, the courts have established some presumptions as to when a material breach occurs. One of those situations is, like here, the failure to make a progress payment in a construction contract.

The most important consequence of declaring a breach material is that the innocent party is entitled legally to suspend his or her remaining duties of performance. Restatement 2d § 237. This suspension of performance lasts either until the material breach is cured, waived, or transforms into a "total breach." Once the breach is total, the innocent party's duties under the contract are discharged. Restatement 2d § 243.

Here, when Linda failed to make the progress payment, it was a material breach. That means that Morris was legally entitled to walk off the job, and committed no breach in doing so.

(B), (C), and (D) are incorrect.

These answers are incorrect for the reason that (A) is correct. The innocent party, here Morris, may legally suspend his performance in light of the other party's material breach until the material breach is either cured, waived or becomes total. Hence, Morris was under no obligation to perform after Linda failed to pay the progress payment, and was not in breach for refusing to continue.

Answer to Question 15

(C) is the correct answer.

As set forth in the explanation to the previous question, Linda committed a material breach when she refused to make a progress payment. However, material breaches can be "cured." When properly cured, material breaches are transformed into immaterial ones. Restatement 2d § 237. That is, the breaching party has still committed a breach (for "any nonperformance [of a contractual duty] is a breach" under Restatement 2d § 235(2)), but the breach is no longer a material one.

The consequence of there being an immaterial breach is that, while the innocent party can sue for any damages resulting from the immaterial breach, that party no longer can suspend performance without consequence. As such, once Linda tendered the payment, and given that the delay caused Morris no inconvenience, she cured her material breach and Morris became obligated to complete the pool. His unwillingness to do so was a material breach, making (C) the correct answer.

If Morris had, e.g., taken another job when Linda refused to pay him and could not do both jobs, then, perhaps, her cure would not have been effective. A non-breaching party is obligated only to accept a reasonable (to him, her, or it) cure. Note also that while Linda has immaterially breached the contract, if Morris went back to work and finished on time, it may be a situation in which a breach does not cause any damages to the innocent party. But even if that's so, Linda did not perform fully under the contract, and so her one day delay was a "breach." Restatement § 235(2).

Morris's breach, however, *is* material since he walked off the job and refused to return after Linda's material breach had been cured.

(A) is incorrect.

While Linda's breach was transformed into an immaterial because her tender of the check cured her material breach, Morris's walking off the job is a material breach.

(B) is incorrect.

While Linda's breach becomes immaterial because her tender of the check cured her material breach, Morris's walking off the job is a material breach. If Morris was genuinely concerned about payment, his option was to demand reasonable assurances of payment by Linda. Restatement 2d § 251. While requests for reasonable assurances are generally thought of as a UCC doctrine under UCC § 2–609, and are often studied as a UCC principle, the concept is also available under common law agreements. Restatement 2d § 251.

(D) is incorrect.

Initially Linda committed a material breach, but the tender of the $10,000 progress payment cured the material breach and made it an immaterial one. Further, once she tendered the payment, Morris became obligated to finish the pool.

Answer to Question 16

(B) is the correct answer.

Once a material breach has occurred, there are generally only three possible future scenarios: (1) the material breach can be cured; (2) the material breach can be waived; or (3) the material breach can be transformed into a total breach. Although there are other ways to do it, generally a material breach will ripen into a total one if enough time occurs without the material breach being cured. Restatement 2d § 243.

Here, three months have passed since the material breach and Morris has taken on other work for the next year. As such, the breach cannot be cured by paying the progress payment this late, so the material breach has been transformed into a total breach.

A total breach "discharges the injured party's remaining duties to render . . . performance." Restatement 2d § 243. Since Morris is the injured party, the total breach discharges his duties to finish construction of the pool.

(A) is incorrect.

(A) is incorrect because Linda can no longer cure the breach, both because of the passage of time and because Morris has taken on additional work.

(C) is incorrect.

The duties of the innocent party (here Morris) are not discharged when the other party only immaterially breaches. Discharge only occurs upon a total breach Restatement 2d § 243 (upon a material breach, the innocent party's duties are suspended under Restatement 2d § 237).

(D) is incorrect.

Linda has committed a total breach and thus Morris's duties have been discharged and he would not be required to finish the pool.

Answer to Question 17

(B) is the correct answer.

The failure to put in a pool light on a $25,000 pool would be an immaterial breach by Morris. It would be a breach because Morris has not performed fully. Restatement 2d § 235(2). It would be an immaterial one because of the weighing of the factors listed in Restatement 2d § 241, but mostly because Linda has received most of the benefit under the contract. As such, Morris is responsible for the bulb and its installation. Under modern law, Linda need not pay the $3,000 and then sue for the cost of the bulb and its installation; rather, she can simply offset the cost from the amount she owes from the final payment.

(A) is incorrect.

As noted above, even though it is an immaterial breach, Morris is still obligated for the cost of the pool light and its installation, and that amount should be offset from the amount of the final payment otherwise owed to Morris.

(C) is incorrect.

(C) is incorrect because the failure to install the pool light is only an immaterial breach. If Morris had done something (or failed to do something) which constituted a material breach, then Linda would be justified in suspending her unexecuted duties under the contract, and withholding payment until the material breach was cured or transformed into a total breach.

(D) is incorrect.

(D) is incorrect because Morris's breach was immaterial, not material.

Answer to Question 18

(B) is the correct answer.

Many define "waiver" as "an intentional relinquishment of a known right." Others define it as an excused non-occurrence of a constructive condition of exchange. Although the latter is more technically accurate under contract law, the former will answer most of the questions that come up under that doctrine.

Here, Linda knew she had a right to make Morris install the light, but voluntarily relinquished her right to insist upon it. Hence, she waived her right to sue for its installation failure.

(A) is incorrect.

(A) is incorrect because an "election" is a particular type of waiver that occurs <u>after</u> performance has passed and the breach could no longer be cured. Here, the lack of the light bulb installation occurred during the scheduled final inspection, and could still be cured by Morris if he wanted to.

(C) and (D) are incorrect.

Part performance and divisibility are synonyms when used in the conditions context. They provide that if the contract itself can be split into a series of corresponding part performances, the contract should be enforced as to the parts that have been performed. An example would be if a baseball fan ordered three packs of baseball cards for $30 and only got one. While there has been a material breach (two-thirds of the value of the contract is missing), a court would find that performance could be split into three corresponding performances, each worth $10, and require the buyer to accept and pay for the one pack that was delivered. Here, there is no equal way to divide the pool light from the pool.

Answer to Question 19

(A) is the correct answer.

As set forth in the explanation to (A) to Question 18, an election is a special kind of waiver that takes place after performance has passed and the breach could be cured. Here the time for performance has long since passed. Hence, Linda's "waiver" is really an "election."

(B) is incorrect.

The failure to install the light bulb was an immaterial breach; therefore there could be no waiver of a "total" breach under these facts.

(C) and (D) are incorrect.

Part performance and divisibility are synonyms when used in the conditions context. They provide that if the contract itself can be split into a series of corresponding part performances, the contract should be enforced as to the parts that have been performed. An example of this is given in the explanation to (C) and (D) in the preceding question.

Answer to Question 20

(C) is the correct answer.

The concept of breaches being "material" and "immaterial" is only relevant when there are executory (unperformed) duties remaining for the innocent party. This is because the principal consequence of a finding of materiality is that the innocent party can suspend performance until the breach is cured or becomes a total breach. Restatement 2d § 237. Here, Morris has completed performance—he built the pool. Thus there are no duties for him to suspend. As such, Linda's breach is neither material nor total; it is just a breach, entitling Morris to damages.

Similarly, the consequence of a "total" breach is that the innocent party's duties are discharged. Restatement 2d § 243. Here, because Morris fully performed under the contract before the breach, his duties were already discharged by performance. Restatement 2d § 235(1). Hence, again, Linda's breach is not "total"—it's just a breach.

(A), (B), and (D) are incorrect.

These answer choices are incorrect for the reasons that (C) is correct as explained above.

Answer to Question 21

(A) is the correct answer.

This question is based on *Jacob & Youngs v. Kent*, 129 N.E. 859 (1921). There, a contract called for a specific type of copper pipe to be used, and an equivalent pipe was inadvertently substituted in its stead. Justice Cardozo stated two rules: (1) inadvertent or not, there still was a breach (although an immaterial one); and (2) where there was substantial performance of the contract, coupled with an inadvertent breach, the general damage rule that the innocent party is entitled to the cost to remediate (or repair) the property as the measure of damages would be suspended when the value of the repair was economically disproportionate to the economic benefit received from the repair. Instead, if all those criteria were met, the damage rule would be the difference between the value of what was promised less the value of what was received. In *Jacobs & Young*, that was the difference between the value of a house with all Reading brand pipe less the value of the house with a combination of Reading and Cohoes pipe, which was likely nothing.

Here, all the elements of the "substantial performance" doctrine are met. There was a breach by Morris as he did not live up to the terms of the contract calling for all Acme brand gunite. However, the breach was inadvertent, and Morris substantially performed the contract by giving Linda what she bargained for (a built pool). To rip out the gunite and repair the damage would be $20,000, whereas there would be little, if any, economic benefit to Linda from having an all Acme brand gunite pool. As such, she is entitled only to the difference in value between what she was promised (the value of a pool with all Acme brand gunite) and what she got (the value of a pool with mixed Acme and Beta brand gunite), which might well be nothing.

(B) is incorrect.

The substantial performance rule does not provide that there was no breach. In fact it holds just the opposite. There was a breach because Linda did not receive what she bargained for under the contract—all Acme brand gunite. What often occurs in substantial performance construction cases is that there are often no recoverable *damages* caused by the breach.

(C) is incorrect.

(C) is incorrect because under the substantial performance rule, the breach is immaterial, not material, and has special damage rules as described in the explanation to (A). But more fundamentally, this choice is wrong because for there to be a breach at all, it must be because one party did not do something that was called for under a contract. But not all breaches are material.

(D) is incorrect.

(D) is not correct because it sets forth the general damage rule allowing an innocent party to recover the costs of repair upon a breach in a construction contract. Where the special "substantial performance" rules apply, as described in the explanation to (A) above, the damage rule is different.

Answer to Question 22

(D) is the correct answer.

This question turns on an excuse of a condition. That is, assume the parties are in a contract where one party's duties are subject to an express or implied condition. Usually, if that condition does not occur, the duty does not become enforceable. But there are situations, some of which stem from the general duty of good faith and fair dealing that apply to all contracts as set forth in Restatement 2d § 205, in which contract law will excuse the condition, interpret the promise as *unconditional* instead of conditional, and require performance of the promise even though the condition does not occur. In the language of the Restatement 2d, this occurs when the non-occurrence of the condition is caused by a party's "wrongful prevention, hindrance, or noncooperation." Restatement 2d § 245, Cmt. a. As the text of Restatement 2d § 245 provides, "[w]here a party's breach by non-performance [of the duty of good faith and fair dealing] contributes materially to the non-occurrence of a condition of one of his duties, the non-occurrence is excused."

Here, Mary was under a good faith obligation to at least seek a loan from First Bank. Restatement 2d § 205. Indeed, it is that good faith obligation which saves the promise from being illusory. So while she was under no obligation to *obtain* a loan, she was under an obligation to *apply* for it. Her failure to apply "contribut[ed] materially to the non-occurrence of a condition of one of [her] duties"—namely her duty to pay. As such, the "non-occurrence is excused." Thus, instead of the contract reading, in essence, "Mary must purchase the boat for $25,000 on the condition she gets the described loan," the contract will be interpreted as providing an unconditional promise to pay, i.e., as if it provided, "Mary must purchase the boat for $25,000."

(A) is incorrect.

(A) is incorrect because all conditions, express or implied, can be excused by a party's "wrongful prevention, hindrance, or noncooperation" in the non-occurrence of a condition. Restatement 2d § 245, Cmt. a. By not applying for the loan, Mary breached her duty of good faith and wrongfully prevented, hindered and failed to cooperate in getting the loan.

(B) is incorrect.

(B) is incorrect because the obligation of good faith and fair dealing supplies consideration supporting the promise because it will imply a duty in Mary at least to apply for the loan under Restatement 2d § 205, which is a legal detriment she did not otherwise have to do before signing the contract, thus constituting a bargained-for exchange necessary for consideration. Restatement 2d § 71.

(C) is incorrect.

   (C) would be correct under traditional "but for" causation rules. That is, if John can show Mary breached her contract by not applying for the loan, he typically would also have to show that breach was the but for cause of his loss of a sale, i.e., that if she had applied for the loan, she would have obtained it, and thus the breach caused the damage. But Restatement 2d § 245 sets forth a different consequence when, as here, the breach is a breach of the implied duty of good faith. In that situation, the consequence of the breach is to make the formerly conditional promise an unconditional one, such that Mary becomes unconditionally obligated to purchase the boat, whether she would have qualified for the loan or not. It is a deliberately chosen consequence by contract law to punish bad faith behavior.

Answer to Question 23

(C) is the correct answer.

   This problem is governed by a special rule set forth in Restatement 2d § 243(3), which provides, "where at the time of the breach the only remaining duties of performance are those of the party in breach and are for the payment of money in installments ... his breach of non-performance as to less than the whole, whether or not accompanied or followed by a repudiation, does not give rise to a claim for damages for total breach."

   Here, Creditor had already performed (made the loan) so the only remaining duties of performance are for the payment of money in installments by Debtor, the breaching party. Debtor was obligated in month seven to pay less than the whole remaining balance, and so only breached a part of the entire loan repayment. As such, Creditor is limited to only suing for the installment that was breached, and not for the remaining balance. Creditor would have to wait until the end of the loan period to sue for all the payments at once, or sue for each missing loan payment plus interest every month.

   Note that the rule of Restatement 2d § 243(3) is only a default rule in the absence of any specific contractual provision on the issue. To protect against this situation, many lenders insist on an "acceleration clause" in the loan documents providing that if the debtor misses two or three installments in a row, the debtor agrees that the entire debt is accelerated and is thereafter immediately due and owing.

(A), (B), and (D) are incorrect.

These choices are incorrect because of the rule designed for these types of cases set forth in Restatement 2d § 243(3), as described above in the explanation of (C).

Answer to Question 24

(C) is the correct answer.

Maid's not showing up in January is a material breach of contract. As such, Moneybags's duties to employ and pay her were suspended, until the breach was either cured, waived, or transformed into a total breach. Restatement 2d § 237. Here, Moneybags waived the breach, i.e., he intentionally relinquished his right to terminate the contract. Restatement 2d § 246. As such, the contract became enforceable for the remaining eleven months on its terms.

It is not relevant to the answer to this problem, nor is it clear from the facts, but Moneybags's waiver could be a waiver of the material breach and a decision to treat it as an immaterial one (in which case he could sue Maid for any damages he suffered as a result of her missing January, e.g. the difference between her fee and the fee of her replacement), or as a waiver of his right to sue her at all. Which of the two options would be true in this situation would depend on Moneybag's intent, expressed at the time of the waiver.

(A) is incorrect.

(A) is incorrect because it is incomplete. Maid did commit a material breach, but, as explained above, Moneybags waived the breach.

(B) is incorrect.

(B) is factually incorrect because the problem states that Maid was reinstated under the terms of her contract with Moneybags, which required good cause for termination.

(D) is incorrect.

Maid did not cure her breach by showing up in February, for she did nothing to make up for the lost services she owed Moneybags for January. Rather, she offered to continue working from then on under the contract if Moneybags was willing to overlook (waive) her material breach in January.

Answer to Question 25

(D) is the correct answer.

Statement II is correct because Brian was obligated to deliver three records and only delivered one. Therefore he breached the contract and would be liable for his failure to deliver the two missing albums.

Statement III is correct because of the "part performance" rule of Restatement 2d § 240. That rule states that a portion of a contract might be enforceable even if there has been a material breach by the other if it is possible: (1) to apportion the agreement into corresponding pairs of part performances; and (2) to regard the parts of each pair as agreed equivalents. Restatement 2d § 240.

Applied here, the contract is divisible because it is possible to apportion the agreement into three separate pairs of part performance ($100 payment for each record). Therefore, payment for the first record he received is an agreed equivalent once the part performances are separated into three separate acts, and he must pay for the record delivered and cannot suspend his performance for that one claiming a material breach of the whole.

Note that if there were reasons why all three albums were linked together, e.g., they were a set by the same artist, or they were a complete set of a live rock concert, etc., then Statement IV would be correct. But there is no factual support for any such linkage in the problem. Indeed, the problem provides that the records are by three separate artists, in three separate musical genres.

Statement I is incorrect because a buyer need not pay the contract price if he or she does not receive all the benefits under the contract.

Note that even though this problem deals with goods, i.e., records, it is still governed by Restatement/common law principles because there is no specific rule under the UCC dealing with divisible contracts. UCC § 1–103(b).

(A), (B), and (C) are incorrect.

Only Statements II and III are correct, as discussed above.

Answer to Question 26

(D) is the correct answer.

Courts allow for the excuse of a condition by wrongful prevention, hindrance, and noncooperation by the party benefited by the condition. This is because the party who benefits from the condition has breached his or her duty of good faith and fair dealing with regard to the condition. Restatement 2d § 205. The court will not allow a party to benefit from his or her own wrongful conduct. (A) is an example of an inaction leading to wrongful prevention or hindrance of the occurrence of a condition. (B) is an example of an affirmative wrongful prevention of a condition and is loosely based on *Barron v. Cain*, 4 S.E.2d 618 (N.C. 1939).

Courts will also excuse a condition if: (1) enforcement of the condition will lead to disproportionate forfeiture; and (2) the condition is not as to a material part of the bargained-for exchange. Restatement 2d § 229. (C) is an example of when a condition is not material to part of the bargained-for exchange, because the material exchange is to have piping of a certain quality installed in the home, not the exact brand installed. Restatement 2d § 229, Cmt. a, Ill. 1. *See Jacob & Youngs v. Kent*, 129 N.E. 889 (N.Y. 1921).

(A), (B), and (C) are incorrect.

As described in the explanation of (D), all of the answer choices are correct.

Answer to Question 27

(C) is the correct answer.

(C) is correct because of the constructive condition of tender. At the time the contract was made, the parties were in an enforceable agreement, but the duties under that agreement were not enforceable. The duties were conditioned on each party tendering performance. Because they did not expressly agree on that term, it is known as a <u>constructive</u> condition. That means, until and unless tender occurs, neither party's duty is enforceable.

Tender means a manifestation of the ability and willingness to perform. Restatement 2d § 238. Thus, Buyer has no enforceable duty to pay unless and until Seller shows up at the appointed time and establishes that he or she is willing and able to deliver the laptop. Similarly, Seller has no enforceable duty to transfer possession of the laptop unless and until Buyer shows up at the appointed time and establishes that he or she is able and willing to pay.

Under the UCC, the buyer must tender payment first, and once that is done, seller must tender delivery. This concept is set forth in UCC § 2–511(1), which provides, "tender of payment is a *condition to the buyer's duty to tender* and complete delivery," (emphasis added) and in UCC § 2–507(1), which provides that seller's "[t]ender of delivery is a condition to the buyer's duty to accept the goods and . . . to his duty to pay for them."

Here since neither party showed up at the appointed time and demonstrated a willingness and ability to perform under the agreement, i.e., tendered, the duties of neither party were enforceable, and hence neither was in breach for failing to perform.

(A) is incorrect.

(A) is incorrect because Buyer had no duty to make the payment because Seller had not tendered performance. As noted above in the explanation to (C), Buyer's duty would not become enforceable until Seller tendered performance by showing Buyer the laptop and showing a willingness to proceed with the deal. Here, this did not occur because Seller did not show up at the agreed time and place. Therefore, Buyer had no duty to Seller, so Seller cannot prevail against Buyer for breach of contract.

(B) is incorrect.

(B) is incorrect for the same reasons that Choice (A) is incorrect. Buyer does not have a duty to perform, because Seller has not tendered the laptop. Therefore, there has been no breach and Seller will not prevail, regardless of when Buyer makes payment.

(D) is incorrect.

(D) is incorrect because Seller also does not have a duty to perform. Seller's duty would not become enforceable until Buyer tendered payment, and this has not occurred. Thus, it does not matter that Seller did not provide the laptop, because he had no obligation to do so.

Answer to Question 28

(A) is the correct answer.

(A) is correct because the constructive condition of tender has not been fulfilled. As stated in Restatement 2d § 238, in a bilateral contract with executory (unperformed) duties, neither party's unexecuted duties become enforceable until the other has tendered performance. This rule is also set forth in UCC § 2–507(1), which states that tender of payment by the buyer is a condition to the seller's duties, and UCC § 2–511(1) which states that tender by the seller is a condition to the buyer's duties. Tender occurs when a party offers performance, and manifests a present ability to perform, as stated in Restatement 2d § 238. Here, neither party has tendered performance because Seller did not show Buyer the laptop, and Buyer did not show Seller the payment. That is, there was no demonstrated ability and willingness of either to perform. Legally it is the same as if neither showed up. Therefore, neither party's duties have become enforceable, so Buyer has not breached the contract.

(B) is incorrect.

(B) is incorrect because Seller did not have any enforceable obligation to provide the laptop because Buyer had not tendered payment.

(C) is incorrect.

(C) is incorrect because Buyer did not have an enforceable duty to make the payment at this time. The constructive condition of tender was not fulfilled because Seller did not tender performance by showing Buyer the laptop, and manifesting a present willingness to go forward with the sale. UCC § 2–511. Therefore, Buyer had no duty to provide payment, and Buyer has not breached.

(D) is incorrect.

(D) is incorrect for the reasons stated above. Buyer's duties are not enforceable because Seller has not tendered performance. Therefore, Buyer has not breached the contract.

Answer to Question 29

(B) is the correct answer.

(B) is correct because the constructive condition of tender has been fulfilled at this point. As stated in the previous question, Restatement 2d § 238, UCC § 2–507(1), and UCC § 2–511(1), provide that the Buyer and Seller must tender performance before the other party's duties become enforceable. Here, Buyer has tendered performance because he showed Seller the money and said "I am willing to proceed." At this point, Seller's performance became due, and when Seller refused to perform, there was a breach of the enforceable duty to deliver the laptop, which constituted a breach of contract.

(A) is incorrect.

(A) is incorrect because Buyer did not have a duty to perform at this time. This is because Seller did not tender performance by showing the laptop and manifesting a present willingness to proceed with the sale. However, Seller has breached because Buyer did tender performance when he presented the payment and said he was willing to proceed. Therefore, Seller's delivery obligation became enforceable and Seller has breached the contract when he left without delivering the laptop.

(C) is incorrect.

(C) is incorrect for the same reasons that (A) is incorrect. Buyer did not have any duty to give Seller the payment, because Seller had not tendered performance. Because Buyer had tendered performance, it was Seller who had the enforceable duty to perform, and Seller breached the contract when he left without delivering the laptop.

(D) is incorrect.

(D) is incorrect for the same reasons explained above. When Buyer showed the payment and said, "I am willing to proceed," this was the tender of performance. At this time, the Buyer's constructive condition of tender was fulfilled, and Seller's obligations became enforceable. UCC § 2–511(1). Thus, Seller's failure of performance constituted a breach of contract.

Answer to Question 30

(B) is the correct answer.

In the contract to sell the car, each party's performance was subject to a constructive condition of the other party's performance. This rule is set forth in UCC § 2–507(1) and UCC § 2–511(1). Under UCC § 2–511, the tender of payment is a constructive condition to the seller's duty to tender (and complete) delivery. Hence, as assumed by this answer, if the buyer tendered payment, the duty of the seller to tender and complete delivery became enforceable, and if Seller failed to deliver the car after such tender, Seller is in breach.

(A) is incorrect.

(A) is incorrect because Buyer is not required to actually perform by paying the $10,000. Rather, Buyer need only to tender performance by presenting payment and manifesting a present willingness to proceed with the deal.

(C) is incorrect.

(C) is incorrect because, under the UCC, tender of payment is a condition to the buyer's duty to tender and complete performance. UCC § 2–511. So Buyer must tender the payment before Seller is required to tender the title.

(D) is incorrect.

The contract stated that November 1 was the date for the sale to take place. The failure of Seller to tender the title on November 1 is a breach of contract, so long as Buyer tenders the purchase price and fulfills the constructive condition of tender under UCC § 2–511 by November 1. The fact that there was no "time is of the essence" clause may result in a finding that Seller's breach was only a minor or immaterial breach, but it is still a breach and Buyer is entitled to whatever damages were caused by the delay.

Answer to Question 31

(D) is the correct answer.

In this problem, Buyer waived the express condition when he promised to go forward with the contract even if the condition (delivery on September 1) was not fulfilled. Under common law, waivers were treated as modifications and required new consideration in order to be enforceable, with some exceptions. Restatement 2d § 89. However, under the UCC, there is no consideration necessary to enforce a modification and, so long as it is in writing (and e-mails count) it is enforceable. UCC §§ 2–209(1),(3), 1–306. Therefore, the waiver/modification is valid even though Seller did not give consideration to support it.

(A) is incorrect.

(A) is incorrect for the reasons stated above. Under common law, the modification would be ineffective for lack of consideration (absent an exception under Restatement 2d § 89), but under the UCC there is no consideration necessary for an effective waiver/modification.

(B) is incorrect.

(B) is incorrect because Buyer already made an effective waiver during Buyer and Seller's August 20 e-mail exchange. Therefore, there is no need to find an implied-in-fact waiver on the day of delivery for the agreement to be enforceable. Certainly, even in the absence of the e-mail exchange, if Farmer had delivered the apples on September 15 and Buyer accepted them, there would be an enforceable waiver. But this answer choice uses the word "unless" and, as discussed above, the implied-in-fact waiver is not the only way an enforceable waiver can be found.

(C) is incorrect.

This choice sets forth one of the common law exceptions to the requirement that consideration be given to enforce a modification or waiver of a condition. However, the waiver was enforceable upon its making under the UCC, because the UCC does not require consideration (or reliance) in order for a waiver to be enforceable. UCC § 2–209(1). Once again, the use of the word "unless" in the answer choice makes it incorrect.

Answer to Question 32

(A) is the correct answer.

This is a contract for the sale of goods (refrigerators), so the UCC applies. (A) is correct because under UCC § 2–209(5), a waiver can be withdrawn, so long as the other party has not relied on the waiver and so long as reasonable notice is given. Here, the facts say that Buyer has not relied on making the payments late—just that it is convenient for it to do so. Therefore, so long as Seller gives reasonable notification that it is retracting the waiver, the waiver is effectively withdrawn.

(B) is incorrect.

(B) is incorrect because it suggests that conditions cannot be waived. Conditions can be waived, and here an implied waiver occurred when Seller repeatedly accepted late payment without objection. Therefore, a waiver did occur, but Seller can retract the waiver by giving Buyer reasonable notification.

(C) is incorrect.

(C) is incorrect because the waiver (and the course of performance that runs from it) can be retracted for the reasons stated above and set forth in UCC § 2–209(5). Therefore, the waiver of the condition does not preclude Seller from ever strictly enforcing the delivery condition, he or she must simply provide reasonable notice before doing so.

(D) is incorrect.

(D) is incorrect because a waiver can be enforced without consideration under UCC § 2–209(1).

Answer to Question 33

(D) is the correct answer.

(D) is correct under the perfect tender rule, set forth in UCC § 2–601. The perfect tender rule provides that in single lot contracts (contracts in which the goods are delivered in one shipment) if either the goods or tender of delivery fail in <u>any</u> respect to conform to the contract, the buyer may: (a) reject the entire shipment; (b) accept the entire shipment; or (c) accept any commercial unit or units in the shipment, and reject the rest. Here, this was a single lot contract because the goods were to be delivered at one time. Therefore, when one headband was missing, this constituted a breach allowing Buyer to accept 200 headbands (200 commercial units) and reject the rest.

Note that, given the extraordinary rights given to the buyer under the perfect tender rule, there are a number of exceptions or limitations to it—none of which apply here. These exceptions include: (1) the ability of the seller to cure under UCC § 2–508; (2) different standards if the contract was an installment, and not a single lot, contract under UCC § 2–612; (3) different standards for revocation of acceptance under UCC § 2–608; (4) (according to some courts) inapplicability of the rule where the good involved was a "complex machine"; (5) (according to some courts) inapplicability of the rule where the goods involved were specially made goods and the problem was only a late tender, not a deficiency in the quantity or quality of goods; and (6) different standards when there is an applicable usage of trade, course of dealing or course of performance under UCC § 1–303.

(A) is incorrect.

(A) is incorrect because under the UCC perfect tender rule, every breach by the seller in a single lot contract is treated as if it is a material breach, and the buyer is entitled to the remedies under UCC § 2–601. Hence, Buyer does not have to accept the incomplete shipment.

(B) is incorrect.

(B) is incorrect because under UCC § 2–601, Buyer may accept some commercial units and reject the rest. Hence, its options are not only to accept or reject what was submitted.

(C) is incorrect.

(C) is incorrect because with single lot contracts under the UCC, it does not matter whether the breach substantially impairs the value of the shipment. A seller's failure to render the promised performance in <u>any</u> respect gives the buyer the right to reject the shipment. UCC § 2–601.

Answer to Question 34

(B) is the correct answer.

(B) is correct because installment contracts, where goods are to be delivered in more than one shipment under the contract, are treated differently under the UCC than are single lot contracts. As described in the answer to the previous question, single lot contracts are governed by the perfect tender rule. UCC § 2–601. However, installment contracts (which applies here because the headbands were to be delivered in two shipments), are governed by UCC § 2–612. Under that provision, a buyer may reject a particular shipment due to a non-conforming tender only if the non-conformity substantially impairs the value of that shipment, and either the non-conformity cannot be cured, or the seller refuses to give adequate assurances that it will be cured. Thus, Buyer may not reject the shipment because the facts state that the missing headband does not substantially impair the value of the shipment to Buyer.

(A) is incorrect.

(A) is incorrect for the reasons stated above. Because this is an installment contract, it is governed by UCC § 2–612. The only way a buyer is entitled to reject the entire shipment in an installment contract situation is if the value of the shipment is substantially impaired, and the non-conformity cannot be cured or an offer of a cure is not forthcoming. Here, the problem provides there is no substantial impairment to Buyer.

(C) is incorrect.

(C) is incorrect because under UCC § 2–612(3), a buyer may cancel the entire installment contract only if the cumulative impact of the imperfect tender in the various shipments "substantially impairs the value of the whole contract." Here, the problem provides that the 249 headbands in the first shipment did not even substantially impair the value of that shipment, let alone the value of the contract *as a whole.* Therefore, Buyer was not entitled to cancel the entire contract, despite Seller's breach.

(D) is incorrect.

(D) is incorrect for the reasons stated above. Under UCC § 2–612, this is an installment contract and Buyer must accept the whole shipment because the one missing headband does not substantially impair the value of the shipment. If this was a single lot contract governed by UCC § 2–601, Buyer would be entitled to accept some and send back the rest.

Answer to Question 35

(B) is the correct answer.

This problem turns on the seller's right to cure a breach under UCC § 2–508, and the effect of cure on the perfect tender rule set forth in UCC § 2–601.

Under the perfect tender rule, Buyer was entitled to reject the motorcycle because the motorcycle had a defect (the missing GPS made it a lack of perfect tender) in a single lot contract. However, one of the limitations on the perfect tender rule is that the seller has some rights to cure the defective tender.

If the time for performance has not passed, the seller has an absolute right to cure. UCC § 2–508(1). Where, as here, cure will not occur until after performance was due (tender was due on Friday and cure wouldn't be effected until the following Monday), the seller has the right to cure so long as: (a) the seller had reasonable grounds to believe what was tendered would be acceptable; and (b) the cure is reasonable under the circumstances and will not cause the buyer undue inconvenience. UCC § 2–508(2). Here, (a) Seller believed the motorcycle had contained the GPS device since Seller ordered it with that equipment, and (b) Buyer was not too inconvenienced by picking up the motorcycle with the GPS device on Monday.

(A) is incorrect.

While it is true under the perfect tender rule that Buyer initially had a right to reject the motorcycle because of the GPS defect, as explained above, Seller had the ability to cure the breach under UCC § 2–508(1).

(C) is incorrect.

This choice sets forth the rule in installment contracts where a buyer may reject any installment whose nonconformity substantially impairs its value, if the conformity cannot be cured. UCC § 2–612. However, even under this rule, if the seller gives adequate assurances of cure, the installment must be accepted as long as the nonconforming installment does not substantially impair the value of the entire contract. This is irrelevant, though, because this contract is a single lot contract because the motorcycle would be delivered at one time, and the missing GPS device can be cured.

Note also that the substantial impairment test is also the standard for revoking acceptance under UCC § 2–608(1). However, as Buyer never accepted the motorcycle, revocation of acceptance does not come into play.

(D) is incorrect.

(D) is incorrect because the perfect tender rule applies equally to merchant and non-merchant sellers, as does the concept of cure.

Answer to Question 36

(B) is the correct answer.

(B) is correct because the restaurant may reject this shipment under UCC § 2–612(2), which provides a buyer in an installment contract may reject a particular shipment due to a non-conforming tender if the non-conformity "substantially impairs" the value of that shipment, and the seller refuses to give adequate assurance of cure. Here, this is an installment contract because there will be monthly shipments of heads of lettuce over three years. The non-conformity in this shipment also substantially impairs the value of the shipment because 130 of the 150 heads of lettuce are spoiled. Further, the seller refuses to give adequate assurance of cure by refusing to send replacements. Thus, under UCC § 2–612(2), the restaurant may reject this shipment.

However, though the restaurant may want to cancel the contract and hire a more reliable supplier given the problems with the very first shipment, it may not do so at this time. Under UCC § 2–612(3), a buyer may declare a material breach of the whole contract and cancel the remainder only when the failure of tender in a particular shipment or shipments "substantially impairs the value of the whole contract." Further, UCC § 2–612, Cmt. 6 provides that an uncertainty as to completeness of future performance based on a seller's past shipments is not enough, in and of itself, to justify cancellation of the entire contract. It is rare that an imperfect tender in the first shipment of an installment contract can substantially impair the value of the whole contract as called for in UCC § 2–612(3). Therefore, because only the first shipment of a three-year monthly contract was imperfectly tendered, it is unlikely that the restaurant may cancel the entire contract at this time.

Note that the restaurant may send a request for reasonable assurances under UCC § 2–609. After sending a request for reasonable assurances, if farmer does not supply the requisite assurances, the restaurant may treat the farmer's lack of adequate response as an anticipatory repudiation of the contract.

(A) is incorrect.

(A) is incorrect because the imperfect tender of the first shipment has not substantially impaired the value of the whole contract, as needed to cancel the remainder of the contract under UCC § 2–612(3). That is, because only the first shipment in the three-year monthly contract was imperfectly tendered, the restaurant may not cancel the entire contract at this time. UCC § 2–612, Cmt. 6.

(C) is incorrect.

(C) is incorrect because, while the restaurant may accept the shipment if it desires, it does not have to accept the shipment. As stated in UCC § 2–612(2), a buyer may reject a shipment that is imperfectly tendered if the imperfect tender substantially impairs the value of that shipment, and the seller refuses to give adequate assurances of cure. Here, 130 of the 150 heads of lettuce were spoiled, so the imperfect tender substantially impaired the value of that shipment. Further, the seller refuses to cure by sending replacements. Thus, the restaurant may accept, but it also may reject the shipment.

Note, however, that if the restaurant accepts the shipment it does not need to pay for the spoiled heads of lettuce. This rule is stated in UCC § 2–717, which says that a buyer may deduct damages resulting from breach of contract from the price still due under the same contract so long as he or she notifies the seller.

(D) is incorrect.

(D) is incorrect because the restaurant may accept the shipment, but also may reject the shipment for the reasons stated above. The restaurant also does not need to pay for the spoiled heads of lettuce, as stated in UCC § 2–717.

Answer to Question 37

(D) is the correct answer.

(D) is correct because, as here, once the date for performance has passed, a seller does not have the absolute right to cure. It only has the ability to cure if: (a) seller had reasonable grounds to believe its tender would be acceptable; and (b) cure would be reasonable in light of buyer's needs. UCC § 2–508(2). Here, the Academy would have no use for the monitors received after the date of the Oscar broadcast, and thus condition (b) above is not satisfied.

(A) is incorrect.

(A) is incorrect because it does not matter whether Seller was at fault or not. Any time a party does not fully perform under a contract, there is a breach under Restatement 2d § 235, and an imperfect tender under the perfect tender rule. UCC § 2–601.

(B) is incorrect.

(B) is incorrect because the presence or absence of a time is of the essence clause is not determinative. Such clauses help establish that a breach is a material one, but the circumstances may also do so as well, and here, the Academy no longer needed the monitors on February 21.

(C) is incorrect.

(C) is incorrect because Seller's right to cure does not turn on whether it knew of the purpose of the contract. The question under UCC § 2–508(2) is whether the cure is "reasonable" in light of the buyer's needs. Since the Academy has no use for the monitors on February 21, the proffered late tender cure is not "reasonable" under the circumstances, and thus not effective. Seller has breached and the Academy does not have to accept the proposed cure.

Answer to Question 38

(B) is the correct answer.

(B) is correct because Seller does not have an absolute right to cure under UCC § 2–508(1). Seller's ability to cure is judged under UCC § 2–508(2) because the date for performance under the contract has passed. Under that provision, the seller has the ability to cure if: (a) seller had reasonable grounds to believe its tender would be acceptable; and (b) cure would be reasonable in light of buyer's needs. Both criteria are met in the problem's facts and in (B).

(A) is incorrect.

(A) is incorrect because Seller does not have an absolute right to cure under UCC § 2–508(1). That provision provides that a seller has the absolute right to cure if the time for performance under the contract has not passed. Here, the time has passed, because the goods were due on August 1, and any cure would have to be accomplished after that date. Therefore, Seller will have to turn to UCC § 2–508(2) to attempt to prove that it has the ability to cure.

(C) is incorrect.

(C) is incorrect because, while the storeowner may be able to reject the shipment under the perfect tender rule, the Seller may be able to establish that she has the ability to cure under UCC § 2–508(2), the conditions of which are set forth in (B).

(D) is incorrect.

(D) is incorrect because it misstates the law. The storeowner does not need to accept a brand of mp3 player he or she did not order, even if the substitute brand is of the same value and quality as the brand he or she ordered.

Answer to Question 39

(A) is the correct answer.

(A) is the best choice because under these facts, the time for the contract has expired because the shirt was not delivered until the end of the day on July 25, the last date for contract performance. Therefore, the sporting goods store does not have an absolute right to cure under UCC § 2–508(1), and must rely for its ability to cure on UCC § 2–508(2). Under UCC § 2–508(2), the seller has the ability to cure if: (a) seller had reasonable grounds to believe its tender would be acceptable; and (b) cure would be reasonable in light of the buyer's needs.

While One Stop probably acted in good faith because it ordered from a reputable manufacturer and expected that the shirt would be acceptable, in this scenario, the buyer would be unduly inconvenienced by the delay in receiving the cured tender. Here, because Jackie is leaving the next morning and cannot receive the shirt by mail, Jackie would not be able to wear the shirt on her trip, so waiting for a cure would cause too much inconvenience. In other words, cure under UCC § 2–508(2) turns on the needs of, and convenience to, the buyer, and not the good faith of the seller.

(B) is incorrect.

(B) is incorrect because the focus in determining a cure's availability is the reasonable needs of the buyer, not the knowledge of those needs by the seller. Since Jackie needed the shirt before her trip, she would be unduly inconvenienced by the late tender.

(C) is incorrect.

(C) is incorrect because, while One Stop Sporting Goods probably did act in good faith, Jackie would suffer too much inconvenience in waiting for a cure.

(D) is incorrect.

(D) is incorrect because it does not matter if the manufacturer is at fault; it is too late for the store to cure its imperfect tender.

Answer to Question 40

(C) is the correct answer.

Statement III is correct based on *Zabriskie Chevrolet, Inc. v. Smith*, 240 A.2d 195 (N.J. Super. 1968), which ushered in the "shaken faith" doctrine as a limitation to the <u>type</u> of cure available. There, the court held that because the purchase of a car is such a large investment and the breach dealt with the buyer's health and safety, once the buyer's "faith" in the car is "shaken" by the defective tender (there was a transmission problem in *Zabriske* similar to the one described in this problem), then the only acceptable cure is by replacement, i.e., a new car, and not a cure by repair, i.e., by taking a transmission form another car.

The general rule is that a seller who is entitled to cure may do so either by repair or by replacement. In other words, it is up to the seller how it wants to effect the cure. However, if the breach comes under the "shaken faith" rule, only a replacement good is acceptable as a cure.

The shaken faith doctrine has proven to be pretty limited—essentially to cases where the defective tender reasonably makes a purchaser fear his or her health and safety. So if, e.g., a flat screen television has a greenish-tinged picture, the seller can cure by repairing the defective part, even if the buyer would prefer a brand new TV.

(A), (B), and (D) are incorrect.

These choices are incorrect because only statement III is correct as explained above.

Answer to Question 41

(B) is the correct answer.

David properly rejected the rug because it was imperfectly tendered. However, under UCC § 2–602(2)(a), a rejection is no longer effective if the buyer exhibits "any exercise of ownership [over the goods]." When David accepted the check made payable to himself from the painters, David exercised ownership over the rug. At that point, his rejection failed and he became the "owner" of the rug.

Note that if David had accepted a check made payable to Randy's, the rejection would still be effective.

(A) is incorrect.

(A) is incorrect because David would have a reasonable time after delivery to reject under UCC § 2–602(1). Therefore, it does not matter that David had already taken the rug home. The issue here is that David exercised indicia of ownership over the goods when he accepted the check.

(C) is incorrect.

(C) is incorrect because once David accepted the check he could no longer reject the goods for the reasons stated above.

(D) is incorrect.

(D) is incorrect because it does not matter that David had already notified Randy's that he was rejecting the rug. Once he accepted the check he could no longer reject the rug.

Answer to Question 42

(B) is the correct answer.

(B) is correct because a buyer can revoke an acceptance under UCC § 2–608(1)(a) if the goods were accepted with knowledge of their non-conformity, so long as: (a) they were accepted with a reasonable expectation that the seller would cure the non-conformity, and (b) the defect substantially impaired the value of the good to the buyer herself. Here, Buyer accepted the bookcase because Seller told her that it would mail the missing shelf to cure the imperfect tender, and the missing shelf substantially impaired the value of the unit to Buyer.

Revocation must occur within a reasonable time, but the problem directs that three weeks was reasonable.

Note that there is a split of opinion as to whether the seller has the right to cure in a revocation situation. But in this case, the facts provide that the store did not effect a timely cure in any event.

(A) is incorrect.

(A) is incorrect because Buyer has accepted the unit when she started using it. UCC § 2–606(1)(b),(c). Once accepted, the bookcase cannot be rejected. UCC § 2–607(2).

(C) is incorrect.

(C) is incorrect because Buyer can revoke her acceptance of the bookcase, as set forth in the explanation to (B) above.

(D) is incorrect.

(D) is incorrect because UCC § 2–608(2) states that revocation must occur before the buyer has made any substantial change in the condition of the goods. Therefore, if the buyer substantially changed the bookshelf by painting it, Buyer would no longer be able to revoke her acceptance.

Answer to Question 43

(A) is the correct answer.

(A) is correct because all of the requirements for revocation of acceptance under UCC § 2–608 have been met under these facts. UCC § 2–608(1)(b) requires a buyer to prove that the goods were accepted without knowledge of their non-conformity in order to have a viable revocation. Here, the non-conformity was unknown because it was difficult or impossible to discover initially. Buyer accepted the bicycle without knowledge of the non-conformity, because it was difficult for him to know that there was a problem with one of the "wheel nuts" on the axle rod as it took a week for them to loosen enough to fall off.

UCC § 2–608 also requires that the buyer prove: (a) the non-conformity substantially impairs the value of the goods to the buyer, (b) that revocation is occurring within a reasonable time after buyer has discovered grounds for it, and (c) that revocation must occur before any substantial change in the condition of the goods has occurred. Here, Buyer can no longer ride his bike to work, which is the reason he bought the bicycle, and the facts set forth that the non-conformity substantially impairs the value of the bike to him. Buyer is also returning the bike only a week after he purchased it, and immediately after the "wheel nut" fell off, which would be within a "reasonable time." Further, the facts state that Buyer has made no substantial change to the bike. Thus, Buyer may revoke his acceptance at this point in time.

(B) is incorrect.

(B) is incorrect because there is no requirement under UCC § 2–608 that a seller give the buyer permission to revoke his or her acceptance. Because the requirements under UCC § 2–608 are met, Buyer is entitled to revoke his acceptance.

(C) is incorrect.

(C) is incorrect because, although Buyer accepted the bike by using it for a week UCC § 206(1)(b),(c), Buyer is still entitled to revoke that acceptance if the elements of UCC § 2–608 are met, which is the case here as set forth in the explanation to (A) above.

(D) is incorrect.

(D) is incorrect because it misstates the law. UCC § 2–608 requires that the non-conformity substantially impair the value of the good <u>to the particular buyer</u>. Therefore, substantial impairment is a subjective, not an objective, test for revocation.

Answer to Question 44

(D) is the correct answer.

(D) is correct because the facts of this question demonstrate another "exception" to the perfect tender rule. Although lawyers use the phrase "perfect tender rule" when discussing UCC § 2–601, the statute itself does not use the words "perfect tender." Rather, it says that the buyer can reject a shipment if it fails to "conform to the contract." Therefore, the usage of trade, course of dealing, and course of performance may modify the seller's duties, and a shipment may be perfectly tendered even if it does not conform to the express words of the contract if it is acceptable under accepted usages of trade. UCC § 1–103.

Here, it is customary in the trade to weigh buttons, rather than counting them. Thus, even though the exact number of buttons did not match the number stated in the contract, because Seller followed the trade custom, the tender of buttons "conformed to the contract," and Buyer is obligated to pay the contract price and may not prorate it.

(A) is incorrect.

(A) is incorrect for the reasons stated above. Because Seller followed the custom in the industry, the tender "conformed to the contract."

(B) is incorrect.

(B) is incorrect for several reasons. First, Buyer may not reject the shipment for the reasons stated above. Second, this was a single lot contract, because the buttons came in one shipment. Therefore, it is irrelevant whether the imperfect tender substantially impairs the value of the shipment. Third, even if this were an installment contract, the test is whether the imperfect tender substantially impairs the value of the shipment to a reasonable person. Thus, it would not matter that Buyer subjectively felt that the value of the shipment was substantially impaired.

(C) is incorrect.

(C) is incorrect because there has been no breach in this instance because Seller conformed to the contract by tendering "perfectly" within the usage of trade, and thus Buyer must pay the contract price, and not the prorated price based on the number of buttons actually received. In other words, Seller was only obligated to send twenty 10-ounce shipments of buttons under the agreement, which it did, and thus Seller is entitled to full payment for full performance.

CHAPTER 15
ANTICIPATORY REPUDIATION

ANSWERS

Answer for Question 1

(A) is the correct answer.

It wasn't until the 1850s before contract law had a remedy for the innocent party when the other party indicated he or she would breach a contract in the future. The doctrine of anticipatory repudiation was ushered in by *Hochster v. De La Tour,* 118 Eng. Rep. 922 (Q.B. 1853).

Now, when one party unambiguously tells the other that he or she will not be performing under a contract with executory (unperformed) duties of both parties remaining under the contract, the innocent party can immediately bring suit for anticipatory repudiation. Restatement 2d § 253(1); UCC § 2–610.

To have a viable anticipatory repudiation claim: (1) there must be a bilateral contract with executory duties remaining by both parties; (2) the repudiated duty must amount to a total breach if it is never performed; and (3) the repudiation must be definite and unequivocal. Here, Dennis unequivocally said he would not do any work (a total breach) under a bilateral contract where both parties had remaining duties. Since the elements for the repudiation to be effective are satisfied, Parker would be entitled to bring suit for the breach now under the anticipatory repudiation doctrine.

(B) is incorrect.

(B) represents what Parker must do if there was not an effective anticipatory repudiation. That is, he would have to wait until the performance was due to bring suit for the breach. While it is true that, technically, there is no "breach" until a party fails to perform an obligation when due, contract law will not make the innocent party wait and allows a suit for anticipatory *repudiation* before the date performance is due under the contract if the other elements are met.

(C) is incorrect.

There is no rule limiting suit for only damages upon the unequivocal repudiation of material duties due to be performed in the future under a bilateral contract, as occurred here.

(D) is incorrect.

Dennis has anticipatorily repudiated the agreement. It is up to Parker, as plaintiff, to establish the amount of damages to which he is entitled, and one way to do that is by finding another landscaper willing to do the work for a higher price. But even if he cannot find another landscaper, Parker is still entitled to at least nominal damages. Restatement 2d § 346(2).

Answer to Question 2

(D) is the correct answer.

A valid anticipatory repudiation claim requires the existence of a bilateral contract with executory duties remaining by <u>both</u> parties. Restatement 2d § 253(1); UCC § 2–610. Here, Seller has already completely performed; he has given up possession of the watch to Buyer. As such, Seller has no anticipatory repudiation claim and must wait until July 1, when Buyer's performance was due, before bringing suit.

(A) is incorrect.

Where, as here, there is not a bilateral contract with unperformed duties <u>on both sides</u>, no anticipatory repudiation claim can be established, no matter how unequivocal the repudiation of the "breaching" party. In such a case, the innocent party must wait until performance was due to sue for breach of contract.

(B) is incorrect

The anticipatory repudiation doctrine does not apply in situations where one party to the contract has already completely performed. Hence, Seller has no anticipatory repudiation claim. Note that <u>if</u> Seller *did* have such a claim, there is no rule limiting suit to damages only.

(C) is incorrect.

There is no requirement to seek out an alternative buyer. The problem with Seller's anticipatory repudiation claim here is that Seller has already completely performed under the contract and thus, must wait until performance was due to sue for breach.

Answer to Question 3

(B) is the correct answer.

Anticipatory repudiation has significant consequences to a contractual relationship. If one party repudiates, the other can declare the contract over, will not have to perform, and can immediately bring suit for breach. As such, to invoke the anticipatory repudiation doctrine, the repudiating party must *unequivocally* refuse to perform an executory duty. Restatement 2d § 250(a); UCC 2–610.

Here, Seller has only made a request for modification; he has not actually anticipatorily repudiated the contract. That is, Seller did not unambiguously say he would not perform. He merely noted the rising prices, questioned whether he would be able to perform, and asked if Buyer would be willing to kick in a little more money to help him earn a small profit. However, Seller never gave an unambiguous statement that he would not perform under the terms of the original contract.

(A) is incorrect.

Seller did not make an unequivocal statement that he would not perform; therefore there was no anticipatory repudiation. Instead, Seller has made only a request for modification of the price under the agreement.

(C) is incorrect.

Seller has neither breached nor repudiated. "Repudiation" requires an unequivocal statement that the party will not perform, and a "breach" cannot occur until performance is due.

(D) is incorrect.

Losing a little money per ton on a ten ton contract is insufficient "impracticability" to invoke the commercial impracticability doctrine. UCC §§ 2–613–615.

Answer to Question 4

(C) is the correct answer.

When a good faith difference of opinion as to the meaning of the contract exists, a party will not have anticipatorily repudiated because he or she denies the duty existed. Dave was not refusing to perform an undisputed duty under the contract; rather he was honestly disputing whether there <u>was</u> a duty to paint the guest house under the contract.

(A) is incorrect.

Dave has not anticipatorily repudiated his duties, but rather has raised an honest and legitimate dispute as to the scope of his duties owed under the contract.

(B) is incorrect.

While one element of proving that an effective anticipatory repudiation occurred is that the duty repudiated must be "material," (since the repudiated duty must lead to a total breach if it remained unperformed), simply because it is material to one party does not mean that it is actually a duty owed under the contract. In other words, it first has to be established that a duty existed before it becomes relevant whether it is material to give rise to a total breach or not.

(D) is incorrect.

Whether an unjust result might occur is not a determinative factor in finding whether an effective anticipatory repudiation has taken place or whether the painting of the guest house was a duty under the contract.

Answer to Question 5

(C) is the correct answer

Up until this point in this chapter, the route to anticipatory repudiation has been of the "classic" common law variety, i.e., one party unequivocally stating it would not perform a material duty under a bilateral contract with executory duties remaining for both parties. However, there is another route to a valid anticipatory repudiation claim which is illustrated by this question, namely the failure to provide reasonable assurances in response to a valid request for reasonable assurances. UCC § 2–609; Restatement 2d § 251. This process is explained below.

If one party has "reasonable grounds for insecurity" to believe the other will perform under a bilateral contract, that party can ask for "reasonable assurances" of the other party's willingness and ability to perform. If such assurances are not forthcoming within a "reasonable time," (under UCC § 2–609, the "reasonable time" cannot exceed thirty days), then the party requesting the assurance can treat it as an anticipatory repudiation of the agreement.

Each step of the process needs to be analyzed. The first question is when is there "reasonable grounds for insecurity" justifying a party's request for reasonable assurances? The answer is that there is no one test, but know that the threshold for insecurity is low. As set forth in

UCC § 2–609, Cmt. 3, "a report from an apparently trustworthy source" that there might be problems with the other party's performance is sufficient. Here, the *Wall Street Journal* article is a report from a trustworthy source, especially when coupled with Buyer's statement about hoping he would have the money to pay. Hence, Seller had reasonable grounds to demand assurances.

Note that the grounds for insecurity need not turn out to actually be true, they just need to reasonably appear to be true at the time an insecure party makes a request for reasonable assurances. UCC § 2–609. Here, although the *Wall Street Journal* article was incorrect and the comments by Buyer were a joke, the grounds for insecurity would still appear to be true at the time Seller requested them.

Once reasonable grounds are established, Seller is entitled to demand "adequate assurances" from Buyer of Buyer's "willingness and ability" to perform when performance was due in September. Buyer was obligated to respond, and when he did not, Seller was justified in treating the absence of a response as an anticipatory repudiation: "After receipt of a justified demand [for assurances] failure to provide within a reasonable time not exceeding thirty days such assurance of due performance as is adequate under the circumstances of the particular case is a repudiation of the contract." UCC § 2–609(4).

Here, Seller demanded the assurances on May 2, and so on June 5, when it did not receive any assurances within thirty days, it was entitled to treat the agreement as repudiated, cease performance under the agreement, and immediately bring suit. UCC §§ 2–609, 2–610; Restatement 2d § 251. Once again, Buyer was not excused from providing reasonable assurances because the grounds for insecurity were incorrect. So long as Seller was justified in asking for the assurances, Buyer had to respond or Seller was justified in treating the agreement as repudiated.

(A) is incorrect.

The *Wall Street Journal* article and the statement of Buyer gave the Seller reasonable grounds for insecurity. The fact the article was untrue and the statement a joke is irrelevant so long as it reasonably appeared to give the Seller grounds to demand assurance. UCC § 2–609; Restatement 2d § 251.

(B) is incorrect.

The failure to respond to a justified demand for assurances can be treated as an anticipatory repudiation by the insecure party. UCC § 2–609(4); Restatement 2d § 251(1).

(D) is incorrect.

Upon an anticipatory repudiation, the seller is entitled *either* to complete the machine and try to sell it to another, or immediately cease working on it and sue for the damages caused thereby, so long as the decision is commercially reasonable. UCC § 2–704.

Answer to Question 6

(A) is the correct answer.

An insecure party with the right to demand assurance may not effectively demand a particular kind of assurance; it is up to the *receiving* party to determine what type of assurances will be adequate. An insecure party certainly can *ask* for a particular kind of assurance and say that if you send me this, that will satisfy me. But what the insecure party cannot due is *demand* a particular kind of assurance and state that "if you do not send me exactly what I demanded, I will treat you as having committed an anticipatory repudiation."

In other words, just because Seller demanded Buyer's P/L, it does not mean Seller could only provide assurances with that document. All that is necessary is the assurances Buyer chose are "adequate" to alleviate the insecurity, as judged by a reasonable party. A credit report from a reputable company showing financial stability is sufficient in this kind of situation.

(B) is incorrect.

Although Seller demanded the P/L, Buyer would not be required to provide assurances only with that document.

(C) is incorrect.

It does not matter whether the P/L is a reasonable type of assurance. The question is whether what was eventually supplied by the Buyer—the credit report—was "adequate."

(D) is incorrect.

The question is not whether a party acts in good faith in sending "something" in response to a justified demand for reasonable assurance. If there is a dispute, a court will have to later determine whether what was sent was "adequate" assurance. If it was not, an anticipatory breach can be alleged.

Answer to Question 7

(D) is the correct answer.

When a party has reasonable grounds for insecurity and demands assurance, he or she may suspend performance while waiting for a response. UCC § 2–609(1). Hence, here, after Seller requested assurances, it was entitled to suspend work on the sign until it heard from Buyer. If such a suspension causes the insecure party to delay its final performance under the agreement, that delay is excused, and does not constitute a breach.

Further, Buyer likely has not anticipatorily repudiated the contract because it responded within a reasonable time. A party must respond to a request for reasonable assurances within a *reasonable time* not exceeding thirty days. UCC 2–609. Here, Buyer got Seller the new credit report in five days, which the facts state is the fastest it possibly could get the report, and so neither party repudiated or breached the contract.

Note that if Seller had seen the report or otherwise knew of a shaky credit status of Buyer *before* entering into the contract, Seller could not legitimately demand reasonable assurances of performance. That is because a demand for reasonable assurance can only legitimately be based on facts or rumors learned *after* the contract had been made. UCC § 2–609.

(A) is incorrect.

Under UCC § 2–609(1), any delay caused by reasonably suspending performance while waiting for assurances is excused. The five day delay in completion of the project would be excused since it took five days for Buyer's assurances to arrive.

(B) is incorrect.

This choice is incorrect because there was no breach by Seller. A Seller is entitled to suspend performance while waiting for adequate assurances, and if there is a delay in the performance under the contract due to the suspension, the delay is excused. UCC § 2–609(1).

(C) is incorrect.

By responding as fast as it could, Buyer provided adequate assurances within a reasonable time, and thus did not anticipatorily repudiate the contract.

Answer for Question 8

(B) is the correct answer.

The best way to think of a party's unequivocal anticipatory repudiation is that it is only an offer to repudiate the contract. That is because the innocent party can simply do nothing in response to the repudiation and/or urge the repudiating party to reconsider. In that case, there is simply an offer to repudiate that is outstanding, and like most offers, that offer can be retracted before the date on which performance is due. If the "offer" is effectively retracted, the other party is given a reasonable time to complete performance, but the contract is back on and the other party is obligated to perform. UCC § 2–611; Restatement 2d § 256.

However, there are two situations in which the repudiating party loses the ability to effectively retract the repudiation. The first is when the non-repudiating party "accepts" the offer of repudiation by communicating with the repudiating party to the effect that "the contract is over" or "I am treating your repudiation as final." That did not occur here.

The second way the repudiating party loses the right to retract the repudiation is when the non-repudiating party materially changes position in reliance on the repudiation. UCC § 2–611(1); Restatement 2d § 256. Here, Seller has taken on new work that will require all of his time for the next two years. He thus materially changed his position in reliance on Buyer's repudiation and Buyer can no longer retract the repudiation.

(A) is incorrect.

The repudiation was made irrevocable when Seller materially changed his position in reliance on the repudiation. UCC § 2–611(1); Restatement 2d § 256. As such, Seller would not be repudiating by refusing to perform because Buyer cannot retract her previous repudiation.

(C) is incorrect.

(C) correctly sets forth the outcome of an effective retraction of a repudiation, i.e., the non-repudiating party is obligated to perform, but would be granted a reasonable time beyond the contract due date to complete performance. However, the attempted revocation of the repudiation was not effective because Seller materially changed position in reliance on Buyer's repudiation.

(D) is incorrect.

Buyer did not effectively retract her repudiation because Seller's reliance on the revocation by taking on the other job made the revocation irrevocable.

CHAPTER 16

IMPOSSIBILITY, COMMERCIAL IMPRACTICABILITY, AND FRUSTRATION OF PURPOSE

ANSWERS

Answer to Question 1

(B) is the correct answer.

Impossibility is a "defense to performance" in a breach of contract suit, asserted by someone who did not perform what that person promised to do in a contract. To illustrate how impossibility works and why contract law needs it, assume A has contracted to sell a race horse to B. Unknown to both, the race horse dies in the stable shortly after the contract was made because, completely unexpectedly, a tractor at the adjacent farm blew up and a piece of shrapnel from the tractor pierced the horse's heart. A cannot now deliver the horse; it is impossible for him to do so. Since we don't want to penalize A for not doing something that is impossible to do and was not his fault, contract law has to find some mechanism to discharge his duties and let him off the hook.

Without the impossibility-causing event, A would be obligated to tender the horse to B. When performance became impossible, contract law says A does not have to fulfill his tender obligation, i.e., it is "excused" or, in the words of the Restatement 2d, his duty is "discharged." So B's obligation to pay never arises because A never tendered the horse, but A is not liable for his failure to tender the horse because his tender obligations under the contract are discharged.

So if A is sued by B for breach of contract, impossibility gives him a defense to the breach action by discharging his duty to tender the horse. In other words, A is not liable because he no longer had to do the act which is asserted to be a breach.

The next question is when does impossibility apply to discharge a duty? A party asserting the defense must prove four elements: (1) an event must occur which makes the performance of the duty objectively impossible, (2) the nonoccurrence of the event was a mutually shared basic assumption of the contract, (3) the event was not the fault of the party asserting the defense, and (4) the party asserting the defense did not explicitly or implicitly assume the risk of the occurrence of the event. Restatement 2d § 261. (The elements for impossibility are the same under the UCC in UCC §§ 2–613, 2–615, even if it is not immediately clear from the wording of those provisions).

With regard to the racehorse example: (1) an event occurred (*the death of the horse*) which makes the performance of the duty objectively impossible; (2) the non-occurrence of the event was a mutually shared basic assumption of the contract (i.e., *both parties shared the assumption that the horse would still be alive until delivered to the buyer*); (3) the event was not the fault of the party asserting the defense (*we are assuming the seller of the horse had no reason to know about the problems with his neighbor's tractor*); and (4) the party asserting the risk did not explicitly or implicitly assume the risk of the occurrence of the event (*the seller was not a guarantor against farm equipment maladies from another farm*). Since all four elements are met, the seller's duties were discharged and a breach action by the buyer fails because the seller had no enforceable obligation to deliver the horse, and therefore did not "breach" anything.

Here, the question is whether impossibility will allow Dwayne to argue that his duty to provide Paula with a building in good condition for her play is discharged. It would because: (1) an event occurred (*the lightening strike and subsequent fire*) which made the performance of the duty objectively impossible, (2) the non-occurrence of the event (*the continued existence of the building*) was a mutually shared basic assumption of the contract, (3) the event was not the fault of the party asserting the defense (*there was nothing Dwayne could do to prevent the fire*), and (4) the party asserting the defense did not explicitly or implicitly assume the risk of the occurrence of the event (*Dwayne did not assume the risk under the contract that a lightning strike would burn the building down*).

If you think the last element is arguable (how do we know Dwayne did not implicitly assume that risk under their contract?), you understand impossibility pretty well and see where many impossibility defense arguments fail. The last element is always a contested matter of proof, and it is difficult to state for certain that the party asserting the defense did not implicitly assume the risk without more facts. However, this problem is based on the facts of *Taylor v. Caldwell*, 122 Eng. Rep. 309 (1863) where the court found impossibility excused a music hall owner's duty to furnish a suitable building to a musical producer on similar facts.

(A) is incorrect.

Misunderstanding involves parties to a contract attaching different meanings to the same term in a contract. Restatement 2d § 20. It is a defense *to formation* of a contract and does not play a role here. Impossibility is a defense *to performance* under a contract.

(C) is incorrect.

As will be explained further in this chapter, frustration of purpose is typically a defense asserted by a <u>buyer</u> of goods, services, interests in real estate, etc., and not by the supplier of those goods, services or interests in real estate. The gist of the doctrine is that the party can perform, but the purpose for which he or she entered into the contract is frustrated and, because of an event, it does not make any sense to perform. Here, Dwayne could not perform. It's not that the purpose for which he entered in the contract could still be accomplished but was frustrated; rather his obligation to deliver the hall in good condition was rendered impossible.

(D) is incorrect.

Commercial impracticability is related to impossibility and has similar elements. However, commercial impracticability is relevant when performance of the contract becomes much more expensive as a result of an unforeseen event. Here, we know the performance is impossible due to the fire, not just more costly. Restatement 2d § 261; UCC § 2–615. Impracticability is discussed further in the next question.

Answer to Question 2

(D) is the correct answer.

This question is also based on a real series of cases, known as *The Westinghouse Cases*, 405 F. Supp. 316 (M.D.L. 1975). Westinghouse had agreed to supply nuclear reactors to about thirty utilities around the country, which obligated it to supply close to seventy million pounds of uranium. Because of a price-fixing conspiracy, it would have lost over $2 billion had it fulfilled the contracts. On its face, this would seem a good candidate for the commercial impracticability defense, which Westinghouse asserted. However, that defense was disallowed by the courts, as explained below.

When applicable, commercial impracticability works the same way as impossibility, as explained in the answer to the previous question. That is, it acts to discharge the duties of a party under the contract, and so is a defense to a breach of contract action.

The elements of commercial impracticability are similar to impossibility: (1) an event must occur which makes the performance of the duty commercially impracticable, (2) the nonoccurrence of the event was a mutually shared basic assumption of the contract, (3) the event was not the fault of the party asserting the defense, and (4) the party asserting the defense did not explicitly or implicitly assume the risk of the occurrence of the event. Restatement 2d § 261; UCC § 2–615.

The first issue in *The Westinghouse Cases* was thus whether performance was "commercially impracticable." There is no definition of that term in either the Restatement 2d, the UCC, or its comments, but the thought is that the party asserting the defense must suffer a huge, unconscionable loss before this element is satisfied. Something like six to ten times the costs reasonably allocated when the contract was formed is considered the floor by many commercial scholars. Without holding definitively that a $2 billion loss (in 1975 dollars) was sufficient to meet the "impracticability" standard, the court said that it was willing to accept that performance was sufficiently impracticable, because the defense failed for other reasons.

The second issue was whether the absence of a world-wide price fixing cartel was an assumption that both parties shared. The court held that it was.

The third issue was whether Westinghouse was at fault for the illegal cartel. It was not.

Where Westinghouse lost was on the last element—whether it expressly or *impliedly* accepted the risk of the cartel. The court held that while there was no express assumption by Westinghouse, there <u>was</u> an *implied* assumption of that risk because it agreed to supply the nuclear power plants for a fixed price. That is, if the nuclear fuel rods were the most expensive component, it knew that the price for uranium could increase for any number of reasons—shortages, increased demand, etc. So while maybe it was unfair to hold that it could have foreseen a price fixing cartel, it was not unfair to conclude that it should have protected itself by putting in a clause that said, in effect, "Westinghouse will supply a nuclear power plant for $20 million, *providing the price of uranium does not go above "X" price.* Since it did not do that, and since it agreed to supply the plants at a fixed price, the court concluded the fourth element of impracticability was not met and the defense was unavailable to Westinghouse.

Author's Note:

The above answer is in great detail to illustrate the analysis in an impracticability case. In all likelihood, if you see a multiple choice question on analogous facts, the call of the question

would be "What is the best defense for Westinghouse?" Of the answer choices presented, probably commercial impracticability would be a better choice than impossibility, frustration, fraud, etc. However, real world application of these doctrines is very complicated.

Note that both the Restatement and the UCC do not have separate tests for "impossibility" and "impracticability," viewing them as two ends of the same spectrum. Nevertheless, courts still make the distinction, and each is discussed separately in this book.

(A) is incorrect.

Performance under the contract is not impossible, just more costly than initially thought. Without the event making performance *objectively impossible*, the defense is improper.

(B) is incorrect.

As explained above, commercial impracticability was the defense relied on by Westinghouse but rejected by the court.

(C) is incorrect.

(C) is incorrect for the same reasons given above. Frustration of purpose also has the element that the party attempting to assert the defense must not have explicitly or impliedly assumed the risk of its occurrence.

Answer to Question 3

(B) is the correct answer.

This problem follows a fact pattern in a series of cases known as "The Coronation Cases," *See Krell v. Henry,* 2 K.B. 740 (C.A.) (1903). In *Krell,* a man rented a flat for one day at a premium because it offered a great view of the expected coronation of an English King. The King got the flu, however, and cancelled the coronation. The owner of the flat argued that impossibility could not apply since the renter certainly <u>could</u> pay the agreed fee. The renter, of course, said the only reason he agreed to rent the flat was to watch the coronation, and he should not have to pay once it was cancelled.

The court agreed with the renter and ushered in the "frustration of purpose" doctrine. Frustration works the same way as impossibility and impracticability—it acts as a defense to a breach of contract action by discharging the duties of the party asserting it. It also has similar elements. The party asserting the defense must establish: (1) An event occurred which frustrates a principal purpose for which the party entered the contract, (2) the non-occurrence of the event causing the frustration was a mutually shared basic assumption of the parties, (3) the party asserting the defense was not at fault in causing the event, and (4) the party asserting the defense did not explicitly or implicitly assume the risk of the event's occurrence. Restatement 2d § 265. (Frustration is not explicitly mentioned in the UCC, but there is an indication in Cmts. 3 and 9 to UCC § 2–615 that frustration is contemplated under the UCC, and many courts have used the doctrine in UCC cases).

Here, (1) the principal purpose for which Denise rented the apartment (to watch the concert) was substantially frustrated when the concert was canceled. She did not want to rent the apartment for the view of the park in general, she wanted the view of the sold out concert. The concert occurring on that day was (2) a mutually shared basic assumption of both parties, after all, that is the whole reason Peter decided to rent the apartment that day. Denise has no part in cancelling the event, so she (3) cannot be said to be at fault. Finally, (4) the risk of the event not occurring as scheduled had not been fairly assumed by Denise (or at least that is what the court said about the renter in *Krell*; although some have argued that the renter (like Denise here) could have made her payment expressly conditional on the coronation's (concert's) occurrence). Thus, she will be excused based on frustration of purpose.

(A) is incorrect.

(A) is incorrect because it is not impossible for Denise to perform. She still could take possession of the apartment for the day for $5,000. The real issue is her purpose in wanting the apartment is for an event that was cancelled.

(C) is incorrect.

For the reasons discussed in (B), Denise would likely be excused from her duties to lease the apartment May 5.

(D) is incorrect.

(D) is incorrect because Denise's payment obligations would be discharged due to frustration, and so she would owe nothing to Peter.

Answer for Question 4

(D) is the correct answer.

Derek will want to argue frustration of purpose excuses his duties to rent the retail space under the contract, i.e., the laws restricted firework sales so much he should not open a firework store, thus has no need for the space. However, the argument fails for two reasons. First, there must be substantial frustration for the doctrine to apply. Seeing as though he could, in fact, continue selling the legal fireworks, it is unlikely that sufficient frustration exists. Further, the rental property could still be used for any other retail endeavor as well. Thus the broad purpose of the contract was not frustrated (i.e., operation of a retail store) even if Derek's personal expectations of opening a successful firework shop were. Restatement 2d § 265.

Second, it is likely that Derek would have assumed the risk that these laws and regulations would be passed prohibiting some fireworks. The facts state that the firework industry was booming because of the debates about passing new laws, i.e., people were buying up what they could while it was available. This being a reason Derek wanted to get into the firework retail industry, it is likely he will be deemed to have assumed the risk the laws ultimately are passed and the industry will become less profitable.

This question is based on the facts of *Lloyd v. Murphy,* 153 P.2d 47 (Cal. 1944). There, Lloyd leased retail space, which had no qualification on its use, just before World War II. He planned to open a car dealership, but once the war started, he could not get any cars to sell since most of the domestic steel, rubber, etc. industry was diverted to the war effort. The California Supreme court held the lack of substantial frustration (he could still use the space for other retail purposes) and the assumption of risk (at the time he entered the lease, the U.S. entering the war was certainly a much discussed issue) meant frustration of purpose could not be successfully asserted.

(A), (B), and (C) are incorrect.

These answer choices are incorrect because of the reasons given in Choice (D). Derek's potential frustration of purpose defense would likely fail under *Lloyd v. Murphy*.

Answer to Question 5

(C) is the correct answer.

The Danbury Hotel's primary purpose of entering into the contract was to provide visitors of the hotel additional entertainment during their stay in an effort to boost the desirability of their hotel. Following the fire, it could no longer take additional guests, and thus had no need for water park access with no guests at the hotel. The non-occurrence of a fire destroying the hotel was a basic, mutually shared assumption of both parties. The facts state that the fire was not due to any fault of The Danbury, and it had not fairly assumed the risk of fire occurring. With all of the requirements being met, The Danbury will thus likely be able to have its payment obligations discharged because of frustration of purpose. This question was based on *LaCumbre Golf and Country Club v. Santa Barbara Hotel,* 205 Cal. 422 (1928), where a hotel had a similar arrangement with a local golf course, and where the hotel's duties were discharged on frustration grounds after it burned down.

(A) is incorrect.

(A) is incorrect because while it may be impossible for The Danbury to have guests in the burned hotel, it is not impossible for it to make the payments under the contract. It was not its contractual duty that became impossible as a result of the unforeseen events, but rather the purpose for which it entered the contract that became frustrated.

(B) and (D) are incorrect.

The Danbury's duties will likely be discharged under a frustration of purpose theory as explained in (C).

Answer to Question 6:

(D) is the correct answer

While it is true that it is theoretically possible for Dwayne to follow through on the contract and face the legal consequences for doing so, contract law will not require a contracting party to commit an illegal act to complete performance under a contract, even if that act was legal at the time the contract was entered into.

The mechanism by which it accomplishes that goal is to discharge the duty to do the illegal act under an impossibility theory. Restatement 2d § 264; UCC § 2–614(2).

(A) is incorrect.

As discussed in the explanation to (D), contract law will not compel an illegal act to avoid a breach. As such, Dwayne would not be required to perform. It is not relevant whether Parker agrees to pay any potential fines in determining if Dwayne must perform.

(B) is incorrect.

Parker will not prevail because his duties under the contact were discharged by supervening illegality under the impossibility doctrine.

(C) is incorrect.

Parker will lose the suit because of impossibility due to the performance becoming illegal. Whether he attempted to find alternative means to replace Dwayne as a fishing guide is irrelevant.

Answer to Question 7

(A) is the correct answer.

This question illustrates the difference between objective and subjective factors in an impossibility analysis. To assert a valid impossibility defense, an event must occur that makes performance *objectively* impossible, e.g., like the arts center burning down or the race horse dying. Restatement 2d § 261. Here, it may have been subjectively impossible for Start–Up to manufacture the computer, but it could be done by another, Apple. Hence, the performance of the contract was not objectively impossible and Start–Up has no impossibility defense. It also has no such defense because it impliedly assumed the risk of being liable to Government if it was unable to complete performance. This case is based on *U.S. v. Wegematic Corp.*, 360 F.2d 674 (2d Cir. 1966).

(B) is incorrect.

(B) is incorrect for the reasons given in the explanation of (A).

(C) is incorrect.

(C) is incorrect because Start–Up implicitly accepted the consequence of the risk of being unable to perform when it signed the contract.

(D) is incorrect.

Start–Up may have been frustrated by not being able to complete the contract, but it is the supplier of services, not the purchaser, and hence is unable to assert frustration as a defense. Also, the purpose for which the contract was entered into was not frustrated; it is just that Start–Up could not finish what it promised.

Answer to Question 8

(B) is the correct answer.

This choice sets forth the rule of UCC § 2–615(b), i.e., upon an impossibility event which destroys only some of the supplier's inventory, a supplier with existing contracts must allocate the remaining inventory to its contracting parties on a pro rata basis.

(A) is incorrect.

If all the lithographs were destroyed, the duties under the contracts would be discharged, but since some of the lithographs survived, they must be allocated to those with whom the seller is contractually obligated to supply the lithographs. UCC § 2–615(b).

(C) is incorrect.

Pro rata allocation in a situation such as described in this question is mandatory, not discretionary. UCC § 2–615(b).

(D) is incorrect.

This is an issue of impossibility, not commercial frustration.

Answer to Question 9

(C) is the correct answer.

This choice sets forth the rule of UCC § 2–616. That is, while the seller must *offer* a pro rata allocation to a party in the position of Gallery #1 under UCC § 2–615(b) (as explained in the previous question), the buyer need not *accept and pay for* the allocation under UCC § 2–616(a). In other words, the law does not require a buyer to accept less of a good than it contracted for.

(A) is incorrect.

The buyer is not obligated to accept the pro rata allocation of a seller in such a situation. UCC § 2–615.

(B) is incorrect.

(B) is incorrect as it sets forth an erroneous statement of law. A buyer who contracts for apples does not have to accept bananas as a "substituted performance," even if the apple crop were wiped out by an unexpected fungus.

(D) is incorrect.

(D) is incorrect because (C) is correct.

Answer to Question 10

(A) is the correct answer.

An example of force majure clause would be:

Neither party shall be held responsible if fulfillment of any terms or provisions of this contract are delayed or prevented by revolutions or other civil disorders, wars, acts of enemies, strikes, floods, fires, acts of God, or by any other cause not within the control of the party whose performance is interfered with, and which by the exercise of reasonable diligence the party is unable to prevent, regardless whether the class of such cause is enumerated above.

The purpose of such a clause is to allow the parties to agree in advance what sorts of events will discharge their obligations under the contract. That way they do not have to rely on courts to decide whether the event triggers impossibility, frustration, etc., making (A) correct.

(B) is incorrect.

(B) is incorrect because force majure clauses protect both sellers and buyers.

(C) is incorrect.

(C) is incorrect because force majure clauses, like the example above, often include acts of God.

(D) is incorrect.

(D) is incorrect because both (B) and (C) are incorrect.

CHAPTER 17
THIRD PARTY BENEFICIARY CONTRACTS

ANSWERS

Answer to Question 1

(A) is the correct answer.

With any potential third party beneficiary situation, the first step is to identify the parties. Star is the promisor, for she is obligated to do an act (in this case, pay money) that will benefit a third party. Jane is the promisee, for she bargained for the promisor's promise. Bill is the beneficiary, for he will benefit from performance of Star's promise to make the payment.

At common law, beneficiaries were identified as either "creditor," "donee," or "incidental" beneficiaries. The Restatement 2d changed the classification to just "intended" or "incidental" beneficiaries in Restatement 2d § 302. However, courts continue to classify intended beneficiaries, even under the Restatement 2d, as either "donee-like intended beneficiaries" or" creditor-like intended beneficiaries," for reasons explained in the answer to Question 2 below.

Here, Bill is an intended beneficiary because the purpose of the Jane–Star contract was to benefit Bill, and thus "recognition of a right to performance of a promise in the beneficiary is appropriate to effectuate the intention of the parties." Restatement 2d § 302(1).

Buyer is a donee-like intended beneficiary because "the circumstances indicate that the promisee intends to give the beneficiary the benefit of the promised performance." Restatement 2d § 302(1)(b). That is, Jane was making a gift of the money to Bill thus Bill is a donee of that promise.

(B) is incorrect.

The requirement to be a creditor-like intended beneficiary is that, "the performance of the promise will satisfy an obligation of the promisee to pay money to the beneficiary." Restatement 2d § 302(1)(a). In other words, for Bill to be an intended creditor-like beneficiary, the third party beneficiary contract would have to have been entered into to satisfy a previous obligation of Jane to pay money to Bill, which was not the case here.

(C) is incorrect.

The purpose of the Jane–Star contract was to benefit Bill, making him an intended beneficiary, not an incidental one.

(D) is incorrect.

(D) is incorrect because Bill is an intended third party beneficiary.

Answer to Question 2

(A) is the correct answer.

An intended third party beneficiary always has the right to sue the promisor (here Star) for breach of the promisor's promise. That is often the central purpose of such agreements and after all, Star received bargained-for consideration (the necklace) in return for the promised payment.

However, an intended donee-like beneficiary acquires no rights against the *promisee* (here Jane) arising from the formation of a third party contract. That is, Jane was just making a gift to Bill. If she had just promised to give Bill the necklace, that gift promise would not be enforceable by Bill contractually because it lacks consideration. Bill acquires no additional rights just because Jane makes a gift of the proceeds from the sale of the necklace.

This question illustrates the major difference between a "donee-like" intended beneficiary and a "creditor-like" one, and the reason courts continue to use the terms "creditor-like" and "donee-like" as modifiers to the term "intended beneficiary." By definition, a creditor-like beneficiary already is under an obligation to pay money to the promisee. Restatement 2d § 302(1)(a). As such, if the promisor does not perform, the beneficiary can still sue the promisee; not because of any rights granted under the third party beneficiary contract, but to enforce the pre-existing obligation. But because no contractual rights to enforce a gift promise exist, if the promisor does not perform, the donee-like intended beneficiary cannot sue the promisee.

(B) and (C) are incorrect.

As explained in the explanation to (A) above, as a donee-like intended beneficiary, Bill has no rights against the promisee, Jane.

(D) is incorrect.

(D) is incorrect because Bill, as an intended beneficiary, is entitled to bring suit against the promisor, Star, for the reasons explained in (A).

Answer to Question 3

(A) is the correct answer.

The issue in this question turns on the rights of the promisor and promisee to modify the third party beneficiary contract to the detriment of the intended beneficiary. The majority view, which is also the view adopted in the Restatement 2d, provides the beneficiary's rights vest either: (a) upon creation of the promisor–promisee contract if it contains a valid no modification clause, Restatement 2d § 311(1); (b) upon a material change of position by the beneficiary in justifiable reliance on the promisor's promise, Restatement 2d § 311(3); or (c) upon the intended beneficiary's assent to beneficiary status at the request of either the promisor or promisee, Restatement 2d § 311(3). Without one of these exceptions applying, the promisor and promisee can freely modify the agreement to the detriment of the intended beneficiary.

Accordingly here, once Bill enrolled at college in reliance on the payment by Star, Jane and Star were without the power to effectively modify the contract to Bill's detriment under Restatement 2d § 311(3). This meant that Star still owes Bill the money even though she has already made the payment to Jane. Since Jane wasn't entitled to the payment, Star can sue her for unjust enrichment for its return, but Star nevertheless continues to owe Bill $30,000.

As noted above, the Restatement position is the majority view. The other two common law views are: (1) an intended beneficiary's rights vest upon creation of the third party beneficiary contract, regardless of a no modification clause, and so the agreement may never be effectively modified by the promisor and promisee to the beneficiary's detriment; and (2) an intended beneficiary's rights vest only upon knowledge by the promisor and promisee of the beneficiary's reliance in receiving performance by the promisor.

(B) is incorrect.

As explained in the answer to the previous question and in the explanation of (A) above, Bill (the donee-like intended beneficiary) has no rights to sue Jane (the promisee) under the third party beneficiary contract because Jane simply made a gift promise to Bill of the proceeds from the sale of the necklace. It is possible that Jane could be liable for a tort like interference with contract. However, the problem limits the question to considerations of "breach of the Jane–Star contract only."

(C) is incorrect.

This answer is incorrect because Bill cannot sue Jane for breach of the Jane–Star contract as explained in the answer to (B).

(D) is incorrect.

(D) is incorrect because Bill, as an intended beneficiary, has a valid claim against Star, the promisor.

Answer to Question 4

(B) is the correct answer.

To be a creditor-like intended beneficiary, "the performance of the promise will satisfy an obligation of the promisee to pay money to the beneficiary." Restatement 2d § 302(1)(a). Here, the Jane–Star contract was entered into to satisfy a pre-existing (i.e., existing before the third party beneficiary contract came into existence) obligation of the promisee (Jane) to pay money to the beneficiary (Bill).

(A), (C), and (D) are incorrect.

These answer choices are incorrect for the reason (B) is correct.

Answer to Question 5

(C) is the correct answer.

Bill is entitled to sue Star for $30,000 because he is an intended beneficiary of a third party beneficiary contract, and Star is a promisor in that contract who failed to perform. The rule is that an intended beneficiary is entitled to sue the promisor for breach. Restatement 2d § 304.

Bill is also entitled to sue Jane for failure to repay the loan when due. In other words, the underlying debt between Bill and Jane was not extinguished just because Jane entered into a third party beneficiary contract with Star.

(A), (B), and (D) are incorrect.

These answers are incorrect for the reason (C) is correct.

Answer to Question 6

(A) is the correct answer.

The agreement between Donna and Rhonda is a third-party beneficiary contract with Donna as promisee, Rhonda as promisor, and

Hairstylist as an intended beneficiary because recognizing Hairstylist's right to payment from Rhonda is necessary to effectuate the intent of the promisor and promisee when they entered into the agreement. Restatement 2d § 302.

Hairstylist is simultaneously both a creditor-like and a donee-like intended beneficiary. She is a creditor-like intended beneficiary because "the performance of the promise will satisfy an obligation of the promisee to pay money to the beneficiary," (for the $500 debt). Restatement 2d § 302(1)(a). She is a donee-like intended beneficiary because "the circumstances indicate that the promisee intends to give the beneficiary the benefit of the promised performance." (for the $250 tip). Restatement 2d § 302(1)(b).

An intended third-party beneficiary may enforce the contract in an action against the promisor, and is entitled to the value of the promisor's performance, here $750. It is irrelevant that the debt was only $500, and Rhonda agreed to pay $750 for the painting and cannot escape that obligation by claiming the extra $250 was a gift from Donna.

(B), (C), and (D) are incorrect.

These answers are incorrect for the reasons (A) is correct.

Answer to Question 7

(A) is the correct answer.

Home Depot was only an incidental third party beneficiary of the Moneybags–Gardner agreement. The definition of an "incidental beneficiary" under Restatement 2d § 302(2) is a catchall—it is any beneficiary which is not an intended beneficiary.

A beneficiary is an intended beneficiary if recognition of a right to performance in the beneficiary is appropriate to effectuate the intention of the promisor and promisee, and either: (a) the performance of the promise will satisfy an obligation of the promisee to pay money to the beneficiary; or (b) the circumstances indicate that the promisee intends to give the beneficiary the benefit of the promised performance. Restatement 2d § 302(1). Because performance of the Moneybags–Gardner contract will not satisfy an obligation of Moneybags to pay money to Home Depot, nor is it the case that Moneybags intended to give Home Depot, or any other retailer, the benefit of the promised performance at the time he entered into the agreement with Gardner, Home Depot is only an incidental beneficiary under Restatement 2d § 302(2). As such, it cannot sue the promisor for breach of the promisor's duty. In other words, Moneybags's deal was only intended to benefit Gardner. Any benefit realized by a retailer on the sale of the tractor was only incidental to that intent.

(B) is incorrect.

Home Depot's obtaining inventory for sale will not obligate Moneybags where no obligation existed before. Home Depot *might* be able to state a claim against Gardner for reliance on Gardner's promise, although it is unlikely it can successfully do so. But it has no claim against Moneybags whatsoever, since it is only an incidental beneficiary of the Moneybags–Gardner agreement.

(C) is incorrect.

(C) is incorrect for the reasons that (A) is correct, i.e., Home Depot is not an intended beneficiary of the Moneybags–Gardner contract, but rather an incidental beneficiary. Restatement 2d § 302(2).

(D) is incorrect.

Gardener was not acting as Moneybag's agent. Gardner was buying the tractor for himself. Moneybags was just going to pay for it.

Answer to Question 8

(D) is the correct answer.

The overwhelming majority rule is that citizens are presumptively only incidental beneficiaries of contracts between municipalities and third parties with whom the municipalities contract to perform required city services. One reason is that ordinarily it is not the case that the city and the private party intended to confer on the citizen an enforceable right to the private party's promised performance, and so the situation does not meet the definition of an intended beneficiary under Restatement 2d § 302.

There is also a policy reason for the presumptive rule. If citizens are allowed to sue private parties such as Contractor, every citizen would have a right to sue whenever he or she believed the roadway was not built correctly, and facing the threat of an onslaught of litigation would act as a disincentive for private companies to contract with municipalities, which could lead to a decline in public services. Restatement 2d § 313, Cmt. a. *See also Moch Co. v. Rensselaer Water Co.*, 159 N.E. 896 (N.Y. 1928).

(A) is incorrect.

The citizen cannot be a creditor-like beneficiary because City's duty to the citizen is not one to pay money, as required under Restatement 2d § 302(1)(a).

(B) is incorrect.

The majority view, as explained in the answer to (D) above, is that citizens are only incidental beneficiaries of contracts between municipalities and third parties with whom the municipalities contract to perform city services.

Note that there is a minority view holding that citizens should be considered donee-like beneficiaries to a contract between municipalities and third parties for the performance of city services, because the public service is a type of gift bestowed on the citizen, but this theory has not gained much traction with the courts and is a distinctly a minority view.

(C) is incorrect.

The class action status of the suit is irrelevant. The problem is that courts simply do not recognize a citizen's rights as a beneficiary to enforce a contractor's promise to perform a municipal duty.

Answer to Question 9

(A) is the correct answer.

Under Restatement 2d § 309(1), "A promise creates no duty to a beneficiary unless a contract is formed between the promisor and promisee; *and if a contract is voidable or unenforceable at the time of its formation, the right of any beneficiary is subject to the infirmity*" (emphasis added).

In the vernacular of contract law, Sister, as the beneficiary, "stands in the shoes" of the promisee (Brother) and is subject to any defenses the promisor (Buyer) could assert in a breach of contract lawsuit brought by the promisee (Brother). In the words of Restatement 2d § 309(1), Sister is *"subject to the infirmity"* in the Buyer–Seller contract. Under contract law, a contract is voidable and subject to rescission even if a misrepresentation was innocent, so long as it was material. Restatement 2d § 164(1). Thus, Buyer may apply the defense of misrepresentation in a suit by Sister because he could assert that same defense in a breach of contract suit brought against him by Brother for non-payment.

(B) is incorrect.

(B) is incorrect because Sister is not an incidental beneficiary, but rather an intended one because the contract was entered into to benefit her. Restatement 2d § 302.

(C) is incorrect.

(C) is incorrect for the reasons that (A) is correct and is also a misstatement of law. Any defense that the promisor has against the promisee may be brought against the beneficiary as well.

(D) is incorrect.

Restatement 2d § 164(1) provides that a contract is voidable even if the misrepresentation is innocent, so long as it is "material." Here, being given the wrong provenance of the painter is certainly "material," i.e., a reasonable person in the buyer's position would consider it important in deciding whether to purchase the painting. Thus, the contract is voidable regardless whether the misrepresentation is innocent, negligent or fraudulent.

Answer to Question 10

(D) is the correct answer.

The obligation of Buyer is to pay Sister, because she is an intended third party beneficiary. The question in this problem turns o who can enforce that payment obligation. The answer is that both Sister and Brother can sue Buyer to enforce his obligation to pay Sister. But because the payment is due Sister, Brother must turn over any proceeds he recovers from the lawsuit to Sister.

(A) is incorrect.

(A) is incorrect for the reason (D) is correct. Sister, as an intended beneficiary is not the only party that may sue under the contract for non-performance by the promisor. She could file an action, but so can Brother, the promisee.

(B) is incorrect.

Sister is not an incidental beneficiary but an intended one, and both she and Brother, the promisor, have a right against Buyer to enforce Buyer's obligation to pay Sister if he fails to do so.

(C) is incorrect.

Although this answer choice recognizes that Brother, as promisee, may sue Buyer as promisor, it neglects the fact that Sister, as an intended beneficiary, is still entitled to the benefit of performance or any recovery from a suit for non-performance.

Answer to Question 11

(B) is the correct answer.

The issue in this question turns on the ability of Buyer and Seller (the promisee and promisor) to validly modify a third party beneficiary contract to the detriment of Creditor (the intended beneficiary). The general rule is that the promisor and promisee retain the power to modify the agreement to the beneficiary's detriment, even so far as to terminate an intended beneficiary's rights under the contract. Restatement 2d § 311(2).

However, that general rule is subject to three exceptions: (a) the promisor–promisee contract has a valid no modification clause, Restatement 2d § 311(1); (b) before receiving notice of the modification or discharge, the beneficiary materially changes position in reliance on the contract, including bringing suit on it, Restatement 2d § 311(3); and (c) the beneficiary manifests assent to the contract at the behest of either promisor or promisee, Restatement 2d § 311(3). None of the exceptions apply to this problem, and so the modification, as set forth in Choice (B) would effectively deprive Creditor of any rights as an intended beneficiary under the Buyer–Seller agreement.

(A) is incorrect.

(A) is incorrect because an intended third-party beneficiary does not have to notify either the promisor or the promisee that the beneficiary "accepts" the benefits of the contract. Note that if either the promisor or promisee asks the beneficiary to do so, the beneficiary's rights vest, and the promisor and promisee may not thereafter modify the contract to the beneficiary's detriment. Restatement 2d § 311(3).

(C) is incorrect.

An intended beneficiary does not need to provide consideration to attain rights under the promisor–promisee contract. If that were the case, there could never be a third party beneficiary agreement where a donee-like intended beneficiary could enforce the agreement. However, this choice is not only legally wrong, but factually wrong as well. In creating the debt owed by Seller, Creditor did give consideration to Seller.

(D) is incorrect.

The general rule is that a contract for the transfer of land cannot be enforced if oral. Restatement 2d §§ 125–129. However, all that means is that if Seller did not wish to follow through with the deal, he or she could not be compelled to transfer the title. But if the parties wished to go forward, they could. In other words, such an oral contract is voidable, not void.

Here, however, the oral nature of the agreement as suggested in this answer choice is irrelevant because the transfer of title took place. Hence, <u>if</u> Creditor had a claim as an intended beneficiary, Creditor would be able to enforce it since the contract was performed and the obligation of Buyer to pay money was enforceable.

Answer to Question 12

(C) is the correct answer.

The main distinction between an assignment and a third party beneficiary situation is that in the latter, only one contract is involved (i.e., at the time of the making of the third-party beneficiary contract, an intended beneficiary gains rights). In an assignment, there are two contracts: the original agreement, followed by a second contract in which contractual rights obtained under the first agreement are assigned to a third party.

Here, Creditor does not obtain rights until after the original contract was formed and only did so by means of a separate agreement. Therefore, it would be considered an assignment with the roles of the parties identified in the answer.

(A) and (B) are incorrect.

Both of these answer choices treat the roles of the parties as if the contract were a third-party beneficiary contract in which Creditor is some form of intended beneficiary. As explained in the answer to (C) above, that is incorrect.

(D) is incorrect.

(D) is incorrect because the answer assumes there had been a delegation of a contractual duty (and not the assignment of a right to receive contractual performance) to perform to a third party, which is not the case here. This was an assignment. One way to remember the rule is that duties are delegated; rights are assigned.

CHAPTER 18
ASSIGNMENTS

ANSWERS

Answer to Question 1

(B) is the correct answer.

When a party enters into a contract, it acquires rights. When it gives (or sells) those rights to a third party, it is known as an assignment. Once the right is assigned, the party who originally owned the right, but later gave (or sold) it away (known as the *assignor*) no longer has the right; and the third party who got the right (known as the *assignee*) now has the right to that performance. The party who used to owe a performance obligation to the assignor, but now owes that performance to the assignee, is known as the *obligor*.

Assignments are described in Restatement 2d § 317 fairly technically: "[a]n assignment of a right is a manifestation of the assignor's intention to transfer it by virtue of which the assignor's right to performance by the obligor is extinguished in whole or in part and the assignee acquires a right to such performance."

One of the key things to look for in an assignment is a transfer of an existing contractual right, with no other action necessary, for only existing contractual rights with no other action needed can be assigned. *Id.* Even then there are restrictions stating that some rights cannot be assigned. Restatement 2d § 317(2). Questions as to these restrictions are found below in this chapter.

(B) is correct because an assignment took place when Tom transferred his existing contractual right to collect the $800 to a third party (Liz). Tom is the <u>assignor</u> because he originally had the right to collect $800 and gave it away. Sandy is the <u>obligor</u> because she is the party that initially promised performance to the assignor (when she promised to pay $800), but now owes that duty of performance to Liz. Liz is the <u>assignee</u>, because she was not a party to the initial assignor/obligor contract, and received from Tom the <u>right</u> to receive $800.

There are two types of assignments: (1) gratuitous assignments, where the assignor is making a gift of the contractual right to the assignee; or (2) assignments for value, when the assignor has received consideration for the assignment. Here, Tom made a gratuitous assignment of the right to collect the $800.

Author's Note:

Note that some cases call the "assignor" the "obligee" or the "promisee." Similarly, there are older decisions which refer to the "obligor" as the "promisor." However, most modern cases and treatises use the terms "assignor," "obligor" and "assignee" to refer to the three parties in an assignment, and that will be the convention used in this book.

(A) is incorrect.

(A) is incorrect because Liz was not a third party beneficiary. This is because the contract between Tom and Sandy *had already been formed* and Tom <u>later</u> decided to transfer his contractual right to receive payment to Liz via a second agreement. Thus, an assignment took place.

A third party becomes a beneficiary under a third party beneficiary contract when that party receives the right to performance at the time the first and only contract was entered into. In other words, if *at the time the Tom/Sandy contract was made,* Tom said "I'll sell you my laptop for $800, and pay the money to Liz," there would be a third party beneficiary situation.

But because Tom and Sandy entered into the contract first, and <u>later</u>, Tom told Sandy to pay the $800 to Liz, it is an assignment situation. In other words, in a third party beneficiary situation, there is only one contract, and a third party obtains rights in its performance at its formation. In an assignment situation, there are two agreements— the original one between the assignor and obligor; and a second one, formed later, in which the assignor's rights under the first contract are transferred to the assignee.

(C) is incorrect.

(C) is incorrect because the parties are incorrectly identified. Tom is the assignor, Sandy is the obligor, and Liz is the assignee, for the reasons stated above in the explanation for (B).

(D) is incorrect.

(D) is incorrect because this problem sets forth the transfer of a contractual <u>right</u>, and not the transfer of a contractual <u>duty</u>. A transfer of a contractual duty is known as a delegation. Restatement 2d § 318. Rights are assigned and duties are delegated.

Here, Tom transferred his contractual right to receive $800, rather than his contractual duty to hand over his laptop. Therefore, an assignment took place.

Answer to Question 2

(A) is the correct answer.

In this problem, Amy is the assignor, Brenda is the assignee, and Carly is the obligor.

(A) is correct because Amy's purpose in making the assignment was to give Brenda a gift. Had Brenda given consideration to Amy for the right to receive the $5,000, this would have been an assignment for value, but because Brenda did not give Amy any consideration, this was a gratuitous assignment.

Note that it is irrelevant to the classification as a "gratuitous assignment" or "assignment for value," that the $5,000 came from a previous debt. The only relationship to examine is the one between Amy (the assignor) and Brenda (the assignee).

(B) is incorrect.

(B) is incorrect because an assignment for value is one in which the assignee has given consideration to the assignor for the assignment. Here, Brenda (the assignee) has not given Amy (the assignor) any consideration in order to receive the $5,000.

(C) is incorrect.

(C) is incorrect because there is no consideration necessary between the assignor and assignee in a gratuitous assignment. Gratuitous assignments are supported by whatever consideration existed in the agreement between the assignor and obligor. Therefore, the consideration that Amy gave to Carly when she gave her a loan supports the assignment from Amy to Brenda.

(D) is incorrect.

(D) is incorrect because the assignee does not have to give any consideration to the obligor in order to have an effective assignment.

Answer to Question 3

(B) is the correct answer.

In this situation, Peter is the assignor, Mary is the assignee, and Paul is the obligor. The question turns on the rules for what kinds of rights can be effectively assigned.

The rules governing the types of contracts that can be assigned are found in Restatement 2d § 317(2). The structure of that provision is that all assignments are effective <u>unless</u> the assignment runs afoul of one of the exceptions in Restatement 2d § 317 (2)(a), (b) or (c). Specifically it provides:

A contractual right can be assigned unless:

(a) the substitution of a right of the assignee for the right of the assignor would materially change the duty of the obligor, or materially increase the burden or risk imposed on him by his contract, or materially reduce its value to him, or

(b) the assignment is forbidden by statute or otherwise inoperative on grounds of public policy; or

(c) assignment is validly precluded by contract.

This case is an example of an assignment being prohibited because Paul's (the obligor's) burden in performing his duty (cleaning a home) would be materially increased by the assignment. Restatement 2d § 317(2)(a). That is, rather than cleaning a 3,000 square foot home for $300, after the purported assignment Paul would have to clean a 17,000 square foot mansion for that same $300.

(A) is incorrect.

(A) is incorrect because an obligor does not need to formally accept an assignment for it to be valid, so this choice is an incorrect statement of law. This choice is also incorrect because the assignment here is substantively invalid because it materially increases the burden to the obligor, Paul, and is thus prohibited under Restatement 2d § 317(2)(a).

Note that if Paul wanted to accept the assignment, he certainly could waive any protections provided for him by contract law and if he were willing to clean the mansion for $300, nothing would prevent him from doing so and agreeing to a modification of the original contract. Nevertheless, the purported assignment of the right would still itself be invalid.

(C) is incorrect.

Restatement 2d § 327(1) requires that the assignee, here Mary, assent to the assignment before it is enforceable. Hence, if Mary objected, there would be another reason why the assignment would not be enforced. However, Choice (C) provides that the assignment is enforceable "*unless*" Mary objects. Hence it is incorrect because even if Mary did not object, the assignment would still not be enforceable because it materially increased Paul's duties as a result, and is thus invalid under Restatement 2d § 327(2)(a).

(D) is incorrect.

(D) is incorrect because the purported assignment (which was manifested by Peter) is invalid for the reasons stated above, i.e., it materially increased the burden of the obligor. Restatement 2d § 327(2)(a).

Answer to Question 4

(C) is the correct answer.

Restatement § 317(2)(c) provides that a contractual right cannot be assigned if assignment is validly precluded by contract. However, courts disfavor anti-assignment clauses. Courts interpret such clauses very narrowly and uphold them in only a very few circumstances.

First, courts interpret anti-assignment clauses as prohibiting only delegations, unless the circumstances indicate otherwise. Restatement 2d § 322(1). Second, courts interpret anti-assignment clauses as benefiting the obligor, so the obligor can waive the protection. Restatement 2d § 322(2)(c). And finally, and most relevant to this question, courts tend to interpret anti-assignment clauses as a promise, not a condition. Therefore, if there is an assignment under a contract with a no assignment clause, the assignment is still valid, but the assignor is liable to the obligor for breach of contract. Restatement 2d § 322(2)(b).

Thus, Fruity Farm's assignment to Big Bucks Bank is effective, but Fruity Farms is liable to Whistling Winery for breaching the covenant not to assign. Whether there are damages flowing from this breach is unknown from the facts in the question. But nevertheless, a valid assignment, along with a breach, has occurred under modern assignment rules.

(A) is incorrect.

(A) is incorrect because the assignment to Big Bucks Bank is still effective for the reasons stated above. Rather, Fruity is liable to Whistling Winery for the breach of the covenant not to assign.

(B) is incorrect.

(B) is incorrect because the covenant not to assign <u>did</u> have legal effect. Fruity Farms will be liable to Whistling Winery for breach of contract due to the assignment to Big Bucks Bank.

(D) is incorrect.

(D) is incorrect because it misstates the law of assignments. Covenants not to assign apply to both buyers and sellers of goods. Therefore, Fruity is still liable to Whistling Winery for the breach of the covenant not to assign for whatever damages it can establish.

Answer to Question 5

(D) is the correct answer.

(D) is correct because one of the requirements for an effective assignment is that there be an assignment of an existing contractual right "without further action or manifestation of intention by the obligee." Restatement 2d § 324. Here, because Sasha promised to transfer the right *in the future* and *upon a certain condition*, there is not a present intention to transfer the right. Therefore, no assignment has taken place. This is only a promise to assign a "future right," as provided for under Restatement 2d § 321(2).

(A) is incorrect.

(A) is incorrect because Sasha's promise would need further action in order for an assignment to occur. Therefore, an effective assignment has not taken place because Sasha does not have a present intention to transfer the right without further action.

(B) is incorrect.

(B) is incorrect because no assignment has taken place for the reasons stated above. The validity of the purported assignment is not dependent upon the future payment of Sasha.

(C) is incorrect.

(C) is incorrect because Rita is the obligor, and a manifestation of assent is not required by the obligor in order for an assignment to be effective. The reason why there was no effective assignment here is that there was no immediate assignment of an existing right—just a promise to do so in the future. Restatement 2d § 321(2).

Answer to Question 6

(C) is the correct answer.

In this situation, Ashley is the assignor, Barry is the assignee, and Stretch, Inc. is the obligor. (C) is correct because Restatement § 327(1) provides that before an assignment becomes effective, the *assignee* must manifest his or her acceptance to the assignment.

While there are exceptions to this rule—when the assignment is for value provided by a third party and where there is some writing or token associated with the thing assigned that is sent with the assignment to a third party (Restatement 2d § 327(1)(a), (b))—this problem does not raise any of the exceptions. Thus, Barry must manifest an acceptance to the assignment before it can become effective.

(A) is incorrect.

(A) is incorrect for the reasons Choice (C) is correct. Under Restatement 2d § 327(1), Barry must manifest an acceptance to the assignment before it becomes effective.

(B) and (D) are incorrect.

(B) is incorrect because Stretch, Inc. is the obligor, and obligors do not need to manifest an acceptance to an assignment; rather, only assignees need manifest such agreement. Restatement 2d § 327(1). Since Choice (B) is incorrect, Choice (D) must also be incorrect.

Answer to Question 7

(A) is the correct answer.

In this problem, Larry is the obligor because he is the promisor of the payment of money to David, David is the assignor because he originally had the right to the money, and Frieda is the assignee because she is the party that is being assigned the right to collect the money.

As stated in Restatement 2d § 327, the general rule is that the assignee must agree to the assignment to make it effective. However, there are two exceptions to this rule. The first is if a third party other than the assignee has given the assignor consideration for the assignment. Restatement 2d § 327(1)(a). That is what occurred here. Mary (a third party other than the assignee), agreed to paint David's bedroom (gave consideration) in exchange for David assigning the right to Frieda. Therefore, (A) is correct because Frieda does not need to accept the assignment in this situation to make it effective.

(B) is incorrect.

(B) is incorrect because the assignment takes place once David and Mary agree to it, not once Mary performs, under the rule of Restatement 2d § 327(1)(a).

(C) is incorrect.

(C) is incorrect for the reasons stated above. While the general rule is that an assignee must manifest acceptance of the assignment to make it effective, Restatement 2d § 327(1), this situation is one of the exceptions to the rule. Because Mary, a third party to the assignment, gave David, the assignor, consideration for the assignment, Frieda does not need to manifest acceptance to the assignment. Restatement 2s § 327(1)(a).

(D) is incorrect.

(D) is incorrect because the obligor of an assignment never needs to manifest acceptance to the assignment in order to make it effective.

Answer to Question 8

(D) is the correct answer.

In this problem, Amy is the assignor, the lottery commission is the obligor, and Dianne is the assignee.

While Restatement 2d § 327(1) states the general rule that assignees must manifest acceptance to the assignment before they are effective, this problem illustrates one of the exceptions to the rule.

An assignment is irrevocable and effective when there is a delivery of a writing or token to a third party evidencing the assignment. Restatement 2d § 327(1)(b). Here, there is a valid assignment because of the delivery of a writing (the lottery ticket) to a third party, Dianne. Therefore, Dianne need not assent to the assignment to make it effective.

(A) is incorrect.

(A) is incorrect for the reasons stated above. While Restatement 2d § 327(1) provides that an assignee generally must assent to the assignment to make it effective, the situation presented by this question falls under one of the two exceptions to the rule. Thus, no acceptance by Dianne is necessary to make the acceptance effective.

(B) and (C) are incorrect.

(B) and (C) are incorrect because obligors do not need to assent to an assignment in order for it to be effective nor would their objections make an assignment ineffective. Therefore, it does not matter that the lottery commission has not assented, and it would not matter if it objected to the assignment.

Answer to Question 9

(D) is the correct answer.

In this problem, Tom's is the assignor, Bank is the assignee, and Elizabeth is the obligor.

(D) is correct because when an assignment has taken place, the assignee "stands in the shoes" of the assignor. Therefore, any defenses that the obligor could have asserted against the assignor (if the assignor brought suit) can be asserted against the assignee. Restatement 2d § 336(1). Thus, Elizabeth can assert any defenses she had against Tom's (in this case, misrepresentation) against Bank, because Bank has "stepped into Tom's shoes."

(A) is incorrect.

(A) is incorrect because Elizabeth (the obligor) can assert any defenses she had against Tom's (the assignor) against Bank (the assignee). It does not matter that no one from the Bank made any misrepresentations to her.

(B) is incorrect.

(B) is incorrect because the defenses available to Elizabeth do not turn on whether the assignment was gratuitous or an assignment for value. Following the assignment, Elizabeth can assert any defenses she had against Tom's against Bank.

(C) is incorrect.

(C) is incorrect because it does not matter whether Bank was aware of the misrepresentation. Bank has "stepped into Tom's shoes" and Elizabeth can assert the misrepresentation defense against it.

Answer to Question 10

(A) is the correct answer.

In this problem, Manufacturer is the assignor, Big Bank is the assignee, and Fred's is the obligor.

As indicated in the *Author's Note* associated with the question, this problem and Question 11 test students' knowledge of the "holder in due course" ("HDC") exception to normal assignment rules.

The HDC rule is complicated even just to state:

When an assignee has purchased the right to receive payments under a "negotiable instrument" (a check or a promissory note—

anything that is payable "To the Order of . . ." rather than just "Payable to . . ."):

(a) which does not bear any evidence of forgery, irregularity or incompleteness, and

(b) if the purchase was made in good faith by the holder, for value, and without any actual knowledge by the holder of defenses to enforcement against the instrument,

then the obligor cannot assert any of the defenses he or she has against the assignor in a suit brought by the assignee.

The definition of a holder in due course is set forth in UCC § 3–302. Under this rule, Big Bank has met all of the requirements and is a "holder in due course." Thus, Big Bank will prevail because Fred's will be unable to assert the defenses (lack of consideration; rejection; etc.) it had against Manufacturer in the lawsuit.

(B) is incorrect.

(B) is incorrect because the issue here is that Big Bank was a "holder in due course." It is irrelevant that Big Bank did not make any representations to Fred's regarding the computer.

(C) is incorrect.

(C) is incorrect because Big Bank was a "holder in due course" of a negotiable instrument as set forth in UCC § 3–302. Therefore, as described in (A), Fred's cannot assert the defenses it has against Manufacturer against Big Bank.

(D) is incorrect.

(D) is incorrect because any objection by Fred's, as obligor, has no effect on the validity of the assignment or the defenses Fred's is entitled to assert in a lawsuit by Big Bank as a "holder in due course."

Answer to Question 11

(C) is the correct answer.

In this scenario, Bob is the assignor, Big Bank is the assignee, and Ann is the obligor.

This question tests knowledge regarding how federal law has prohibited the use of the "holder in due course" ("HDC") rules when the defendant is a consumer. Here, Ann is a consumer, so Big Bank cannot become a holder in due course. Therefore, Ann can assert against Big Bank any defenses she had against Bob (if Bob had brought suit), as would be true under the normal rules of assignments. Restatement 2d § 336(1). It is important to note that not all first year contracts classes cover this concept, so if this is the first time you have heard about HDC, there might not be a reason to learn a rule your Professor has not assigned.

(A) and (B) are incorrect.

(A) and (B) are incorrect because the HDC exception only applies in merchant-to-merchant situations. Because Ann (the obligor) is a consumer, the rule does not apply and Ann can assert any defenses she had against Bob against Big Bank.

(D) is incorrect.

(D) is incorrect because it misstates the law. It does not matter whether Big Bank made the misrepresentations to Ann. Ann can assert any defenses against Big Bank that she had against Bob.

Answer to Question 12

(A) is the correct answer.

In this problem, DD is the assignor, First Bank is the assignee, and Andrew is the obligor.

(A) is correct because when an assignment occurs, the assignee "steps into the assignors shoes" viz-à-viz the obligor. Therefore, Andrew would be able to assert any defenses against First Bank (the assignee) that he would be able to assert against DD (the assignor) had DD brought suit. Restatement 2d § 336(1). Thus, Andrew can assert the fraud defense against First Bank.

(B) is incorrect.

(B) is incorrect because it does not matter whether First Bank knew about the fraud. Andrew can assert the defense against First Bank for the reasons stated above.

(C) is incorrect.

(C) is incorrect because Restatement 2d § 336(1) provides that the obligor may assert any defenses he or she has against the assignor against the assignee.

(D) is incorrect.

(D) is incorrect because it does not matter whether the assignment is gratuitous or for value, Andrew can assert the fraud defense against First Bank for the reasons stated above.

Answer to Question 13

(A) is the correct answer.

In this problem, Al's is the assignor, Credit Bank is the assignee, and Bob is the obligor.

This question tests a student's knowledge about the implied warranties that accompany every assignment for value. In Restatement 2d § 332, an assignee who is paid for the assignment warrants he or she will do nothing to defeat or impair the value of the assignment, and that the assigned right actually exists. However, the assignor does <u>not</u> warrant that the obligor is solvent, or that he or she will perform the obligation. Restatement 2d § 333(2).

Thus, Al's did not impliedly warrant that Bob would perform his obligation (make his payments), making (A) the correct answer. In other words, non-payment by the obligor is one of the risks that an assignee for value takes when he, she or it enters into the assignment for value transaction and, presumably, that risk is factored into the price paid by the assignee.

Note there are no such implied warranties made by an assignor in gratuitous assignment situations.

(B) is incorrect.

(B) is incorrect because it misstates the law. Assignors cannot assert defenses against the assignee that the obligor would have against the assignee. Further, there are no facts to support a finding that Bob had any defenses against Credit Bank.

(C) is incorrect.

(C) is incorrect because assignments for value are the only assignments that have warranties, but there is no warranty that the obligor will perform.

(D) is incorrect.

(D) is incorrect because Credit Bank will lose because Al's did not warrant that Bob would pay as explained under Choice (A) above.

Answer to Question 14

(C) is the correct answer.

Under Restatement 2d § 333(1)(a), the assignor in an assignment for value impliedly warrants that he, she or it, "will do nothing to defeat or impair the value of the assignment and has no knowledge of any fact that will do so." Here, Al's knew that the refrigerator didn't work when it sold the refrigerator to Bob and when it assigned the contract to the bank. As such, it had knowledge of a fact which impairs the value of the assignment, making Choice (C) correct.

(A) is incorrect.

(A) is incorrect because Al's did, in fact, impliedly warrant that it will not impair the value of the assignment under Restatement 2d § 333(1)(a).

(B) is incorrect.

(B) is incorrect because it misstates the law. Assignors cannot assert defenses against the assignee that the obligor would have against the assignee.

(D) is incorrect.

Al's breached the implied warranty under Restatement 2d § 333(1)(a) and has no defense for that breach on these facts.

Answer to Question 15

(C) is the correct answer.

In this problem, Alex is the assignor, Dan is the assignee, and Jack is the obligor.

This question deals with the rights of the assignor and obligor to modify and/or cancel the contract to the disadvantage of the assignee. The structure of Restatement 2d § 332 starts by saying that gratuitous assignments are modifiable unless one of the exceptions set forth in the section apply. But there are many exceptions in the provision, and so, in truth, the rights of the assignor and obligor to modify the agreement are fairly circumscribed.

(C) is correct because one of the exceptions to the revocability of gratuitous assignments is when the assignment is made in writing, as this assignment was. Therefore, Alex and Jack may not modify the assignment. Restatement 2d § 332(1)(a).

Note that assignments for value are never modifiable by the assignor and obligor. They are only modifiable if the assignee agrees, and even then, any modification is judged under normal modification rules. Restatement 2d §§ 73, 89.

(A) and (B) are incorrect.

(A) and (B) are incorrect for the reasons stated above. When a gratuitous assignment is made in writing, it is not modifiable by the assignor and obligor. Restatement 2d § 332(1)(a).

(D) is incorrect.

(D) is incorrect because it misstates the law. An obligor does not need to assent to the modification of a gratuitous assignment. However, this assignment is irrevocable because it was in a writing that was signed and delivered by the assignor.

Answer to Question 16

(B) is the correct answer.

This question tests knowledge of priorities with regard to multiple assignments of the same right from the same assignor. Under the Restatement 2d, which came from rules established in Massachusetts, the general rule is that the first assignee takes priority over all subsequent assignees, regardless of the knowledge or notice of the assignees. Restatement 2d § 342.

As always, however, there are exceptions to that rule. That is, the subsequent assignee has priority over the first when:

(a) the first assignment is ineffective, revocable, or is voidable by the assignor or by the subsequent assignee; or

(b) the subsequent assignee in good faith and without knowledge or reason to know of the prior assignment gives value and obtains:

   (i) payment or satisfaction of the obligation;

   (ii) judgment against the obligor;

   (iii) a new contract with the obligor by novation; or

   (iv) possession of a writing of a type customarily accepted as a symbol or as evidence of the right assigned.

Restatement 2d § 342.

The situation in this question is governed by Restatement § 342(b)(i), i.e., satisfaction of the obligation has already been given to the second assignee, Mary. As such, Mary has priority, making Choice (B) correct.

(A) is incorrect.

(A) is incorrect because notice is not important under the Massachusetts/Restatement 2d rule.

Note that the first assignee to notify the obligor has priority over all other assignees of the same right under the so-called "English Rule" of establishing priorities.

(C) is incorrect.

(C) is incorrect because, while the first assignee generally prevails under Restatement § 342, there are four exceptions to this rule, and Mary falls under one of the exceptions.

(D) is incorrect.

(D) is incorrect because the filing of a financing statement is unimportant under the Massachusetts/Restatement rule. Rather, this becomes important in secured lending situations under Article 9 of the UCC.

Answer to Question 17

(D) is the correct answer.

Not all contract rights are assignable. The restrictions as to what rights cannot be assigned are set forth in Restatement 2d § 317(2). One of the restrictions was asked about in Question 3 above—a right cannot be assigned when the assignment will materially increase the duties of the obligor. Another restriction, set forth in Restatement 2d § 317(2)(b) is that an assignment cannot be made if it violates public policy. All fifty states have outlawed the assignment of wages by the employee. The reason is that if employees assign their wages, they may not work as hard at work. Accordingly, an assignment of wages is not effective as violation of public policy.

Of course, after receiving her wages, Sally is certainly entitled to pay 50% (or some other amount) of it to Bank. It is just that she cannot assign her wages so that payment is made by her employer before she sees the money.

(A), (B), and (C) are incorrect.

These choices all go to procedures necessary to make an effective assignment. The problem is that the assignment of wages is substantively invalid, making these choices incorrect.

CHAPTER 19
DELEGATIONS

ANSWERS

Answer for Question 1

(A) is the correct answer.

The applicable rule is set forth in Restatement 2d § 328(1): "[A]n 'assignment of the contract' . . . is an assignment of the assignor's rights and a delegation of his unperformed duties under the contract.". Hence, when Tom's "assigned the contract" to Super Vacations, it acted as both an assignment of its rights under Brett's contract and a delegation of its duties under that agreement. Hence, because of the delegation, Super Vacations now has the duty to book Brett on a round trip charter flight to Prague and a week at the Hilton. On the other hand, due to the assignment of the rights under that contract, Super Vacation also now has the right to collect the $1,400 from Brett.

(B) is incorrect.

The party who is owed a duty under a contract by one party but who, after the delegation, is owed that duty by another party, is known as the "obligee." Here, that party is Brett. Initially he was owed the duty by Tom's and, after the delegation, he is owed that duty by Super Vacation. The obligee need not assent to or even be aware of a delegation for it to be effective.

(C) is incorrect.

This contract concerns the right of an individual, but it is not a "personal services" contract within the meaning of that term under assignment and delegation law. On the delegation part of this transaction, a "personal services" contract means a contract in which the obligee (Brett) has a "substantial interest" in seeing that the party with whom he has contracted is the party who performs the contract, e.g., if a studio books Jack Nicholson for a movie, Jack cannot delegate his duty to act in the movie to Jane Seymour because the studio has a "substantial interest" in having Jack perform the role. Restatement 2d § 318(2). There are no facts which suggest that Brett has any "substantial interest" in having Tom's, as opposed to Super Vacations, book a plane flight and a hotel reservation or that Tom's was in any way chosen for its special skills or talents as is required to establish a "substantial interest."

Similarly, with regard to the assignment part of the transaction, the rule against assigning a "personal services" contract means an assignment will not be allowed where Brett's chances of getting what he contracted for will be "materially impaired" if Super Vacations is given the task to book the vacation versus Brett's chances of getting the vacation he contracted for if Tom's does the booking. Restatement 2d § 317(2)(a). There is no evidence that such is the case on these facts.

(D) is incorrect.

The phrase "assigning the contract" acts as both an assignment and a delegation of the Tom's–Brett contract. Restatement 2d § 328(1). As set forth in the explanation to (C) above, both the assignment and the delegation were effective.

Answer to Question 2

(C) is the correct answer

One of the first steps in a delegation analysis is to identify the parties. There are three parties to a delegation:

(1) The <u>delegating party</u>, which is the party who transfers a duty of performance under the contract to another. Here that is Tom's, since Tom's had a duty to book Brett's vacation that it transferred to Super Vacation. (Note that some older cases called the "delegating party" either the "obligor" or the "delegator.")

(2) The <u>obligee</u>, which is the party who was in the contract originally with the delegating party and was initially owed the duty by the delegating party but which, after the delegation, is owed that duty by another. Here, that is Brett because Brett originally was owed a duty to have a vacation arranged by Tom's and who, after the delegation, is owed that duty by Super Vacation.

(3) The <u>delegate</u>, which is the party who was not a party to the original contract, but who owes the obligation of performance to the obligee after the delegation. Here, that is Super Vacation because it was not a party to the original contract but who, after the delegation, now has the duty to book Brett's vacation.

Here, Statement I is incorrect because Nick's was not involved in the contracting transaction at all. All it did was suggest that Brett go to

Tom's. To be a delegating party, one must be in a contract under which it owes a duty of performance to the obligee.

Statement II is correct because Super Vacation is the delegate as it is the party which owes the duty of performance to Brett after the delegation.

Statement III is correct because Tom's is the delegating party since it delegated the duty to book Brett's vacation to Super Vacation.

Statement IV is incorrect, and Statement V is correct, as Brett is the obligee, i.e., he is the party who originally was owed the obligation by the delegating party (Tom's) but who, after the delegation, is owed the duty by the delegate (Super Vacation).

(A), (B), and (D) are incorrect.

These choices are incorrect for the reasons set forth in the explanation to Choice (C) above.

Answer to Question 3

(D) is the correct answer.

Absent evidence to the contrary, when a party "assigns the contract" or "all their rights under the contract" to another party, it acts as both an assignment of rights and a delegation of duties under the existing contract. Restatement 2d § 328; UCC § 2–210(4). Since Ted's has assigned its contract to Sport's, it would have both assigned the right to receive the $1,000 payment from Paul, and delegated the obligation to secure Paul's tickets. Further, there is no reason based on the facts as to why either the assignment or the delegation would be ineffective or prohibited.

(A) and (B) are incorrect.

(A) and (B) are individually true, making (D) the better answer.

(C) is incorrect.

When a party uses language such as "assigns the contract" or "all their rights under the contract," this demonstrates the parties' intent to both assign the rights and delegate the duties under the contract unless evidence to the contrary is shown.

Answer to Question 4

(B) *is the correct answer.*

When the obligee has a "substantial interest" in having a particular party perform the promised acts, the duty to perform those acts cannot be delegated. Restatement 2d § 318(2); UCC § 2–210(1). When performance depends on the particular skills, character, training, taste, etc., of the party attempting to delegate the duty, it is less likely the delegation will be effective. As indicated in the answer to the previous question, Jack Nicholson cannot effectively delegate his duties to act in a film to Jane Seymour because the studio has a "substantial interest" in having Jack perform.

Pat also had a "substantial interest" in having Wild Things perform, since she contracted with the band for their particular skills and talents as performers. If Pat were forced to accept the performance by the lesser known local hip-hop group, Pat would not receive what she had bargained for. As such, the attempted delegation is ineffective, making Choice (B) correct.

(A) *is incorrect.*

The assignment is not effective because Pat had a "substantial interest" in having Wild Things perform, and any retention of control by the delegating party over the delegate is irrelevant and does not make the delegation effective. Restatement 2d § 318(2); UCC § 2–210(1).

(C) *is incorrect.*

Typically the obligee need not assent to the delegation to make it effective, but where the obligee (Pat) has a "substantial interest" in having the delegating party perform under the contract, her consent (waiver of her right to object) is necessary to make the delegation effective.

(D) *is incorrect.*

The issue is not whether <u>Wild Things</u> can show a substantial interest in having the hip-hop group perform, but rather whether *Pat* has a "substantial interest" in having Wild Things perform. Restatement 2d § 318(2); UCC § 2–210(1).

Answer to Question 5

(C) is the correct answer.

(C) accurately sets forth the legal effects of a delegation—it gives the delegate the right, but not the obligation, to render performance to the obligee. Restatement 2d § 318(3). As Gardener delegated the duty to Landscaper, Landscaper gained the right to perform to Owner, but does not have the obligation to perform. This means that if neither Landscaper nor Gardner perform the required landscaping, Owner's only remedy is to sue Gardner, because only Gardner has the <u>obligation</u> to perform under the contract.

Note that if Gardner wanted to be off the hook under the contract and have Owner only be able to recover from Landscaper for performance, the parties would need to enter into a transaction known as a "novation" under Restatement 2d §§ 279(2), 280, not a delegation under Restatement 2d § 318.

(A) is incorrect.

Landscaper did not become obligated to perform after the delegation, he simply had the enforceable right to perform. Restatement 2d § 318(3).

(B) is incorrect.

After the delegation, it is Gardener who has the <u>duty</u> to perform, not Landscaper. Both have the <u>right</u> to perform. Restatement 2d § 318(3).

(D) is incorrect.

The obligee need not know of, or consent to the delegation in order for the delegate to acquire the right to perform.

Answer to Question 6

(A) is the correct answer.

Anti-delegation clauses are routinely enforced by courts, and so an attempted delegation in a contract that has an anti-delegation clause is unenforceable.

In this respect, anti-delegation clauses are treated very differently from anti-<u>assignment</u> clauses, which face judicial hostility. Restatement 2d § 322.

(B) is incorrect.

(B) states a frequent occurrence under anti-<u>assignment</u> clauses, i.e., courts will frequently allow the assignment but hold it was a breach of contract. Restatement 2d § 322(2)(a). But anti-delegation clauses are typically enforced and attempted delegations judged unenforceable in agreements with such a provision.

(C) is incorrect.

Anti-delegation clauses are generally enforced by the courts and a court would not prevent an assignment just because the agreement has an anti-delegation clause.

(D) is incorrect.

Anti-delegation clauses are generally enforced by the courts regardless of the suitability of the putative delegate.

Answer to Question 7

(A) is the correct answer.

When a third party has offered performance in exchange for a promise to release the original party from his duty to perform, and the obligee agrees to the arrangement, a "novation" has taken place. Restatement 2d §§ 279(2), 280. In a novation, the obligee (here Preston) can no longer sue the original contracting party in the event of a breach. Here, by agreeing to a novation, i.e., by allowing Jerry to perform in place of Dan and discharging Dan's obligation to perform, Preston has given up his right to sue Dan in the event of a breach.

Note this is in contrast to the normal delegation situation in which the delegate acquires only the right to perform, not the obligation to do so. In the normal situation , the delegating party is the only party liable under the contract. So if all that took place in this question was that Dan had delegated the landscaping job to Jerry, and no one showed up on March 20, Preston would only have been able to sue Dan, the delegating party, for only Dan would have had the obligation to perform. But, by releasing Dan and putting Jerry in his place, Preston's novation made it such that only Jerry had the obligation to perform the landscaping services.

(B) is incorrect.

(B) sets forth what the result would be if there had been a delegation of Dan's duties to Jerry. Here, however, the parties entered into a novation, meaning Dan was off the hook for the non-performance.

(C) is incorrect.

(C) represents the proper result if there had been a delegation by Dan of the duties under the contract, coupled with an assumption of the obligation by Jerry. In such a case, Dan, the obligee, would have been owed two enforceable duties, one from Dan and one from Jerry, and could have sued either. But there was a novation instead, meaning that Dan was off the hook.

(D) is incorrect.

Whether Preston has a claim at all against Jerry does not depend on Dan's insolvency.

Answer to Question 8

(B) is the correct answer.

This problem requires analysis under two different theories: delegations and third party beneficiary contracts, for the <u>same transaction</u> gives rise to different rights and responsibilities under each theory.

First the transaction analyzed as a delegation" Thomas is the delegating party; John is the obligee; and Dillon is the delegate. Thomas has delegated to Dillon his duty to pay $10,000 to John. Under the normal delegation rules, Thomas, as the delegating party, remains liable to John for the payment, making Statement I true. Dillon, as the delegate where there is no novation, does not owe John the money, for a delegate only acquires the right, but not the duty, to perform.

Now the same transaction analyzed as a third party beneficiary contract: Thomas was the promisee; Dillon was the promisor; and John was an intended third party beneficiary of the contract between Thomas and Dillon. An intended third party beneficiary is entitled to enforce the promise against the promisor. Restatement 2d § 304, 315. Hence, John can sue Dillon for breach of the promise to pay the $10,000. This is not due to Dillon's status as a delegate, but rather due to Dillon's status as a promisor under a third party beneficiary contract. This makes Statement II correct.

There was thus both a delegation and a third party beneficiary contract formed in this situation, making Statement IV correct.

Finally, Thomas, as promisee, is entitled to sue Dillon, the promisor, for breach of the third party beneficiary contract, making Statement III true.

(A), (C), and (D) are incorrect.

These choices are incorrect for the reason that (B) was correct.

Answer to Question 9

(C) is the correct choice.

There has been an effective delegation by the President. The President is the delegating party; American Express the obligee; and the viewing audience the delegates. Upon an effective delegation, the delegates acquire the right to perform, so American Express must accept payments of the President's bill from anyone in the viewing audience because each of them has the <u>right</u> to perform the President's obligation under the contract with American Express. Restatement 2d § 318. However, the viewers do not have the duty to perform, and so if no one sends in a payment, the President is still on the hook. *Id.*

(A) is incorrect.

A delegation can be effective even if oral.

(B) is incorrect.

Because the delegates have the right to perform after an effective delegation, American Express is required to accept any payment sent in to pay the President's bill. Restatement 2d § 318.

(D) is incorrect.

A delegate acquires the right to perform after an effective delegation, but not the obligation to do so. So if no one pays, American Express can only look to the President to enforce the payment obligation.

CHAPTER 20
REMEDIES

ANSWERS

Answer to Question 1

(C) is the correct answer.

The apples in this problem are fungible goods, which can easily be purchased elsewhere by the Buyer. In these types of situations, a buyer can easily go into the market and purchase replacement goods from a third party and require the breaching party to pay the difference in price ("cover") under UCC § 2–712; or use the relevant market price and sue for market differential damages under UCC § 2–713. If the innocent party can easily be made whole by damages, an order for specific performance (an equitable remedy) cannot be awarded.

Here, no credible argument can be made that Buyer was depending on the particular type of apple from Seller's farm (the facts say there is no special characteristic of the Seller's apples) nor was the Buyer bargaining for a guaranteed supply of apples over a long period of time, as is true in a requirements contract, both of which would justify specific performance. UCC § 2–716, Cmt. 2.

(A) is incorrect.

While specific performance is somewhat easier to get under the UCC than at common law, it is still not the standard preferred remedy awarded in breach actions, and monetary damages are still the norm. As an equitable remedy, specific performance is not obtainable when damages are adequate to put the non-breaching party in as good a position as it would have been in had the contract been performed.

(B) is incorrect.

While future contracts may be subject to the equitable remedy of specific performance, it is still not the preferred choice of remedy. Although it is possible to impose specific performance in future contracts, courts will typically only do so if it is shown that money damages would not adequately compensate the innocent party for the breach.

(D) is incorrect.

There is no rule that specific performance is not available in an anticipatory repudiation situation.

Answer to Question 2

(D) is the correct answer.

This question is based on the facts of *Walgreen Co. v. Sara Creek Property Co.*, 966 F.2d 273 (7th Cir. 1992). There, the court found a permanent prohibitory injunction against the owner of the mall, prohibiting it from leasing to a competitor of its tenant with a no competition clause, would be proper. The court reasoned that money damages would be inadequate to compensate the innocent party because any calculations of damages would be a guess, lacking sufficient accuracy. That is, there simply was not a practical way to predict accurately how much damage having a competitor within the mall would cause over a ten-year period.

(A) is incorrect.

For the reasons discussed in (D), money damages are inadequate in the given situation. Without a way to predict what damages will occur over the ten years remaining on the lease, simply awarding money damages is improper because it is impossible to know that the damages awarded would accurately reflect SS's losses due to OE's presence in the mall.

(B) is incorrect.

It is true that interests in real estate are considered unique for purposes of specific performance. So if, e.g., MM signed a lease with SS and denied SS the right to move into the leased space, SS might well be able to sue for specific performance to force MM to give it its leased premises.

However, this is a question about breaching a non-competition clause in a lease. The breach of any clause in a lease agreement does not automatically provide specific performance just because it is in a lease. Where, as here, the clause does not deal with providing an interest in property, it is a question of money damages. As such, money damages are still the typical form of remedy used.

The issue presented in this question is that money damages could not be awarded with sufficient certainty, making the *result* set forth in (B) correct, but for an incorrect <u>reason</u>.

(C) is incorrect.

The court in *Walgreen* examined the argument that imposing an injunction poses too great a burden on the court. Courts will deny injunctions if the burden of supervision is too great. Restatement 2d § 366. However, the *Walgreen* court found that the injunction there imposed only a minimal burden on the court, namely, ensuring no other competitor store is opened in the mall.

Answer to Question 3

(B) is the correct answer.

At early common law the goods had to be truly "unique" and one-of-a-kind before specific performance was granted. However, the UCC loosened this requirement, stating that specific performance was allowed where the goods were unique or "in other proper circumstances." UCC § 2–716.

One of these "other proper circumstances" is where tracking down a replacement would entail a considerable burden. As the court in *Sedmak v. Charlie's Chevrolet*, 622 S.W.2d 694, 700 (Mo. Ct. App. 1981) put it, specific performance should be awarded when replacement goods can be obtained, if at all, only with "considerable expense, trouble, great delay, and inconvenience."

Here the facts indicate these guitars are very rare (only forty in the world) and no others are currently being advertised for sale. In order to get replacement goods, Buyer would either have to spend considerable time and money to convince another owner to part with his or her guitar, or wait a long time for another owner to offer his or hers for sale (the facts indicate it would be a few years). In light of the trouble, inconvenience, and expense that would be required of Buyer to find replacement goods, specific performance is proper under UCC § 2–716.

(A) is incorrect.

Specific performance is not the typical remedy used for breach of contract cases. While it may seem like a more equitable remedy to enforce exactly what is bargained for, it is only done in extraordinary cases where monetary damages are insufficient to fully compensate the innocent party or there would be too much difficulty in tracking replacement goods down, i.e., where the goods are unique or "in other proper circumstances." UCC § 2–716.

(C) is incorrect.

While it is true that monetary damages are the typical remedy used in breach of contract cases, this question describes one of the extraordinary situations where monetary damages are inadequate. As discussed under (B), it is the difficulty in determining the proper amount of damages which would put the innocent party in as good a position as if the contract had not been breached that is the problem here, due to the relative uniqueness of the goods involved and the hassle of finding a replacement.

(D) is incorrect.

A buyer who is otherwise entitled to specific performance will be entitled to it even without seeking to cover the goods in the breached contract.

Answer to Question 4

(B) is the correct answer.

Generally a court will not issue an order requiring a contract for personal services to be specifically performed. Restatement 2d § 367. The contract involved in this question is a personal services contract because its performance depends upon a particular person's skills, character, training, and talents, i.e. it matters more *who* is actually performing the contract rather than performing *what* has been contracted for. Restatement 2d § 318.

Andrew was hired to be the star of the film based on his skills, character, training, and talents that set him apart from other actors. Hence, it is a personal service contract and an order of specific performance requiring Andrew to work for Producer will not be granted. As the Restatement puts it, specific performance will not be granted when "its probable result will be to compel a performance involving personal relation, the enforced continuance of which is undesirable." Restatement 2d § 367. In other words, if Andrew wanted to work on the other project, telling him he has to work for Producer and work in Producer's film might well make for a poor film, which is "undesirable," and a court would have too many problems trying to figure out whether Andrew was violating its order to use his best efforts in working on Producer's film. Restatement 2d §§ 366, 367.

Note that it is likely that Producer is entitled to an injunction prohibiting Andrew from working on any other project during the four-month exclusivity period. But a specific performance order requiring Andrew to work with Producer would likely not be issued both because of the personal nature of Andrew's services and the fact that such an injunction would force people to work together who may not wish to do so.

(A) is incorrect.

The fact Andrew has specific talents is part of the reason the contract involved in this problem is a personal service contract, making specific performance unavailable. As discussed under (B) above, it is Andrew's unique talents, skills, and characteristics that make this a personal service contract, and since courts do not want to force people to work together when they do not want to, an order of specific performance is unavailable. Restatement 2d § 367.

(C) is incorrect.

The fact Andrew could complete both projects is irrelevant to whether specific performance is available to the Producer. The contract called for his exclusive services and working on another movie breaches that term.

(D) is incorrect.

While Andrew performing the contract may achieve an equitable result, the court will not force him to do so. Doing so would create an undesirable relationship between the Producer and Andrew, which should be avoided. Producer would need to seek an injunction prohibiting Andrew from working on any other project during the four month exclusivity period, and, of course, could sue for money damages arising from the breach if Producer chose to do so and could prove such damages. Restatement 2d § 367.

Answer to Question 5

(A) is the correct answer.

A covenant not to compete is generally not favored in the law. Some states, like California, ban such clauses by statute, with a few exceptions exemplified in other questions and explanations in this chapter.

However, if it is narrowly drawn, a covenant not to compete is enforceable so long as it is freely negotiated and voluntarily assumed. Narrowly drawn means: (1) it does not last too long, (2) does not prohibit competing employment in too great a geographic area, and (3) does not prohibit too broad a type of activity.

Here the covenant is too broad on a number of grounds. First, it spans the entire West Coast. It is very unlikely that John will be in competition with, and taking clients from, his former employer if he sets up shop in Sacramento, 400 miles away, let alone if he relocated to Seattle or some other West Coast city presumptively covered by the clause that is even further away from Los Angeles. Second, while the Los Angeles employer may have some grounds to protect its specialized cleft palate teeth replacement procedures, it has no interest in prohibiting John from engaging in general dentistry since it does not engage in that practice. And finally, telling professionals they cannot ply their trade for eighteen months is likely too lengthy a period under modern law. The reason is that enforcement of the covenant prohibits individuals from making a living in the trade where they have taken training, and creates an economic incentive to bind them to their first employer, rather than promote free employment opportunities. Further, it deprives John's potential patients from being able to choose the dentist of their choice.

Courts will accept slightly more broadly drawn covenants where trade secrets are involved. Indeed, even a state which otherwise prohibits covenants not to compete like California will allow them when trade secrets are involved (another such exception is discussed in the next question). Accordingly, if the covenant had been to prohibit John from engaging in the practice of replacing teeth in cleft palate patients in the Los Angeles area for six months, it would have had a better chance to be enforced because it would have protected the trade secrets of the Los Angeles employer for a reasonable time and in a reasonable market.

One last point—it used to be that employers would draft covenants as broad as possible, relying on courts to narrow them to legal limits. This was known as "blue penciling" since edits used to be made with blue pencils and the courts would thus "blue pencil," or edit, the overbroad covenant to make it comply with the law. In the past few decades however, courts have begun refusing to blue pencil such agreements, rejecting their role as editors of deliberately overbroad agreements. Instead, they will either enforce the covenant as written (if it is drawn narrowly enough) or will strike it completely, as would be done here.

(B) is incorrect.

As discussed above, a covenant not to compete is enforceable if it is sufficiently narrow. And although John did agree voluntarily to the terms of the contract, including the covenant, the covenant is unenforceable as a matter of policy because it is too broad.

(C) is incorrect.

(C) is incorrect for the same reasons as (B) is incorrect.

(D) is incorrect.

Covenants not to compete can have broader terms when the former employee has knowledge of trade secrets. However, here the facts state that it is not likely that John will use the trade secrets in his new office, and even so the covenant is too broad to be enforced under modern law.

Answer to Question 6

(C) is the correct answer.

Courts are generally more receptive to enforcing broader covenants not to compete when the person subject to the covenant is the seller of a business. This is because, much of what the purchaser is bargaining for in a business purchase is the reputation and goodwill (clientele) of the business established by the seller. Hence, prohibiting the former owner from opening a competing shop nearby and welcoming in his or her former customers for some period of time is thought to be more reasonable.

However, to say courts are more receptive to enforcing such clauses when the burdened individual is the seller of the business is not to say that such clauses will be enforced no matter the terms. Reasonable restrictions are okay; unreasonable ones are not. To ban an owner of a business from ever being able to ply his or her trade is unenforceable under modern cases. The goodwill of the former shop and the customer base loyal to that former owner decreases every year, and at some point, the seller is entitled to get back into the same line of business if he or she wants.

(A) is incorrect.

While limiting the covenant to the same competitive geographic market is required to make a covenant not to compete enforceable, it is not the only requirement to make it valid. That is, simply because the covenant is reasonably geographically limited can't alone make it enforceable, and as noted under (C) above the covenant at issue in this question lasts too long to be enforceable.

(B) is incorrect.

Providing the buyer with what the buyer bargained for (goodwill, reputation, and clientele of the former business) is one of the major concerns in determining whether a covenant not to compete is enforceable. But the courts are also very concerned about whether enforcement would leave the former owner with no adequate means of income in his or her profession. To balance both of these concerns, courts use the geographic, temporal and scope limitations on enforceability. Here, a lifetime prohibition is simply too long.

(D) is incorrect.

As discussed above in (A) to the previous question, the modern trend is for courts either to uphold the covenant as written or to strike it altogether. Here, Seller violated the geographic restriction in the covenant. But because the covenant as a whole was for too lengthy a period, it would be struck down completely and none of its provisions would have prohibitory effect.

Answer to Question 7

(D) is the correct answer.

This question is based on *Peevyhouse v. Garland Coal & Mining Co.*, 382 P.2d 109 (Okla. 1962). There, the court denied a request for specific performance where the cost to remediate the land was approximately $29,000, and the increase in the fair market value of the land after remediation was only $300. The court ruled the $29,000 cost to convey only a $300 benefit was so disproportionate that specific performance, an equitable remedy, would not be ordered and the landowners would be limited to monetary damages instead. Restatement 2d § 364(1)(b). Here, the facts indicate that it would cost as high as $40,000 to remove the stumps for a net property benefit of only $500 and thus, specific performance would not be granted.

Author's Note:

Some professors (and students) believe *Peevyhouse* to be incorrectly decided. If your professor is in that camp, you may want to check with him or her as to how to answer an objective question based on similar facts.

(A) is incorrect.

The fact that the remediation clause was fully negotiated and freely bargained for alone will not justify a grant of equitable relief, as was true in *Peevyhouse*.

(B) is incorrect.

In a similar situation, the court in *Peevyhouse* determined that monetary damages would be the proper remedy, finding requiring specific performance would impose disproportionate economic impact on the breaching party and create an inequitable result.

(C) is incorrect.

Peter would not be required to seek cover if equitable relief was otherwise proper.

Answer to Question 8

(B) is the correct answer.

Expectation damages are intended to put the non-breaching party in as good a position as if the contract had been performed. That is, the goal is to award the innocent party the amount he or she could reasonably have expected had the deal gone through.

Generally speaking, expectation damages are composed of three components: (1) Loss of value, as measured by the difference between the performance promised and the performance actually received; (2) Consequential damages, which are economic losses other than lost value suffered as a consequence of the breach, such as lost profits; and (3) incidental damages which are out-of-pocket expenditures caused by, but incurred *after* the breach in an attempt to mitigate its effects.

Note that in calculating expectation damages there are two items which, if present, must be subtracted from the sum of the lost value, consequential, and incidental components. The first of these is any "cost avoided," as a result of the breach. These consist of costs which the innocent party would have had to bear had the contract gone forward as planned, but which are avoided because of the breach. For example, suppose the non-breaching buyer was obligated to drive to Indianapolis to pick up the merchandise in the original contract. Assume that, a result of the breach, he or she no longer has to make the trip. The cost of the Indianapolis trip would have to be subtracted from the recoverable damages to arrive at the proper expectation damage figure.

The second component that has to be subtracted is "loss avoided" as a result of the breach. Losses avoided are generally the scrap value of the components purchased by the non-breaching party before the breach, which either can be resold by the innocent party or used by the innocent party in future transactions. For example, suppose an upholster was contractually obligated to recover a couch for a customer. Assume the upholsterer purchased some expensive fabric in preparation for the job before the buyer unjustifiably breached. If the fabric can be resold, or can be used by the upholsterer in recovering the next couch, the value of the fabric must be subtracted from any expectation damage recovery.

The reason both of these items must be subtracted is that, if they were not, the innocent party would be in a better position than he or she would have been had the contract been performed. That is, in the first example, whatever profit the buyer would have made under the original contract would have been offset by the cost of the Indianapolis trip. To make it "even," the costs of the trip that will no longer have to be taken must be subtracted to arrive at the correct expectation damage figure. Similarly, if the upholsterer can use the fabric on another couch, its value must be subtracted else the upholsterer would have an unearned economic advantage in the costs of construction of the second couch.

(A) is incorrect.

This answer is a statement of the reliance measure of damages, not the expectation measure.

(C) is incorrect.

When non-breaching parties do not reasonably mitigate damages following a breach they are *not* automatically <u>completely</u> barred from *any* recovery, which is what this answer provides. Rather, the amount of damage award is simply reduced by the amount that could have been reasonably avoided. Restatement 2d § 350(1).

(D) is incorrect.

(D) is incorrect for the reasons that (C) is incorrect.

Answer to Question 9

(C) is the correct answer.

Expectation damages are designed to put Contractor in the position he would have been in had the contract been performed. Restatement 2d § 347. If Contractor had completed the project, he would have made $1.5 million profit, but spent some money ($8.5 million) to get there. Here, to put him in the same position he would have been in upon completed performance, he would need to recover the $1.5 million profit, but to make a profit that is "free and clear," he will have to be reimbursed for the amount he has already expended, i.e., $2.5 million. Thus he needs to be awarded $1.5 million plus $2.5 million to allow him to "walk away" with the same $1.5 million profit he would have received from full performance of the contract.

(A) is incorrect.

This answer only takes into account what the contractor's expected profit from the completed contract was. Since the contract was breached the contractor would need to be reimbursed for his existing expenses in addition to his expected profit.

(B) is incorrect.

(B) is incorrect because the formula does not correctly calculate Contractor's expectation interest. The answer choice presumes Contractor is entitled to the full amount for which other contractors would have bid the job, plus his expenses to date, which is not the correct measure of the expectation interest. Once the contract was signed, Developer was obligated to pay damages based on the values in the contract with Contractor in any breach action, and what other contractors might charge is irrelevant in that situation. Further, recovery under the formula set forth in this answer would vastly overcompensate Contractor based on what Contractor would have realized from complete performance under the original contract, i.e., a $1.5 M profit.

(D) is incorrect.

While Choice (D) incorporates many of the correct values used in determining the expectation interest, it incorrectly subtracts out the $2.5 million in expenses.

Answer to Question 10

(B) is the correct answer.

Reliance damages are the out of pocket damages expended by the innocent party under the contract up to the time of the breach. Restatement 2d § 349. Here, Contractor had spent $2.5 million in labor and materials up through the time of the breach, and that is the value of his reliance interest. The fact that another builder would have only spent $2 million is irrelevant.

(A) is incorrect.

(A) incorrectly assumes Contractor would be entitled to the amount of the whole contract price at which other contractors would have bid the job. What other contractors would have charged is not relevant to reliance damages suffered by the innocent party. As explained in (B), the relevant amount is what the contracting party spent under the breached contract.

(C) is incorrect.

(C) is incorrect because it sets forth the difference between Contractor's bid and what other contractors in the area would have bid. This figure is irrelevant for reliance interest.

(D) is incorrect.

(D) includes future expenses, which are irrelevant to the reliance interest which measures the amount expended by the non-breaching party *up to* the time of the breach. Restatement 2d § 349.

Answer to Question 11

(B) is the correct answer.

Restitution is based on the unjust enrichment of a benefit conferred on one party by the party seeking recovery. Restatement 2d § 371. Here, Contractor provided Developer some services before Developer breached. Developer hasn't paid for them, and would be unjustly enriched if he retained the value of those services without compensation. The question is how such services should be valued.

The measure of the services under the "Net Benefit" method calls for the difference in fair market value of the property before and after the services provided. Restatement 2d § 371(b). Here, the value of the land was $5 million before Contractor began working, and $6.8 million at the time of the breach. The difference between those figures is the restitutionary interest as valued under the "Net Benefit" method.

(A), (C), and (D) are incorrect.

These answers are incorrect for the reasons that (B) is correct, as explained above. Note that (D) expresses the correct value of the restitutionary interest as valued under the "Cost Avoided" theory as explained in the answer to the next question.

Answer to Question 12

(D) is the correct answer.

Restitution is based on the unjust enrichment of a benefit conferred on one party by the party seeking recovery. Restatement 2d § 371. Here, Contractor provided Developer some services before Developer breached. Developer hasn't paid for them, and would be unjustly enriched if he retained the value of those services without compensation. The question is how such services should be valued.

The measure of the services under the "Cost Avoided" method is the "cost" the benefitted party "avoided" from having to pay to receive the benefits provided by the party seeking restitution. Restatement 2d § 371(a). The "cost" is measured not by the costs of the party seeking restitution, but by the average cost of those services by others in the area. In other words, it is the average cost that is the value of the enrichment.

Here, Contractor valued his services at $2.5 million, but the average cost of providing those services by others in the area is $2 million. Hence, the correct measure of the restitutionary interest as measured by the "Cost Avoided" method is $2 million.

(A), (B), and (C) are incorrect.

These choices are incorrect for the reasons that (D) is correct, as explained above.

Answer for Question 13

(B) is the correct answer.

Expectation damages are designed to put Paul in the position he would have been in had the contract been performed. These damages include the lost value to him, plus incidental and consequential damages, less any cost or other loss that he has avoided by not having to perform. Restatement 2d § 347. Paul would have made a $200,000 profit and has already spent $500,000. Thus he needs to be given $700,000 to "walk away" with the $200,000 profit.

However, he has already been paid $100,000, so that figure needs to be subtracted from any recovery he would get at trial, making the expectation recovery *at trial* would equal 200,000 plus 500,000 minus 100,000, because he keeps the $100,000 already paid to him.

To clarify, his total expectation interest is $700,000 but the problem asks about his proper recovery *at trial*. That is only $600,000 because he already received $100,000 and that must be taken into account in calculating his proper recovery. If he recovered $700,000 at trial and got to keep the $100,000 he's already been paid, he would be overcompensated.

(A), (C), and (D) are incorrect.

These choices are incorrect for the reasons Choice (B) is correct. Note that choice (D) sets forth the proper value of Paul's expectation interest, but it does not take into account the $100,000 he has already been paid, which he gets to keep and thus must be subtracted from his recovery at trial.

Answer to Question 14

(C) is the correct answer.

Reliance damages are the out of pocket costs expended by the breaching party up to the time of the breach in reliance on the contract. Reliance damages include any expenditures made in preparation for performance or in performance, less any loss that the party in breach can prove with reasonable certainty the injured party would have suffered had the contract been performed. Restatement 2d § 349.

Here Paul spent $500,000 in labor and materials up through the time of the breach, and that is the value of his reliance interest. However, as explained more fully in the explanations in the previous question, since Paul has already been compensated $100,000, this amount must be subtracted from his recovery after trial because he gets to keep that amount.

Note that if this was a losing contract, e.g., if David could prove that Paul had underbid the job and would have lost money completing the contract, the amount of that loss would have to be subtracted from any award as well under Restatement 2d § 349.

(A), (B), and (D) are incorrect.

These answers are incorrect for the reasons (C) is correct. Note that (A) incorrectly uses the value that other contractors would have spent to do the work that Paul has completed. For reliance damages the proper figure is the amount *Paul* has spent up to the time of the breach. (B) sets forth the correct value of Paul's reliance interest, but does not take into account the $100,000 already received. (D) incorrectly subtracts the value that Paul would have to spend to complete the project, which plays no role in reliance damages.

Answer to Question 15

(A) is the correct answer.

Restitution is based on the unjust enrichment provided by the party seeking recovery. Restatement 2d § 371. Here, Paul provided David some services before David breached. David hasn't paid for them, and would be unjustly enriched if he retained the value of those services without compensation. The question is how such services should be valued.

The measure of the services under the "Net Benefit" method calls for the difference in fair market value of the property before and after the services provided. Restatement 2d § 371(b). Here, the value of the land with Paul's partially completed structure on it is $750,000, and the value before the project started was $400,000. The difference between those figures, $350,000, is the restitutionary interest as valued under the "Net Benefit" method.

Restitution attempts to put the parties in the position they were in before the contract was entered into. As such, if Paul wants restitution for the services he provided, he must return to David the value of whatever David has benefitted him under the contract. Restatement 2d § 384. This is known as "mutual restitution," and the slang developed from this requirement is, "to *get* restitution, you must *do* restitution."

After trial, there does not have to be a mutual exchange of a check provided by David of $350,000 and one provided by Paul of $100,000. Rather, the $100,000 Paul has already received is simply subtracted from the amount Paul would receive from David.

(B), (C), and (D) are incorrect.

These answers are incorrect for the reasons that (A) is correct.

Answer to Question 16

(A) is the correct answer.

Restitution is based on the unjust enrichment provided by the party seeking recovery. Restatement 2d § 371. Here, Paul provided David some services before David breached. David hasn't paid for them, and would be unjustly enriched if he retained the value of those services without compensation. The question is how such services should be valued.

The measure of the services under the "Cost Avoided" method is the "cost" the benefitted party "avoided" from having to pay to receive the benefits provided by the party seeking restitution. Restatement 2d § 371(a). The "cost" is measured not by the costs of the party seeking restitution, but by the average cost of those services if they were provided by others in the area. It is this average costs which measures the amount of the enrichment by the defendant.

Here, Paul valued the services at $500,000, but the average cost of providing those services by others in the area is $600,000. Hence, the correct measure of the restitutionary interest as measured by the "cost avoided" method is $600,000.

Restitution attempts to put the parties in the position they were in before the contract was entered into. As such, if Paul wants restitution for the services he provided, he must return to David the value of whatever benefit David has conferred on him under the contract. Restatement 2d § 384. This is known as "mutual restitution," and the slang developed from this requirement is, "to *get* restitution, you must *do* restitution."

After trial, there does not have to be a mutual exchange of a check provided by David of $600,000 and one provided by Paul of $100,000. Rather, the $100,000 Paul has already received is simply subtracted from the amount Paul would receive from David.

(B), (C), and (D) are incorrect.

These answers are incorrect for the reasons that (A) is correct, as explained above.

Answer to Question 17

(A) is the correct answer.

The expectation damages here consist of the $600,000 in costs spent up to the time of breach, plus the $400,000 expected profit. By awarding Pam the profit under the contract, plus what she expended up to the time of the breach, she would walk away with $400,000 profit, which is exactly the position she would have been in had the contract been completed.

The $500,000 in costs spent after breach cannot be collected by Pam because a party may not recover damages that the injured party could have avoided or mitigated without undue risk, burden or humiliation. Restatement 2d §350. Since Pam was told to stop work and that the project was not going forward, she could have easily avoided these additional costs, and as such they will not be recoverable. This problem is loosely based on *Rockingham County v. Luten Bridge Co.*, 35 F.2d 301 (4th Cir. 1929). There, the court would not allow recovery for costs incurred when a contractor continued to work after being told to stop building a bridge because those costs were post-termination.

(B) is incorrect.

(B) is incorrect because it erroneously includes the $500,000 in avoidable costs incurred after the breach.

(C) is incorrect.

(C) is incorrect because while the "extra" $500,000 spent by Pam after termination is not recoverable, it need not be subtracted from her recovery. She spent the money and just can't recover for it, but it does not affect how much she is entitled to recover from Daredevil. In other words, she is simply out of pocket the $500,000.

(D) is incorrect.

Choice (D) does not take into account the lost profits on the contract. The $600,000 represents Pam's reliance interest (the amount she has spent thus far) and since she has sued for expectation damages the lost profits on the contract must also be included in a recovery at trial.

Answer to Question 18

(D) is the correct answer.

If an injured party has taken reasonable steps to avoid a loss, but those steps prove not to be the most inexpensive way to "cover" the breach, he or she may still be entitled to recover the full amount of loss suffered. Restatement 2d § 350(2).

Paula is entitled to the $3,000 difference between the new bid she accepted and Dan's original bid. In other words the mitigation rules do not require the innocent party to scour the area for the most inexpensive option or even to take the most inexpensive option offered. Here, she only needed to take *reasonable* steps in mitigation of the damages, and contacting five other contractors for a bid is likely reasonable.

Saying she could have avoided the costs because someone somewhere would have done the work for cheaper places an unreasonable burden on the innocent party to contact an unreasonable number of contractors. So long as Paula acted reasonably, her recovery will not be limited by avoidability.

(A) is incorrect.

(A) would be correct if Dan were able to successfully argue that Paula had the duty to find the cheapest alternative possible which could have mitigated his damage by avoiding the additional costs. As discussed in (D)., However, Paula acted reasonably in her mitigation attempt by contacting five other builders and choosing the cheapest one of the five, and as such her recovery would not be limited simply because a cheaper option existed.

(B) is incorrect.

(B) is incorrect, since the components of the formula given in this answer wrongly assume that the bid Paula accepted should be subtracted from the average bid price she received. The average bid price is irrelevant to a calculation of her damages here.

(C) is incorrect.

(C) is incorrect for similar reasons that make (B) incorrect. That is, it incorrectly uses the average bid price of $25,000 as a measure for Paula's damages.

Answer to Question 19

(C) is the correct answer.

Pattie cannot recover any lost profits because she cannot prove what her profits would have been with the requisite degree of certainty. In addition to avoidability, another limitation on expectation damage recovery is that the amounts sought by the innocent party must be reasonably certain. Restatement 2d § 352. Here, Pattie's profits were based entirely on royalties, and since this is her first book, there is no way to gauge exactly how many people would have purchased the book had the contract been completed. As the Restatement puts it, any lost profits she would have received are based entirely on the "uncertain tastes of the public," and since those uncertain tastes cannot be reliably quantified, no recovery for them is permitted. Restatement 2d § 352, Cmt. a, Ill. 1.

(A) is incorrect.

Whether Pattie sought cover is irrelevant to whether the consequential damages are recoverable in this case. The problem is that the royalties are too uncertain, which prevents any recovery, regardless of any reasonable attempt to cover.

(B) is incorrect.

Pattie would be entitled to lost profits, but only if she could prove what they would have been with sufficient certainty. Restatement 2d § 352. Since she cannot, as this was her first book, this answer choice is incorrect.

(D) is incorrect.

Lost profits are a foreseeable result of the breach on these facts; clearly by not publishing the book Pattie would not be able to collect any potential royalties she may have received. So the problem is not that the lost profits were not foreseeable, but rather, as stated in the explanation of (C), that the foreseeable lost profits cannot be established with sufficient certainty.

Answer to Question 20

(B) is the correct answer.

This problem is based on *Hadley v. Baxendale*, 156 Eng. Rep. 145 (Ex. Ch. 1854). The court found damages similar to those presented in this question to be indirect consequential damages, which were not sufficiently foreseeable to be collectable as consequential loss.

Consequential damages are economic damages that are not based on the lost value of the performance contracted for, but rather are economic losses suffered as a consequence of the breach. That is, the "lost value" of the services in this question would be the difference between the charge for expedited shipping which was promised and the charge for the regular shipping that was actually provided. In other words, the contract was for services worth $200, and Parts received services worth $50. The difference is the "lost value" under the contract.

In addition to not getting what it bargained for, parties like Parts can also suffer additional economic damages as a consequence of the lost value of performance—like lost profits. Such damages are the "consequential damages" of contract law.

In *Hadley,* the court divided consequential damages into two types: direct and indirect. Direct consequential damages are those that clearly would result in the ordinary course of events following a breach. These are now codified in Restatement 2d § 351(2)(a). Indirect consequential damages are those that result from a special circumstance beyond the ordinary course of events, and thus need to be brought to the attention of the other party before contracting in order to be recoverable. These are now codified in Restatement 2d § 351(2)(b).

The lost profits here, as in *Hadley,* were indirect consequential damages. That is, at the time of contracting, an ordinary person in Direct Delivery's shoes would not know the consequence of failing to make a timely delivery, i.e., a reasonable person would not know it was risking paying lost profits of Parts if it breached. In other words, all Direct knew was that it was had contracted to get a package, containing *something,* to Direct, not that if it didn't get the package there in time, it Delivery Direct was going to be liable for the company's lost profits for every day it was late. The idea is that without knowledge of the consequences of the breach, it had not contemplated the risk of paying such damages in setting its price or even in deciding whether it wanted to enter into the contract at all.

Because these were indirect consequential damages, they will not be recoverable unless Delivery Direct was made aware of the consequence by the employee from Parts. It was not. As such, those damages would not be recoverable.

(A) is incorrect.

As discussed above, the lost profit damages were caused by the breach, but they are indirect consequential damages and thus not recoverable unless Delivery Direct was made aware of the consequences of a breach at the time of the contract's making.

(C) is incorrect.

As the court in *Hadley* held, these are not direct consequential damages. After all, without any further information, the shutdown of a factory seems very unlikely as a result of delayed delivery of one package.

(D) is incorrect.

Equity is relevant when a party seeks an equitable remedy such as specific performance. Consequential damages are money damages which are subject to different rules.

Answer to Question 21

(D) is the correct answer.

All contract damages must be proven with reasonable certainty to be recoverable. Restatement 2d § 352. Under the reasonable certainty test, the more a non-breaching party's lost profits depend upon the "uncertain tastes and preferences" of the public, the less likely the damages can be established with reasonable certainty. Here, Paper is going to be making unique greeting cards, the sales of which depends wholly on what the public favors and buys. Also, as a new company, it has no track record to establish those sales. As such, the lost profits cannot be determined with reasonable certainty.

(A) is incorrect.

Although it is likely foreseeable that Paper would lose profits while unable to move into its offices, the damages for this new company remain unprovable to a reasonable certainty, and thus are unrecoverable.

(B) is incorrect.

Lost profits are available as a result of a construction contract breach. But these damages must still meet the limitations of reasonable certainty, foreseeability, and avoidability. Restatement 2d §§ 350–352.

(C) is incorrect.

While Paper's claim would not fail due to avoidability because it made reasonable efforts to mitigate the resulting damage, it does fail because any damages suffered cannot be proven with sufficient certainty.

Answer to Question 22

(A) is the correct answer.

The longer a business has been in operation and has an established track record, the more likely its lost profits can be determined with reasonable certainty. Where, as here, the company has been in operation for 10 years, Peter's supermarket could easily show historical data for its profits that would satisfy the damages requirement that the proof be reasonably certain.

(B) is incorrect.

(B) is incorrect because there are many situations where lost profits will not be granted. Lost profits are subject to the limitations of certainty, foreseeability, and avoidability. Restatement 2d §§ 350–352.

(C) is incorrect.

Breaches under contract law are "strict liability" events. It does not matter that a party was reasonable or not. The only question is whether one contracting party failed to do what it promised and has thus breached the contract.

(D) is incorrect.

As noted above in the explanation of Choice (A), courts are willing to use the historical figures to determine lost profits with a reasonable certainty.

Answer to Question 23

(C) is the correct answer.

When determining the expectation damages for breach by the builder in a construction contract, there are special rules for determining lost value. Normally the cost of completion or repair may be used to calculate the lost value component. However, if the cost of repair is so much greater than the diminution in fair market value, then the innocent party must use the decrease in fair market value as "lost value." It is only when the disparity of the two values is very large and they are "clearly disproportionate" that this limitation of remedy is imposed. Restatement 2d § 348(2)(b).

(A) is incorrect.

(A) is incorrect because the correct calculation of), the lost value component is the decrease in the fair market value, not the cost of repair or completion.

(B) is incorrect.

The difference in the cost of materials is irrelevant to the determination of lost value. It is the difference in fair market value of the property that is potentially relevant.

(D) is incorrect.

While the value of the difference in fair market value as a consequence of the breach is slight, there still is some difference and that difference is recoverable. This fact distinguishes this situation from a case like *Jacobs & Youngs v. Kent*, 230 N.Y. 239 (1921) where the contractor used a different kind of pipe that was exactly equivalent in price *and* quality.

Answer to Question 24

(C) is the correct answer.

The proper valuation under the "American Rule" in land sale contracts is the difference between the purchase price and the fair market value of the property, plus the return of any down payment that has already been paid. Here, this would be the $120,000 fair market value minus the $100,000 purchase price, plus the $10,000 down payment Buyer originally paid. Under the "American Rule" Buyer would not be entitled to the expenses related to title insurance and inspections because he would have incurred these costs had the contract gone forward to realize the $20,000 gain on the purchase. Awarding these costs would thus put Buyer in a better position than he would have been had the contract gone forward.

(A) is incorrect.

(A) is incorrect because it erroneously allows Buyer to recover for the expenses of title insurance and inspections that he would have incurred had the contract gone forward. That is, he would have had to make those expenditures to recover the $20,000 benefit of the bargain.

(B) is incorrect.

(B) is incorrect because it is a representation of the "English Rule" regarding land sale contracts, where recovery is limited to the expenses incurred in reliance of the contract, plus any down payment paid.

(D) is incorrect.

(D) is incorrect because it erroneously assumes that collectable damages consist only of the expected gain on the bargain. It thus neglects the fact that Buyer has already paid a $10,000 down payment prior to the breach by Seller, which is recoverable under the "American Rule."

Answer to Question 25

(B) is the correct answer.

Under the "English Rule" for recovery for a breach of a land sale contract, a purchaser is only entitled to recover his or her reliance damages such as down payments, plus out of pocket expenses spent under the contract up to its breach. However, a purchaser will not receive any expectation damages.

Here the buyer is entitled to the $2,000 spent on title insurance and inspections as well as the $10,000 down payment. Buyer would not be allowed to recover any of the benefit from the bargain he made based on the difference between the fair market value and contract price of the property.

(A) is incorrect.

(A) is incorrect because it inaccurately awards Buyer the lost benefit of his bargain. That type of damage is not recoverable under the "English Rule."

(C) is incorrect.

(C) is incorrect as it sets forth the proper amount of recovery under the "American Rule," not the English Rule. For an explanation of recovery under the American Rule," *see* the explanation of (C) in the previous question.

(D) is incorrect.

(D) is incorrect because it awards the benefit of the bargain to the Buyer by granting the difference between the fair market value of the property and the contract price. This is not recoverable under the "English Rule."

Answer to Question 26

(B) is the correct answer.

In breach of contract cases, typically emotional distress damages are not recoverable. Restatement 2d §353. This reasoning is partially from a desire to separate tort and contract law and to leave personal injuries and their attendant emotional distress to be settled as part of a tort claim. It is also because contract law is more commercial in nature, and contract law does not want recovery from a breach to exceed the value of the expectation, reliance or restitutionary interests, none of which includes an emotional distress component into their respective formulas. Restatement 2d § 351(3).

There are two recognized exceptions to the general rule regarding the unavailability of emotional distress in contract-based claims. The first involves instances where the harm is "particularly likely" to result from the breach, e.g., mishandling of corpses, mistaken delivery of death notices, "bad faith" breach by insurance companies, and, in some jurisdictions, wrongful termination of employment. Restatement 2d § 353. The second involves cases where the breach of contract causes personal injury, including, but not limited to breach of warranty cases under the UCC. Restatement 2d § 353; UCC § 2–715(2)(b).

Stress from having to scramble for an upcoming car sale does not fall into either category excepting it from the general rule.

(A) is incorrect.

(A) is incorrect because with the few exceptions mentioned above, emotional distress damages are not available in breach of contract cases. The certainty of such damages is irrelevant.

(C) is incorrect.

One exception to the general rule that emotional distress damages are not collectable in contract breach cases is if the emotional distress is "particularly likely" to result from the breach. But this is a limited exception and has only been applied in cases where, e.g., a mortuary mishandles a corpse, mistaken death notifications, where an insurance company acts in "bad faith" to breach and, occasionally in wrongful termination cases. Restatement 2d § 353.

(D) is incorrect.

Simply because the buyer was able to cover is not determinative in whether emotional distress damages are available to him or her. As discussed earlier, absent one of the exceptions to the general rule, a plaintiff is not entitled to emotional distress in breach of contract cases, even if such distress was actually suffered.

Answer to Question 27

(D) is the correct answer.

A contract breach which is also associated with a physical injury is one of the exceptions to the general rule that emotional distress damages will not be awarded. Restatement 2d § 353; UCC § 2–715(2)(b). The rationale is that the legal system is more willing to reward a plaintiff for an interference with his or her emotional wellbeing when personal injuries are involved than when only economic harms are involved.

(A) is incorrect.

The expectation interest under contract law is made up of the lost value of the bargain, consequential damages and incidental damages, accompanied by certain set offs. Restatement 2d § 347. Emotional distress is not part of that interest.

(B) is incorrect.

The general rule is that emotional distress damages are not awarded in breach of contract cases. Restatement 2d § 351(3). However, this problem presents one of the exceptions to the general rule, i.e., where the breach is accompanied by physical injury.

(C) is incorrect.

Comparative negligence of the plaintiff does not act as an offset in breach of contract actions. Besides, Dr. Darren was licensed to do the procedure, and thus it was not negligent for Pauline to go to him, even if there were other doctors with better success rates in the area.

Answer to Question 28

(B) is the correct answer.

An award of punitive damages would almost always put a non-breaching party in a better position than he or she would have been had the contract been performed. This would frustrate the goal of expectation damages, thus the general rule is punitive damages will not be awarded in contract actions. Restatement 2d § 355.

(A) is incorrect.

In contract terms, this is not a "bad faith" breach. It is an intentional breach, but all intentional breaches are not bad faith ones. In fact, under the "efficient breach" doctrine, Seller should have breached, as long as it was willing to pay the Buyer cover damages.

(C) is incorrect.

(C) is incorrect because modern courts have actually become more willing to award punitive damages if there is particularly egregious "bad faith" conduct involved in the breach. It is also incorrect because punitive damages were not awarded for breach of contract actions at common law.

(D) is incorrect.

The amount Seller received from the new buyer is irrelevant to determining the amount of punitive damages, assuming the court found punitive damages appropriate at all. Punitive damages are to be determined on the bases of the wealth of the defendant and the egregiousness of the defendant's actions, among other things.

Answer to Question 29

(D) is the correct answer.

One of the exceptions to the no punitive damage rule for breach of contract actions is a "bad faith" breach by an insurance company under a life insurance contract. Often refusing to pay the policy will lead an innocent party to settle for less because he or she needs the money now, rather than after a lengthy, costly, litigation. Also the innocent party may never even sue and could even lose at trial, and during that time the insurance company will gain the benefits of the interest on the sum owed to the innocent party. Due to these incentives for the insurance company to wrongly refuse payments, punitive damages become necessary to counter the benefits the Insurance Company would receive from a "bad faith" breach.

The other exception to the no punitive damages rule for breach of contract recognized in some (but not all) states is bad faith wrongful termination of employment. Such cases fit within the exception set forth in Restatement 2d § 355 allowing for punitive damages in contract law when, "the breach is also a tort for which punitive damages are recoverable."

(A) is incorrect.

Punitive damages are generally not awarded for breach of contract, but "bad faith" breaches of life insurance contracts are an exception to the general rule.

(B) is incorrect.

This is not the type of breach the "efficient breach" doctrine refers to. This breach was done in "bad faith" to attempt to manipulate innocent parties to settle for less than they are owed under the contract. One of the attributes of an "efficient breach" is that the breaching party must be willing to pay damages to the innocent party.

(C) is incorrect.

Just because there was an intentional breach does not mean that it was a "bad faith" breach. There are numerous justifiable reasons for breaching a contract that would not amount to "bad faith." Without a finding of bad faith by the breaching party, punitive damages are not likely to be awarded.

Answer to Question 30

(D) is the correct answer.

I is correct because Patti will be able to get pre-judgment interest from the time performance is due until the date of judgment because the suit was for a liquidated, or fixed, sum of money. Restatement 2d § 354. In all other cases, where the exact sum of money recoverable from the breach is not certain, the court has discretion to award pre-judgment interest if it believes it is just to do so, but the trend it not to do so. Restatement 2d § 354(2). It is for that reason that IV is incorrect.

III is correct because any party with a viable judgment is entitled to post-judgment interest on the award from the date the judgment is officially entered to the date the judgment is "satisfied" or paid by the breaching party.

II is incorrect because, when suing for a liquidated, or fixed sum of money, pre-judgment interest runs from the date performance was due, not the date suit was filed.

(A), (B), and (C) are incorrect.

These answers are incorrect for the reasons given under (D) above.

Answer to Question 31

(D) is the correct answer.

The majority rule is that the non-breaching party is entitled to pre-judgment interest so long as the amount in dispute is for a liquidated, or fixed, sum of money under the contract. Restatement 2d § 354. Here the claim was for emotional distress damages. Such damages, are not fixed under the contract, but rather can only be determined in the discretion of the trier of fact based on what the trier deems Penny's emotional distress was.

By contrast, had the award been for the cost of the weed whacker that failed, which was known to the parties under the contract, then the suit would have been over a liquidated, finite sum, and the award of pre-judgment interest would be likely. Therefore, even though the jury fixed an amount, it was not an amount that could be calculated before the lawsuit began, which is what is necessary to be a "liquidated" sum.

(A) is incorrect.

The $20,000 award given in the claim for emotional distress damages was a discretionary amount determined at trial by the jury based on the type and amount of distress suffered. Prior to the trial, and under the contract itself, there was no finite amount that Penny was claiming, so Penny's emotional distress damages were not "liquidated" as that term is used in contract law, and only liquidated damages are eligible for mandatory pre-judgment interest.

(B) is incorrect.

The foreseeability of the emotional distress is not relevant to whether pre-judgment interest would be given on the sum awarded. The key is whether the amount of the award was liquidated, i.e., fixed, before trial started and under the contract itself.

(C) is incorrect.

The rule given in this answer choice is for collection of post-judgment interest, not pre-judgment interest.

Answer to Question 32

(C) is the correct answer.

When a party receives a judgment for damages based on future payments, contract law reduces the total value of the payments to their present value for immediate payment. Each state has its own method of calculating the present value and the reduction rate of the future values, but the idea is that a dollar paid today is worth more than a dollar paid ten years from now.

For example, if the plaintiff invests the money so that the dollar paid today will be worth more than a dollar ten years from now, the plaintiff would realize more than he or she would have had the contract been performed, thus going against expectation damage principles. Similarly, the defendant could invest $0.75 today and have $1.00 ten years from now. So making the defendant pay the full dollar today makes the defendant pay more damages than he or she would have had to pay had the contract been performed.

(A) is incorrect.

Granting Seller the entire contract price would put Seller in a better position than he would have been if the contract had been performed. The $100,000 payment ten years from now is likely worth less than $100,000 paid today. Additionally any money paid today could be invested to increase its value ten years from now beyond the initial payment of $100,000.

(B) is incorrect.

When a contract calling for future payments is breached, the payments are reduced to a present value payable immediately.

(D) is incorrect.

When the defendant is a debtor and the judgment is only to pay money, specific performance is never granted. The reason is that a specific performance order is an order of the court. If any party disobeys a court order, the party is subject to contempt of court, which could include imprisonment. Because parties who are judged to owe money sometimes do not have the money to pay, or have other reason why they are not paying, America does not imprison them. Our society has eliminated debtor's prisons.

Instead, when the defendant is a money debtor, the court system simply enters a judgment against that individual, which is not a court order to pay, punishable by contempt. If defendants do not satisfy a judgment, society will allow levying their assets, or renewing the judgment until the particular defendant has assets which can be collected. But jailing a defendant for failing to pay is not done. Hence, judgments can be entered, but specific performance cannot be ordered.

Further, as discussed under (C) above, any judgment would have to be reduced to present value, and so even if an order of specific performance was possible, it would not be for $1,000,000, but rather for less than that as the $1,000,000 would have to be reduced to present value.

Answer to Question 33

(B) is the correct answer.

As this question involves the sale of goods, it is governed by the UCC. The first question is whether buying the thirty-six-inch sets was a proper cover. The UCC requires only that the buyer act reasonably in effecting cover, and provides that the covered goods can be more expensive and even slightly better quality if exact replacement goods are not readily available. Assuming that the buyer acted in good faith, the cover here is valid.

The next issue is how to calculate cover damages. The formula given in UCC § 2–712 provides: (Cost of Cover) – (Contract Price) + (Incidental Damages) + (Consequential Damages) – (Expenses Saved in

Consequence of the Breach). The cost of cover was $21,000, and the contract price was $20,000.

Incidental damages are out-of-pocket costs expended after the breach, which the non-breaching party reasonably incurred trying to cure or otherwise because of the breach. UCC § 2–715(1). Here, the $400 spent on express shipping to receive the shipment in a timely manner is an incidental damage.

The consequential damages incurred are the lost profits suffered by Pristine as a result of the delayed delivery, or $250. This is recoverable because it is foreseeable that a commercial seller will lose sales (and hence profits) upon a delay in supplying inventory. Further, Pristine made Darren's aware of the consequences of a breach, "delivery as Pristine told Darren that it was out of inventory for the sale."

Finally the expenses avoided as a result of the breach would be the $300 Pristine will not have to spend picking up the televisions from Darren's. That is, the $300 was a cost it would have had to incur under the contract as originally written, but which it avoids having to pay as a result of the breach. It need not send someone to pick up the TV's from Darren's when it is, instead, going to receive the covered TV's from another seller by express mail.

(A) is incorrect.

(A) is incorrect because it only takes into account the difference between the price of the goods used to cover and the original price. It neglects to account for any incidental or consequential damages and the expenses saved as a result of the breach.

(C) is incorrect.

(C) is incorrect because it does not include the consequential lost profits from the breach.

(D) is incorrect.

Choice (D) fails to account for the consequential damages and the expenses saved as a result of the breach.

Answer to Question 34

(A) is the correct answer.

The problem with market differential damages under the UCC is that there are often different market prices involved in the equation, i.e., the price can shift from day-to-day, the price might be different in the market where the seller is located than where the buyer is located, etc. Hence, the first step is to select the proper market.

The Code itself provides the correct temporal and geographic markets. Buyer's market differential damages are governed by UCC § 2–713. UCC § 2–713(1) provides that the proper temporal market is the market "when the buyer learned of the breach."

The proper geographic market is the market "of the place of tender or, in cases of rejection after arrival or revocation of acceptance . . . the [market price as of the] place of arrival." UCC § 2–713(2).

Since Seller informed Buyer that he would not be delivering the lemons on February 28, the proper temporal market for determining market differential damages is February 28, and the proper geographic market is that of the seller, since the goods are to be tendered at Seller's farm. Hence, (A) is correct.

Note there is an argument that February 28 is the date the seller learned of the *repudiation*, and not necessarily the *breach*, i.e., the "breach" didn't occur until May 1. This argument has been rejected by the courts for situations like those presented in this question, i.e., where fungible commodities are sold on a national market. *Oloffson v. Coomer*, 296 N.E.2d 871 (Ill. App. Ct. 1973).

(B) is incorrect.

$640 is the market price at the contracted delivery date, and UCC § 2–713 provides that the proper temporal market is the one when the Buyer learned of the breach.

(C) is incorrect.

The $602 market price comes from the date the suit was initiated, which is improper. It should be the date on which the Buyer learned of the breach. UCC § 2–713(1).

(D) is incorrect.

Choice (D) is incorrect because it utilizes the incorrect market in determining the market differential damages. The proper market is the Seller's market (the place of tender) and not the Buyer's market. UCC § 2–713(2).

Answer to Question 35

(D) is the correct answer.

Determining the proper market price requires both the proper temporal and geographic market. When the goods have not been delivered, the proper geographic market is the place of tender and the proper temporal market is the time "when the buyer learned of the breach." UCC § 2–713(1), (2). Buyer learned of the breach on May 1, and under the contract, tender was to take place at Seller's farm, making (D) the correct choice.

(A) is incorrect.

(A) is incorrect because $615 was not the market price on the proper date for determining the market differential damages, as explained in (D).

(B) is incorrect.

(B) is incorrect because it uses an erroneous geographic market price for the lemons. The figure $640 is from the Buyer's market. As discussed above the proper market is the place of tender which is Seller's market. UCC § 2–713(2).

(C) is incorrect.

Choice (C) is incorrect because it uses the wrong geographic and temporal markets. $602 was the market price on December 1 in Buyer's market; however, the proper market was Seller's market on May 1, as explained in(D).

Answer to Question 36

(B) is the correct answer.

Where the buyer rejects the goods after arrival, the market price is determined at the place of arrival, on the day the buyer learned of the breach. UCC § 2–713(1), (2). The proper geographic market becomes the Buyer's market, because the lemons were delivered to Buyer on May 1, where they were rejected. It was on that day the buyer learned of the breach because it was upon their arrival that the lemons were discovered to be substandard. Thus, $640 is the proper market price for determining market differential damages, and that figure should be subtracted from the contract price under UCC § 2–713(1).

(A) is incorrect.

(A) is incorrect because it utilizes the wrong temporal market.

(C) is incorrect.

(C) is incorrect because it uses the wrong temporal market, using the market price on the day the suit was initiated, rather than the market price on the date the buyer learned of the breach.

(D) is incorrect.

(D) is incorrect because it erroneously uses the Seller's market for the market differential calculation. When there is breach *before* delivery, the place of delivery under the contract determines the market price for the calculation. However, the same is not true where the goods are rejected *after* delivery. Since Buyer rejected the goods at the time they arrived, the place of arrival becomes the proper geographic market under UCC § 2–713(2).

Answer to Question 37

(C) is the correct answer.

The important fact in this problem is that Peter has decided to keep the computer. Once he accepted the good and decided to keep it, Peter limited his recovery to warranty damages under UCC § 2–714. Under that provision, he will be able to collect the value of the goods as warranted less the value of the goods received, or $10,000 minus $1,500.

Note that in breach of warranty damages, it is the value, and not the contract price, that controls. The formula constitutes the *value* of what was promised (which may or may not equal the contract price, and here is $10,000) minus the *value* of what was received (here $1,500).

(A) is incorrect.

Cover damages are awarded to a Buyer who does not have the goods at the time of suit, either because he or she rejects them, revokes his or her acceptance of them, or has never received them. UCC §§ 2–711(1), (2); 2–712. As noted, in this problem, Peter accepted the computer and decided to keep it.

(B) is incorrect.

Market differential damages are awarded to a buyer who does not have the goods at the time of suit, either because he or she rejects them, revokes his or her acceptance of them, or has never received them. UCC §§ 2–711(1), (2); 2–713. It is an alternative remedy to cover. As noted, in this problem, Peter accepted the computer and decided to keep it.

(D) is incorrect.

For the reasons given in the explanations to Choices (A) and (B) above, Peter does not have his choice of any of the three remedies; he is limited to breach of warranty damages once he decided to accept and keep the computer.

Answer to Question 38

(D) is the correct answer.

When a Seller can establish that any attempts to resell the goods would be unavailing, he or she may collect the full contract price without attempting to go in the market and resell the goods. UCC § 2–709(1)(b). An example of this situation is set forth in this question, i.e., when there is a custom good tailored for a specific buyer so that the good has little appeal to others in the market. Here we know the statue is a custom statue of Buyer. Likely any attempt to sell the statute to someone else would be unavailing. Thus, Seller is entitled to the full contract price ($250,000) under UCC §2–709(1)(b).

(A) is incorrect.

Seller is entitled to the full contract price. The formula in (A) incorrectly compensates him for only the difference between the contract price and his expenses and labor. In other words, he has already spent the $10,000 in materials and $9,000 in labor to make the statue. If these amounts are subtracted from his recovery, Seller will not be made whole.

(B) is incorrect.

When a seller can prove that any attempts to go out in the market and attempt to resell the good would be unavailing, the seller is entitled to the full contract price, regardless of whether he or she makes any attempt to resell.

(C) is incorrect.

(C) is more akin to pure reliance damages, as it only awards Seller his out of pocket expenses for materials and labor spent in reliance on the contract up to the time of the breach. Seller would recover no profit if his recovery were limited to the formula set forth in (C).

Answer to Question 39

(B) is the correct answer.

When a buyer wrongfully rejects conforming goods, the seller may collect damages for the difference between the resale price and the contract price, so long as the resale is done in a good faith, commercially reasonable manner. UCC § 2–706(2)–(4). By giving Buyer notice of its plans and offering Buyer the chance to match the $750/unit price, Seller acted in good faith and in a commercially reasonable manner.

Under UCC § 2–706, the equation to compute "seller's cover" damages is: (Unpaid contract price) – (Resale Price) + (incidental damages) – (expenses saved as a result of the breach). Here, contract price minus resale price was $5,000. In addition, Seller incurred incidental damages (an out-of-pocket expenditure made after and because of the breach) of $300 to ship the goods back, which is also recoverable. UCC § 2–710. Therefore, Seller's damages would be $5,000 plus $300.

(A) is incorrect.

All that is required is that Seller act in a commercially reasonable manner. The fact that at trial the buyer can show some other company would have been willing to pay more for the computers does not limit Seller's recovery. The innocent Seller only has to act reasonably; he does not have to search the area for the best deal to mitigate the breaching buyer's damages.

(C) is incorrect.

(C) is incorrect because its formula erroneously neglects to include recovery of the incidental damages from shipping the goods back.

(D) is incorrect.

The $200 expense saved in storage was an expense saved by *Buyer*, the breaching party. This does not belong in the Seller's calculation of damages.

Answer to Question 40

(B) is the correct answer.

Since this is a sale of goods, it is governed by the UCC. Whenever market differential damages are involved, the correct market must be selected. For example, the market price may vary from day-to-day, and even on the same day, the price may be different where the seller is located versus where the buyer is located.

The UCC directs what market to use. What is often frustrating to students (and practitioners) is that the correct market to use when the seller is the plaintiff (as set forth in UCC § 2–708) is different from the correct market to use when the buyer is the plaintiff (as set forth in UCC § 2–713).

Here, where it is the buyer who wrongfully rejects conforming goods, the seller is the plaintiff. The correct market under UCC § 2–708(1) is "the market at the time and place for tender." Since under the contract the goods were to be tendered in Oregon on June 1, the market price of $0.20 is the correct figure for determining the damages.

Under UCC § 2–708, the correct formula is: (unpaid contract price) – (market price) + (incidental damages) – (expenses saved in consequence of the buyer's breach). Thus, Seller's market differential is ($0.25 – $.20) × 50,000.

(A) is incorrect.

(A) is incorrect because its formula erroneously uses the market price as of the place of delivery, and not the place of tender, which is called for under UCC § 2–708.

(C) is incorrect.

(C) is incorrect because its formula uses an incorrect temporal and geographic market by taking the figure from the date of delivery (rather than the date of tender), and the delivery location rather than the location of tender, as called for under UCC § 2–708.

(D) is incorrect.

(D) is incorrect because its formula erroneously uses the market price pending on the date of delivery, not the date of tender, as called for by UCC § 2–708.

Answer to Question 41

(D) is the correct answer.

Seller is a "lost volume" seller, and as such would be entitled to recover the lost profits from the missed sale under UCC 2–708(2).

Under the UCC, a seller is entitled to proceed under § 2–708(2) only after it is determined that proceeding under UCC § 2–708(1) is inadequate to put the seller in as good a position as if performance were completed. Hence, in a case where UCC § 2–708(2) might be an issue, calculation of seller's damage under UCC § 2–708(1) first is necessary.

The formula under UCC § 2–708(1) subtracts the contract price from the resale price. Here that would be $500 (contract price) minus $500 (resale price), leaving the seller with nothing. Because proceeding under UCC § 2–708(1) would not leave the seller in as good a position as performance would have, proceeding to UCC § 2–708(2) is appropriate.

A lost volume seller situation under UCC § 2–708(2) occurs when a seller could have made two sales to two different buyers, but, because of the original buyer's breach, has only made one sale to the second buyer. Because it lost out on a sale, the buyer is entitled to the profit it would have made on that lost sale, not the purchase price. Awarding it the latter would put it in a better position than it would have been had both contracts been fulfilled.

The formula under UCC § 2–708(2) is described as: "the profit (including reasonable overhead) which the seller would have made from full performance by the buyer, together with any incidental damages provided in this Article (Section 2–710), due allowance for costs reasonably incurred and due credit for payments or proceeds of resale." The formula is thus set forth in the following equation: [(profit) + (incidental damages) + (costs incurred) – (payments already received from buyer) – (proceeds of resale)].

Note that the "due credit for . . . proceeds of resale" language in UCC § 2–708(2) is universally acknowledged as a mistake in lost volume seller situations and should be read out of the formula when calculating damages for a lost volume seller. If it were to be included in the formula here, Seller would recover nothing. The formula would be [($100) + (0) + (0) – (0) – ($400)], or a negative $300. Hence, do not subtract the proceeds of resale when calculating the damages under a lost volume seller.

To be a "lost volume seller," the seller must have enough inventory to make the two sales. For example, say a consumer contracts to sell her only car to Bob for $10,000. Bob breaches and an hour later she sells the car to Dan for $10,000. She is not damaged because she only had one car to sell and so by selling the car to Dan for the same price an hour later, she got everything she would have received had the contract with Bob continued.

Here, Seller had more than one couch in inventory. Seller could have made two sales had Buyer not breached, thereby qualifying Seller as a lost volume seller. Although Seller was able to sell the very same couch to another party shortly after, as a lost volume seller, the $500 sale after the breach is not like a "cover." As a lost volume seller, Seller lost out on one sale, and hence is entitled to the profits lost as a result of the breach of the initial contract.

(A) is incorrect.

(A) is incorrect because as a lost volume seller, the second sale is not treated as a cover mitigating damages. Since the Seller had enough inventory on hand to make the second sale, had there been no breach the

Seller would have had two sales, thus the second sale is not treated as a cover of the first even though it was a sale of the same couch.

(B) is incorrect.

(B) is incorrect because providing the entire contract price to Seller for the lost sale would unjustly enrich him since all he lost was the profit from the second sale.

(C) is incorrect.

(C) is incorrect for the same reason that (B) is incorrect, i.e., if Seller were given the entire acquisition cost he would be in a better position than he would have been had the contract been performed since all he lost was the profit from the second sale.

Answer to Question 42

(A) is the correct answer.

When a seller is part way through the manufacture of a good for a buyer who breaches, the seller has the option either to finish the good and try to sell it to another, or to stop production and immediately sue for damages, so long as the seller acts in a commercially reasonable manner in making its selection. UCC § 2–704.

Here, Seller decided to stop manufacturing the product. Damages are calculated in such a situation under the formula set forth in UCC § 2–708(2).

The formula under UCC § 2–708(2) is: "the *profit* (including reasonable overhead) which the seller would have made from full performance by the buyer, together with any incidental damages provided in this Article (Section 2–710), due allowance for *costs reasonably incurred* and due credit for *payments or proceeds of resale*" (emphasis added). Thus Seller is entitled to the $500 *profit*, plus the $2,500 in *costs reasonably incurred* up to the time of breach, less $700 as implied *proceeds of resale* since $700 worth of mahogany is salvageable in other projects and thus is deemed "resold" to the innocent Seller to be used in other projects.

(B) is incorrect.

(B) is incorrect as the formula provides Seller only with the profits he lost on the contract, and does not compensate Seller for all the expenses he has already incurred. If Seller only got the profit, he would lose money because he has spent more for raw materials than what he would recover under the formula in this answer.

(C) is incorrect.

(C) is incorrect because the answer sets forth Seller's reliance damages only, i.e., the out-of-pocket costs spent by Seller in reliance on the contract before the breach. Here, Seller is also entitled to the profits lost as a result of the breach. UCC § 2–708(2).

(D) is incorrect.

Since $700 of the costs expended up to this point is mahogany that can be used in other contracts for furniture, it must be deducted from the costs recovered in an award of damages. Otherwise Seller would be overcompensated because he either would be paid for that mahogany again by the purchaser of whatever cabinet was made with the salvaged mahogany, or he would be able to offer that piece of furniture at a less than market value since he would be using "free" mahogany on another piece of furniture paid for by the breaching buyer described in this question.

Answer to Question 43

(B) is the correct answer.

The $250K Clause is a liquidated damages provision, meaning that it is a clause that provides for a set amount of damages upon a breach, without the plaintiff having to prove the actual damages suffered. Liquidated damages are not favored by courts, which generally prefer to award the expectancy interest, i.e., the exact amount which would put innocent parties in the position they would have been in had the contract been completed.

Further, if the liquidated amount is more than a party's actual damage, it acts as a "penalty" for a breach, and if the liquidated amount is less than the actual damage, courts worry that it becomes too easy to breach the contract. Neither situation is welcomed by contract law damage theory.

At common law, one requirement to enforcement of a liquidated damages clause was that the actual damages be reasonable in light of the harm anticipated when the contract was entered into. Under that test, the $250K Clause would be unenforceable because it was a $250,000 promise for a breach that would have been worth $20,000 (the value of the house) at the time the contract was entered into.

However, under Restatement 2d § 356(1), a liquidated damages clause is enforceable if it is reasonable (in amount) in light of the harm anticipated *or* the harm actually caused. Since the actual harm caused in this case is the loss of receiving a $220,000–$280,000 house, the liquidated damages clause would be enforceable. In other words, it does not matter that at the time of contracting it was only thought the breach would cause $20,000 in harm since the actual damage at the time of the breach was much greater.

The second requirement for a liquidated damages provision to be enforceable is that actual damages be difficult to prove with precision. Restatement 2d § 356(1). Here, different appraisers cannot agree on the exact worth of the house, so proving the amount of damages with precision to award money damages would be difficult.

(A) is incorrect.

As discussed above, the Restatement 2d states that the amount the amount of the liquidated damages provision being reasonable in light of the actual harm is an alternative to the requirement that it be reasonable in light of the harm anticipated. Restatement 2d § 356. Satisfying either will suffice.

(C) is incorrect.

(C) is incorrect because the clause calls for $250,000 in damages for a $220,000–$280,000 loss; this difference is negligible.

(D) is incorrect.

Pierre need not prove that his services were worth $250,000. He made a contract with Daphne whereby she agreed to turn over her house in ten years. Therefore, they have agreed on the worth of his services (the value of the house). The question here is whether a breach of the turn-over-the-house promise is roughly equivalent to $250,000, the amount of payment due upon breach of the house promise under the liquidated damages clause.

Answer to Question 44

(D) is the correct answer.

A requirement of an enforceable liquidated damages clause is that the actual damages must not be easily determined and provable. Restatement 2d § 356(1). Here, Phillip remained on the utility grid for an extra month. However, the utility bills its customers monthly, so Phillip's damages can be determined with precision—whatever he was billed from the utility for the period from March 1–April 1. Since the exact amount of damage caused by the delay is calculable, an award based on the liquidated damages clause in improper.

(A) is incorrect.

Regardless of its reasonableness, this liquidated damages clause cannot be enforced because the actual damages can be easily determined.

(B) is incorrect.

(B) is incorrect for the same reasons (A) is incorrect.

(C) is incorrect.

If a liquidated damages clause is otherwise enforceable, there is not a cap on the amount of damages based on the profits of one party under the contract.

Answer to Question 45

(A) is the correct answer.

A clause is enforceable when it provides two alternative means of performance. Here, the clause provides that Buyer may perform under the contract and satisfy it by either the annual purchase of $200,000 in helium or the payment of $40,000. The difference between a liquidated damage clause and an alternative performance clause is that in the former, a payment is triggered by the breach of the contract, whereas under the latter, there are alternative methods of performing under the contract without a breach.

To give an illustration, suppose there are two contracts. One says Seller must deliver an apple for $1, and if she does not, she must deliver a banana to Buyer. The banana clause would be a liquidated damages provision because seller would not be obligated to provide a banana unless the contract was breached. Now assume there is a contract whereby for $1, the buyer can choose whether she wants an apple or a banana. This would be an alternative performance clause, whereby the buyer can choose how to perform under the contract without any breach occurring. Alternative performance clauses are favored in the law because they are not triggered by any breach, and thus do not raise any overcompensation or undercompensation concerns arising from a breach as do liquidated damages provisions.

Courts state that they examine alternative performance clauses carefully to ensure that they are not disguised liquidated damages clauses. Factors include: the intent of the parties, the disparity between the amounts of alternative performances, the good and bad faith of the parties, etc. However, despite these admonitions, actual examples of situations in which alternative performance clauses are overturned as disguised impermissible liquidated provisions are few and far between.

(B) is incorrect.

(B) is incorrect because the clause involved is not a liquidated damages clause, but rather an alternative performance one.

(C) is incorrect.

(C) is incorrect because it erroneously applies the liquidated damages requirement standard, i.e., that the damages must not be easily determinable and provable, to an alternative performance provision.

(D) is incorrect.

(D) is incorrect because the clause is an alternative performance clause, not a liquidated damages clause.

CHAPTER 21

DISCHARGE BY SUBSEQUENT AGREEMENT

ANSWERS

Answer to Question 1

(C) is the correct answer.

This chapter deals with "subsequent" agreements, i.e. agreements made after a first contract is entered into between the parties. The questions addressed in the problems in this chapter are: (1) what happens to the original agreement as a result of the second one; and (2) is the second agreement enforceable?

This question deals with a subsequent agreement that attempted to modify the original one. After an effective modification, the original agreement is in force, just with one or more different terms. Here the question is whether the modification is effective. It is not.

Gil had promised to fix the car for $600. Then he got Terry's agreement to pay him $750 to do the same work. This is a contract for service, meaning that it is governed by common law/Restatement rules, rather than the UCC. Under the Restatement 2d, modification of a contract for services must be supported by consideration to be enforceable (Restatement 2d § 73), or an exception to the consideration rules must apply. Restatement 2d § 89.

There was no new consideration to support the modification by virtue of the pre-existing duty rule, i.e., in the attempted modification, Gil promised to do the same job, just for an increase in price. If Gil had promised to something more in the subsequent agreement, e.g., also do a wheel rotation or something, there would be consideration supporting the new agreement. But no such promise was forthcoming here, so there was no consideration.

No exception under Restatement 2d § 89 applies, either. That is, there is no evidence that outside circumstances changed from the time the contract was made as Gil examined the car thoroughly before he began working on it and there was nothing supporting Gil's increased price request other than his desire to make more money, nor any reliance by Gil on the modification. Restatement 2d § 89(a), (c).

Gil might try to argue that what happened was an agreement to discharge the original $600 agreement and substitute the $750 agreement in its place. This won't work because a subsequent agreement discharging the original one requires consideration or an exception to the consideration rules. Restatement 2d § 273.

Note that the reason for this rule is that the risk of entering into a fixed price contract is that the work will cost more than anticipated at the time of the making of the agreement. Gil bears that risk—of course Gil gets the benefit if the work costs less than he anticipated. Also, if circumstances changed from the start of the contract, contract law might allow the subsequent agreement to be enforced and replace the original one. Restatement 2d § 89(a). But none of those theories can be factually supported, making Choice (C) the correct answer.

(A) is incorrect.

An accord and satisfaction occurs when the parties make an agreement that a new agreement will take the place of their first one, on the condition that the second one is actually performed. Restatement 2d § 281. This isn't what happened here. Here, there was simply an (unsuccessful) attempt at an enforceable modification of an existing agreement.

(B) is incorrect.

Reliance on a modification can serve as an exception of the pre-existing duty rule requiring new consideration upon modification. But there are no facts to support its application here. Under Restatement 2d § 89(c), the reliance exception is only applicable upon a showing of a "material change of position in reliance on the promise." Here, Gil did not materially change any position in reliance of the promised increased payment. Gil may say he wouldn't have fixed the car without the increased promise, but he had already agreed to fix it for $600 and his change of mind is not reliance. For example, in *Alaska Packer's v. Domenico*, 117 F. 99 (1902), sailors on a ship refused to go forward without additional payment when their ship was in the middle of the Pacific. The promise of the owner to pay them an additional wage was not enforceable under the pre-existing duty rule, even if it could be said that the sailors, in some respect, relied on the promise to complete the voyage.

(D) is incorrect.

The modification of a service contract need not be in writing even if the original was in writing as long as the contract, as modified, is not within the Statute of Frauds. If the promise were otherwise enforceable, it wouldn't be rendered unenforceable simply because it was oral.

Answer for Question 2

(B) is the correct answer.

This is an example of a special kind of accord and satisfaction by check that is endorsed by UCC § 3–311, as explained below. Note, however, that the result would be supported by Restatement 2d §§ 273, 281 as well.

An "accord" is an agreement to discharge an original agreement and put in its place a new agreement. This is also what "substituted performances" and "substituted contracts" do as well. What makes an accord different, is that in an accord, the parties agreed to something like the following: "We will wipe out our first agreement and put a second agreement in its place, *but only if the debtor actually performs what he's agreed to do in the second agreement. If not, then I (the creditor) get to decide whether to sue for breach of the original contract, or the second agreement.*" Restatement 2d § 281; UCC § 3–311. In other words, in an accord and satisfaction situation, the accord (second agreement) is enforceable, but it only wipes out (discharges) the first agreement if the accord is actually "satisfied," or performed. If it is not, the debtor can sue under either the breached original agreement or breached subsequent agreement.

With substituted performances and substituted agreements, the parties agree that they will immediately discharge their first contract and will immediately agree to put something else in its stead. Restatement 2d §§ 278, 279. So if the second agreement is not performed by the debtor, the only remedy by the creditor is under the second agreement because the debtor's duties under the first have been discharged in the making of the second agreement.

One thing that all three such agreements (accords, substituted performances, and substituted contracts) require is consideration to be enforceable. Here, consideration exists because there is a bona fide dispute and the amount of damages is not liquidated, i.e., the exact amount of damage is uncertain, or liability is genuinely contested. This is an accord situation because the original $2,500 debt is only extinguished if Contractor collects the money signified by the check.

The special issue regarding accord and satisfaction with checks arises in cases just like this question. The debtor offers a part payment (which is an offer for an accord—"I am proposing a new deal whereby we will wipe out our original $2,500 agreement and put a $500 agreement in its stead"), but only if the creditor accepts the offer as a full and complete settlement of the dispute. The creditor sees the partial payment as "his" money and wants to take the partial payment and still retain his rights to sue for the remainder. Contract law has gone back and forth on this over the years, but under UCC § 3–311, contract law now says that if the creditor cashes the check, that is an acceptance of the offer for an accord on the debtor's terms, regardless whether the creditor crosses out the "settlement" language, so long as the settlement language is prominent. When the check is honored by the bank, and the money given the creditor, the "accord" is "satisfied."

This case is loosely based on *County Fire Door Corp. v. C.F. Wooding Co.*, 520 A.2d 1028 (Conn. 1987).

(A) and (C) are incorrect.

Both (A) and (C) presume that there is not a valid accord and that Contractor may recover under the original contract. These choices are thus incorrect for the reasons that Choice (B) is correct.

(D) is incorrect.

Because there was a valid accord, it would not matter if Contractor was acting in good faith in performing the contract. He is not rewarded extra for his good faith and again, it does not overcome the fact that there is an enforceable accord and satisfaction.

Answer to Question 3

(D) is the correct answer.

A substituted performance describes a transaction in which a party owing a duty under a contract arranges to discharge the duty under the first, original contract, by making a different performance. Restatement 2d §278. Substituted performances require consideration to be enforceable. *Id.*

When Thomas told Serena that he would accept the pies in lieu of payment, in essence he made an offer to enter into a unilateral contract, whereby Serena's performance acted as acceptance. Therefore, consideration is present as Serena bound herself to something she didn't have to do (delivering the pies), and Thomas forewent something he had a right to do (enforce the debt), and Serena's act and Thomas's promise were bargained for and sought in exchange for one another. Thus, when Serena delivered the pies, a substituted performance has taken place and Serena's debt to Thomas is discharged.

Note that had Serena not delivered the pies, Thomas would only be able to sue for the $200 under his original bill, and not to enforce delivery of the pies because Serena has not *promised* to make the delivery. Their agreement is only that *if* Serena delivers the pies, the debt will be discharged.

Note also that to be a valid substituted performance, the obligor must agree to discharge the existing duty upon actual performance only. If the duty is discharged on the basis of a *promised* performance, e.g., if Thomas had said "if you *promise* to deliver five pies to my next Friday," it would be a substituted <u>contract</u> or accord situation, and not a substituted <u>performance</u> one. Restatement 2d § 279.

Finally, note that a substituted performance has similarities to, and differences from, an accord and satisfaction situation. The similarities are that under both, the parties agree to discharge their obligations under the first contract only if the second contract is actually performed. But in an accord situation: (1) the second contract can be formed by promise, and need not be unilateral; and (2) if the second agreement is breached, the creditor can sue for either breach of the first or of the second contract. Restatement 2d § 281.

(A) is incorrect.

Consideration is present in Serena's act in delivering the pies and this choice is incorrect.

(B) is incorrect.

As set forth in the explanation of (D) above, Serena's obligations under the first contract were discharged when she accepted Thomas's offer for a substituted performance by delivering the pies.

(C) is incorrect.

This choice is incorrect because it is not when Thomas offers to accept a substituted performance that Serena's obligations are discharged; rather, it is when she performs on (and accepts) the offered unilateral contract that her duties discharged.

Answer to Question 4

(B) is the correct answer.

A substituted contract is a transaction in which a party owing a duty under a contract discharges it by *promising* a different performance than that originally called for under the contract. Restatement 2d § 279. A substituted contract is itself a separate bilateral contract, and thus must be formed by a separate offer, acceptance and consideration to be enforceable. The offer in these situations is a promise to discharge a debt upon the promised performance of an act that is separate from a preexisting duty, and the acceptance is the promise to do the act called for in the offer. Each party's bargained for promise serves as the consideration to support the second agreement.

There are two categories of substituted contracts that depend on whether the party to perform the new obligation is the original promisee or a third party. Where the original promisee makes a new promise, it is called a "substituted contract," which is what is illustrated by this problem. Restatement 2d § 279. The other category, where a third party makes a new promise, is called a "novation" and is governed by the Restatement 2d § 280.

When Alex offered to give Vanessa his concert tickets, it was an offer for a substituted contract, which she immediately accepted. At that point there was a valid substituted contract. The rule regarding these contracts is that, when the contract was formed, Alex's obligation to pay $1,000 under the original debt was immediately discharged and Vanessa may only sue him for breaching the promise for Alex to leave the tickets at will-call. Restatement 2d § 279(2). Thus, although Vanessa will win, she can only recover for the value of the concert tickets, as the duty to repay the $1,000 under the original computer debt was discharged.

(A) is incorrect.

This choice erroneously assumes that Vanessa can still recover under the original agreement. As explained above, this would be an example of a valid substituted contract. The rule is that when a substituted contract is formed, the obligations of the original parties are discharged and the obligations under the subsequent agreement only are enforceable.

(C) *is incorrect.*

This choice is incorrect for the same reasons answer (A) is incorrect. It erroneously assumes that Vanessa can recover on both the original agreement and under the substituted contract. She cannot, as explained under (B) above.

(D) is incorrect.

This answer is incorrect because consideration is present in the new bargained-for exchange, namely, Alex's promise to leave the tickets for Vanessa, and Vanessa's promise to release the debt.

Answer to Question 5

(A) is the correct answer.

This question tests knowledge of a special type of "substituted contract" known as a "novation." A novation occurs when a new contract is entered into in which the duties under the original contract are discharged because one party has agreed to accept the promised performance by a third party in its stead. Restatement 2d § 280. Upon the making of the second agreement, the duties under the first are discharged and thus if the third party does not perform the second agreement, the only remedy for the original contracting party is to sue the third party for breach of the second agreement. Restatement 2d § 279(2).

Here, when Vanessa accepted Alex's and Zack's offer for Zack to perform services on her car, she entered into a valid novation. Therefore, Alex's obligation to pay the $1,000 was immediately discharged. This means that when Zack did not perform, Vanessa's only recourse is to sue *Zack* for his failure to perform as promised because she can no longer enforce Alex's promise to repay the $1,000, and Alex owes her no duties whatsoever after the novation.

(B) is incorrect.

This answer choice is incorrect because it erroneously assumes that Alex has remaining duties to Vanessa, which, as set forth in the explanation of Choice (A) above, is not the case. Alex's obligations were discharged upon the formation of the valid novation.

(C) is incorrect.

This answer is incorrect for the same reasons (B) is incorrect, i.e., because Alex's obligations were discharged upon formation of the novation, Vanessa may only recover from Zack, not Alex.

(D) is incorrect.

This answer is incorrect because it not only assumes that Alex is still liable for any failure on Zack's performance under the novation, but it also assumes that Vanessa can still recover on the original debt, which is incorrect. The original debt was immediately discharged upon formation of the novation.

Answer to Question 6

(C) is the correct answer.

The parties have entered into an accord based on the facts of this question. It is an accord because they have made an agreement to discharge their original agreement by means of a second agreement, but their agreement provides that the duties under the first agreement will only be discharged *if* the second agreement is actually performed, i.e., if the "accord" is "satisfied." Restatement 2d § 281.

In an accord situation, the original agreement is suspended until the parties have a reasonable opportunity to complete performance of the second agreement. So upon their agreement, Zack had a reasonable time to fix Vanessa's car, and during this reasonable time period, Vanessa cannot sue Alex for the original $1,000 debt because that obligation suspended. Once that reasonable time period ends, Vanessa can sue on *either* of the agreements. She can choose to sue Zack for failure to fix the car, or sue Alex on the original debt that is revived upon the failure of the accord to be satisfied. She can only collect on one of the two obligations, but it is her choice which to pursue.

Note that this is an accord involving a third party. When a third party is promising performance under a substituted contract, it is known as a "novation." Restatement 2d § 240. However, when a third party is involved in an accord situation, there is no special name for it.

Note that there need not be a third party involved. For example, if the agreement was that Vanessa would allow Alex to fix her car in lieu of the $1,000 payment, but the discharge was contingent on Alex actually doing fixing the car, it would still be an accord, and if Alex did not fix the car, Vanessa could sue Alex for his breach of the $1000 debt promise, or for his breach of the fix the car promise.

(A) and (B) are not the best choices.

As explained above, both (A) and (B) are both correct, which making (C) the correct answer.

(D) is incorrect.

(D) is incorrect because Vanessa can only sue Alex for the original contract.

Answer to Question 7

(D) is the correct answer.

Mutual rescission is an agreement whereby each party in a bilateral contract agrees to discharge all the remaining unexecuted duties of the other. It is enforceable when it has the attributes of a separate contract, i.e., an offer, an acceptance, and consideration. Restatement 2d § 283. In order to be an effective rescission, the parties must be in a bilateral contract with executory duties *remaining on both sides* at the time the rescission agreement is reached, otherwise there is no consideration for their promises. As a general rule, an oral mutual rescission is enforceable. Restatement 2d §§ 283, Cmt. b; 277(1).

Here, the parties agreed to discharge their remaining executory duties to a bilateral contract. A valid offer to discharge was made by Brett; that offer was accepted by Michael; and there was consideration because each party discharged a legal duty. Restatement 2d §§ 71, 73.

(A) is incorrect.

As set forth in the explanation of Choice (D) above, this is a case of mutual rescission and does not require a writing.

(B) is incorrect.

The agreement to rescind a legal relationship is sufficient for consideration. Restatement 2d §§ 71, 73.

(C) is incorrect.

This choice assumes that the original agreement would require a writing, but the agreement does not come within the Statute of Frauds since it is a sale of goods agreement for less than $500.

Note, however, that the mutual rescission of a duty to transfer an interest in land must be in writing as an application of the Statute of Frauds. Restatement 2d §§ 148, 283, Cmt. b.

Answer to Question 8

(A) is the correct answer.

Sometimes, a party who is supposed to get the benefit of a performance under a contract is willing to give up that benefit. But what if the party changes his or her mind? At common law, unilateral renunciations were unenforceable for a lack of consideration. However, the Restatement 2d changed the rule to make a unilateral renunciation enforceable even without consideration so long as the renunciation is in writing. Restatement 2d § 277(1). Therefore, when Michael renounced his right to payment in writing, the statement became enforceable and Michael cannot effectively demand payment.

Another similar manner in which Michael could give up the benefit of the bargain is through a "release," which is an enforceable promise by a party that he or she is discharging a duty owed to him or her immediately *or upon the occurrence of a condition*. Restatement 2d § 284. At common law, to be effective, a release needed to be supported by consideration (Restatement 2d § 284, Cmt. b), but most states today have statutes that provide a release is binding even in the absence of consideration.

(B) is incorrect.

As set forth in the explanation for (A) above, at common law, this answer choice would be correct, but under the Restatement 2d, the renunciation would be enforceable because the renunciation agreement was in writing.

(C) is incorrect.

Although Michael is receiving a $400 benefit from the original agreement, Michael is within his rights to give up his right to that benefit and thus the renunciation would be enforceable.

(D) is incorrect.

The original agreement need not be in writing, as it was for a sale of goods for less than $500. UCC § 2–201.

CHAPTER 22
APPLICABILITY OF ARTICLE 2 OF THE UCC

ANSWERS

Answer to Question 1

(A) is the correct answer.

Article 2 of the UCC is not limited to merchants. Since many cases involving the UCC deal with merchants, some students mistakenly believe there is a requirement that one of the parties must be a merchant. Note that there are nineteen provisions of the UCC which deal specifically with merchants, but the other provisions apply just as much to parties selling goods to their friends as they do to transactions between merchants. Here, neither party is a merchant, but so long as the transaction is for goods, that is irrelevant, and Article 2 will govern the transaction.

(B) and (C) are incorrect.

(B) and (C) are incorrect for the reasons set forth in the explanation of (A). There is no requirement the transaction involve a party who is a merchant for the Article 2 of the UCC to apply.

(D) is incorrect.

A "future good" is a good which is not identified to the contract at the time it was made. UCC § 2–501(1)(b). That is, suppose a buyer purchases an iPod from the Apple Store. At the time of purchase, the sales representative has to go in the back and get an iPod in a box to fulfill the order. At the time of contracting, since no one knows which particular box will be given to the buyer, the iPod is a "future good." Once the sales representative picks the iPod box, it is thereafter "identified" to the contract, meaning that it is the particular good which is to be sold under the contract.

However, both contracts for identified goods and contracts for future goods are governed by Article 2 of the UCC. UCC § 2–501.

Answer to Question 2

(C) is the correct answer.

For the first thirty years or so of its existence, there was much debate as to whether Article 2 of the UCC would apply to transactions for leases. Article 2 provides that it applies to "transactions in goods," (UCC § 2–102), and one faction argued that a lease was a "transaction" and a car was a "good," so Article 2 applied. Opponents argued that almost all the substantive provisions of Article 2 use the terminology "contract for sale" and speak in terms of "seller" and "buyer" and not "lessor" or "lessee," and thus Article 2 was not intended to cover leases.

In 1987, Article 2A was enacted to resolve the conflicting opinions. Titled "Uniform Commercial Code—Leases," Article 2A governs the formation, operation, and performance of contracts regarding leases. UCC § 2A–101.

Here, there was a lease for a vehicle that, before the passage of Article 2A, would have sparked debate as to whether Article 2 applied. But under modern law, Article 2A of the UCC will govern the transaction for a lease.

Note that Article 2A has not solved all problems with leases. The definition of a lease under Article 2A is: "'Lease' means a transfer of the right to possession and use of goods for a term in return for consideration." UCC § 2A–103(j). Certainly it would cover an individual leasing a car from a car rental company, as was the issue in this question. But controversy has remained, e.g., long term leases. For example, suppose Joe enters into a 3 year "lease" for a television from a "Rent to Own" place, where, after three years of "lease" payments, he has the option to purchase the television for $1. Is that a lease (which should be governed by Article 2A) or really a disguised sale (which is governed by Article 2)? The cases are split on this issue.

(A) is incorrect.

(A) is incorrect for the reasons given in the explanation of Choice (C), namely, the issue has been resolved such that Article 2A governs contract for leases.

(B) is incorrect.

The rules of UCC Article 2A apply to this transaction, not common law contract rules.

(D) is incorrect.

(D) is incorrect for two reasons. First, the provisions of the Restatement 2d are not "the law" anywhere as they are not statutes but rather general rules authored and adopted by the American Law Institute as being representative of the majority position throughout the country. Hence, they would never "govern." It is also incorrect because here, the rules of Article 2A would govern the transaction, as explained above.

Answer to Question 3

(D) is the correct answer.

Article 2 of the UCC applies to "transactions in goods." UCC § 2–102. The term "transaction" is not defined in Article 2, although clearly sales transactions are Article 2 transactions. After all, Article 2 is titled "Uniform Commercial Code—Sales." UCC § 2–101.

"Good" is defined, however, as a thing that is movable at the time of identification to the contract (UCC § 2–105), i.e., something that can be picked up and moved from one place to another as opposed to, e.g., land or a service or intellectual property. In general, this means an Article 2 "good" is personal property.

An RV, even one being used as a residence, is a movable thing at the time it is identified in the contract, i.e., at the time the seller says "this particular RV is the one I am selling you." UCC § 2–501(1). Thus, the RV would qualify as a "good" and its sale would be governed by Article 2 of the UCC.

(A) is incorrect.

The RV is a "good" as defined under UCC § 2–105(1). It would be movable at the time it was identified under the contract, and thus Article 2 would apply.

(B) is incorrect.

As discussed in the explanation in (D), just because it will be used as a residence does not prevent classifying the RV as a "good". The RV meets the definition of UCC § 2–105(1) and as such will be classified as a "good" for UCC applicability purposes.

(C) is incorrect.

(C) is incorrect because in order for the UCC to govern the transaction, the contract must be for "goods." The UCC will not govern regardless of classification as a "good" or not.

Answer to Question 4

(B) is the correct answer.

"Identification" occurs at the time when "goods are shipped, marked or otherwise designated by the seller as goods to which the contract refers." UCC § 2–501(1)(b). That is, identification occurs once the particular good that is to be sold is selected or identified by the seller as the good that will be the subject of the particular transaction.

Sometimes there is no gap between the time of contracting and the time of identification to the contract. For example, if a buyer contracts to buy a car on the lot, the particular car that is the subject of the contract is "identified" at the time the contract is made.

Sometimes, as is the case here, the particular good that will be given to the buyer is not identified at the time of the making of the contract, but will be identified later. This is known as a contract for the sale of "future goods." UCC § 2–501(1)(b).

Regardless of *when* the good is identified, so long as it is "movable" *at the time it is identified*, it is a "good" for Article 2 applicability purposes, making the sale of the stereo a "transaction in goods" under UCC § 2–202, meaning Article 2 applies.

(A) is incorrect.

The requirement for Article 2 applicability is that the item must be movable when it is identified to the contract (whenever that is) to be a "good" under Article 2. UCC §§ 2–105(1), 2–501.

(C) is incorrect.

(C) is incorrect for the same reasons that (A) is incorrect. It is not relevant whether the good was movable at the time of purchase; it is whether it is movable at the time of *identification* that matters for Article 2 applicability. UCC §§ 2–105(1); 2–501.

(D) is incorrect.

(D) is incorrect because a stereo is in fact a "good" under UCC § 2–105(1) since it is "movable" at the time of its identification under a sales contract.

Answer to Question 5

(A) is the correct answer.

Sometimes there are "hybrid" contracts in which a buyer contracts for both goods and services in the same transaction. The question arises whether these transactions should be looked at as "goods" transactions, governed by Article 2 of the UCC (with its four year statute of limitations, warranty protections, etc.) or whether they should be regarded as services transactions, and thus governed by common law rules (for example, the statute of limitations for negligence in most states is either one or two years). Contract law has come up with two distinct tests to make the goods or services determination, and often, as here, application of one test will come up with a different answer than by applying the other test. The names of the tests are: (1) the "Predominant Purpose" test; and (2) the "Gravamen [of the cause of action]" test.

Under the "Predominant Purpose" test, the court must determine whether the principal purpose of the Buyer in entering the contract was for the purchase of goods or for services. If it is determined the purpose was for goods, then Article 2 will govern all parts of the transaction. If it is determined the purpose was for services then none of the transaction will be governed by Article 2.

Here, the contract called for both services and goods, the installation (service) and the dishwasher itself (goods). It appears Buyer's purpose is to get a dishwasher, i.e., the purchase of the goods, while the installation is secondary (and costs less than the good itself). Thus, Article 2 will govern the entire contract.

(B) is incorrect.

(B) is incorrect for the reasons discussed in (A). The predominant purpose of the contract was to obtain the dishwasher, not to receive the installation services.

(C) is incorrect.

(C) is incorrect because it focuses on what caused the problem. This is what is done under the "gravamen" test, as will be explained in greater detail in the answer to the next question 6.

(D) is incorrect.

(D) is incorrect for the same reasons as Choice (C) is incorrect.

Answer to Question 6

(D) is the correct answer.

Under the "Gravamen" test, the court determines what caused the problem, and then will apply either Article 2 or common law rules to the situation. In applying this test, courts look to whether the injury arises out of some problem with the goods, or out of some negligence in the services provided under the contract. If the claim is from non-conforming goods, then Article 2 will govern; if it is from negligent services then common law tort principles will govern.

Here, the cause of the flooding was from negligence in installing the dishwasher. Thus, Article 2 will not govern the claim, making Choice (D) correct.

(A) is incorrect.

(A) is incorrect because it applies the "Predominant Purpose" test in determining the governing law. The court will look to what caused the claim, not what the purpose of the contract was, under the "gravamen" test.

(B) is incorrect.

(B) is incorrect for the same reasons as (A) is incorrect.

(C) is incorrect.

(C) is incorrect because the gravamen of the cause of action is the negligent provision of services, not some product defect with the dishwasher itself.

Answer to Question 7

(C) is the correct answer.

When there is a sale of something attached to real property, a special set of rules determines whether Article 2 will govern the transaction. For the sale of minerals (including oil and gas) and structures that are attached to real estate, Article 2 governs if the *seller* is to sever it from the property. UCC § 2–107(1). The sale of crops, timber, and anything else capable of severance without material harm to the property and not included in the first rule, is governed by Article 2 regardless of who severs it. UCC § 2–107(2).

Here, the transaction is for oil, so Article 2 applicability is governed by the rule set forth in UCC § 2–107(1). Under that provision, in order for Article 2 to govern the transaction, the oil would need to be severed by Seller, not Buyer. Since the contract calls for Buyer to harvest the oil, the transaction is not governed by Article 2 of the UCC.

(A) is incorrect.

(A) is incorrect as it sets forth the rule of UCC § 2–107(2); but this transaction, involving the sale of oil, is governed by UCC § 1–107(1).

(B) is incorrect.

(B) is incorrect because of the reasons set forth in (C). Since Buyer is severing the oil, it is not an Article 2 transaction under UCC § 2–107(1).

(D) is incorrect.

This is not a transaction for real property, it is a transaction for the oil (which is a "good" because it is movable) currently attached to the property that will be severed for sale. UCC § 2–107(1).

CHAPTER 23
WARRANTIES

ANSWERS

Answer to Question 1

(C) is the correct answer.

Under UCC § 2–315, a buyer can establish that the implied warranty of fitness for a particular purpose has been made, so long as he or she proves that: (1) the buyer had an unusual or particular purpose in mind for the good, (2) the seller had reason to know of this particular purpose, (3) the seller has reason to know that the buyer is relying on the seller's skill or judgment to select or furnish goods that will meet the buyer's needs, (4) the buyer in fact relied on the seller's skill or judgment in selecting suitable goods; and (5) the goods did not perform as warranted. (Note there is also a "notice" requirement for a successful claim under UCC § 2–607(3) which is discussed later in this chapter)

Here, Brianna (the buyer) has a particular purpose in mind for the good because she planned to compete in an extreme marathon in South Africa. Shady Sellers (the seller) had reason to know of this particular purpose and had reason to know that Brianna is relying on the seller's skill to select goods, because Brianna told Shady's employee the reason that she needed the shoes and asked them to select a pair of appropriate shoes for her. Brianna relied on the seller's skill in selecting suitable goods. Finally, the goods did not perform as warranted because the goods were not appropriate for the extreme marathon. Thus, because all five requirements are met, there was a breach of the implied warranty of fitness for a particular purpose with regard to the shoes.

(A) is incorrect.

(A) is incorrect because Shady Sellers made no express warranties with regard to the shoes. The act of the employee giving Brianna the shoes is not deemed sufficient as a representation of fact under warranty law to make it an actionable representation.

(B) is incorrect.

Brianna did have an implied warranty of merchantability under the transaction, but this warranty was not breached given the facts. Under

UCC § 2–316(2)(c) goods are merchantable if they are "fit for the ordinary purposes for which such goods are used." Here, the cloth shoes would have been fit for an ordinary running purpose. The problem in this instance is that there was a breach of an implied warranty of fitness for a particular purpose, for the reasons stated in Choice (C).

(D) is incorrect.

(D) is incorrect because there was a breach of the implied warranty of fitness for particular purpose under UCC § 2–315.

Answer to Question 2

(D) is the correct answer.

(D) is correct because Shady Sellers made no express warranties to Brianna, the implied warranty of merchantability has not been breached, and there is no implied warranty of fitness in this scenario.

First, Shady Sellers did not expressly warrant anything with regard to the shoes because its sales representative said nothing, and there were no signs, or videos in the store describing the properties of the shoes.

Second, while there was an implied warranty of merchantability because Shady Seller's is a merchant, the warranty was not breached because the shoes would pass without objection in the trade as ordinary running shoes. Therefore, under the UCC § 2–314(2)(c), the goods are merchantable because they are "fit for ordinary purposes for which such goods are used."

Finally, there is no implied warranty of fitness for a particular purpose, because the requirements for this warranty are not present. Under UCC § 2–315, an implied warranty of fitness requires: (1) the buyer had an unusual or particular purpose for the goods, (2) the seller had reason to know of the particular purpose, (3) the seller had reason to know the buyer was relying on the seller's skill or judgment to furnish the goods, (4) the buyer relied on the seller's skill or judgment, and (5) the goods did not perform as warranted. Although Brianna did have a particular purpose for the goods (the extreme marathon), because Brianna picked the shoes out without talking to anyone, she did not give the seller any reason to know of this particular purpose nor that she was relying on the seller's judgment to furnish the goods. Therefore, there is no implied warranty of fitness.

(A) is incorrect.

(A) is incorrect because Shady Seller's has made no express warranty with regard to the shoe.

(B) is incorrect.

(B) is incorrect because the implied warranty of merchantability was not breached because the call of the question states that the shoes would have been adequate for ordinary running use, as explained in (D).

(C) is incorrect.

(C) is incorrect because it is not supported by the facts. Brianna did not give Shady Seller any reason to know that she had a particular purpose for the shoes, or was relying on seller's judgment to furnish the goods, as explained in (D).

Answer to Question 3

(B) is the correct answer.

The only warranty breached here is an express warranty. The implied warranty of merchantability deals with whether the good is of average quality, or fit for ordinary use for which such goods are made. Here, Bianca's complaint is not that the document with the lyrics on it is not fit for the ordinary purpose, but rather that factual representations that Sasha made about the document with the lyrics on it, on which Bianca relied in making the purchase, turned out to be false.

An actionable express warranty was made by means of an "affirmation of fact or promise made by the seller which relates to the goods," when Sasha promised Bianca that the document with the lyrics on it was authentic. UCC § 2–313(1)(a). In order for a valid breach of express warranty claim, the affirmation must also become part of the "basis of the bargain." UCC § 2–313(1).

There are three theories as to what the term "basis of the bargain" means. The first is that it means that the buyer relied on the affirmation in making the purchase. Here, Bianca only purchased the document with the lyrics on it because Sasha assured her that the document was authentic. Therefore, Bianca relied on the affirmation in deciding to make the purchase.

The second theory is that "basis of the bargain" means the affirmation was made during the negotiation process, before the sale took place. Here, Sasha made the affirmation that the document with the lyrics on it was authentic before either party tendered performance, so the affirmation became a "basis of the bargain" under this theory as well.

The third theory is a bit of an amalgamation of the first and second. It posits that "basis of the bargain" means reliance. However, it presumes that the buyer relied on every factual statement made by the buyer during the pre-sale negotiations, and places the burden on the seller to prove the buyer did not, in fact, rely on any particular statement. Support for this theory comes from UCC § 2–313, Cmt. 3. Here, that would mean the burden would be on Sasha to show that Bianca did not rely on her statements of authenticity in order to defeat Bianca's claim, and there are no facts which support this in the problem.

Therefore, there is no claim for an implied warranty of merchantability, but there is an actionable breach of express warranty making (B) correct.

(A) is incorrect.

(A) is incorrect because there was no breach of the warranty of merchantability, because Bianca has no complaints about the documents with the lyrics on it not being fit for their ordinary purpose. Rather, the complaint is that Sasha made a representation with regard to the lyrics and the representation turned out to be false.

(C) is incorrect.

(C) is incorrect because there was no breach of the warranty of merchantability, as explained in (A) and (B).

(D) is incorrect.

(D) is incorrect because Bianca has an actionable breach of an express warranty, for the reasons set forth in (B).

Answer to Question 4

(C) is the correct answer.

Under UCC § 2–313, an express warranty can be made if there is: (1) an affirmation of fact or promise that relates to the goods, (2) a description of the goods, or (3) a sample or model. Here, Seller described the goods as able to cut through any food and as self-sharpening, therefore a representation was made based on a description of the goods.

To have a claim for breach of express warranty, the description of the goods must also become a part of the "basis of the bargain." There are three theories of what "basis of the bargain" means. The first is that it means the same as reliance. This would mean Buyer must have relied on Seller's description in deciding whether to purchase the good in order for there to be a breach of express warranty claim. Here, Buyer relied on Seller's representation because the facts say Buyer was "so impressed with Seller's description that he buys four sets of the knives." Thus, under the first theory for what "basis of the bargain" means, Seller's description of the knives became a basis of the bargain.

The second theory is that "basis of the bargain" means the affirmation was made during the bargaining process, before the sale took place. Here, Seller's description of the knives was made before Buyer purchased the knives, so the description became a basis of the bargain under this theory as well. Therefore, Buyer has a claim for a breach of express warranty against Seller based on Seller's description of the goods.

The third theory, like the first, posits that "basis of the bargain" means reliance. However, it presumes that the buyer relied on every factual statement made by the buyer during the pre-sale negotiations, and places the burden on the seller to prove the buyer did not, in fact, rely on any particular statement. Support for this theory comes from UCC § 2–313, Cmt. 3. Here there are no facts which would support Seller's claim that Buyer did not rely on Seller's representations.

(A) is incorrect.

(A) is incorrect because Seller provided Buyer with a description of the goods, and Buyer relied on that description in purchasing the knives. Therefore, Buyer will have an express warranty claim against Seller based on Seller's description of the knives. UCC § 2–313.

(B) is incorrect.

(B) is incorrect because Buyer did not have to test the knives before purchasing them in order for a viable express warranty to be established. Here, Seller provided Buyer with a description of the knives, and Buyer relied on that description in deciding to purchase the knives. Therefore, there was an express warranty under UCC § 2–313.

(D) is incorrect.

(D) is incorrect because Seller does not have to sign anything for an express warranty to exist. Buyer has an express warranty claim against Seller for the reasons stated in the explanation in (C).

Answer to Question 5

(B) is the correct answer.

(B) is the correct answer because under UCC § 2–313(1)(c), an express warranty can be created by a model or sample. Here, the video of the Spick-and-Span model that the store used constituted an express warranty that the vacuum would work as well as in the video if Buyer purchased it and used it at home.

To have a claim for an express warranty, the sample or model shown to the buyer as representative of the goods must become part of the "basis of the bargain." Again, there are three theories for what "basis of the bargain" means. The first is that "basis of the bargain" means that the buyer relied on the representation in deciding whether or not to purchase the good. Here, Buyer relied on the vacuum model because he was impressed with the vacuum's abilities and purchased it. The second theory regarding the meaning of "basis of the bargain" is that the representation was made before the sale took place. Here, Buyer examined the video before buying it, so the sample became a basis of the bargain under this theory. The third theory presumes that the buyer relied on every factual statement made by the buyer during the pre-sale negotiations, and places the burden on the seller to prove the buyer did not, in fact, rely on any particular statement. UCC § 2–313, Cmt. 3. Here, there are no facts which would support a lack of reliance by Buyer. Thus, Buyer has a breach of express warranty claim based on the Spick-and-Span video he viewed in the store.

(A) is incorrect.

(A) is incorrect because the Seller does not have to sign anything, the Seller made a representation to Buyer based on the Spick-and-Span video, and Buyer relied on that representation when he decided to purchase the vacuum.

(C) is incorrect.

(C) is incorrect. Seller made a representation based on the Spick-and-Span model in the video and Buyer relied on that representation (which was also made prior to the purchase) when he decided to purchase the vacuum. The fact that the manufacturer produced the video means that Buyer may also have a claim against the manufacturer. But Seller showed the video in its store and so is also responsible for the representation made in the video since it was part of its marketing efforts in the vertical retail distribution chain.

(D) is incorrect.

(D) is incorrect because Buyer relied on the video and the representations demonstrated in it, and otherwise satisfied "basis of the bargain" requirement, when he purchased the vacuum as explained in Choice (B).

Answer to Question 6

(C) is the correct answer.

This problem presents the issue as to what happens when a seller makes an oral express warranty, but then later attempts to disclaim that warranty in a bill of sale. The issue is controlled by UCC § 2–316(1). The general rule is when a sale has, "[w]ords or conduct relevant to the creation of an express warranty and words or conduct tending to negate or limit [that warranty]" then the "negation or limitation is inoperative..." However, that rule is "subject to the provisions of this Article on parol or extrinsic evidence (Section 2–202) . . ." UCC § 2–316.

What that means is that *if* both the warranty and the warranty disclaimer are in evidence, the warranty controls and the words of negation of the warranty are inoperative. But, there is a question of whether the oral words of warranty ever can be introduced into evidence. This is because the oral warranty is not consistent with the disclaimer, and under the parol evidence rule, an oral agreement made during negotiation that is not a "consistent additional term" with a term of the written agreement is excluded from evidence. UCC § 2–202.

Many courts find this a harsh result. After all, if the sales representative orally affirms some attribute of the product while the consumer is still deciding whether to purchase it, an ordinary consumer would rely on that representation and not expect that it will be "disclaimed" by some writing at the end of the deal. So courts will find the disclaimer unconscionable or otherwise unenforceable, and there will be no parol evidence problem because, with the disclaimer gone, the warranty is not an "inconsistent" term. But there are a number of cases which exclude the oral warranty on parol evidence grounds, and so if Buyer loses, it will likely be for that reason.

(A) and (B) are incorrect.

Both of these answers are incorrect as they are misstatements if the law. When both a warranty and a disclaimer are in evidence, it is the disclaimer that is inoperative under UCC § 2–316, not the warranty.

(D) is incorrect.

(D) is incorrect as there is no rule that says a buyer may not rely on a statement made by a representative during contract negotiation. Indeed, the creation of express warranty section, UCC § 2–313, provides the opposite.

Answer to Question 7

(A) is the correct answer.

Under UCC § 2–314 a buyer can sue for breach of an implied warranty of merchantability if the buyer can prove that: (1) the seller of the good was a "merchant," (2) the goods sold by the seller were not "merchantable," and (3) the breach caused the buyer damage. (There is also a "notice" requirement for a warranty claim under UCC § 2–607(3) which is discussed later in this chapter).

A merchant is someone who deals with goods of the kind, or holds himself or herself out as having skill or knowledge to the practices or goods involved in the transaction by virtue of his or her occupation. UCC § 2–104(1). Here, Box Store is an electronics retailer, so she is a merchant.

Goods are merchantable if they "pass without objection in the trade." UCC § 2–314(2)(a). The television would not pass without objection in the trade because it does not work. And the failure to turn on caused Buyer damage, since he has paid for a non-working set. Therefore, Buyer would have a claim for a breach of the implied warranty of merchantability.

(B) is incorrect.

(B) is incorrect because Buyer had no particular purpose for the television that was different than the ordinary purpose of a television, and furthermore, Seller was not aware of any particular purpose that Buyer may have had for the television, as is necessary for a fitness warranty claim under UCC § 2–315. Therefore, there was no implied warranty of fitness under these facts.

(C) is incorrect.

(C) is incorrect because Buyer has a claim for breach of the implied warranty of merchantability, for the reasons stated in the explanation of (A).

(D) is incorrect.

(D) is incorrect because even though Seller did not expressly warrant that the television would work, Buyer has a claim of breach of the implied warranty of merchantability, for the reasons stated in the explanation of (D).

Answer to Question 8

(D) is the correct answer.

Barry does not have a claim for the implied warranty of merchantability because Sarah is not a merchant. Under UCC § 2–314, in order to establish a breach of the implied warranty of merchantability, the buyer must prove that the seller of the good was a "merchant." A merchant is someone who deals with goods of the kind, or holds himself or herself out as having skill or knowledge to the practices or goods involved in the transaction by virtue of his or her occupation. UCC § 2–104(1). Here, Sarah is not a merchant because she does not deal in cars, and does not hold herself out as having any special skill or knowledge in regards to cars. Thus, there is no claim for breach of the implied warranty of merchantability.

Barry also has no claim for a breach of express warranty, because Sarah made no promises to Barry with regard to the attributes of the car (although see the explanation to (B) below for a different perspective). UCC § 2–313. Therefore, there is no claim for breach of an express warranty.

Finally, Barry has no claim for breach of an implied warranty of fitness because Barry had no special purpose for the car and gave Sarah no reason to know that he had a special purpose for the car or that he was relying on her to furnish a car with those attributes. UCC § 2–315. Thus, Barry has no warranty claims against Sarah.

Barry can get his money back from Sarah under a misrepresentation and/or unjust enrichment theory, but there is no breach of warranty claim on these facts.

(A) is incorrect.

(A) is incorrect because Barry has no claim for breach of an implied warranty of merchantability, as explained in Choice (D).

(B) is not the best choice.

(B) is not the best choice. One *could* argue that by advertising a "car" for sale, Sarah made an implied representation that she is selling a vehicle that could drive down the street. A few courts have used this kind of argument, but it remains a stretch of the majority rule in UCC decisions.

(C) is incorrect.

(C) is incorrect because Barry has no claim for breach of an implied warranty of fitness for the reasons stated in the explanation of Choice (D).

Answer to Question 9

(D) is the correct answer.

Because Sarah is a merchant, there would ordinarily be a breach of the implied warranty of merchantability under UCC § 2–314. However, UCC § 2–316(3)(a) provides that "all implied warranties are excluded by expressions like 'as is,' 'with all faults' or other language which in common understanding calls the buyer's attention to the exclusion of warranties and makes plain that there is no implied warranty." Hence, the "as is" warranty disclaimer means that no warranty of merchantability attached to the sale, and there is, again, no warranty claim.

(A) is incorrect.

(A) is incorrect because Barry has no claim for breach of an implied warranty of merchantability, for the reasons set forth in the explanation of (D).

(B) is not the best choice.

(B) is not the best choice. One *could* argue that by advertising a "car" for sale, Sarah made an implied representation that she is selling a vehicle that could drive down the street. A few courts have used this kind of argument, but it remains a stretch of the majority rule in UCC decisions.

(C) is incorrect.

(C) is incorrect because Barry has no claim for breach of an implied warranty of fitness, both because the elements of the claim are not present on these facts, and because the "as is" disclaimer disclaims all implied warranties, including the implied warranty of fitness for a particular purpose.

Answer to Question 10

(A) is the correct answer.

As with the previous few questions, this question also deals with a warranty disclaimer. However, the disclaimer in this question only disclaims the implied warranty of fitness for a particular purpose, and not the implied warranty of merchantability. That is, under UCC § 2–316(2), "Language to exclude all implied warranties of fitness is sufficient if it states for example, 'There are no warranties which extend beyond the description on the face hereof.'"

To specifically exclude the warranty of merchantability, UCC § 2–316(2) provides, "to exclude or modify the implied warranty of merchantability or any part of it, the language must mention merchantability." Here, there was no "as is" or "without all faults" language which would exclude *all* implied warranties under UCC § 2–316(3)(a) nor was there a disclaimer which mentioned "merchantability," which is necessary to exclude the implied warranty of merchantability under UCC § 2–316(2). As such, because Barry purchased the car from a merchant, and because the car did not work, it did not pass without objection in the trade, and Barry has a claim for breach of the merchantability warranty. UCC § 2–314.

(B) is not the best choice.

(B) is not the best choice. One *could* argue that by advertising a "car" for sale, Sarah made an implied representation that she is selling a vehicle that could drive down the street. A few courts have used this kind of argument, but it remains a stretch of the majority rule in UCC decisions.

(C) is incorrect.

(C) is incorrect because Barry has no claim for breach of an implied warranty both because the elements of the claim are not present in this question and because the warranty disclaimer given disclaims the warranty of fitness. UCC § 2–316(2).

(D) is incorrect.

(D) is incorrect for the reasons that make (A) is correct.

Answer to Question 11

(C) is the correct answer.

In order to establish a claim for breach of the implied warranty of merchantability, a buyer must establish that the seller of the good was a "merchant," that the goods sold by the seller were not "merchantable," and that the breach caused the buyer damages.

Seller is a merchant because Seller deals in farm supplies and holds himself out as having special knowledge by virtue of his occupation. UCC § 2–104(1). However, fungible goods are merchantable if they are of "fair average quality." UCC § 2–314(2)(b). Here, the facts say to assume that the grain was of average quality. Therefore, Buyer would have no claim for breach of the warranty of merchantability, even though Buyer is not pleased with the goods.

(A) is incorrect.

(A) is incorrect for the reasons stated in (C). It does not matter that Buyer does not believe that the grain is of the same quality that he is used to, the grain is of average quality, so the warranty of merchantability has not been breached.

(B) is incorrect.

(B) is incorrect because a breach of warranty of merchantability does not require the buyer to prove that he or she has a particular purpose for the good. Therefore, it does not matter that Buyer did not feel he could use the goods for farming, the warranty of merchantability was not breached because the grain was of average quality.

(D) is incorrect.

(D) is incorrect because it misstates the law. There can be a warranty of merchantability for fungible goods, and the warranty is breached if the goods are not of "fair average quality." UCC § 2–314(2)(b).

Answer to Question 12

(D) is the correct answer.

(D) is correct because the warranty of merchantability can be disclaimed under the authority of UCC § 2–316(2) or under the authority of UCC § 2–316(3). Under the former, a disclaimer is effective to disclaim the implied warranty of merchantability if it prominently uses the term "merchantability," making (A) correct. Under UCC § 2–316(3), a warranty disclaimer is effective to disclaim all implied warranties, including the implied warranty of merchantability, if it uses the term "as is," making (B) correct.

(A) and (B) are incorrect.

(A) and (B) are incorrect for the reasons explained in (D), namely, both answers are effective modes of disclaiming an implied warranty of merchantability.

(C) is incorrect.

(C) is incorrect because this disclaimer neither uses the word "merchantability," to disclaim the warranty of merchantability under UCC § 2–316(2) nor does it use the terms "as is" or "with all faults" or like language to be an effective disclaimer of all implied warranties under UCC § 2–316(3).

Answer to Question 13

(A) is the correct answer.

UCC § 2–607(3) states that a buyer must notify the seller of any breach of warranty within a reasonable time after either the breach was discovered or should have been discovered. If no such notice is given, the buyer is "barred from any remedy" for breach. Therefore, Buyer had a duty to notify Seller of the breach of the implied warranty of merchantability within a reasonable time.

UCC § 2–605(1) provides that a buyer who does not particularize the defect on which a rejection is based is "preclude[ed] . . . from relying on the unstated defect to justify rejection or to establish breach." Here, Buyer only said, "These computers stink," which does not particularize the problem.

The reason for both of these requirements is to allow the seller to know of the problem as early as possible and attempt to cure. Also, the notification requirement under UCC § 2–607(3) allows the seller to begin negotiating to settle the dispute as well. UCC § 2–607(3), Cmt. 4.

(B) is incorrect.

(B) is incorrect for the reasons stated in the explanation of (A). Where consumers (as opposed to merchants) are involved, courts often hold that the filing of litigation meets the notice and particularization requirement on the theory that consumers often do not know of these duties. However, the requirements are more strictly enforced in business-to-business disputes. Because both Buyer and Seller are businesses, likely the notice requirement would be enforced.

(C) is incorrect.

(C) is incorrect because it misstates the law. It does not matter whether Seller was in the wrong. Buyer has a duty to notify Seller of the breach of warranty within a reasonable time after it discovers the breach, and to particularize the problems to justify the rejection. UCC §§ 2–607(3), 2–605(1).

(D) is incorrect.

(D) is incorrect for the reasons stated in the explanation of (A). In ordinary consumer transactions some courts do hold these notice requirements unconscionable. This is because ordinary consumers are usually unaware that they will be barred from recovery if they fail to notify the seller of a breach of warranty within a reasonable time or do not particularize the defects when they send the goods back. However, the notice requirements are more strictly enforced in business-to-business transactions. Thus, likely the notice requirement would be enforced in this situation.

Answer to Question 14

(C) is the correct answer.

Although the rule varies among jurisdictions, it is generally held that there are two complete defenses to a breach of warranty claim: (1) assumption of the risk, and (2) unforeseeable misuse. Assumption of the risk is a complete defense to a warranty suit if a seller can prove that the plaintiff knowingly and voluntarily undertook a known risk in purchasing and using the product, understanding the extent of the risk at the time it was taken.

Here, Buyer removed the guard with a clear warning on it, and chose to voluntarily encounter the risk by taking the guard off. Hence Seller likely has a complete defense to the breach of warranty claim.

(A) is incorrect.

(A) is incorrect because Seller will likely have a complete defense to a breach of warranty claim for the reasons stated in the explanation of (C). Further, there are no facts which would support an implied warranty of fitness for a particular purpose claim.

(B) is incorrect.

(B) is incorrect because Seller will likely have a complete defense to a breach of warranty claim for the reasons set forth in the explanation of (C).

(D) is incorrect.

(D) is incorrect because this is a situation in which there has been assumption of the risk, not merely comparative negligence.

Answer to Question 15

(C) is the correct answer.

While UCC § 2–312(1) states that in a contract for the sale of goods there is a warranty by the seller that the title conveyed is good title, this rule is subject to subsection (2), which provides that there is no warranty of title if the buyer has reason to know that the person selling it "does not claim title in himself." Here, Dennis made it clear to Paula that there may be competing claims to the antique. Therefore, Paula would not have a claim for breach of warranty of title under UCC § 2–312.

(A) is incorrect.

(A) is incorrect for the reasons set forth in the explanation of (C). Because Dennis made it clear to Paula he could not guarantee that there were no other claims to the revolver, Paula would not have any claims against him for breach of the warranty of title.

(B) is incorrect.

(B) is incorrect for two reasons. First, because of the reasons set forth in the explanation to (C). Second, because even if Paula did have a claim for breach of the warranty of title, she would not be entitled to the

$2,000 payment because she did not lose the suit against Anne and she still has the revolver.

(D) is incorrect.

(D) is incorrect because the issue here is that Dennis told Paula there may have been other claims to the revolver, not that Paula won the suit against Anne. If Dennis had not disclosed to Paula that there may be competing claims, and Anne had a colorable claim to the revolver, Paula still could have recovered the attorney's fees expended in the suit brought by Anne under UCC § 2–312.

Answer to Question 16

(A) is the correct answer.

Under UCC § 2–312, Paula has a claim for breach of the warranty of title even if she does not win the suit against Anne, so long as Anne has a colorable claim to the revolver. Therefore, Paula would be awarded the attorney's fees expended in the suit versus Anne. Note that if Paula would have lost in the suit brought by Anne, and Anne was awarded the pistol, Paula would also be entitled to recover the $2,000 cost of the pistol from Dennis.

(B) is incorrect.

(B) is incorrect because Paula would only be awarded attorney's fees. Paula would not be refunded her $2,000 payment because she still has the revolver, since she won in the suit against Anne.

(C) is incorrect.

(C) is incorrect because Paula had no reason to know that there was another claim to the revolver, so this is irrelevant to whether Paula could recover for a breach of warranty of title. If Paula had reason to know that Dennis did not claim to have title, then she could not recover for a breach of warranty of title, but this did not occur.

(D) is incorrect.

(D) is incorrect because it does not matter that Paula prevailed in the suit against Anne. So long as Anne had a colorable claim to the good, Paula will be able to recover attorney's fees under UCC § 2–312.

Answer to Question 17

(D) is the correct answer.

(D) is correct because Paul can only prevail in a breach of warranty title if he loses to Alfred, or if Alfred has a colorable claim to the cell phone. Therefore, because Alfred had no reason to believe the cell phone was his, Paul would have no colorable claim for breach of the warranty of title.

(A) and (B) are incorrect.

(A) and (B) are incorrect for the reasons set forth in the explanation of Choice (D). Because Alfred did not have a colorable claim, Paul is not entitled to recover from Dan's for breach of the warranty of title.

(C) is incorrect.

(C) is incorrect because the issue here is that Alfred did not have a colorable claim to the cell phone, not that Paul won the suit against Alfred.